The Emergence of Stability
in the Industrial City

The Emergence of Stability in the Industrial City: Manchester, 1832-67

MARTIN HEWITT

SCOLAR PRESS

Published by
SCOLAR PRESS
Gower House
Croft Road
Aldershot
Hants, GU11 3HR
England

Ashgate Publishing Company
Old Post Road
Brookfield
Vermont 05036-9704
USA

British Library Cataloguing in Publication Data
Hewitt, Martin
  The emergence of stability in the industrial city: Manchester, 1832-67
  1.Manchester (England)—History—19th century
  2.Manchester (England)—social conditions
  I.Title
  942.7'3'081

  ISBN 1-85928-276-8

Library of Congress Cataloging-in-Publication Data

Hewitt, Martin
  The emergence of stability in the industrial city: Manchester,
1832–67/Martin Hewitt
  p. cm.
  Includes bibliographical references and index.
  ISBN 1-85928-276-8 (cloth)
  1. Manchester (England)—Social conditions. 2. Manchester
(England)—Politics and government. 3. Industries—England—
Manchester—History—19th century. 4. Working class—England—
Manchester—History—19th century. I. Title.
HN398.M27H48 1996
306'.09427'33—dc20   95–47155
                                        CIP

ISBN 1-85928-276-8 (cloth)

Printed in Great Britain at the University Press, Cambridge

Contents

Tables and Figures

Tables

Figures

Preface

When I commenced work on this study a decade ago, the years it covers were paradoxically the subject of what amounted almost to scholarly overkill conjoined with academic neglect. The study of chartism was still being driven to new insights by the work of Dorothy Thompson, Gareth Stedman Jones, and their students and fellow travellers. At the same time, the post-chartist period, notwithstanding a spate of work on the labour aristocracy, languished in neglect. Even when the thesis, of which this book is a revision, was submitted in 1991, it was necessary to go back to Frances Gillespie's *Labor and Politics in Britain, 1848–67*, (1927) to find a detailed appraisal of the post-chartist period. Although there was no shortage of books which purported to cover 1848–67, this period was largely unoccupied ground, over which historians of the early nineteenth century and of the later nineteenth century fought for rights of annexation.

This situation is rapidly changing. Recent years have seen a spate of new studies of both the period and the problem addressed in this study, most notably Eugenio Biagini's *Liberty, Retrenchment and Reform*, (1992), Margot Finn's *After Chartism*, (1993), James Vernon's *Politics and the People*, (1993), and Miles Taylor's *The Decline of British Radicalism* (1995). All, in their various ways, have addressed one of the central questions of British nineteenth century history, and indeed of the history of all industrialising societies, namely the roots of the transition, apparently almost revolutionary in its pace and absoluteness in Britain, from the decades of social instability of the early industrial revolution, to the social and political stability of the maturing industrial economy.

We are thus suddenly much better placed than we have ever been to unravel the conundrum of the collapse of chartism and radicalism, and to explain the evolution of social and political forms which in Britain appeared to preclude the maintenance of radical challenges to the *status quo*, choked the growth of Marxism or socialism, and buttressed the power of traditional elites. And yet, on examining this scholarship what is most striking is the absence of any new explanatory consensus, any new theoretical construction, that might provide a new orthodoxy to settle, at least for the time being, the question which has so vexed scholars since E.P. Thompson's discovery of a class-conscious working class in the early nineteenth century created the historical whodunnit of this class's sudden and tragic disappearance. There has been some attempt in the past few years to side-step this question, by suggesting that class never became the central paradigm of social identity in nineteenth century Britain. However, in chapter one I endeavour to show why I remain unconvinced by the arguments of the 'linguistic turn'.

Instead, this study attempts to work within the broad confines of Thompsonian culturalism, while adopting lines of inquiry which reveal considerable sympathy with the questions and subject matter of the scholars of the 'linguistic turn'. Chapters two and three discuss the development of Manchester during the mid-nineteenth century, establishing the foundations of working-class identity and of middle-class reformism. Chapters four, five and six then examine the struggle to shape the intellectual cultures of the working class, arguing that despite the overt aims of 'embourgeoisiement' or intellectual hegemony, there is little evidence that the middle class was able successfully to construct mechanisms which might explain a collapse of class consciousness. Chapters seven, eight and nine proceed to examine the nature of working-class consciousness and politics in the light of these conclusions. They argue that there are marked continuities of attitude and belief among the working classes across the chartist and post-chartist period, but that a clear shift can be detected in working-class perceptions of the efficacy of the traditional tactics of platform radicalism. This shift, which accurately reflected the more difficult terrain of political culture in the 1840s and 1850s, helps explain the collapse of chartism and the weakness of its successors, but it amounts to no more than a strategic reorientation of working-class political aspirations, and the operational difficulties caused by this reorientation.

During the course of writing this book (and before that the thesis on which it substantially draws), I have accumulated numerous debts. The Economic and Social Research Council provided me with two years of funding, and Nuffield College, Oxford generously supplemented this with a third, as well as providing a host of benefits during the four years I was attached to the College. I have received guidance and encouragement particularly from Asa Briggs, Chelly Halsey, Tony Howe, Neville Kirk, Maxine Berg, Keith Nield, Mike Turner, Robin Pearson, Douglas Reid, David Richardson and Christine Hallas, as well as useful comments from seminars in Oxford, Hull and Manchester. I have also benefited from the guidance and assistance of the staff of various libraries and archives, particularly the Manchester Central Library.

Over the years my parents have helped both spiritually and practically in countless ways. Above all, however, this book finally sees the light of day as a result of the constant encouragement and monumental patience of Mary-Clare. I hope I have done her justice.

Menston
1995

Abbreviations

Repositories

BL	British Library
MCL	Manchester Central Library
MCLA	Manchester Central Library, Archives Department
MJRL	John Rylands University Library, Manchester
MRC	Modern Records Centre, Warwick
UCL	University College, London

Newspapers and other series

BH	*Beehive*
EASAR	Educational Aid Society, *Annual Report*
HO	Home Office Papers, Public Record Office
IRSH	*International Review of Social History*
LL	*Lankeshur Loominary*
MC	*Manchester Courier*
MCCP	Manchester City Council, *Proceedings*
MCMAR	Manchester City Mission, *Annual Report*
MCMM	*Manchester City Mission Magazine*
MCN	*Manchester City News*
MG	*Manchester Guardian*
MSA	*Manchester and Salford Advertiser*
MSp	*Manchester Spectator and Commercial Gazette*
MSTR	*Manchester and Salford Temperance Reporter and Journal of Progress*
MTPAR	Manchester Ministry to the Poor, *Annual Report*
MWA	*Manchester Weekly Advertiser*
MWT	*Manchester Weekly Times*

MX	*Manchester Examiner and Times*
NR	*National Reformer*
NMW	*New Moral World*
NS	*Northern Star*
OSMFR	*Operative Stone Masons, Fortnightly Returns*
PMG	*Poor Man's Guardian*
PP	*Parliamentary Papers*
PPL	*Pitman's Popular Lecturer*
PPr	*People's Paper*
RWN	*Reynold's Weekly Newspaper*
SWN	*Salford Weekly News*
TAHP	*Trades Advocate and Herald of Progress*
TMSS	*Transactions of the Manchester Statistical Society*
TUM	*Trade Union Magazine*
WCM	Manchester Corporation, Watch Committee "Minutes", MCLA
WMC	*Wheeler's Manchester Chronicle*
XR	*Christian Review*

Please note that the following convention has been used with reference to newspaper citations. Where a name appears in quotation marks, this indicates the source is a letter in the newspaper over this signature. Where a name appears without quotation marks, this indicates words attributed to an individual in a report.

Pagination of *Parliamentary Papers* refers to the printed page numbers of each report (which is referenced), not to the manuscript numbers added to the volumes.

Chapter One

Introduction

A mid-century watershed?

Until recently it would have been impossible to conceptualise British history in the nineteenth century without acknowledging the presence of a fundamental watershed at around mid-century, involving what Trygve Tholfsen has described as 'the swift transition from the militant working class radicalism of the 1830s and 1840s to the relative quiescence of the age of equipoise'.[1]

The debate which existed – and it existed in profusion – concerned the genesis and significance of this transition. Did it, as G.M. Young once suggested, mark merely a return to normality, so that '[a]fter all the alarms and agitations of thirty years, the State had swung back to its natural centre'.[2] Or did it, as many later historians, especially of the Left, argued, constitute a more decisive moment of definition for British political culture, 'a change of atmosphere', as David Kynaston puts it, 'so fundamental that it gave the British labour movement a reformist character of apparent permanence'.[3]

In the last decade, however, the established depiction of mid-century discontinuity has been challenged, largely by two bodies of research emanating from Cambridge and Manchester, which we might describe as the 'Cambridge School'[4] and the 'Manchester School'[5] (with

---

[1] T. Tholfsen, *Working Class Radicalism in Mid-Victorian England*, (1976), 11.

[2] G.M. Young, *Portrait of an Age: Victorian England*, (1983 [original 1932]), 69.

[3] D. Kynaston, *King Labour: The British Working Class, 1850–1914*, (1975), 11. Of course this perception is, despite recent criticisms, still current, especially among historians writing broadly from the left; hence Margot Finn talks about 'the profound caesura of working-class radicalism in these years', M. Finn, *After Chartism. Class and nation in English radical politics, 1848–74*, (1993), 141; cf. T. Koditschek, *Class formation and urban-industrial society. Bradford, 1750–1850*, (1990), especially chapter 18.

[4] Gareth Stedman Jones, 'Rethinking Chartism', *Languages of Class. Studies in English working class history 1832–1982*, (1983), 90–178, E. Biagini and A. Reid, eds, *Currents of Radicalism: Popular Radicalism, Organized Labour and Party Politics in Britain, 1850–1914*, (1991), E.F. Biagini, *Liberty, Retrenchment and Reform: Popular Liberalism in the Age of Gladstone, 1860–1880*, (1992), Miles Taylor, *The Decline of British*

apologies to Richard Cobden and his allies). The Cambridge School, concentrating on studies of the ideologies and practices of chartism and working-class or reforming liberalism, has argued the defeat of the chartists in 1848 and their subsequent decline were not as significant as hitherto suggested, because chartism was not the revolutionary class-conscious movement it had been painted. The reformist lib-labism enshrined in the Gladstonian Liberal party did not mark a break with the past, but rather the culmination of traditions of radicalism stretching back into the eighteenth and seventeenth centuries. 1848 was not a watershed, but merely a staging post on the long climb towards the summit of Gladstonian Liberalism. Taking a complementary perspective, which is focused on local rather than national politics, and on political culture rather than political action, the Manchester School has stressed the multiple meanings and gradual evolution of rituals, symbols and ideas, in such a way as to question both the significance of class, and the validity of the Thompsonian narrative of the formation (and then presumably the destruction or demobilisation) of the English working class.

It is easy, as Robbie Gray has recently pointed out, to take joy in demolishing the familiar landmarks of historical chronology, to uncover elements of continuity with which to soften sharp breaks in the historical narrative.[6] It is almost as easy, of course, to cling to established ways of thinking, especially ways which have for so long defined the questions asked, and the approaches taken, by many historians. What recent scholarship has done, amongst other things, is to draw our attention to the need for care in evaluating the nature of the transition in mid-nineteenth century Britain. It has challenged a chronological bifurcation which had become almost institutionalised,

Radicalism, 1847–1860, (1995), plus much of the prodigious output of Gregory Claeys, in particular, *Machinery, Money and the Millennium. From moral economy to socialism,* (1987), *idem, Citizens and Saints. Politics and anti-politics in early British Socialism,* (1989). Although not directly the product of Cambridge, Dror Wahrman's work, in particular his *Imagining the Middle Class. The Political Representation of Class in Britain, c.1780-1840,* (1995), also reveals a considerable intellectual debt to Stedman Jones.

[5] P. Joyce, *Visions of the People: Industrial England and the Question of Class, c.1848–1914,* (1991), *idem, Democratic Subjects. The self and the social in nineteenth century England,* (1994), J. Vernon, *Politics and the People. A Study in English Political Culture, c.1815–1867,* (1993), F. O'Gorman, 'Campaign Rituals and Ceremonies: the social meaning of elections in England, 1780–1860', *Past & Present,* 135 (1992), 79–115.

[6] R. Gray, 'Class, politics and historical revisionism', *Social History,* 19 (1994), 212.

particularly within British labour history, in which studies tended to deal either with chartism, or with the post-chartist period, and which in the process exaggerated the mid-century hiatus.

However, despite the powerful continuities which the new scholarship traces, it has neither denied nor fully explored the dramatic differences in almost all aspects of political and cultural life between the turbulent antagonisms of the chartist years and the complexly negotiated relations of the 1850s and 1860s.[7] (This period, as contemporaries were not slow to recognise, saw the emergence of stability in industrial society.) Nor has it done much to bridge the historical chasm of 1848; with a few honourable exceptions, 1848 remains a watershed that historians of the nineteenth century working below the level of broad survey seem reluctant to traverse.

In response, one of the aims of this study is to confront the period from the 1830s to the 1860s as a whole, through detailed use of primary material from across the period. In this way it seeks to contribute to this process of re-examination, not by denying the dramatic nature of change at mid-century, but rather by uncovering some of the complex inter-relationships between change and continuity which only close study across the 'watershed' can reveal.

Marxism and the dynamics of transition?

The renewal of debate over the nature of the mid-century transition has taken place within the context of sustained debate over its causes. Until the mid-1980s this debate might be characterised as comprising a series of internal disagreements within marxist and *marxisante* labour history over the causes of the failure of the working class to live up to its revolutionary mission, and a more general disagreement between these historians, and those of a more social democratic (if not conservative) frame of reference, who advanced a number of rival arguments, anticipating in many cases some of the themes of the Cambridge School.[8]

---

[7] At best it is an exuberance of language to argue that 'Once we place mid and late-Victorian working class Liberal and Labour activists back into their own political context…enough continuity in popular radicalism can be demonstrated to make the search for social explanation of major changes unnecessary', Biagini and Reid, 'Introduction', *Currents of Radicalism*, 5.

[8] There is no space, nor indeed any great need, to rehearse these debates in full here; a

The main features of these debates can be quickly caricatured. For many historians mid-Victorian stability was, as Bill Lancaster put it, the 'simple and unsurprising' result of prosperity.[9] Not only did the incidence of cyclical unemployment decrease, and wage levels rise, but the structural dislocation of the early nineteenth century made way both for more stable employment conditions, and the establishment of new supervisory and intermediate grades, whose greater rewards and status contributed to the fragmentation of the working class and the emergence of an aristocracy of labour.[10] The greater prosperity of the post-1850 period also provided scope for a more general 'liberalisation' of upper- and middle-class attitudes, building on the legislative concessions of the 1840s, and the fiscal reforms of the 1850s. This both opened up a vista of gradual improvement within the existing political system, and suggested a more accommodating stance towards the working classes on the part of those with political power.

At the same time the diversity of prosperity was emphasised by the cultural accretions, especially the trade unions but also religious, educational, provident and recreational societies, which, as Burgess puts it, 'acted to confirm the process of working class differentiation'.[11] These institutions in many cases functioned as part of a process of social control, or embourgeoisiement, and hence as one wing of the wider processes by which the middle classes controlled and transformed working-class culture, the other wing of which (characterised by Robert Storch's picture of the policeman as 'domestic missionary') were those campaigns and initiatives backed up by the

very full and sensibly critical account is provided in N. Kirk, *The Growth of Working Class Reformism in Mid-Victorian England*, (1985), 1–31, plus the works there cited, in particular, H.F. Moorhouse, 'The Marxist Theory of the Labour Aristocracy', *Social History*, 3,1 (1978), 61–81, and R. Gray, *The Aristocracy of Labour in Nineteenth Century Britain, c.1850–1914*, (1981).

[9] W. Lancaster, *Radicalism, Co-operation and Socialism*, (1987), 53–4.

[10] For technological dislocation and later stability, see D. Goodway, *London Chartism, 1838–48*, (1982), 154–218, R.A. Sykes, 'Popular Politics and Trade Unionism in S.E. Lancashire, 1829–42', (PhD thesis, University of Manchester, 1982), J. Foster, *Class Struggle in the Industrial Revolution. Early Industrial Capitalism in Three English Towns*, (1974), 224–37. For contrasting marxist and non-marxist uses of fragmentation see E.J. Hobsbawm, 'The Labour Aristocracy', *Labouring Men: Studies in the History of Labour*, (1964), R. Harrison, *Before the Socialists. Studies in Labour and Politics, 1861-1881*, (1965), A.E. Musson, 'Class struggle and the labour aristocracy, 1830–1860', *Social History*, 3 (1976), 334–56, K. Brown, *The English Labour Movement, 1700–1951*, (1982), 74–6.

[11] K. Burgess, *The Challenge of Labour*, (1975), 23, 24.

coercive arms of the state, the law, the magistracy, the police, and the poor law guardians.[12]

When, during the 1970s, the concept of social control came under sustained theoretical attack, it was replaced by Gramsci's theory of hegemony, which for all its more sophisticated theoretical underpinnings, has often been used in a purely analogous fashion, for describing a means by which, whatever the viscidity of the process, the working classes were prevented from developing or sustaining radical ideas, and were either incorporated into the capacious ranks of respectable culture,[13] or were left inchoate and leaderless by the failure to sustain an intellectual challenge to bourgeois society.[14]

In one sense the notion of hegemony, in that it generally argued for the creation of a significant, albeit fragile and limited, consensus between middle and working classes, is part of a wider suggestion that mid-Victorian stability was based on a core of shared values, perhaps deriving from the institutions of respectability and self-help;[15] perhaps emerging out of the complex processes of learning based on the practical lessons of the structures of everyday working-class life, the shape of the family, the overwhelming presence of authority, the symbolic lessons of the physical environment;[16] perhaps the result of the common intellectual heritage of radicalism. Hence for Brian Harrison and Patricia Hollis, the career of Robert Lowery demonstrated the rationality of chartism's absorption by liberalism.[17]

---

[12] Robert D. Storch, 'The Policeman as Domestic Missionary: Urban Discipline and Popular Culture in Northern England, 1850-80', *Journal of Social History*, 9,4 (1976), 481-509; F.C. Mather, *Public Order in the Age of the Chartists*, (1959), *passim*, J. Saville, *1848. The British State and the Chartist Movement*, (1987), *passim*, Goodway, *London Chartism*, 99-142.

[13] R.Q. Gray, 'Bourgeois Hegemony in Victorian Britain', in J. Bloomfield, ed., *Class, Hegemony and Party*, (1977), G. Eley, 'Reading Gramsci in English: Observations on the Reception of Antonio Gramsci in the English-speaking world, 1957-1982', *European History Quarterly*, 14 (1984), 441-78. The most extreme expression of the uses to which hegemony has been put is Roger Cooter's *The Cultural Meaning of Popular Science: Phrenology and the organisation of consent in nineteenth century Britain*, (1984).

[14] T. Nairn, 'The English Working Class', *New Left Review*, 23 (1964), 43-57, *idem*, 'The Fateful Meridian', *New Left Review*, 60 (1970), 3-35, P. Anderson, 'Origins of the Present Crisis', *New Left Review*, 22 (1964), 26-53, Kynaston, *King Labour*, 30-44, Burgess, *Challenge of Labour*, 19-20, 31-6.

[15] G. Best, *Mid-Victorian Britain*, (1971), T.W. Laqueur, *Religion and Respectability. Sunday Schools and working class culture 1780-1850*, (1976).

[16] Burgess, *Challenge of Labour*, 20-23, 28-9, Joyce, *Work, Society and Politics*, *passim*.

[17] B. Harrison and P. Hollis, 'Chartism, Liberalism and the life of Robert Lowery', *English Historical Review*, 82 (1967). Similarly Trygve Tholfsen has argued that the

While these arguments undoubtedly provided some of the necessary materials for a comprehensive explanation of the emergence of mid-Victorian stability, they present a series of empirical and theoretical problems. Although the improvement of the economy remains undeniable, the ebb and flow of radicalism was never fully synchronised with the economic cycle, even at the height of chartism in 1841. The rapid collapse in 1842, the narrow revival in 1848, and in particular the lack of response to the quite severe crisis of 1857 and the even more disastrous 'Cotton Famine' in the 1860s all call into question any simple connection. Moreover studies of working-class incomes suggest that there was little marked improvement in working-class standards of living and a widespread persistence of working-class poverty into the 1860s.[18] While it is clear that some occupational groups (not necessarily 'skilled' workers) did better out of the post-1850 prosperity than others, the notion of a labour aristocracy remains descriptively imprecise, and the implications of wage differentials on social and political attitudes far from clear.[19]

Undoubtedly, the middle classes did reap economic benefits from the greater stability of the economy after 1842, and this and the lessons of chartism helped encourage reforming legislation, civic philanthropy, and even a degree of political accommodation; but it is easy to over-exaggerate the impact of these. One of the key elements of liberalisation in the 1840s, the 1847 Ten Hours Act, was in practice reneged on as soon as the act was passed: the 10.5 hour settlement enshrined in the acts of 1850 and 1853 was for the cotton operatives as much a symbol of middle-class perfidy as it was of a new humanitarian state.[20] Philanthropy also had its limitations: there was no guarantee, as civic leaders found time and again, that the provision of a library or some drinking fountains could bring more amicable and deferential relations between the classes. While it may well be true, as Joyce has

'overlapping' between the two ideologies made it almost inevitable that the classes would be drawn into a shared vision in which 'the values of the working class sub-culture turned in an unintended and unexpected direction – assimilation to the cultural patterns dominated by the middle class', *Working Class Radicalism*, 84 and *passim*; the notion of overlapping is also invoked elsewhere, see for example D. Thompson, *The Chartists*, (1984), 332–4.

[18] For a useful summary of the debate see J. Rule, *The Labouring Classes in Early Industrial England*, (1986), chapter 1; also see below, chapter 2.

[19] For a recent study of the empirical and theoretical difficulties of the labour aristocracy thesis, with references to the extensive previous work, see T. Lummis, *The Labour Aristocracy, 1851–1914*, (1994).

[20] 'A Manchester Cardroom Operative', *Ashton Standard*, 1 May 1858.

suggested, that there was a much greater chance of success in developing this kind of deferential relationship between an individual master and his workforce within the structures of factory work, the stable factory communities of the North Lancashire towns on which he based his study of factory paternalism were far from characteristic even of Lancashire, the paternalism of the masters was an ambivalent one, and processes which he incorporates into his notion of 'the culture of the factory' were largely the same as those which operated so ambiguously in the wider society.

Indeed, in many cases the reaction of the working classes to the institutions of hegemonic control, whether community- or factory-based, was to avoid them. The greater success of such institutions from the 1850s is as much a symptom of the new basis of class relations as a cause, not least because the operation of these institutions cannot be assumed to be detrimental to the maintenance of distinctive working-class attitudes. As Peter Bailey has demonstrated, working-class participation in such institutions often represented a sophisticated process of role playing, the acknowledgement that certain values and beliefs, and the codes of conduct which went with them, were appropriate in certain situations or at certain times but were far from absolutely binding.[21]

Populism, chartism and liberalism

One of the most striking features of the debate as it had evolved into the 1980s was relative neglect of the actual attitudes and beliefs of the working classes. Many studies failed to move beyond a comfortable behaviourism, making little attempt to examine working-class attitudes themselves, and instead taking the apparent collapse of radicalism and increased working-class participation in the institutions of respectability as *prima facie* evidence of changes in attitude. This was particularly true of the more empirically-inclined non-marxist historians, but it was a danger which even the more sophisticated marxisante historians did not avoid.[22] Hence even the culturalist labour aristocracy studies of

---

[21] P. Bailey, 'Will the Real Bill Banks Please Stand Up? Towards a Role Analysis of Mid-Victorian Working-Class Respectability', *Journal of Social History*, 12 (1978–79), 336–53; this whole topic is considered in greater depth in chapters 5 and 6.

[22] One honourable exception is John Foster's attempt to get at the 'intellectual conviction' of the Oldham working class, Foster, *Class Struggle in the Industrial Revolution*.

Gray and Crossick tended to use 'respectable labour patterns' or 'distinct patterns of behaviour' as a surrogate for attitudes themselves, in the process skirting around the central problem of establishing the full boundaries of the intellectual world in which the working classes lived.[23]

It has been the significant achievement of the 'linguistic turn' in nineteenth century social history, in striving to emphasise the importance of historical languages, to bring the close study of what, amongst others, the mid-Victorian working class actually wrote and said, back to centre stage.[24] In doing so, it has in part taken up the work of the earlier 'consensus historians', and considerably developed their insights. It has also essayed a more fundamental challenge to the dominant traditions of nineteenth century social history, repudiating what is seen as the social determinism of cultural materialism, the assumption that, for all the qualifications which might be invoked, political movements and the attitudes which lie behind them 'are little more than the natural (i.e. causally determined) outgrowths of prior social and economic realities' – that, in Thompsonian terms, there is a direct relationship between social being and social consciousness.[25] Instead, emphasis is placed on the importance of language, symbols, rituals, and the cultural genesis of identities.[26] In the process, the linguistic turn seeks to reorder the priority usually given to class,

---

[23] R.Q. Gray, *The Labour Aristocracy in Victorian Edinburgh*, (1976), 130, G. Crossick, *An Artisan Elite in Victorian Society: Kentish London, 1840–80*, (1978), 110. For a strident critique of the tendency to behaviourism see R.S. Neale, *Class in English History, 1650–1850*, (1981), 155–8.

[24] The notion of the 'linguistic turn' is a useful way of integrating the approaches of the Cambridge and Manchester schools, not least because Gareth Stedman Jones and Patrick Joyce, the leading figures in each school, are the two scholars perhaps most associated with the movement in Britain. However, this should not obscure the significant differences which remain in their positions, as well as in those of their schools. For discussions of the distinctions, and the debates engendered by the linguistic turn, see David Mayfield and Susan Thorne, 'Social history and its discontents: Gareth Stedman Jones and the politics of language', *Social History*, XVII (1992), 167–88, Jonathan Lawrence and Miles Taylor, 'The poverty of protest: Gareth Stedman Jones and the politics of language – a reply', *Social History*, XVIII (1993), 1–16, and various subsequent contributions in this journal, culminating with Patrick Joyce, 'The end of social history?', *Social History*, XX (1995).

[25] J. Lawrence, in Biagini and Reid, *Currents of Radicalism*, 65; for the most sustained development of this position see Wahrman, *Imagining the Middle Class*, *passim*.

[26] For perhaps the best up to date introduction to the international roots of the linguistic turn see Joyce, *Democratic Subjects*, (1994), 1–20.

asserting instead 'the absence of class as the dominant or most meaningful category'.[27]

The repudiation of class proceeds on several levels. Doubt is thrown on the existence of homogenous class positions by reference to the greater complexity currently ascribed to the process of industrialisation in Britain.[28] Detailed empirical investigation of the languages and identities of what might be termed the 'working class', is used to demonstrate that although the language of class is never finally eclipsed, increasingly as the century goes on, 'class is subsumed in broader moral and political values', and complementary vocabularies of, for example, the 'people' are drained of their class connotations, leaving a populist demotic in which languages of class become increasingly prescriptive rather than descriptive, and 'the principal emphasis is not on class, but on the distinctions between rich and poor'.[29] It is suggested that the consciousness of the working class is not the consciousness which is identified in the Thompsonian tradition; i.e., that as the working classes do not focus on economic exploitation, and the replacement of economic individualism by collectivism, they do not demonstrate class consciousness.

Furthermore, the linguistic turn seeks to take issue with the concept of 'experience' which was central to the Thompsonian dialectic of consciousness-formation. For Thompson, experience was the frame in which social being was manifested to the individual, the interpretation of which led to consciousness. In the critiques of the Cambridge and Manchester schools, however, Thompson's notion of 'experience' is demonstrated to be both imprecise and inadequate. Not only does it fail to take into account the different levels of experience (which can include, for example, shared family traditions, as well as personal memory), but it ignores the 'impossibility of abstracting experience from the language which structures its articulation', and indeed through which it is constituted.[30] And if experience is constituted or ordered through language, then the nature of the linguistic processes and available linguistic resources attain a status alongside, if not above,

---

[27] Vernon, *Politics and the People*, 252, cf. Joyce, *Democratic Subjects*, 2.

[28] Wahrman, *Imagining the Middle Class*, 1-10.

[29] Joyce, *Visions of the People*, 56-7, 293, 294. In this he comes almost full circle to the position of historians such as Bedarida, who have long emphasised the populist nature of working class radicalism in this period, and to those who have continued to doubt to utility of class as an analytical concept for this period.

[30] Stedman Jones, *Languages of Class*, 20, Joyce, *Visions*, 9.

those of any prior social reality, which cannot then be said to be their ultimate foundation. This brings into question the whole validity of the distinction between the 'real' and 'representation' of the real. At times this questioning appears to approach a complete rejection of the 'real'; hence in Joyce's *Democratic Subjects*, 'the constitution of the real is seen to be inseparable from representation', while the 'social' is merely 'a historical construct'.[31] Hence, explanations of the rise and then collapse of chartism, and of the emergence of popular Liberalism, need to be sought through a close examination of the practices, and especially the languages, of politics, for it is here that perceptions of the social are shaped, identities forged, and political programmes promoted.

With respect to chartism, the foundations of this historiographical revolution lie in the work of Gareth Stedman Jones.[32] In its initial formulation Jones' argument identified a failure of chartist ideology, suggesting that its collapse in the late 1840s derived from its inability to come to terms with the changed economic structure of mid-Victorian industrialisation, that its backward-looking artisanal demands, based on long-standing radical notions of 'Old Corruption' and class legislation, became increasingly irrelevant in a world where 'Old Corruption' was waning, and the state was requiring a more neutral, reformist, face. Later he suggested that at root this was a problem not so much of ideology, as of language – that the incapacity of chartism to develop an ideological assault appropriate to industrial society was because the existing structures of language were incapable of encompassing the new experiences of the working class.

Although there were moves to develop these insights during the 1980s, in the works of Robbie Gray, Alastair Reid, and Gregory Claeys, it is really with the publication in 1991 of Patrick Joyce's *Visions of the People*, and the subsequent publications of students and colleagues of Stedman Jones and Joyce, that a new interpretative frame has come to be established.[33] Above all, this frame seeks to emphasise the shared heritage and shared values of chartism and liberalism. Chartism is portrayed not just as a movement which failed to develop an economic critique, but one whose critical frame was rooted in the centuries-old tradition of English radicalism. Even if it employed the

---

[31] Joyce, *Democratic Subjects*, 154, 5.
[32] Stedman Jones, *Languages of Class*, 90–178.
[33] See notes 4 and 5 above.

language of class, and imbued other languages, including those of the 'people', with class meanings, its values (democracy, freedom, independence, honour and manliness) were not essentially class values. Although chartism was 'a repository for all sorts of disparate campaigns and movements', in the support of its mainstream for Free Trade (even if only after the Charter), and its radical anti-statism, it was ideologically close to middle-class radicalism, and its tactics were more akin to the constitutionalism of middle-class radicalism than the rhetorics of physical force might at first suggest.[34]

Alongside this re-evaluation of chartism has come a re-evaluation of liberalism. Instead of mid-Victorian liberalism being portrayed as a largely bankrupt political force, presented with power as a result of the fragmentation of Peel's Conservative party but unable, before the absorption of the Peelites after 1859 and the subsequent emergence of Gladstone as leader, to overcome the gulf which separated the dead weight of whiggism from the fragmented reformism of the radicals, it has been rediscovered as a movement of ideological cohesion which already by the later 1850s had become 'the natural, respectable ruling force in Britain'.[35] Not only did liberalism appeal explicitly to collectivities other than class, in an attempt 'to transcend and negate what were seen as [class's] divisive and destructive effects', but in emphasising local, provincial and national identities, and in sustaining the central narratives of English radicalism and its values, it was easy for it to be seen by former chartists as 'completing the business of Chartism'.[36] Working-class liberalism 'was not the fruit of the success of "bourgeois ideology" during the mid-Victorian decades, but rather of the institutionalisation of older and genuinely plebian traditions'; and indeed, Liberalism was increasingly permeated with 'diluted Chartism'.[37]

Rereading the 'linguistic turn'

This amounts to a full scale assault on the mode of social history dominant in Britain since the 1960s, cultural materialism, and a

[34] Taylor, *Decline of British Radicalism*, 101.
[35] J.P. Parry, *The Rise and Fall of Liberal Government in Victorian Britain*, (1993), 167.
[36] Joyce, *Visions*, 55, 37.
[37] Biagini and Reid, 'Introduction', *Currents of Radicalism*, 10; Parry, *Rise and Fall of Liberal Government*, 209.

wholesale reordering of the dominant interpretative framework of mid-nineteenth century British social history. Unfortunately, although it provides important notes of caution as to the reductionist tendencies of some materialist history, it does so in part by claiming an undue novelty for its own approaches, and in part by developing an epistemology which does not itself provide a more satisfactory explanatory framework for historical change.

Empirically, the biggest problem is how to account for the juncture of ex-chartists and Liberals given the deep differences which split them over parliamentary reform. For Biagini, '[n]o single issue illustrates the continuity between chartism and working class liberalism better than popular commitment to the enlargement of the franchise'.[38] Yet as Parry and Taylor have recently stressed, what marked the Liberal party at the national level, and most provincial liberals, was their extreme lack of enthusiasm for any further substantial measure of franchise extension – parliamentary reform was needed to increase the influence of urban radicals in the House of Commons, not the influence of the urban working class over the election of MPs.[39] Indeed, despite the appearance of cosy cohabitation which it might be possible to portray for the 1870s, the creation of this relationship needs detailed explanation.

In truth, a clutch of integrative forces have been identified as pushing forward this reconciliation. Stedman Jones stressed the importance of the changing nature of the state: chartism, as an ideology of political exclusion was only believable as long as social conditions 'could convincingly be assigned political causes'; '[o]nce, however, the evidence suggested that real reform was possible within the unreformed system...then radical ideology could be expected to lose its purchase over large parts of its mass following'.[40] This theme, of an apparently increasingly neutral state undermining the force of the chartist analysis, has been taken up almost universally.[41]

Moreover, it is suggested, if the state was never entirely above radical suspicion and resentment, such responses were rooted in historical narratives (a key concept for the new social history of

[38] Biagini, *Liberty, Retrenchment and Reform*, 257.
[39] Parry, *Rise and Fall of Liberal Government*, 209–14, Taylor, *Decline of British Radicalism*, 25–40, 158–89.
[40] Stedman Jones, 'Rethinking Chartism', 106.
[41] Biagini, *Liberty, Retrenchment and Reform*, 7–8, Taylor, *The Decline of British Radicalism*, 301–6, 338–9.

identity) which could be used to emphasise the identity of lower and middle classes. One such narrative was the struggle of the 'people' against the idle and profligate, which encouraged '[p]lebian radicals' as Biagini puts it, 'to accept political messages which centred on a "democratic crusade against the privileged orders"'.[42] Another, perhaps even more powerful, was that of the nation (and its local counterpart, the community). Given the strong influence of European affairs on late chartism and mid-Victorian radicalism, both the cohesive force of the idea of the nation, and the practical benefits of organised co-operation between ex-chartists and middle-class radicals, 'ultimately helped to reconcile liberals to labour'.[43]

The contribution of organisational change is not fully clear. At a national level, the Gladstonian Liberal party was created not merely by compromises over policy, but also through the more general acceptance of the overriding importance of the stability of Liberal government.[44] At the local level, less acknowledgement is given to the role of party, not least because of the prevalence of powerful suspicions of party and party activists, although Vernon suggests that the gradual spread of party organisation was one element in the disciplining of popular political culture which he traces in this period. More important than formal organisation were the personalised symbols and rituals of leadership. Politics was dramatised in terms of leadership and the cult of the leader and his qualities; Bright – the 'plain man' – and Gladstone – the 'Grand Old Man' – helped to constitute both political identities and programmes.[45]

Yet it is difficult to see how this can amount to repudiation of cultural materialism. In emphasising the changing nature of the state (and it is clear that he is arguing for a changed state, and not just a different perception of the same state), Stedman Jones is basing his argument on material transformations, and experiences of them, even if these transformations are political rather than economic. While this takes us some way beyond Thompson's unduly circumscribed and underdeveloped notion of 'experience', it does not provide an alternative to the experience-consciousness dialectic.

---

[42] Biagini, *Liberty, Retrenchment and Reform*, 12.
[43] Finn, *After Chartism*, 227.
[44] Taylor, *Decline of British Radicalism*, 309–35.
[45] Vernon, *Politics and the People*, esp. 258–70; Joyce, *Democratic Subjects, passim*.

Likewise, in considering the role of organisational co-operation over matters such as European liberalism and the American Civil War, or in suggesting the powerful influence of changing cultures of politics, recent scholars have illuminated the complexities of the contingencies between social being and consciousness, especially as these relate to self-identification; yet there is little that is controversial in this. It can be argued that despite the potential dangers of Marx's formulation that 'in the final instance' consciousness is determined by social position, the bulk of recent cultural materialist history has approached the large theoretical gulf inherent in this position with a full sensitivity to the complex contingency of the relationship between social being and social consciousness.[46]

Above all, it is difficult to see how recent work on the mid-Victorian period provides a causal foundation for the development of specific languages. The one area of potential here would seem to be an argument that structures of language moulded popular perceptions in directions which encouraged the triumph of particular formulations and identities. However, little attempt is in fact made to address the constitutive role of language: there is no demonstration of the ways in which language moulds subjective experience. Joyce, in fact, is at pains to underline his belief that the linguistic turn does not deny human agency in the way in which some early structuralist writings on language did. A feature of the linguistic turn is its awareness of the flexibilities of languages, of different meanings which can be invested in the same words, the degree to which 'new wine was to be found in old bottles', as Joyce puts it.[47] For the most part the discussion of language degenerates into the study of ideas and belief systems, even if particular sensitivity is shown to the languages in which these are expressed.[48]

There is some suggestion that technologies of communication might have acted to push thinking in certain ways: the press 'actively promoted some ways of seeing the world and relegated others', and the public platform and the political meeting could operate to promote a

---

[46] See N. Kirk, 'History, language, ideas and post-modernism: a materialist view', *Social History*, 19 (1994), 230, 236; this piece considers some of the issues raised by the linguistic turn in greater depth than, but from a similar perspective to, the criticisms developed in the rest of this section, and I am considerably indebted to Kirk's discussion.
[47] Joyce, *Visions*, 29.
[48] A point well made by Caroline Steedman in 'Linguistic Encounters of the Fourth Kind', *Journal of Victorian Culture*, 1,1 (1996), (forthcoming).

particular version of identity. However, this is very 'soft' language, and it is not clear how it takes us much beyond Marx's notion of the importance of the 'means of mental production' in the promotion of dominant ideologies.

Apart from such ideas, the main focus remains on the role of key leaders, whose personalisation and dramatisation of issues and activities serve as the foundations of identity and political unity, both in the chartist and post-chartist periods. But why were these leaders successful? It is not enough to argue, as does Joyce, that political success was based on the articulation of 'effective political languages', or, as Vernon does, that 'new political styles and identities were only successful if they struck a chord with their popular constituencies'.[49] We need to know what made an effective language. Joyce's argument that effective languages 'needed to make sense of people's conditions and outlook' or 'articulated the needs and desires of their audiences' seems to point to the only obvious way out of this impasse – that it is the ability of languages, political or other, to make sense of that inchoate confrontation with the world which we describe as 'experience' which provides their purchase.

Not surprisingly, therefore, despite the epistemological confusions, there appears to be a drawing back from the denial of the real, or even of the social, so that the existence of the real is acknowledged although it 'can only ever be known by terms that are culturally and historically formed', and although 'the self and the social always constitute one another'.[50] Hence, Patrick Joyce, while formally recanting the language of experience which was not fully excised in his *Visions of the People*, is unable to prevent his later *Democratic Subjects* from also being fired through with invocations of experience, and some prior reality which influences it (if couched as 'situations' or 'circumstances').[51]

This retreat – never fully acknowledged – is critical, for if the real exists, then so can the social, or at least that element of the social which under cultural materialism would be described as 'class position',

[49] Joyce, *Visions*, 27, Vernon, *Politics and the People*, 250.

[50] *Ibid*, 26, 14.

[51] *Ibid*, 28, 45, etc; again for a discussion of these confusions see Kirk, 'History, language, ideas and post-modernism', 225–30; however, while Kirk directs his attack at the willingness to collapse the distinction between reality and representation, I would argue that the more recent formulations of *Democratic Subjects* makes this a less tenable position, and that in any case, the ultimate willingness to acknowledge the existence of the real is more damaging to the 'post-modern' position.

the structure which predisposes a pattern of shared experiences. In this case, what is defined in the complex iterations of self and the social is not the social, but rather the self's perception of the social, an important but fundamentally different thing.

In fact, the attempts of Joyce to dismiss class confront quite distinct notions of class. The first considers what in Marxist terminology might be called the 'objective' existence of class, the existence of class *position*. And although it sits uncomfortably with the thrust of the rest of the linguistic critique, there can be no doubt that the unevenness of the process of industrialisation does force historians of class to think more carefully about the processes of class formation (albeit that the Thompsonian position rests not so much on social homogeneity, as on a heterogeneity structured by shared fundamental experiences (of wage labour, alienation and exploitation)). The second addresses the existence of class *consciousness*, or to be more specific the consciousness of class, the sense of class identity. The third confronts more comprehensively the nature of class consciousness, its forms and content. However, in doing so it clearly erects an unduly narrow and prescriptive version of what consciousness ought to be, if it is to be 'class consciousness'.[52] Outside the redundant canons of Marxist orthodoxy, there is no reason why any one idealised form of class consciousness should be privileged over others. If class exists, and subscribes to a set of shared beliefs, those beliefs, whatever they are, but especially if they include some sense of common class identity, can legitimately be described as that class's consciousness.

Towards a model of consciousness and consciousness-formation

It becomes apparent as we delve into the complex debates which mark the scholarship of the chartist and post-chartist periods, that the thread which draws these debates together is the search for an effective, empirically-sound theory which would provide the key to understanding the dynamics of the changes in popular consciousness on which must have rested the collapse or the continuities of working-class radicalism. The question of the nature of consciousness is widely debated within

---

[52] Joyce, *Visions*, 11, 14, 121; see the comments of N. Kirk, 'In Defence of Class. A Critique of Recent Revisionist Writing Upon the Nineteenth Century English Working Class', *International Review of Social History*, 32 (1987), 31.

the sociology of knowledge and social psychology, and this is not the place for an extended discussion of this theorising.[53] Instead a basic position, which draws considerably on what is implicit (rather than explicit) in much current historical writing, but which is informed by the theoretical debate, can be proposed.

It begins from the suggestion that consciousness cannot be treated as an unproblematic or monolithic phenomenon, but must be seen rather as a complex amalgam. Effective examination of consciousnes necessitates disaggregating the form, the content and the status of consciousness. Put over-simply, such a framework might run as follows. Consciousness is an amalgam of various forms of 'knowledge' and belief, which derives from the interaction between experience and the creation of meanings. Experience is patterned in various ways, and given meaning through language and via theoretical understandings of the world. The reflexive process of attempting to comprehend and extract meaning from experience is informed by the theoretical ideas and positions available in society, which circulate in a range of institutions and sites which can be called the 'intellectual matrix'. In particular this matrix provides the resources for the abstraction and generalisation of individual experience into group and class identity. The interaction of individuals and groups and the institutions within which ideas circulate is referential: cultural and political action engendered by theoretical belief can in turn shape the intellectual matrix, which thus remains central to the development and maintenance of group and class consciousness.

As has become clear, the concept of class consciousness remains confused by its role within Marxist theory, in which there is a tendency to focus on the status of class consciousness rather than its content. Too often, an *a priori* ideal type is invoked, which is to be 'attained' or 'acquired' and is then 'possessed'. The consequences of this approach are merely to set up unhelpful distinctions between false and imputed consciousness, and to imply a linear theory of the development of consciousness. Instead, any effective model of consciousness formation must first seek to examine what in pure Marxist terms would be termed the 'social' or 'psychological' consciousness of the working class.[54]

---

[53] For a fuller discussion see M. Hewitt, 'Structures of Accommodation: The Intellectual Roots of Social Stability in mid-nineteenth century Manchester, 1832-67', (DPhil thesis, University of Oxford, 1991).

[54] Neale, *Class in English History*, 17–40.

Consideration of the *form* of consciousness is important to emphasise that consciousness is in part articulated ideas, in part unarticulated practical knowledge, and in part the cultural knowledge involved in the implicit acceptance of social conventions of family, peer group or larger society.[55] It includes both the results of the lessons of personal history, of formal schooling, and of the informal schooling provided by, for example, the material environment. As such, consciousness cannot be reduced to a jumble of 'ideas' and beliefs, which individuals carry around in a kind of mental bag to be dipped into at appropriate moments; there is more to it than the numerical indices of attitudes compiled by some contemporary sociologists.[56] This ensures that although the consciousness can be both articulated and unarticulated, it has a mobility and a reflexiveness which ensure that the consciousness bound up in everyday practice must remain consistent with, and retain the sanction of, articulated concepts and beliefs.

Similar distinctions can be made with respect to content. This can be conceived as comprising practical knowledge which overlaps with the basic factual knowledge accruing from cognition and perception; norms or values which provide the criteria of moral evaluation; theoretical knowledge which orders basic factual knowledge (and provides the means both of comprehending the workings of the world and of judging appropriate means of implementing normative judgements in the light of such judgements); visionary knowledge, or some notion of an ideal social order which will fully manifest normative judgements; strategic knowledge, of the appropriate modes of social action needed to bring about this ideal social order; identity, through which the individual situates himself or herself in relation to the various collectivities which appear to organise the social and political world; and an overall philosophy or *Weltanschauung* which integrates as far as possible these other elements. For example, an individual can have the ability required to hold down a job and earn wages (practical knowledge), an appreciation of the amount of money he (or she) is paid in wages (factual knowledge), a belief as to the justice or fairness of these wages (normative knowledge), a certain understanding of the way in which the level of wages is generated by economic processes (theoretical knowledge), a conception of an alternative way of organising society

[55] For one example of this kind of distinction see A. Giddens, *Central Problems in Social Theory. Action, Structure and Contradiction in Social Analysis*, (1979), 5.
[56] A point made by Gordon Marshall, 'Some Remarks on the study of Working-Class Consciousness', *Politics and Society*, (1983), 263–301.

which would produce a just level of wages (visionary knowledge), a belief as to the most appropriate means of achieving the necessary changes to obtain this state (strategic knowledge), a sense of sharing these conditions and aspirations with others (identity), and a general attitude that it is a nice idea, but 'not the sort of thing that people like me could actually achieve' (*Weltanschauung*).

The formation of group and class consciousness rests in part on the patterning and evaluation of experience. As the 'linguistic turn' has sought to bring to the fore, social position is only one of the ways in which experience is patterned. Gender, ethnicity, generation, religion, and even 'party' (in the Weberian sense) could be proposed as alternatives. However, particularly during the nineteenth century, the commonalities engendered by social position were far stronger, and erected much more formidable accumulations of comparable experience than any other: the experience of the working-class Irishwoman was much more akin to that of the British working-class male than it was either to the middle-class Irishman or the middle-class woman.

The evaluation of experience is the process by which the confrontation of the individual with the world is translated into perceptions, memories, and understandings. The influence of language on this process, rests on its ability to make sense of the world. Hence the importance of the 'intellectual matrix', the sites and practices which furnish the basic conceptual (linguistic) tools whereby experience in its unconstructed reality is abstracted and generalised into forms suitable for memory and articulation, and the theoretical frameworks whereby this experience, its causes and significance, can be comprehended and interpreted.

The shape of these arenas of reflection for a specific period and place can be termed a society's 'intellectual morphology'. Of course political institutions disseminate the conflicting theoretical positions which are used to make sense of reality; but they also act purposefully to articulate grievances and establish programmes of change. Thus the intellectual morphology is especially significant for the abstraction of individual experience into shared experience, the necessary basis of the essentially political processes which create notions of identity, visions of the future, and strategies and tactics to achieve change. The opportunities and constraints offered by the intellectual morphology also provide the terrain on which political groups struggle to establish a coherent platform, gain access to their target groups, and build up support.

Schematically the intellectual morphology can be divided into media, institution, and site. Although communications technology was advancing rapidly during mid-century, revolutionising the transmission of news, the production of newspapers, and the circulation of individuals, media in this period were essentially local and personal, not national and mass. This enhanced the influence over the production and reproduction of ideas of the institutional matrix, both informal (family, peer group, community), and formal (education, religion, voluntary and political organisations). Such institutions often took on the guise of venues (sites) of intellectual activity, and the predominance of direct and personal media placed a premium on access to and control of sites. Such sites would include both the tangible (street, pub, town hall), and the less tangible (the 'public platform', the neighbourhood).

The local focus

Adequate explanation of the course of popular or working-class radicalism in the chartist and post-chartist years thus needs to incorporate some sense of the precise nature of working-class consciousness in this period, its continuities and changes over the period, and the ways in which the intellectual morphology mediated between experience and belief. To this end, this study seeks to analyse the history of Manchester between 1832 and 1867. Manchester appeals in its own right. As the major northern conurbation, it avoids many of the dangers of localities distorted by particular and local conditions. The major industrial city of the North West, it stands at the apex of regional cultural and intellectual activity; this limits the potential for definitive intellectual and cultural trends being developed outside the community under consideration. Manchester was the 'shock city' of the industrial revolution. Contemporaries gravitated towards it as the pre-eminent representative of a new industrial order, and its impact on the national consciousness created an enduring image. It was an image nevertheless, and one which, despite Manchester's importance, modern historical scholarship has little rectified. Both because of its importance to contemporaries, and its neglect by their descendants, nineteenth century Manchester is worthy of detailed study. It also provides a useful counterpoint to many of the locations on which the current picture of the mid-Victorian transformation has been based. In essence, two types of locations have attracted the most attention: factory towns created by the rapid growth of the textiles industry, in the north of England and in Scotland, including Foster's Oldham, Koditschek's Bradford, Kirk's Ashton, and Joyce's Blackburn; or older more established centres of artisanal industry, such as Gray's Edinburgh, Crossick's Kentish Town, or Tholfsen's Birmingham. In many respects Manchester bridges these worlds: although a child of textiles revolution, it was never, despite impressions, a factory town, and its occupational structure was more heterogeneous than has often been accepted; nevertheless, the rise of the commercial sector and the development of engineering notwithstanding, it never lost its factory hands and its unskilled Irish. Nor did Manchester possess the integration of work and leisure which was possible either in the factory town or the artisan community, and it thus provides a more appropriate locus for an examination of the extent to which the interplay of socio-economic conditions and working-class politics was mediated by the intellectual structures of society.

Difficulties exist, particularly of size and definition. By 1831 the population of the township of Manchester itself was 142,026, and including the adjoining townships which made up the parliamentary borough in 1832 and the municipal borough in 1838, its total population was already over 200,000. By 1871 the population of Manchester had increased to 400,804. This scale limits the extent to which demographic and prosopographic techniques can be used, except in the case of selected samples. At the same time, the rapid geographical expansion of the city from 1832 to 1867, and the position of Salford, administratively separate, but appearing by the mid-century as 'a great overgrown suburb or appendage of Manchester rather than a separate, distinct and independent borough', create problems of definition.[57] Intellectual community was no respecter of administrative boundaries, and in light of this, a flexible definition of 'Manchester' will be used throughout this study, allowing inclusion both of Salford and the outlying villages gradually being incorporated into Manchester's urban sprawl during the mid-nineteenth century. As a result of this confusion, consistent statistical information is difficult to acquire: where possible figures for Manchester and Salford (municipal boroughs) will be used; but often information is more readily available for Manchester alone, and will be taken as representative of the wider community.

[57] 'Thomas Davies', *SWN*, 24 February 1866.

Conclusion

Although recent studies of the mid-Victorian period have rightly called attention to the continuities as well as the discontinuities between chartism and post-chartism, there is a danger in pushing this revisionism too far. The temper and shape of working-class radicalism in the 1850s and 1860s were quite distinct from those of the 1840s and 1850s, and this transformation cannot easily be explained by an appeal either to economic improvements, or to the underlying prevalence of populist identities cohabiting with and even overwhelming identities of class. The materialists grossly underestimate the complexities of the relationships between social conditions, attitudes and political action. The proponents of the linguistic turn, for all their emphasis on this contingency, have as yet provided neither an explanation of the success of particular languages over others, nor a discussion which considers the issue of identity within the broader constituents of consciousness. By disaggregating consciousness, and by suggesting the significance of what can be called the 'intellectual matrix' in its formation, a general framework can be established within which to explore with greater precision the nature and significance of the mid-century watershed.

Chapter Two

Manchester: economic growth and social structure

Manchester: image and reality

Manchester magnetised the attention of contemporary observers: from Britain, Europe and America they came to witness the pioneer of a new era. Proclaiming their opinions in diaries, articles, books and novels, they gave the city in the second quarter of the nineteenth century a higher profile than any other in the world. Seeking to comprehend the new reality, commentators produced a powerful image which enthroned Manchester in the public consciousness as the archetype of a new order. Not simply foisted upon them, but in part created by Manchester men themselves, this image powerfully influenced the way in which leading Mancunians thought about their city, and it has endured in the treatment of Manchester by historians almost to the present day. As Richard Dennis has argued, this picture was predominantly an ideological creation; it was designed to explain the rise, for good or ill, of working class radicalism, of socialism and chartism.[1] Nevertheless, it established its own reality.

Manchester confronted contemporaries with a visage of unbounded technological advance. From a distance it was a city of tall chimneys and smoke-laden skies. 'As you enter Manchester from Rusholme', wrote G.J. Holyoake in 1848, 'the town at the lower end of Oxford-road has the appearance of one dense volume of smoke, more forbidding than the entrance to Dante's inferno. It struck me that were it not for previous knowledge, no man would have the courage to enter it'.[2] Scarcely blessed before the 1840s with a single public building worthy of note, it was architecturally dominated by the rows of imposing six and eight storey mills which lined the banks of its rivers and canals.[3] For those whose contacts gained them access to the

---

[1] Richard Dennis, *English Industrial Cities of the Nineteenth Century*, (1984), 49–50.
[2] *Reasoner*, V (1848), 92.
[3] For the development of public and commercial architecture in Manchester see S. Gunn,

interior of a mill, to these impressions was added the overwhelming impact of the heat, noise, and constant movement of the typical factory. Thomas Carlyle wrote in 1839 of 'the awakening of Manchester, at half-past five by the clock; the rushing off of its thousand mills, like the boom of an Atlantic tide, ten thousand times ten thousand spools, and spindles all set humming there – it is perhaps, if thou knew it well, sublime as a Niagara, or more so'.[4]

Nevertheless, awe-inspiring as the technical developments of the factory were, it was the social implications of the new industrial regime that pre-occupied most observers. Disturbingly, the industrial city gathered together a large and heterogeneous population, and crammed them together without order, or any of the normal social institutions of pre-industrial society. Primarily, the cleavage was seen as social, an unavoidable consequence of the rise of large scale factory production. De Tocqueville saw in Manchester, 'a few capitalists, thousands of poor workmen, little middle class', echoing the warning of Manchester doctor James Philips Kay in 1832 that 'the disruption of the natural ties has created a wide gulph [sic] between the higher and lower orders of the community, across which the scowl of hatred banishes the smile of charity and love'.[5] In the 1850s and 1860s and beyond, commentators, especially those from within Manchester society, took the rhetoric of cleavage and made it their own; again and again the dangerous isolation of rich and poor in Manchester was made the rallying cry of social reform.[6] Hence in 1871 James Fraser, recently installed Bishop of Manchester, was doing little more than repeating a local platitude when he called for 'something that would bridge over those prodigious chasms which separated the high from the low, the learned from the ignorant, the refined from the coarse and brutal'.[7]

'The Manchester Middle Class, 1850-1880', (PhD thesis, University of Manchester, 1992), 47–9.

[4] T. Carlyle, *Chartism*, (1839), 83.

[5] A. de Tocqueville, *Journeys to England and Ireland*, (1835), 104, J.P. Kay[-Shuttleworth], *The Moral and Physical Condition of the Working Classes Employed in the Cotton Manufacture in Manchester*, (1969 [or. 1832]), 49.

[6] For example, John Roberton, 'Suggestions for the Improvement of Municipal Government in Populous Manufacturing Towns', *TMSS*, I (1853-54), 81, E. Brotherton, *Popular Education and Political Economy*, (1864), 9-15; cf. the comment of the *MX*, 10 September 1864.

[7] *MCN*, 20 May 1871; the pervasiveness of such ideas in European culture has been nicely explored in A. Lees, *Cities Perceived: Urban Society in European and American Thought, 1820–1940*, (1985).

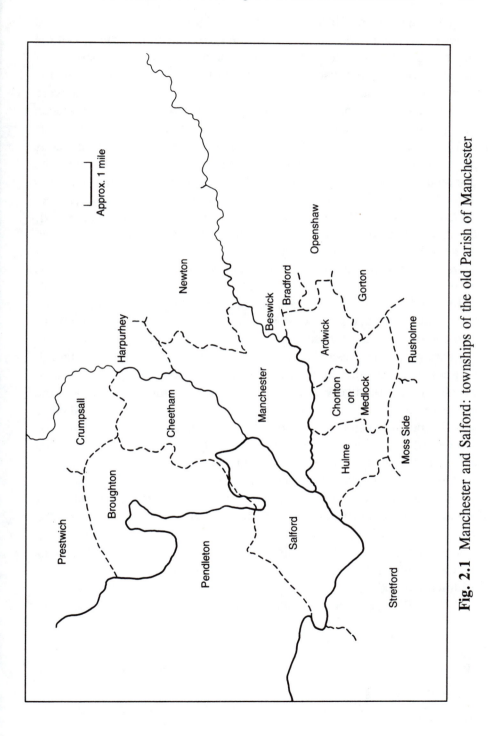

Fig. 2.1 Manchester and Salford: townships of the old Parish of Manchester

In the 1830s it remained the common belief that the fulcrum of social cohesion was the personal contact of the different social orders. But the sheer size of Manchester ruptured this contact and raised the spectre of social dislocation and disorder. The pace of growth from 1800 onwards created fears which may seem exaggerated with hindsight, but were widespread at the time. 'Enormous masses of human beings have been precipitously accumulated', shrieked one Salford clergyman at the start of 1834, fearful that industry had 'drawn together a most heterogeneous population, consisting in no small degree, of the unsettled, the discontented and the depraved; so as to render our trading districts...the moral sewers of the community – a confluence of the scum and offscouring of society'.[8] In these circumstances, it had to be accepted, as Canon Richard Parkinson said, that 'There is far less personal communication between the master...and his workmen...than there is between the Duke of Wellington and the humblest labourer on his estate'.[9]

By the 1840s, this perception of social cleavage was being overlain by a complementary sense of spatial division. Bound by their vision of a dichotomous factory society, contemporaries reduced the social geography of Manchester to the separation of rich and poor. As the full consequences of the uncontrolled expansion of population became visible in the wretchedly unsanitary conditions of the old town, and the overpopulated and underventilated working-class suburbs of Ancoats and Hulme, it became a commonplace of middle-class thought that the growth of the city had created what Layhe called the 'utter and irremediable estrangement' of middle class and working class.[10] According to Cooke Taylor, anti-Corn Law propagandist, and committed protagonist of the factory system, '...the geographical limits of non-intercourse established in Manchester are the greatest of the special evils connected with that town...Ardwick knows less about Ancoats than it does about China'.[11] Engels' picture of Manchester as a city designed to keep the working classes from the sight of the millowners and merchants as they drove in their carriages from Ardwick, Broughton and Pendleton to their offices in the city centre,

[8] 'A Salford Clergyman', *MC*, 18 January 1834.
[9] R. Parkinson, *On the Present Condition of the Labouring Poor in Manchester*, (1841), 13.
[10] *MTPAR*, (1842), 18.
[11] W. Cooke Taylor, *Notes of a Tour in the Manufacturing Districts of Lancashire*, (1842), 160.

merely placed a universal perspective into the context of radical analysis.

Once again, this was an enduring perception. In the 1850s and 1860s it was still part of platform platitude to talk about the 'sifting of the rich from among the poor'.[12] Nor did the sense of beleaguerment felt in the 1830s and 1840s quickly fade. In the 1860s the phenomenon of the 'Ancoats rowdy' fuelled fears that certain parts of the city were becoming no-go areas even for the police, and opposition to further franchise reform could still be based on the fear that 'the inhabitants of all the principal and more respectable streets, and of the innumerable good houses in the suburbs...[would be] swamped by the inhabitant [sic] of back streets, courts and wretched quarters, the less respectable and least intelligent part of the community'.[13]

Not surprisingly, early historians of Manchester seized upon the image of social and geographical cleavage and used it as the framework for their own analysis. Thus, according to Donald Read, writing in 1959, 'society in early industrial Manchester was centred almost exclusively on its cotton industry, and reflected only the basic division within that industry. It lacked all the usual gradations of status or wealth; masters and men faced each other almost alone'.[14] In the early 1960s Asa Briggs called into question the sharpness of this split, and suggested a more complicated social structure than had previously been allowed.[15] Yet despite this, and the lip-service to complexity which has often followed in Briggs' wake, historians have continued to fall into the trap of treating Manchester in dichotomous terms. For some this has been partially mitigated by their own avowed interest as much in the image as in the reality which it attempted to comprehend.[16] In many cases, however, the contemporary picture of Manchester is simply allowed to go by default.[17] In others the longevity of the myth

[12] Rev. John Richardson, 'The Habits of the People', *PPL*, II (1856), 2.
[13] *MCN*, 1 December 1866, 'H.G.', *MG*, 15 March 1860.
[14] D. Read, 'Chartism in Manchester', in A. Briggs, ed., *Chartist Studies*, (1959), 30.
[15] A. Briggs, *Victorian Cities*, (1963), 88–139.
[16] This is perhaps the charitable way to approach Messenger's deeply disappointing *Manchester in the Victorian Age, the Half-Known City*, (1985); see also V. Pons, 'Contemporary interpretations of Manchester in the 1830s and 1840s', in J.D. Wirth and R.L. Jones, eds, *Manchester and Sao Paulo: problems of rapid urban growth*, (1978), and his highly Engels and Cooke Taylor derived account of 'Housing Conditions and Residential Patterns in Manchester of the 1830s and 1840s', unpublished paper, MCL.
[17] For example, F.V. Vigier, *Change and Apathy: Liverpool and Manchester during the Industrial Revolution*, (1970), 132–42, M. Girouard, 'Manchester and the Industrial City', *Cities and People. A Social and Architectural History*, (1985), 256–70.

is less comprehensible. Hence Gatrell in his unpublished thesis acknowledges the complex nature of Manchester society in contrast to contemporary rhetoric; yet the basic thrust of the thesis, as summed up by his published study of the struggle for incorporation is that '...the very depth of the chasm between rich and poor, and the sanctions it acquired in law and ideology, almost guaranteed the rich an inward turning and self-referential mentality'.[18]

Approaches to Manchester which move beyond the cottonopolis image have as yet failed to establish a new orthodoxy. Perhaps the best brief analyses of the heterogeneous nature of Manchester society remain buried in the unpublished PhD theses of Robert Sykes and Simon Gunn.[19] Alan Kidd's introduction to the 1985 volume, *City, Class and Culture* remains the most accessible modern portrayal. Kidd stresses that the Manchester 'social structure, even in the 1830s, could not be reduced to that of mill master and factory hand'.[20] The masters were smaller and less established than had once been assumed, and Manchester, never entirely a mill town, was increasingly dominated by warehouses. Yet the recharacterisation remains tentative: much of the diversification which Kidd cites is located firmly in the second half of the nineteenth century, if not in its final few decades. Kidd is hardly to blame in this, for the narrow range of material which he cites reinforces how little has been done to develop suggestions more than twenty-five years old and assess critically the established image of industrial Manchester. The appearance since Kidd wrote of Lloyd-Jones and Lewis's study of *Manchester and the Age of the Factory* provides an important new source for comprehending early nineteenth century Manchester.[21] Nevertheless, the state of historical scholarship on

---

[18] V.A.C. Gatrell, 'Incorporation and the pursuit of Liberal Hegemony in Manchester, 1790-1839', in D. Fraser, ed., *Municipal Reform and the Industrial City*, (1982), 17; for his more sympathetic analysis of Manchester see Gatrell, 'The Commercial Middle Class in Manchester, 1820-1857', (DPhil thesis, Cambridge University, 1972), 77-106. For a recent readiness to dismiss Manchester as a "factory town" see H.W. Wach, 'The Condition of the Middle Classes: Culture and Society in Manchester, 1815-50', (PhD thesis, Brandeis University, 1987), 9-10 and *passim*.
[19] R.A. Sykes, 'Popular Politics and Trades Unionism in South East Lancashire, 1829-42', (PhD thesis, University of Manchester, 1982), 80-344, Gunn, 'The Manchester Middle Class'.
[20] A. Kidd, 'Introduction: The Middle Class in Nineteenth Century Manchester', in A.J. Kidd and J.W. Roberts, eds, *City, Class and Culture. Studies of social policy and cultural production in Victorian Manchester*, (1985), 7-9; see also his more recent *Manchester*, (1993), 23-32.
[21] R. Lloyd-Jones and M.J. Lewis, *Manchester and the Age of the Factory*, (1988).

Manchester is such that to describe it, as one historian has recently done, even as the 'half-known city' is perhaps over-optimistic.

Manchester: economic development

Manchester was built on cotton, but it was a cotton city and not a cotton town. Nevertheless, at mid-century it still bore many of the signs of its rapid rise on the crest of the industrial revolution. In 1772 it had been a sizeable but compact and unexceptional town of about 25,000 inhabitants, not a manufacturing centre in its own right: its manufacturers were middlemen who supplied cotton and sometimes tools to a predominantly out-working labour force, and then shipped the finished goods to London for export.[22] Only after the harnessing of the steam engine to Crompton's mule freed manufacturing from the edge of the Pennines, and the Napoleonic Wars brought the rapid expansion of the industry, did the town begin to expand rapidly.[23] The importance of textiles (overwhelmingly cotton and silk) for the Manchester economy is revealed by the pattern of employment in Manchester shown by the 1841 census (see Table 2.1). Employment in textiles, at around 40,000, dwarfed all other industrial activity, and much of the employment in other industrial and in retail and commercial sectors was heavily dependent on textiles. The prosperity of Manchester rested on the prosperity of cotton.

Hence the city was intimately involved in the upheavals and depressions of the cotton industry in the 1830s and 1840s, when despite industrial growth, levels of production and profit fluctuated wildly and the structure of the industry was highly unstable. From the early 1830s both spinning and weaving underwent further technological transformation. In spinning, Roberts' self-acting mule was rapidly introduced, particularly for the coarser yarns, and further refinements over the course of the 1840s and 1850s enabled it to produce all but the

[22] S.D. Chapman, *The Cotton Industry in the Industrial Revolution*, (1972), 11–16; L.S. Marshall, 'The Emergence of the First Industrial City. Manchester, 1780–1850' in C.F. Ware, ed., *The Cultural Approach to History*, (1940), 141.

[23] C.H. Lee, *A Cotton Spinning Enterprise, 1785–1840*, (1972), 4–5, Chapman, *Cotton Industry*, 17–32. Fixed capital employed trebled in the first two decades of peace, and then doubled again in the next 20 years; between 1825 and 1836 imports of raw cotton doubled: D.A. Farnie, *The English Cotton Industry and the World Market, 1815–96*, (1979), 52–4, 61–2, 97–105, S. Jones, 'The Cotton Industry and Joint Stock Banking in Manchester 1825–50', *Business History Review*, XX,2 (July 1978), 171.

very finest of counts by 1860. In weaving, handloom outworking lost ground steadily to powerloom production, particularly through further extension of integrated spinning and weaving firms. Only in the 1850s did the industry achieve some kind of technological stability.

Partly for this reason, the years around 1850 can be seen as a turning point for cotton manufacturing. Also important were renewed impetus and much greater stability in the demand for yarn, and the ability of overseas markets, particularly India, to overcome the continuing uncertainty of domestic market for cotton goods. The 1850s saw a further wave of credit-based expansion. Between 1851 and 1861 spindles, looms and employment capacity increased by 44%, 60% and 36% respectively.[24] Notwithstanding problems of cotton supply, measured by raw cotton imports, the industry more than doubled in the third quarter of the nineteenth century.[25] In Manchester, however, cotton production largely stagnated from the early 1850s, and employment in the industry fell (Table 2.1). Although Manchester remained a major centre of cotton production, the premier centre of fine spinning in the country, and a substantial producer of woven cloth, this stagnation marked the steady, albeit gradual, erosion of cotton's overwhelming dominance of the Manchester economy.

In part this reflects Manchester's changing role within the textile economy. By the 1820s it was clear that Manchester was beginning to supplant London as the commercial centre of the cotton goods trade. Between 1820 and 1830 the number of warehouses in Manchester increased from 126 to over a thousand, and the central commercial core of the city began to encroach on the surrounding residential districts.[26] Directories demonstrate the constant increase in the numbers of dealers and agents in the 1830s and 1840s.[27] By 1848 there were 1603 warehouses in the municipal borough, and this figure increased moderately but steadily during the 1850s (see Table 2.2). Employment

[24] Gatrell, 'Commercial Middle Class', 411, C.H. Lee, 'The Cotton Textile Industry', in R.A. Church, ed., *The Dynamics of Mid-Victorian Business*, (1980), 167–73, Farnie, *English Cotton Industry*, 44, 93–6, 105–6, 135, Vigier, *Change and Apathy*, 156–9.
[25] A.E. Musson, *The Growth of British Industry*, (1978), 203.
[26] Jones, 'Joint Stock Banking', 166–7. See also Roland Smith, 'Manchester as a centre for manufacturing and merchandising cotton goods 1820-30', University of Birmingham Historical Journal, IV (1953–54), 63–4.
[27] See Chapman, *Cotton Industry*, 46–50, Jones 'Joint Stock Banking', 172–3.

Table 2.1 Manchester business structure: total employment, 1841–61[28]

	1841	1851	1861
Production			
Textiles	39,081	56,572	55,169
Metals/Engineering	6,518	13,503	19,757
Finishing/Chemicals	5,139	6,059	5,151
Clothing Trades	11,688	22,441	28,971
Building Trades	7,423	10,612	12,811
Food/Drink Processing	2,021	3,898	3,783
Misc. Manufacturing	5,595	12,641	15,374
Extractive Industry	244	749	902
Commerce/Distribution			
Commercial Middle Class	2,229	2,469	2,861
Warehouse Workers	5,086	9,520	12,137
Clerks/Shop Assistants	2,877	4,437	5,222
Transport/Distribution	1,879	5,362	7,920
Retail			
Retail Trades	7,047	12,709	13,935
Pubs and Inns	853	3,295	2,825
Lodging Houses	457	639	848
Services			
Government Officials	1,345	3,091	3,094
Professional Middle Class	1,198	2,360	3,104
Education	681	1,452	1,884
Entertainment	183	472	660
Public Utilities	135	244	659
Domestic Service	14,157	20,166	26,314
Others			
Land and Agriculture	1,294	1,834	2,085
Undefined Labourers	7,404	7,023	6,440
Undefined Mechanics	---	1,001	1,886
Undefined/Miscellaneous	15,847	10,356	10,515

in the warehousing and distribution sectors increased rapidly between 1841 and 1861, the number of warehouse workers increasing from five to twelve thousand, and of clerks from nearly three to over five thousand. Likewise, those employed in transportation, including porters, carters, and railway workers, rose from less than two thousand

[28] From the census occupation tables in *PP*, (1844) XXVII [587], 148–77, *PP*, (1852) LXXXVIII Part II [1691–1], 648–53, *PP*, (1863) LIII Part II [3221], 648–54, occupations reclassified.

to nearly eight thousand (Table 2.1). In the early 1860s Manchester no longer struck the inquiring visitor as the shock factory city of two decades earlier; instead it appeared to the visiting Henry Adams as 'a collection of enormous warehouses, banks and shops set in a broad margin of common brick houses'.[29]

The Manchester economy was also diversifying in other directions. Most directly linked to cotton production were the finishing trades, bleaching, dyeing and printing, which transformed the woven cotton, grey cloth or calico into merchandisable goods. Lloyd-Jones and Lewis found 240 firms engaged in the various finishing trades in 1815 accounting for 2.32% of total rateable value in the city (just over a third of the figure for spinning); by 1825 these figures had risen to 300 and 3%.[30] Many of these firms were involved in other aspects of the cotton industry, particularly commercial ones, and in some cases these would have been warehouses of firms operating outside Manchester in adjacent townships such as Bradford; but despite urban sprawl, many large establishments, such as Thomas Hoyle's Mayfield print works, remained within the borough's boundaries. Figures for 1848 suggest over 40 bleaching and printing works employing 3798 men in the borough of Manchester itself.[31] Within Manchester and Salford, the finishing and chemical sector employed fairly constantly five to six thousand hands between 1841 and 1861, the chemical industry's share being relatively small. Chemicals developed in the area both because of linkages with the finishing trades and the proximity of the main British chemical district, the St Helens – Warrington – Widnes triangle.[32] Twenty-nine chemical producers have been identified for 1815 and although an 1848 survey of 'large establishments requiring water supply', which would have included most if not all of the chemical works in Manchester, identified only eleven, employing a mere 179 workers, this reflected the congregation of the industry just beyond the boundaries of the municipality, particularly to the east, in the townships of Newton and Bradford.[33] In 1859 one survey identified

[29] A.W. Silver, ed., 'Henry Adams Diary of a Visit to Manchester', *American Historical Review*, LI (1945–46), 80.

[30] Lloyd-Jones and Lewis, *Manchester and the Age of the Factory*, Table 3.5, 30, 155–8, 163, 176–8, including Tables 9.3, 9.7, 9.8, 9.9; the large number of 'firms' identified in comparison to later figures based on establishments highlights one of the problems of interpreting the R.V. figures – it is not clear if what is being measured is finishing works, or merely the warehouse of the merchant involved in putting out such work to establishments in most cases well outside Manchester.

[31] Manchester City Council, Watch Committee, *Report of the Chief Constable on Police Statistics*, (1848), 77.

[32] L.E. Haber, *The Chemical Industry during the Nineteenth Century*, (1958).

[33] *Police Statistics*, (1848), 74–5.

Table 2.2 The shape of the Manchester business sector, 1846–60[34]

(Numbers of buildings in each category)

	1848	1850	1852	1854	1856	1858	1860
Textile Mills	126	131	135	140	123	121	126
Print/Dyeworks	42	42	39	36	41	39	42
Machinists/Foundries	89	91	91	103	120	121	116
Hat Manufactures	15	15	14	12	11	11	10
Paper Works	3	3	3	3	4	3	3
Corn Mills	11	11	9	8	12	13	15
Saw Mills	23	27	35	40	52	53	60
Misc. Workshops	749	775	902	931	1214	1217	1128
Warehouses	1603	1619	1663	1708	1743	1756	1758
Shops	5909						7833

Note that these figures are not comprehensive for the non-textile sectors and undoubtedly underestimate their relative importance.

31 chemical works in the immediate vicinity of Manchester, but only three within the city.[35]

The other major spin-off from cotton was engineering.[36] By 1800 Manchester already possessed a diverse and rapidly expanding engineering industry, and after 1800 large and increasingly sophisticated foundries and firms producing advanced machine tools spread along the Ashton and Rochdale canals. In 1815 engineering rivalled the finishing sector in size and in the following decades growth was rapid.[37] Advances in machine tool construction, the development of metal planing machines, slotting and paring machines, and boring machines, along with constant demand for new machinery from the cotton industry, and the opening of new markets with the arrival of the railways, provided the foundation for the growth of large new firms, including Fairbairns, Whitworths and Sharp and Roberts and Co.[38] By 1845 there were over a 100 firms listed as involved in the various engineering classes, and during the 1840s Manchester eclipsed London

---

[34] Calculated from *Police Statistics*, (1846–60).

[35] Survey of John Leigh, *MG*, 4 August 1859; cf. comments on Butler Street, Bradford, in *MTPAR*, (1853), 28–9.

[36] For the linkage effects see Farnie, *English Cotton Industry*, 27–34.

[37] A.E. Musson and E. Robinson, *Science and Technology in the Industrial Revolution*, (1969), 427–72, Lloyd-Jones and Lewis, *Manchester and the Age of the Factory*, 160–3. A good contemporary picture is given by James Naysmith, *Autobiography*, (ed. Samuel Smiles) (1883), 184–207.

[38] A.E. Musson, 'The Engineering Industry' in Church, *Mid-Victorian Business*, 87–92.

as the major engineering centre of the country. In 1851 the engineering/metals sector was already employing nearly a quarter of the number employed in textiles, and apart from the related clothing trades, was the most important industrial sector after textiles (Table 2.1).

Despite the traditional picture of engineering decline after 1850, in many areas of engineering growth continued and Manchester consolidated its position at the head of the British machine-tool industry.[39] The number of machinist/foundry works listed in the Manchester police returns (themselves probably an understatement) increased from 89 in 1848 to 121 ten years later (Table 2.2). At the same time, William Fairbairn spearheaded the advance of heavy civil engineering, and firms such as Beyer, Peacock and Company established themselves as leaders in the supply of railway rolling stock. During this period, although textiles stagnated, the numbers employed in engineering increased rapidly, reaching nearly 20,000 in 1861 and continuing to expand in the 1860s.

By 1870, as Simon Gunn has pointed out, Manchester also possessed a 'plethora of workshops engaged in small-scale textile production – over 700 units employing almost 7000 workers...the "dress trades", including shoemakers, milliners, shirtmakers and tailors'.[40] The extensiveness of these dress trades was one of the marks which distinguished Manchester from the Lancashire cotton towns.

Of course, the ramifications of the textile revolution were not confined to directly ancillary industries such as these. Important in themselves, their sum was greater than their individual parts because in concentrating in and around Manchester they contributed to the creation of a large industrial conurbation, and to the growth of the myriad enterprises integral to the nineteenth century city. Building trades were required to build mills, factories and houses; considerable numbers were employed in clothing, shoeing, and feeding the population. Indeed, the high demand for female labour contributed to the rapid commercialisation of many traditionally domestic functions, such as baking.[41] The retail and food processing sectors expanded

---

[39] *Ibid*, 98–106; see the number of Manchester firms in the leading national firms listed in S.B. Saul, 'The Market and the Development of Mechanical Engineering Industries in Britain, 1860–1914', *Economic History Review*, XX (1967), Table 4, 121; for machine tools see also R. Floud, *The British Machine Tool Industry, 1850–1914*, (1976).

[40] Gunn, 'Manchester Middle Class', 61–4.

[41] The comparatively high concentration of bakers per thousand inhabitants in Manchester is noted in I. McKay, 'Bondage in the Bakehouse? The strange case of the journeymen bakers, 1840–1880', in R. Harrison and J. Zeitlin, eds, *Divisions of Labour: Skilled*

rapidly in line with the growing population. The retail trades employed nearly 14,000 workers by 1861. Within manufacturing, clothing trades employment grew from nearly 12,000 workers in 1841 to almost 29,000 in 1861, and by 1871 the building trades had doubled their 1841 figure of over 7,000. Moreover by 1871 miscellaneous workshop manufacture, mirroring the rise of engineering, was employing more than 25% of the textiles figure, reflecting the cumulative effects of considerable pockets of various important trades, including a flourishing publications trade employing printers and bookbinders, and glass-, cabinet-, and packing-case-manufacture.

Manchester: occupational structure

Manchester was thus a cotton city: it had grown out of the 'take-off' of the British cotton industry, and notwithstanding the variegation of its economic structure its prosperity remained deeply intertwined in the prosperity of the cotton industry. However, it was never a factory town in the way that its satellite cotton towns Ashton or Stalybridge or Dukenfield were. Manchester throughout the period 1832–67 retained a complex occupational structure.

The apex of Manchester's social structure was bourgeois. The aristocrats who had once inhabited the halls with which Manchester and Salford were dotted, had abandoned them during the eighteenth century. The Mosley family sold the rights of the lordship of the manor to the Manchester council in 1846, and the only landed families who retained some vestigial interests in the city were those such as the Egertons of Worsley, and the Ellesmeres, whose influence was predominantly in South Lancashire or Cheshire.[42] This is not to argue that the Manchester elite was wholly urban; as Gunn has noted, '[m]any of the city's leading industrial employer families – McConnel, Kennedy, Murray, Birley, Houldsworth – had landed origins and sustained connections to the gentry through kinship, the county bench and inherited or acquired landholding'.[43] It is rather to suggest that

Workers and Technological Change in the Nineteenth Century, (1985), 49, 76.

[42] Gatrell, 'Commercial Middle Classes', 140–41; for the impact of retained landholdings on the development of Manchester see J.R. Kellett, *The Impact of Railways on Victorian Cities*, (1969), 151–7.

[43] S. Gunn, 'The "failure" of the Victorian middle class: a critique', in J. Wolff and J. Seed, eds, *The Culture of Capital: Art, Power and the Nineteenth Century Middle Class*,

competition between a pre-industrial aristocracy and a new industrial elite played no significant part in the social or political dynamics of class formation in early or mid-nineteenth century Manchester, and to affirm that Manchester had probably as large a middle class as other nineteenth century British cities.[44]

In the early part of this period, manufacturers, both cotton and otherwise, were the backbone of the middle class, but, reflecting the city's diverse economy, even at this period, the middle class was drawn from a wide economic background and included industrialists, merchants, professional men and shopkeepers. In the Waterloo period, economic divisions between spinning and weaving divided the cotton masters, but by the end of the 1820s divisions of economic interest within the industrial middle class had largely been healed, creating an economically coherent group.[45] But these were not the substantial parvenus of legend. The cotton masters themselves were largely drawn from previous merchants and manufacturers of the pre-factory cotton industry, and as Manchester consolidated its commercial supremacy so manufacturing wealth tended to revert to commercial and financial enterprise, and the city's merchants became increasingly pre-eminent.[46]

In the early decades of the century, the distinction between mercantile and manufacturing was blurred by the prevalence of the putting out system. Only as weaving was drawn into the factory, and the international mercantile houses arrived from London, did the commercial community become more distinct. Not that it was economically homogeneous. Entry barriers were low. Many merchants held few stocks, and obtained orders from buyers before purchasing from manufacturers.[47] During periods of credit expansion, it was relatively easy for newcomers with little capital but adequate references to finance quite extensive operations with paper money, with sometimes

(1988), 28.

[44] In this Manchester differed from many contemporary towns and cities. See D.N. Cannadine, ed., *Patricians, Power and Politics in Nineteenth Century Towns*, (1982), D. Smith, *Conflict and Compromise. Class formation in English Society, 1830–1914. A Comparative Study of Birmingham and Sheffield*, (1980), 26–32, and R. Trainor, *Black Country Elites. The Exercise of Authority in an Industrial Area, 1830–1900*, (1993), 87–90. For a simple measure of the proportion of the Manchester population which could be described as middle class, see Gunn, 'Manchester Middle Class', 92–6.

[45] Lloyd-Jones and Lewis, *Manchester and the Age of the Factory*, 63–80, 135–50.

[46] On the origins of the cotton masters see A.C. Howe, *The Cotton Masters, 1830–60*, (1984), 51–61.

[47] G. Anderson, *Victorian Clerks*, (1976), 10.

unfortunate consequences in times of monetary pressure.[48] The proceedings of the bankruptcy courts illustrated the constant flow into and out of the merchant community. The large houses which dominated both in the home and overseas trade, proclaiming their status by the erection in the 1850s and 1860s of grand new warehouses in the centre of the city, were thus the tip of a substantial iceberg.

Similarly, although the cotton, finishing, and engineering industries were dominated by a relatively small number of large firms, in all cases entry barriers were sufficiently low to sustain a considerable number of smaller and more unstable firms, and less prosperous masters.[49] Although the average size of cotton firms increased steadily in the 1840s and 1850s, the increasing importance of small specialised machine tool firms in engineering, the general proliferation of small-scale workshop production in metals and clothing, and the growth of the building trades with their large number of small firms, meant that the industrial middle classes were never dominated numerically by the substantial cotton master.[50] The implication of both Tables 2.2 and 2.3 is that a man such as Robert Rumney, who began life as a grocer's porter and became a manufacturing chemist at Ardwick, member of the Manchester council, and an active educational reformer, was a more typical 'Manchester man' than the merchant princes and master manufacturers, even if the latter usually occupied the more prominent positions in Manchester civic life.[51]

Men such as Rumney provided a bridge to the broader professional groups whose status compensated for their often less favoured economic position. Religion, the law and medicine provided the city with a strong and expanding cadre of professional men, and alongside them were the accountants, commercial and insurance agents, and educationalists.[52]

---

[48] W.R. Callender, *The Commercial Crisis of 1857: its causes and results*, (1858), 27–35.
[49] V.A.C. Gatrell, 'Labour, Power, and the Size of Firms in Lancashire Cotton in the Second Quarter of the Nineteenth Century', *Economic History Review*, XXX,1 (February 1977), 95–113, R. Lloyd-Jones and A.A. Le Roux, 'The Size of Firms in the Cotton Industry in Manchester, 1815–41', *Economic History Review*, XXXIII (1980), 72–82.
[50] Floud, *British Machine Tool Industry*, 32–50.
[51] For Rumney see *MCN*, 31 August 1872; on the openness of the urban elite see J. Garrard, *Leadership and Power in Victorian Industrial Towns 1830–1880*, (1983), 31–5. This is not to subscribe to the Victorian myth of social stability, but to acknowledge as R.J. Morris has done, that limited mobility into the middle classes was a realistic aspiration for many who started life on the boundaries between the middle and working classes.
[52] For the legal professions in early nineteenth century Manchester see V.R. Parrott, 'Manchester Attorneys: Occupation, Communication and Organization: a study of the

Although numerically relatively insignificant (despite steady growth during the period), at least some of this class played important cultural roles. Not surprisingly, religious leaders exercised an influence in the city out of all proportion to their personal wealth. Likewise, the significance of science to many cultural activities, and the importance of the medical schools as educational institutions, provided a ready entré to those trained in medicine. The parallel developments of commerce, industry and the cultural institutions of Victorian city life meant that by 1861 over three thousand inhabitants could be described as belonging to the professional middle classes. Beneath these were the heterogeneous retailers, from the small corner shopowner or market stallholder to the large retailing, wholesaling and eventually publishing businessman Abel Heywood. The numerical strength of this group cannot be ignored. By 1860 there were nearly eight thousand shops in Manchester, compared with less than two hundred large industrial establishments and only 1758 warehouses (Table 2.2). Occupationally, and in terms of wealth, Manchester's non-manual cadre was thus structured like a compressed pyramid with a very broad base.

As Morris has suggested, the gulf which separated the shopocracy from manual workers was cultural as much as economic, but purely in strictly economic terms it was stark enough. Even clerks were subject to long hours and a subordinate position which effectively marked them off from the strata above. Clerks in Manchester's home trade warehouses in the 1830s and 1840s often found themselves at work until ten or eleven o'clock on Saturday night, and these long hours were often worked in confined and far from comfortable conditions. Moreover, even many clerks' salaries were below the earnings of the cream of the skilled workers.[53] Similarly, a shop assistant might work from seven o'clock until perhaps half past nine Monday to Thursday, ten o'clock Friday and midnight on Saturday, and then be expected to attend church and Sunday school.[54] Nevertheless, they could at least

profession before 1838', *TLCAS*, 80 (1992), 87–103, *idem*, 'Manchester Solicitors: Forgotten Provincials in the Development of a Professional Myth', *MRHR*, 8 (1994), 74–82.

[53] For a detailed study of the Victorian clerk with much reference to Manchester, see Anderson, *Victorian Clerks, passim*. Unfortunately, as with so many historical works covering the 'Victorian' period, the source material for Anderson's work is heavily biased to the last two decades of the century and the picture presented can only be applied to the 1830–1870 period with some misgivings.

[54] *MX*, 31 August 1858; one butcher's assistant claimed he had to be up at 5 and could rarely leave the shop before 11 p.m., *MX*, 1 September 1858.

aspire to social advancement within the commercial system, as part of a meritocracy whose leading figures were 'often men of considerable acquirements, and...handsomely paid for their work', according to the *Freelance*.[55] The possession of particular skills of literacy and numeracy, and their clean working environment, encouraged a distinct social identity far more profound than differences of dress.[56] As the number of clerks expanded with the development of Manchester commerce (by 1871 3594 men were listed as 'Commercial Clerk') a distinct petit-bourgeois stratum was established in Manchester society.[57]

Similar comments can be made, *mutatis mutandis*, of non-clerical workers within the warehouse, whose rise in importance as an element of the Manchester workforce naturally mirrored that of clerks. The 1871 census returns suggest that over eight thousand men, not identified as clerks, were employed in Manchester warehouses. These would have included messengers, errand boys, porters, and those employed within the packing departments. The development of hydraulic packing machines in the 1840s established working conditions which changed little before the end of the period, and established the packers as 'the only handicraft trades to be found in the Manchester shipping houses'.[58] Four packers would operate the large hydraulic presses used to compress the bales of cotton goods into as small a volume as possible for shipment, and were aided by a staff of hookers, stitchers, finishers, ticketers, stampers and pressers-off. Immersed in the milieu of warehouse rather than factory or workshop, and able to maintain something of artisan status, clerks and warehousemen were usually linked in contemporary accounts, which set them apart from the rest of the labouring classes. Nevertheless, wage rates among warehousemen varied between jobs and were scarcely comparable with those of the skilled labour aristocrats. In 1856 average wages were stated to be about 15-16/- per week, advancing to 20/- only in very rare cases; although David Chadwick's figures suggest average wages in 1860 of 24/- for packers and 18/- for porters.[59] As such, the packers,

[55] *Freelance*, III (1868), 106.
[56] By the cotton famine they were clearly articulating their sense of distinctness from the working classes below, *MG*, 30 August 1862.
[57] A process somewhat disguised by the failure of the censi before 1881 to have a proper classification of clerks.
[58] For a picture of packing processes see *MCN*, 26 August 1871.
[59] Evidence of D. Chadwick, *PP*, (1860) XII (445), 357; his *On the Rate of Wages in 200 trades and branches of labour in Manchester and Salford, and Lancashire, during*

unionised and among the vanguard of moves towards trade union unity in Manchester in the late 1840s and early 1850s, were prepared to define themselves as working class in a way in which clerks were not.

All workers in the warehouse suffered from the bane of long hours, but not so much as those involved in the commercial distribution system outside the warehouse, particularly carters, railway porters and draymen. Until their successful 1860s short-time movement, transferring goods from the warehouses to the railway stations could take carters from the early evening until four or five a.m., mostly waiting for access to the unloading sheds of the railways.[60] Observers estimated that there were five thousand carters alone in Manchester in 1850; effectively excluded from the cultural life of the city, it is not surprising that they were portrayed as a depressed unskilled group whose conditions, like those of other workers, had been undermined by the influx of rural English and especially Irish migrants into Manchester.[61] In the 1850s wages, at least for porters, seem to have declined, and attempts to reduce hours failed.[62] Only in 1864 was the effective reorganisation of shipping arrangements achieved. This limited shipping to all places except Liverpool to before 6.30 p.m., shifting the bulk of the labour of carters, porters, and railwaymen in the shipping system to predominantly daytime working.[63]

By 1871 employment in the warehouse and distribution system accounted for over 10% of adult male employment in Manchester. It remained dwarfed by the manufacturing sector. In cotton, by 1832 mule spinning was dominant (although throstle spinning of coarser threads by a largely female workforce was never entirely displaced). Both took place in factories. Normal work arrangements consisted of one adult male spinner and one piecer (employed by the spinner) per mule. The spinners were the aristocrats of cotton, skilled workmen, much in demand, and able to earn high wages. However, this position was already coming under threat from the rapid spread, particularly for coarser yarns, of Roberts' self acting mule, by which the winding of

1839–59, (1860), gave wage ranges of between 16/- and 32/- for porters and between 22/- and 36/- for packers.

[60] *MCN*, 26 August 1871, 'Sam Cook', *MG*, 19 February 1861.

[61] J.E. Nelson in *MSp*, 17 August 1850, Cooke-Taylor, *Notes of a Tour*, 11-12, C.E. Lester, *The Glory and Shame of England*, (1841), 178–80.

[62] See details on the rates of pay of railway porters in P.W. Kingsford, *Victorian Railwaymen*, (1970), 89–91.

[63] *MG*, 23 October 1852.

the yarn onto the cop, which had previously been the fulcrum of the spinner's skilled position, was largely automated.

Despite the debate over its impact, it is clear that this innovation brought about a crisis for the spinners, or 'minders' as they became known if tending the self-actor.[64] In Manchester, the spinners' numbers were virtually halved in the 1830s: as the number of spindles on each mule was steadily increased, minders were placed in charge of two mules (with two piecers), and the speed of the mules was also increased. Large numbers of spinners were unable to find work, and when piece rates, by which all spinners were paid, were reduced in line with the productivity of the larger faster mules, the earnings of those on older mules fell (although those on the advanced mules were, at a certain cost in extra effort, able to maintain their earnings).[65] Over the longer term the minders were remarkably successful at maintaining their position as skilled workers with high wages, both because of the continued need for personal adjustment of the self-actor, and via control of the labour supply for piecers.[66] However, minders rarely worked beyond forty, while the coupling of mules created an employment bottleneck, and a constant oversupply of piecers anxious to become minders. This made the minders' status precarious, as well as creating a steady haemorrhaging of labour onto the labour market.[67]

Elsewhere in spinning technical change was less dramatic. By the 1830s the replacement of hand by machine in the preparation of raw cotton for spinning had largely been completed, leaving a few male cardgrinders and strippers in the cardroom, and the rest, scutchers, strippers, drawing frame tenters and bobbin and fly tenters, were lower paid child and female labour.[68]

In weaving also, the widespread introduction of the powerloom saw the almost complete feminisation of factory weaving. Before the 1830s

---

[64] For an account of the technological processes involved see H. Catling, *The Spinning Mule*, (1970).

[65] For the condition of the spinners in this period see Sykes, 'Politics and Trades Unionism', 116–22, M. Huberman, 'The economic origins of paternalism: Lancashire cotton spinning in the first half of the nineteenth century', *Social History*, 12,2 (1987), 177–92, W.E. Lazonick, 'Industrial Relations and Technical Change: the Case of the Self-Acting Mule', *Cambridge Journal of Economics*, 3 (1979). For contemporary comments on the plight of the spinners see J. Leach, *Stubborn Facts from the Factories*, (1844), 28–29, *MTPAR*, (1841), 14. For figures for 1836–44 see *NS*, 11 May 1844.

[66] M. Savage, *The Dynamics of Working Class Politics. The Labour Movement in Preston, 1880–1940*, (1987), 84–91.

[67] *NS*, 2 January 1847.

[68] Sykes, 'Politics and Trade Unionism', 165–8.

Table 2.3 Manchester and Salford: adult male employment, 1841-71[69]

	1841	1851	1861	1871
Production				
Textiles	13,687	17,771	14,012	9,101
Metals/Engineering	4,150	10,856	14,978	15,301
Finishing/Chemicals	4,003	4,370	3,757	4,218
Clothing Trades	5,869	8,170	9,396	9,057
Building Trades	6,596	9,275	11,343	14,557
Food/Drink Processing	1,593	3,052	2,772	2,804
Misc. Manufacturing	3,997	7,833	8,572	9,110
Extractive Industry	188	627	696	810
Commerce/Distribution				
Commercial Middle Class	1,989	2,268	2,510	2,233
Warehouse Workers	3,889	4,954	7,179	8,153
Clerks/Shop Assistants	2,420	3,594	3,894	5,837
Transport/Distribution	1,658	4,691	6,794	8,996
Retail				
Retail Trades	5,170	7,144	9,017	9,505
Pubs and Inns	655	1,482	1,350	1,554
Hotels/Lodging Houses	129	73	173	920
Services				
Government Officials	1,226	2,932	2,824	3,294
Professional Middle Class	1,020	1,741	2,177	2,495
Education	324	511	449	771
Entertainment	141	355	436	186
Public Utilities	129	234	628	870
Domestic Service	1,311	1,583	2,242	1,112
Others				
Land and Agriculture	1,157	1,387	1,646	1,288
Undefined Labourers	6,729	6,301	5,781	7,126
Undefined Mechanics	---	740	1,242	1,425
Undefined Miscellaneous	5,894	2,129	2,942	3,761

most weaving was still done by handloom weavers, domestic
outworkers, who comprised the bulk of the population of many of the
outtownships of Manchester, and large numbers within the borough,
particularly in St George's, Ancoats, and the only partially separated
settlement of Miles Platting, which retained many of the characteristics

[69] From the census occupation tables in *PP*, (1844) XXVII [587], 148–77, *PP*, (1852)
LXXXVIII Part II [1691–1], 648–53, *PP*, (1863) LIII Part II [3221], 648–54,
occupations reclassified.

of the outtownships.[70] Once highly paid, by the 1830s handloom weaving was caught between two pressures which were steadily reducing the weavers to abject poverty: the eventual adoption of the powerloom, capable of substantially higher output and thus steadily depressing piece rates, and the constant oversupply of labour brought by low skill barriers. The competition for employment during a period of already considerable economic difficulty both depressed wages and made full employment all but impossible, save for the more skilled smallware and fancy goods weavers.[71] The transference of the silk industry to the Manchester district in the 1820s and 1830s made little difference. During good times it was possible for experienced weavers to earn a tolerable livelihood, but the inexperienced, as John Layhe, domestic missionary in Miles Platting commented, '...in the best of times earn but a miserable pittance, and if anything happens to throw them out of employment, they are soon plunged into the depths of distress'.[72] The result, during the sustained economic depression of the late 1830s and 1840s was appalling poverty. An average income of 2/6 was all that could be expected in the mid-1840s.[73] Relative prosperity in the early 1850s revived handloom weaving somewhat, but a further collapse of employment in the late 1850s meant that handloom weaver unemployment was still a problem in the north-east of Manchester into the 1860s.[74] In 1871, as well as the handloom silk weavers, there were 681 returned simply as weavers, the remnant of the thousands of the 1830s.

These changes in textiles effected a significant transformation in the pattern of employment in Manchester. A self-employed, domestic workforce with (despite an economically dependent position) considerable control of the labour process and the rhythms of work, and a strong, albeit comparatively recent, sense of craft identity and independence, was replaced by a predominantly female, moderately

---

[70] Survey of police district 2 and part of police district 1, *MG*, 8 November 1834, gave a figure of 27% handloom weavers; J. Heywood, 'State of Poor Families in Miles Platting, Manchester', *Journal of the Statistical Society of London*, I (1838), 34–6.

[71] See D. Bythell, *The Handloom Weavers*, (1969), and the correctives in E.P. Thompson, *The Making of the English Working Class*, (1963), and Sykes, 'Politics and Trade Unionism', 217–59.

[72] *MTPAR*, (1845), 11; Heywood suggested that in 1837 best handloom weavers in Miles Platting could earn 12/- a week for a 14 hour day, 'State of Poor Families', 34.

[73] *MG*, 14 March 1846.

[74] Contrary to some pictures (e.g. Musson, *Growth of British Industry*, 204), Layhe's reports suggest this longevity, *MTPAR*, (1852), 38–9, (1853), 5–6, (1859), 5.

paid, occupationally disorganised workforce effectively subordinated to factory work discipline. Between 1841 and 1861 the percentage of the textiles workforce which was male declined from 35% to 25%, and the indications are that the decline accelerated in the 1860s. This reinforced the transformation effected by the stagnation of textile employment. Because cotton employment became so overwhelmingly dominated by young persons or unmarried females, and because the shape of social identity and working-class culture was largely determined by adult male employment patterns, perhaps more revealing than the aggregate figures are the statistics of adult male employment (Table 2.3). Despite the high age threshold (20), and accepting gender bias in excluding adult female employment, these figures, and particularly their contrast with Table 2.1, are most revealing.

Table 2.3 demonstrates the extent to which the level of adult male employment in cotton was much less preponderate than statistics of total employment might have suggested, and the degree to which the substitution of female labour further diluted the prominence of the cotton factory, reducing the proportion of male employment from 16% in 1841 to 7% in 1871. Taking into account the survival of non-factory weaving in silk and cotton, and the considerable number of engineers employed in the cotton factory, classical male factory workers certainly made up less than 10% of employment in Manchester by 1871.[75] The factory operatives were clearly outnumbered by workers in the indefinable unskilled and semi-skilled labouring trades, comprising not only general labourers, but also large numbers in transport and distribution, and many subsumed in the industrial sectors. The importance of this group, which perhaps accounted for over 20% of adult employment in 1841, also declined during these decades and in 1871 probably accounted for no more than 15% of adult male employment.

By this date, the Manchester economy was dominated by the engineering and building sectors, which together comprised 24% of adult male employment, while the clothing trades and miscellaneous manufacturing both accounted for approximately 7% each. Engineering was a diverse industry and covered numerous distinct trades. Although the rapid technological changes of the first half of the century hindered the emergence of stable occupational groups, and created new groups

---

[75] Chadwick, *Rate of Wages*, 5, suggests that somewhere around a quarter of males employed in cotton factories would be employed within engineering departments.

without long-standing craft traditions, trades such as the boilermakers successfully built on the artisanal traditions of the older iron working trades, a powerful presence in early nineteenth century Manchester. Although fragmented into a multiplicity of small craft groups, concentration on apprentice restriction and the development of workplace custom enabled these trades to establish a privileged position. The status hierarchy into the 1860s, stretched from metalworkers, capable of commanding wages in excess of £2 a week, through a range of mechanics and engineers earning between 28/- and 32/-, to the machine minders, often young men, on 18–22/-.[76] Although Gatrell's statement that '...in the 1830s and 1840s the engineering workers were a stabilising rather than a disruptive force in local society' needs to be qualified, clearly the premium wages which many were able to command, and the preoccupation with union-maintained work practices which butressed their position, marked them off from the cotton workers.[77]

Yet, to a greater or lesser extent, it was an experience shared by many of the other major occupations in the Manchester economy. Certainly this was true of the building trades. The sheer physical growth of Manchester necessitated an extensive construction industry. By 1871, the traditional building trades, excluding labourers, accounted for 750 fewer men than engineering. Labour processes in building remained largely stable during the mid-century. In consequence, industrial relations focused on the maintenance of wages and craft status.[78] Despite almost endemic conflict, the building trades were generally able to improve their status over the period, extracting reductions in hours, the Saturday half-holiday, and wage increases, and repulsing the assault on their workplace autonomy represented by the rise of the large master builders and the associated development of contracting for the whole job and subsequent sub-contracting. Average wages in the building trades at the start of the 1860s were between 26/- and 28/- for the principal crafts.[79] The building trade artisans thus

[76] Chadwick, *Rate of Wages*, 25, P. Rushton, 'Housing Conditions and the Family Economy in the Victorian Slum: a study of a Manchester District, 1790–1871', (PhD thesis, University of Manchester, 1977), 180–82.

[77] Gatrell, 'Commercial Middle Class', 99.

[78] For an overview of the building industry in this period see E.W. Cooney, 'The Building Industry', in Church, *Mid-Victorian Business*, 142–60; labour relations among the building trades are detailed by R. Price, *Masters, Unions and Men: work control in building and the rise of labour 1830–1914*, (1980).

[79] Figures of Chadwick, *PP*, (1860) XII (455), 337.

occupied a pivotal position within the Manchester working classes, their developed craft traditions of work autonomy never removing them from labour conflict or elevating them above a sense of general working-class identity.

Care must be taken in translating census figures into particular groups of working men; for example, evidence from the 1852 strikes suggested that semi-skilled labourers made up 40% of the engineering workforce.[80] This was just one pocket of a vast miscellaneous army of labour of varying degrees of casualness, which subsisted at the bottom end of the social scale, involving not merely male labourers, street sellers, etc., but also varying kinds of semi-domestic female work, washing, mangling, charring etc. Labouring was heavily stocked with Manchester's Irish. In 1851, for example, 84% of the labourers in a sample area of Ancoats were Irish.[81]

Nevertheless, it is clear that the core of the Manchester working class was artisanal rather than factory operative or unskilled labouring. This has several implications. In the first place the diverse nature of the city's working class negates attempts, as far as Manchester itself is concerned, to couch the roots of transition to stability in terms of processes taking place within the factory or within the cotton industry more generally. In Manchester the roots of quiescence were more complex. Secondly, although the cotton workforce was transformed in this period, the cotton factory had never dominated Manchester even in the 1830s. The eclipse of cotton saw both growth in engineering and construction, but was also marked by the emergence of general manufacturing and labouring, and its impact on the Manchester working class was thus ambivalent. In part it would seem that the growth of both old and new artisanal sectors generated increasing social stability through the dead weight of their introverted complacency. Certainly, higher wages set the engineering trades apart; they were never happily assimilated into the mainstream of Manchester working-class life. The same was true, to varying degrees, of trades such as printing, bookbinding, and glassmaking, which could pay between 26/- and 32/- per week, and sometimes as much as 40/-. Moreover, the determination of the skilled trades to maintain the craft limitations from which their wage advantages were derived, undoubtedly brought them into conflict

[80] *RWN*, 1 February 1852. In 1859 it was claimed that whereas skilled mechanics had made up 40–45% of the workforce in 1852, this had declined to only 20–22% by that date, *MG*, 23 August 1859.
[81] Rushton, 'Housing Conditions', 172–4.

with unskilled and particularly semi-skilled co-workers, while their apparent prosperity appeared to blunt the enthusiasm with which they embraced general movements of working-class protest and self-assertion.

The working-class experience

Nevertheless, the absence of a simple occupational dichotomy does not necessitate the repudiation of class. For all the heterogeneity of the Manchester working class, there were sufficient threads of shared economic experience to provide the stuff of class consciousness. The artisan trades were not a thin film of cream floating on a mass of operative milk, but represented rather a substantial proportion of adult male employment throughout the period, so that their position was not as sharply divided from the rest of the working class as conventional assumptions might suggest. Cotton spinners and dressers could boast a status and wage-levels comparable with many skilled groups, while amongst some of the clothing trades, the erosion of barriers to entry was progressing at a rate which undermined the artisanal status of those groups.

Indeed, all sections of the working class were forced in this period to confront the challenge of a labour market overstocked by Irish immigration and handloom weaver unemployment. In many crafts skill barriers were largely artificial and a sustained and difficult rearguard action against the encroachments of unskilled unapprenticed labour was necessary. Except in outcome, the struggles of the boilermaker and the fustian cutter were largely comparable. The experience of the fustian cutters, domestic outworkers whose task was to shear the woven fabric to the required nap to make a variety of cloths commonly used for working-class clothing and under no threat from technology until the 1870s, can be taken as archetypical of the trades threatened by an overstocked labour market. Labour surplus in the 1830s cut fustian cutters' wages by between a third and a half; and wages drifted lower in the 1840s despite the strenuous efforts of the cutters to unionise and bring pressure on the putters-out to maintain 'honourable' prices. By the early 1850s, with piece-lengths increasing, and rates decreasing, many cutters could earn only about 6/- a week, and communal family working was a universal necessity. There was scant improvement over the next 15 years.

This experience was mirrored by the dyers and dressers of the cotton finishing trades, about two thousand strong in Manchester in mid-century.[82] In the 1830s and 1840s the dyers were a cohesive well organised group. Again outworking unamenable to control proved more decisive than the lack of technological threat. During the 1840s their bargaining power was eroded by an overstocked labour market, and the subsequent degeneration of skilled status. Wages fell, the 'cuts' which they had to dye were steadily enlarged, and employment became increasingly irregular. In 1853, although nominal weekly wages were 21-23/-, average earnings over the year were claimed to be only 14-15/-. Though the dyers might have shared in the general increase in wage levels at the end of the decade, their status had declined considerably since the early 1830s.[83]

A large proportion of the working class had to confront the threat of technological change. The introduction of the self-acting mule and the powerloom were merely the best publicised of these. In finishing, while the dyers' position was eroded by labour competition, at the opposite end of the industry, printing was transformed in this period as highly-skilled block printing was, except for some complex and high quality printing, superseded by cylinder printing. Despite the comparably high wages which the minority who were able to make the transition to cylinder printing were able to command, the block printers, particularly in the Lancashire hinterland, shared in the steady technological unemployment of the weavers; in consequence the printers were renowned as among the most violent chartists.[84] Similar processes were also at work in the clothing trades, particularly shoemakers and tailors. Here the 1840s saw the steady breakdown of the 'honourable' trade as master tailors sought profits via a putting out

---

[82] Fustian cutters collection, MCLA; see also Sykes, 'Politics and Trade Unionism', 259-65, Love and Barton, *Manchester as it Is*, (1842), 107, *MG*, 14 January 1852, *PP*, (1865) XX [3473], 19-20; for the eventual supersession of hand cutting see W. Shaw, *Manchester Old and New*, (1894), 26.

[83] Sykes, 'Trades Unions and Politics', 191-7; Chadwick, *Rate of Wages*, 10, *Trades Union Magazine*, (1850-51), 299, *MX*, 2 July 1853.

[84] Cooke Taylor, *Notes of a Tour*, 86, 94-5. For a general overview see G. Turnbull, *A History of the Calico Printing Industry of Great Britain*, (1951), 85-7, 209-12. For printers in general see Sykes, 'Politics and Trades Unionism', 197-211, Chadwick, *Rate of Wages*, 12 (the irregular nature of the printers' work meant that earnings for both groups, but especially block printers, were likely to be considerably below notional wage levels). By the early 1840s less than 10% of all printing work was done by block printing, and 1839-59 the rate of wages for those block printers able to find work had declined from 40-28/-; *MG*, 29 May 1847.

system, or the use of unapprenticed labour in 'sweat shops', tapping the ready supply of cheap unskilled and often Irish labour.[85] The total defeat of the 1834 tailors' strike in Manchester left the trade in no position to resist this development. By 1846 more than 60% of tailors were outworkers, and the sweated workers were often working 16 hours a day.[86] At first, aided by the lack of technological challenge, the distinction between the honourable and sweated trades was not entirely eroded, and with more general employment in the 1850s, the tailors were largely able, at the cost of working long hours, to maintain wage levels.[87] By the 1860s, however, as the adoption of machine sewing threatened a second and more decisive blow to status and conditions, industrial relations began to deteriorate rapidly.[88] By this time the hatters too were confronting the challenge of machinery improvements.[89]

These groups were thus forced to confront a danger which had confronted the shoemakers a decade before, when machine sewing began to be introduced. By this time the shoemakers, like the tailors, had weathered the considerable storm of the 1840s with their craft status intact if under pressure, but although fierce opposition to mechanisation was able to delay the introduction of machinery in many places, shoemakers were finding it difficult to maintain their wage levels by the end of the 1850s.[90] In the same way, Manchester brickmakers, faced with the threat of machine-making of bricks in the 1850s, were forced to undertake a protracted and violent defence of their position in the late 1850s and the early 1860s.[91]

Given that technological change took on the aspect of employer-sponsored attack on working-class positions, the prevalence of the threat of technical change merely strengthened the basic lines of battle

[85] Sykes, 'Politics and Trades Unionism', 61, 302–8; D. Bythell, *The Sweated Trades. Outwork in Nineteenth-Century Britain*, (1978), 65–70.

[86] *MC*, 13 May 1846, *MX*, 14 April 1852.

[87] The picture in Chadwick, *Rate of Wages*, of constant rates of 27/- for coat tailors and 21/- for trouser and vest men in 1839–49–59, must be treated cautiously. Irregular work was a problem and significantly his sample of a Salford district in 1860, although it gives average wages at 28/-, shows tailors concentrated in the lower rental houses, much more so than other groups given a similar wage, *PP*, (1860) XII (455), 337.

[88] *MCN*, 18 August 1866, *MX*, 25 August 1866, *BH*, 25 August 1866.

[89] *MG*, 28 June 1862.

[90] R.A. Church, 'Labour Supply and Innovation, 1800-1860: the boot and shoe-making industry', *Business History*, XII, (1970), 25–45. Bythell, *The Sweated Trades*, 106–11.

[91] R. Price, 'The other face of respectability: violence in the Manchester brickmaking trade, 1859–70', *Past & Present*, 66 (February 1975), 110–32.

which existed between employer and employed. Manchester was never a city of small workshop production. Although there are dangers in overestimating the extent of the barriers, particularly in the early decades of the nineteenth century, the lines between master and man were always more clearly defined than in cities such as Birmingham. As structural developments (as in the building industry), or technical change (as in textiles or engineering) raised the level of capital needed to gain entry as an employer, so the channels of social mobility within trades were stopped, and the focus of working-class ameliorative aspiration was concentrated more exclusively on conditions of employment. As such, although the relative success with which the creation of acceptable bargaining structures varied from the only occasionally ruffled stability of the engineering trades to the periodic violence of the Manchester brickmakers, industrial relations throughout the economy were fired through with an awareness of the essential conflict between the interests of masters and men, a bitterness which employer paternalism could temper but not eradicate (see chapter 7).

At the root of this conflict were wages. Rising wages in the mid-Victorian period have often borne much of the weight of explanations of post-chartist stability. However, such arguments must be treated with extreme caution for several reasons. Not that the materialist argument is empty. When David Chadwick essayed his survey of wage rate movements between 1839 and 1859, the overall picture he painted was one of advance, in some cases quite marked, and he was able, according to his own claim, to defend his statistics before the men themselves.[92] The statistics of G.H. Wood and Deane and Mitchell, particularly for the cotton industry, demonstrate increases in average earnings of over 30% between 1850 and 1874, at least a third of which occurred from 1860 to 1870.[93] Piecemeal evidence from Manchester trade disputes suggests that wage rates in many occupations improved during a similar period, if not to a similar extent.

However, the notion that the decline of chartism can be associated with a substantial improvement in living standards is questionable on a number of levels. The mortality rates computed by Pooley and Pooley suggest that there was little overall decline in death rates in Manchester from the early 1830s to the 1860s. That decline which there was would have been obscured for contemporaries by the successive peaks of the

[92] Chadwick, *Rate of Wages*, *passim*.
[93] See the discussion of this literature in Kirk, *Working Class Reformism*, 79–131.

late 1830s, late 1840s, 1852–3, 1858 and mid-1860s. Significantly, the decline in tuberculosis mortality (perhaps most susceptible to improvements in the standard of living) was marginal before the 1880s.[94] Most crucially, the figures for wage improvement show this to be a feature of the late 1850s, rather than the 1840s, and yet, leaving aside the rather misleading flaring of chartism in 1848, the movement had been in marked decline since, at the very latest, 1842.

Moreover, given the generally unstable level of wages, with successful campaigns for wage increases in one year often being followed quite rapidly by their removal in subsequent years, it is highly unlikely that wage increases would have had any immediate impact on working-class consciousness. Indeed, the perpetual upward and downward readjustments of wages in the light of changing economic circumstances, with their immediate and visible impacts on wage levels, were as significant as any gradual long-term improvements in wage levels discernible between 1832 and 1867. This uneven and conflict-punctuated pattern severely undermines the potential of wage increases as guarantors of a new era of social peace: while perhaps having much to say about the patterns of late Victorian class relations, they say little about the dynamics of the chartist and post-chartist period.

While wage levels might have been rising in the long term, this was often obtained only at the expense of a considerable intensification of the work process. Thus in spinning, wage advances were achieved only at the cost of several-fold increases in the numbers of spindles per mule, and repeated advances in the speeds at which the machines were run. Not surprisingly, in cotton, and elsewhere, marginally improved wage levels were often seen as little compensation for loss of work control, greater pressure, and the indignity of subjection to overlooker, foreman or employer, and in consequence workers faced erosion of working standards. The Manchester working class was thus united in common experience of conflicts both over wages and over control of the work process.

Wage levels are only part of the story. Particularly, they need to be placed against prices, and patterns and stability of employment. In fact, as the figures, first of Wood, and then of Deane and Mitchell, show,

---

[94] M.E. Pooley and C.G. Pooley, 'Health, Society and Environment in Victorian Manchester', in R. Woods and J. Woodward, eds, *Urban Disease and Mortality in Nineteenth Century England*, (1984), 148–77, especially 154–5, 158–60.

prices too were increasing during the mid-1850s, and again in the late 1860s, and in consequence, although wage increases did eventually outstrip prices, this was not until the post-Cotton Famine period in the mid-1860s.[95] Patterns of household employment were particularly important in cotton, where household income was more important than individual wage rates. Here the constant employment of an adult male and two children would have brought quiet prosperity by the mid-1850s. Yet as the male workforce in cotton shrank, the 'typical' cotton worker family became less common, and increasingly child and female cotton employment helped support family economies in which the male bread-winner had a less rewarding, and probably much less stable, labouring or semi-skilled job.

Generous wages were a mixed blessing if they were associated with uncertain employment and periods of unemployment. Yet, of course, the inability of the mid-nineteenth century economy to solve the problems of the slump-boom credit cycle was one of the central features of the period's economic history. In this respect, although Peel's 1844 Bank Charter Act gradually brought a certain stability to the British monetary system, it could neither prevent internal monetary crises, nor insulate Britain from the effects of overseas panics. Thus the crises of the 1830s and 1840s were followed by those of 1847, 1857, and the over-production generated slump which precipitated what became known as the Cotton Famine. The economic fluctuations had a drastic impact on the whole of the Manchester economy. In 1847–48 the numbers cared for by the Manchester Guardians rose by 17,000 to 56,000, and, as W.J. Lowe puts it, 'Manchester faced a serious crisis of dislocation'.[96] Figures for 1857 suggest that at the height of the slump of that year, of 46,384 employees of the textiles, finishing and engineering industries, 8,909 were completely laid off, and a further 19,888 were working short time.[97]

The Cotton Famine was even more devastating, affecting the whole of the local economy. And yet these major economic dislocations were just the most visible troughs of an economy which was fundamentally incapable of providing stable employment. There were scarcely half a

[95] Kirk, *Working Class Reformism*, 100.

[96] W.J. Lowe, *The Irish in Mid-Victorian Lancashire. The Shaping of a Working Class*, (1989), 35, 34–5.

[97] Police returns published in *MG*, 10 December 1857; the figures for machinists, with 1,652 of 6,932 laid off, and a further 2,696 on short time, show the ramifications of such slumps through the whole economy.

dozen years between 1848 and 1867 in which stable conditions of prosperity existed. The reports of John Layhe are studded with references to widespread unemployment. The 1847–48 slump was not finally overcome until 1853; the Crimean War and the 1857 slump both created waves of unemployment; and during the Cotton Famine, widespread difficulties for cotton operatives, shoemakers, dressmakers and building trades, produced 'very great poverty' among many groups.[98]

Moreover, cyclical unemployment disrupted what was already for many of the working classes a fragile balance between comfort and distress. Even in prosperous periods, John Layhe regretted the 'so many trials and struggles' which confronted him.[99] Seasonal unemployment presented problems for both labourers and artisans, particularly in the outdoor trades. According to one city missionary in 1854, although a few in his district were well off, 'as many as a third can only get half sustenance in the winter months'.[100] Meanwhile, the lifecycle itself brought periods of prosperity while children were in remunerative employment, sandwiched between hardship while bringing up young children, or when ageing after the children had grown and left. Layhe admitted that there were large numbers whose earnings would not allow any provision for old age and remarked that many 'working people of average prudence and good conduct...have to struggle on without appearing to make any progress towards improving their condition, or extricating themselves from their difficulties'.[101] And everywhere there was the pervading danger of sickness; James Harrop, one of John Layhe's successors, working in Hulme, noted in 1868 that 'many families of steady, industrious and economical habits, are kept in the greatest straits by the incessant occurrence of sickness in their house', in many cases leading to debts which it took years to repay.[102]

Poverty, or the threat of poverty, was thus virtually a universal experience for the Manchester working class at mid-century, and all sections shaded into the groups below them. Manchester, like other Victorian cities, possessed a large population eking a precarious

---

[98] *MTPAR*, (1845), 5, (1849), 10–11, (1867), 14–15, (1869), 8–12: just some examples among many.
[99] *MTPAR*, (1850), 57–8.
[100] *MCMM*, (November 1854), 155.
[101] *MTPAR*, (1851), 13.
[102] *MTPAR*, (1868), 29. Cf. the impact of accidents, *MCMAR*, (1839), 24–5.

existence through employment in a host of unskilled and often temporary jobs and occupations, headed by building and general labourers, and ranging through night soil men, knockers up, broom sellers, hawkers and pedlars to thieves and prostitutes.[103] Besides representing a constant threat to the status of the working class above them, the unskilled class represented a permanent potential threat to middle-class social and cultural control. Behind the exaggerated rhetoric of mid-century fears about the vice-ridden lower orders was the substantial reality of a large group for whom the transition to mid-Victorian prosperity was an insubstantial shadow. Rarely organised, and even more rarely articulate in the surviving records, the numerical strength of these groups makes their integration into any explanations of the genesis of social stability vital.

Geographical development

Just as Manchester's surprisingly complex occupational structure does not necessarily undermine the emergence of class divisions, so patterns of residential segregation, while much less pronounced than contemporary pictures suggested, nevertheless provided a further basis for the development of class allegiances. Contemporary pictures of cleavage concentrated on two processes: the migration of the haute bourgeoisie out of Manchester, and the creation of large exclusively working-class districts ringing the commercial centre. In both cases there was a substantial grain of truth; but in both cases around this grain accumulated a pearl of dubious quality.

By the 1830s the bourgeoisie had already moved from the centre to a series of suburban enclaves around Manchester, including the prestigious Ardwick Polygon, and adjacent Ardwick Green, the Greenheys and Victoria Park districts of Chorlton-on-Medlock, and the heights of Broughton and Pendleton.[104] In Manchester no middle-class pockets were created and fortified against the spread of the industrial

---

[103] See Gareth Stedman Jones, *Outcast London*, (1971); while contemporary comments (e.g. *Leisure Hour*, 19 March 1857) suggest that Manchester's outcast population was noticeably smaller than London's, it was nevertheless considerable. See, for example, C. DeMotte, 'The Dark Side of Town: Crime in Manchester and Salford, 1815–1875', (DPhil thesis, University of Kansas, 1976).

[104] E. Butterworth, *A Chronological History of Manchester brought down to 1834, including descriptions of boroughs of Manchester and Salford*, (1834), 6–7, 9.

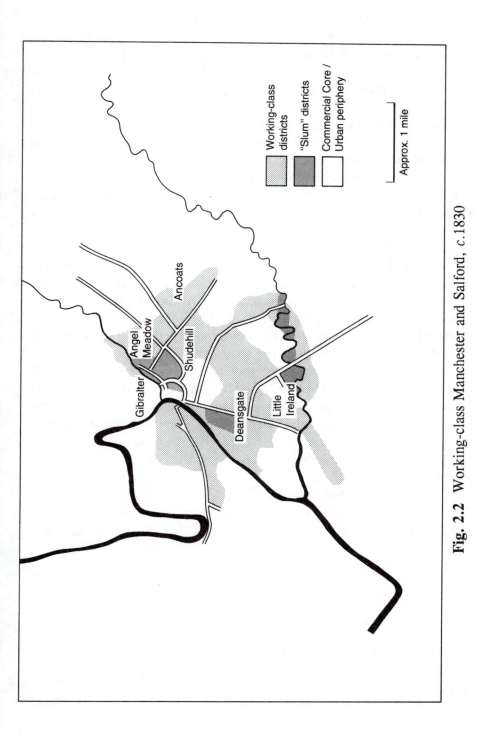

Fig. 2.2 Working-class Manchester and Salford, c.1830

city.[105] Yet the initial suburban developments were in close proximity to the centre of the city, which remained the focus of the social life of the wealthy almost as much as previously, and apart from providing problems in the filling of township offices, the migration had little impact on either the shape of Manchester society or its class relations.[106]

However, as Manchester expanded, these enclosures were in turn quickly swamped. By the 1840s the exclusivity of Ardwick and Chorlton-on-Medlock had been destroyed by the advance of the city, and the area of Manchester between the Ardwick Polygon and the centre was a wide unpaved and unsewered working-class district, rapidly becoming gloomy and decayed as shops and lower quality houses replaced its large residences.[107] Similarly Greenheys, described in 1843 as the most respectable of the Manchester suburbs, lost its old Hall in 1853 and was filled by a dense mass of common brick houses, intersected by narrow streets, which, by the 1860s, were overwhelming the detached suburban villas of the 1820s.[108]

By 1870, even those villages such as Old Trafford, well beyond the boundaries of the borough, were being absorbed into the sprawling city. Although still dominated by 'suburban villas, Belgrave terraces, and other such prettinesses', the abode of 'very respectable respectability', they had been eclipsed by more recent and more distant suburbs.[109] At this time, only Broughton and Cheetham Hill, still the same 'little retreat for the aristocracy, both of merchants and tradesmen' which they had been in the 1840s, remained as enclaves of the upper middle class within the boundaries of Manchester and Salford.[110] For the most part, the upper middle classes had taken advantage of the mobility provided first by the omnibuses and then by the railways to become one stage further removed from the city, to Whalley Range, Bowden, Chorlton-cum-Hardy, Didsbury, Sale, and

[105] *NEM*, (1843), 180–82; this is a significant contrast to the position noted by Savage in Preston, Savage, *Dynamics of Working Class Politics*, 101–7.

[106] For the limited impact of outmigration in this period, see Gunn, 'Manchester Middle Class', 184–210.

[107] L.M. Hayes, *Reminiscences of Manchester and some of its local surroundings from the year 1840*, (1905), 179–80, *MCN*, 17 August 1872.

[108] J. Easby, *Manchester and the Manchester People*, (1843), 13, *MCN*, 18 November 1871.

[109] N. Hawthorne, *Passages from the English Notebooks*, (1870), 354, *MCN*, 17 January 1872.

[110] *NEM*, (1842), 167, *MCN*, 13 April 1872. Even here decay was setting in, *Freelance*, IV (1869), 58.

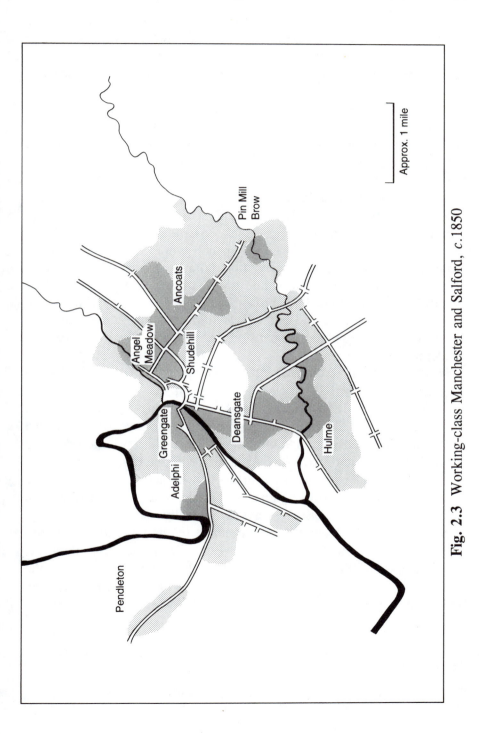

Fig. 2.3 Working-class Manchester and Salford, *c.*1850

even more distant Eccles and Knutsford.[111] It could be said that by this period, the city was bereft of a resident haute bourgeoisie.

Not that the city was without a middle class. Simon Gunn has pointed out that migration to the suburbs did not lead to the withdrawal of the upper middle-class but rather perhaps to a more formal and ritualised relationship with the city and its other classes. This migration provided space for the internal migration of the professional groups few of whom possessed the resources to flee the city. Just as Old Trafford lost its place among the aristocracy of the suburbs and became merely respectable, so Greenheys, particularly the areas most distant from the centre, had acquired a 'professional lustre' by the 1860s.[112] At the same time, growing numbers of retailers and small merchants had begun to move into areas such as the southern end of Chorlton-on-Medlock and Stretford, which were covered with cheap 'middle-class' housing. It was even possible to discern the beginnings of the large clerical suburbs and some of the new working-class suburbs which developed towards the end of the century, including Moss Side and Newton Heath.[113] Within the city, therefore, this period saw both population expansion and a steady, if soft, process of residential segregation.

This movement facilitated the development of the slums so graphically described by social reformers in the 1830s and 1840s. Already, by the 1830s, large areas surrounding the city centre, including medieval Shudehill, St George's and Ancoats, parts of Hulme and Chorlton, Deansgate, and the Regent Road district of Salford were covered in a mosaic of workshops and factories and the densely packed houses of those who worked in them. In the older areas, the combination of overcrowding and old buildings and lack of sanitation quickly created the noisome dens graphically described by Kay[-Shuttleworth] and Engels.[114] Even in some of the more recently built districts – the infamous Angel Meadow or Newtown district along the Irk, Gaythorn, Little Ireland and Pin Mill along the Medlock, and the Salford districts of Blackfriars and Regent Road along the Irwell – low lying waterlogged clayey ground next to rivers which had become open

---

[111] On the impact of transport on the development of the city see Kellet, *The Impact of Railways*, 357–60, and Dennis, *Industrial Cities*, 110–40.

[112] *MCN*, 18 November 1871.

[113] Hawthorne, *English Notebooks*, 379, Shaw, *Manchester Old and New*, 123.

[114] Kay[-Shuttleworth], *Moral and Physical Condition*, F. Engels, *The Condition of the Working Class in England*, (1969 [or. 1845]), *passim*.

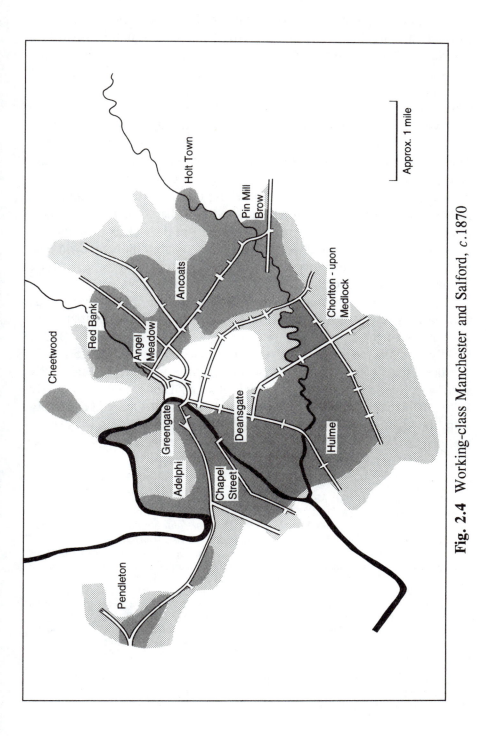

Fig. 2.4 Working-class Manchester and Salford, *c*.1870

sewers, and proximity to noisome industrial premises including catgut works and animal skinners' yards, created equally squalid districts.[115] Districts such as Angel Meadow and Little Ireland, despite the concern of sanitary authorities and the efforts of the city council, remained notorious for the worst housing and most indigent population in the whole city.[116]

Nevertheless, we must avoid falling into the trap of regarding these accounts as an accurate reflection of the working-class districts *in toto*, despite the habit of observers of lumping together the slums with the other working-class districts of the city as though there were little to choose between them, portraying working-class districts as 'seemingly endless streets of houses of one size, and one shape, and one outward semblance'.[117] In part, this merely reflected middle-class prejudice at housing which was undoubtedly less salubrious than their own, in part a desire of social reformers to boost their campaigns by describing neighbourhoods particularly selected to support their views.[118]

Certainly, the constant pressure of immigration and indigenous population growth on the available housing stock did mean that there were parts of the city which, not as bad as Angel Meadow in 1832, rapidly became so during the ensuing years. Kay and Engels both censured the Deansgate district severely; references to its unhealthy state were made periodically in the 1850s and 1860s, and in the early 1870s the area acquired some notoriety as a den of vice and depravity from the writings of the superintendent of a mission hall established in the district.[119] Nevertheless, the conditions created in these areas,

---

[115] J.P. Kay[-Shuttleworth], *Moral and Physical Condition*, 19–21.

[116] *MG*, 6 April 1871, 13 April 1871. For a microcosm see J. Roberts, *Working Class Housing in Nineteenth Century Manchester: A Study of John Street, Irk Town*, (1975).

[117] Rev. John Richardson, 'The Habits of the People', *PPL*, II (1856), 2.

[118] Hence the periodic surveys of working class districts of the mid-century decades concentrated on a small number of favoured localities. Detailed surveys of the Deansgate district (*MX* in 1852, and the Manchester Statistical Society in 1864) focused on the area between Peter Street and Great Bridgewater Street which as a large part of one of the main cholera districts identified by Leigh and Gardiner in 1850 was likely to present an aspect worse than the rest: *MX*, 4 February 1852, H. Oats, 'Inquiry…district in Deansgate', *TMSS*, XII (1864–65), 1–16; see the map accompanying J. Leigh and N. Gardiner, *History of the Cholera in Manchester in 1849*, (1850). Similarly the district of Ancoats, used by the Statistical Society in 1864, had already been identified in 1854 as containing probably the worst housing in the entire district: Oats, 'Inquiry…district in Ancoats', *TMSS*, XIII (1865-66), 1–13, *MX* 15 March 1854.

[119] Engels, *Condition*, 73–4, *MG*, 22 August 1849, 13 October 1849, *MX*, 14 January 1852, A. Alsop, *A Cry for Help from the Slums*, [1870], and *idem, Deansgate Street*, (1876).

although matching those of the older slums, were far from universal, and closer examination uncovers a diversity which mirrored the heterogeneity of the working class itself.

It is possible to outline broad distinctions between different working-class areas. As Pooley and Pooley have demonstrated, the evidence of the census when compared with mortality statistics at enumeration district level, shows a distinct pattern: a steadily expanding commercial core (in which pockets of very high density housing are probably obscured by the district-level analysis), a ring of high density, high mortality districts (especially in the St George's Road and Ancoats registration districts, and along the River Medlock), encased in a zone of lower density/lower mortality districts, whose inner fringes were steadily deteriorating as the period progressed. Even within these distinctions, the pattern was more mixed than these statistical data, or contemporary middle-class conventions, allowed.[120] The Ancoats/St George's Road district provides a good example of the kind of broad social differentiation which could emerge. The degenerating insanitary hollow of the Irk Valley housed the Manchester *Lumpenproletariat*, its thieves, street entertainers, hawkers and casual labourers: from Charter Street to Miles Platting was a huge area occupied by the very poor. In adjacent districts to the immediate west of the Rochdale Road the middle ranks of the working classes were more prominent, those who according to one observer 'are always striving for well-doing, but are never doing well', who represented rather the precarious nature of working-class prosperity even in the 1850s and 1860s; alongside, perhaps most visible on the eastern outskirts, around the engineering works there, were pockets of more prosperous working-class groups.[121]

Focusing on Ancoats, a more detailed picture can be painted. Only partially built up in 1832, the process of the extension out to the boundary of the city continued into the 1870s. Hence, the core of early nineteenth century housing was fringed both by low lying river-side slum districts to the extreme south-east (Pin Mill), and by successively more recent building to the north-east. By 1854 the central districts fringing Great Ancoats Street along Canal Street, Oldham Road and Union Street were full of old, dilapidated buildings, hugely

---

[120] Pooley and Pooley, 'Health, Society and Environment', 161–71.
[121] *MTPAR*, (1866), 16–17.

overcrowded with the lower reaches of the working classes.[122] Bisecting the district, especially along the canals, were also strips of land given over to workshops and mills, including 'a foul tongue of land' along the Newton Heath boundary, containing chemical works, a bone grinding factory and several slaughter houses.[123] In a few districts, such as the land adjacent to Oldham Road Station, landlord neglect had created particular dilapidation.[124] Beyond the core, benefiting from the slightly better housing and more open street plan, along with the gradual action of the city council, were better localities, and beyond these, districts like that to the east of Butler Street, recently built and markedly superior. It was these houses which led to the district being described in the 1860s as predominantly 'small cottage tenements, occupied by operatives...comparatively commodious and healthy'.[125]

Elsewhere, even without the benefit of detailed research in the census enumerators' books, it is clear that residential segregation within the working class was even more patchy and incomplete.[126] In part this was because as working-class housing forced its way into previously middle-class enclaves on the old suburban periphery, the city became ringed with districts with a social mix ranging across the working and middle classes. By the end of the 1860s the once aristocratic and then professional suburb of Greenheys was described as containing 'as complete a combination of wealth and poverty...as could well be got together in a single suburb'.[127] In some areas this kind of social mix had always been present: from the early decades of the century, Pendleton retained both the mansions of the rich, set in large grounds, and the squalid unpaved districts which clustered around the 'conglomeration of collieries, bleachworks, printworks, dyeworks, coachworks, [and] machine shops' in which the working-class population was employed.[128]

[122] MX, 13 March 1854.
[123] MTPAR, (1853), 28–9.
[124] Kellet, The Impact of Railways, 157.
[125] J. Whitehead, The Rate of Mortality in Manchester, (1863), 42. For similar gradations in Chorlton-on-Medlock see John Hatton, A Lecture on the Sanitary Condition of Chorlton-upon-Medlock, January 12 1854, (1854), MCN, 22 April 1871.
[126] For a review of the wider literature on this issue, which supports this contention, see Dennis, Industrial Cities, 201–49.
[127] MCN, 18 November 1871.
[128] MCN, 9 March 1872.

More commonly, the structure of housing tended to throw different strata of the working classes into proximity. Not only did development tend to be piecemeal, producing adjacent housing of different vintages, but the standard back-to-back produced several different levels of housing, those possessing frontages onto thoroughfares, those with frontages onto back-streets, those opening out only into inner courts, and those which were merely cellars.[129] Despite the prohibition on further back-to-back house building introduced in the late 1840s, they remained a substantial proportion of the total housing stock into the late century. Their features were replicated where through-ventilated cottage tenements had front and back rooms let separately and the connecting door boarded up.[130]

A heterogeneous and locally gradated population resulted. In Ancoats, for example, descriptions in the early 1870s traced a clear progression from the 'thin crust of respectability which lines Oldham-st and Great Ancoats-st', via internal thoroughfares such as Bengal Street which 'in spite of its evil reputation [was] tolerably respectable, and, as a rule inhabited by orderly people', to the associated secondary streets such as Primrose Street, full of evil cellars and populations to match, the even more wretched courts which opened off these streets, and the dirty and overcrowded warrens, such as McKay's buildings, which existed in close proximity.[131] Even within narrowly defined geographical precincts, rates of rental varied considerably. David Chadwick's survey of part of the St. Phillip's district of Salford in the 1860s revealed a broad range of house values, and rentals which although more numerous at the lower end were spread relatively evenly from £6 to £11.[132] This segregation occurred not so much on the basis of occupation as of other cultural attributes. St Phillip's was a community stretching from highly paid clerks and moulders to millhands, carters and porters, with average wages which varied from

---

[129] Manchester and Salford Sanitary Association pamphlet on back-to-back housing, M126/1/17, MCLA.

[130] In Ancoats, Oats noted that 66% of the households he surveyed were single room houses with no through passage of air, 'Inquiry...district of Ancoats', 4; on separate letting see A. Ransome and J. Leigh, *Report upon the Health of Manchester and Salford*, (1867), 16.

[131] *MCN*, 5 April 1871.

[132] *PP*, (1860) XII (445), 337. A survey of Red Bank in 1861 found weekly rents varying from 1/9 (£4.7.6. p.a.) to 5/6 (£13.15.0. p.a.), *MG*, 2 January 1861. Rushton, 'Housing Conditions', 95–8, suggests a slight move towards homogenisation between 1829 and 1861.

15/- to 35/- per week. Rather than describe districts by occupation, observers often distinguished districts by character of inhabitant. S. Robinson, Layhe's successor as minister to the poor in Ancoats, divided the district between the undeserving poor, the deserving poor, and the respectable and prosperous.[133] From his portrait it is clear that income or occupation were much less important in determining residence than character, family circumstance, or accidents of health and fortune.

Conclusion

This chapter has taken issue with contemporary pictures of social dichotomy and contemporary assumptions of post-1851 working-class prosperity. Although reliant on cotton, particularly in its growth into an industrial city between 1780 and 1830, both the Manchester economy, and the occupational structure derived therefrom, were more diversified than has previously been accepted, and increasingly so as the century progressed. The growth of engineering and general manufacturing, along with the rapid expansion of Manchester as a commercial centre, produced a society that was multi-layered rather than dichotomous. The complexity of the city's social structure warns against attempts to interpret its social and political history simply in terms of broad socio-economic classifications: even within layers, class positions based on economic position were far from clear cut.

Although the Manchester middle class was bound together by the city's reliance on the cotton trade, the economic interests of spinner, manufacturer, calico-printer, merchant and machine manufacturer were not co-extensive. The interests of the substantial professional and clerical class which the city economy supported were one, and often several, steps further removed, and beneath them ranged a heterogeneous class of tradesmen and shopkeepers, often catering to the middle class, and uneasily spanning middle-class status and working-class location. The working class too was fissured both horizontally and vertically: packers shared status with mechanics and building artisans, but were at the same time enmeshed in occupational relationships with clerks and carters.

[133] *MTPAR* (1866), 17–21.

At the same time, although the relative decline in the importance of the classic cotton factory worker undoubtedly altered the composition of the Manchester working class, this was a change of degree and not kind. Cotton had never been the overwhelming employer and hence there was no massive shift to higher status better paid jobs. Furthermore, although the greater economic stability of the post-1851 period helped to dull the economic imperatives to pre-1851 radicalism, the piecemeal and somewhat delayed nature of the improvement, and the continuing precariousness of the working-class economic position, meant that the condition of the working class remained embattled. Its experience continued to be marked by cycles of poverty and deprivation, which although not as severe as previously, constituted a real barrier to the passive acceptance of the status quo. The result was a working class within which occupational distinctions of status and wage-level co-existed with common experiences of the dynamics of the mid-Victorian economy and their embattled and precarious position within it.

Chapter Three

The genesis of middle-class moral imperialism

Given the recent, and long overdue, rediscovery of the problems inherent in the process of middle-class formation, it is not surprising that the image of Manchester as the central site – and the campaigns against the Corn Laws as the fundamental issue – in the formation of the British middle class has recently come under much scrutiny and revision.[1] Even for those who hesitate to believe with Wahrman that it is 'impossible' to write the history of the creation of the English middle class, the recent studies of Morris, Nenadic, Koditschek and Trainor have demonstrated that the process of class formation was as contingent and complex for the middle class as it was for the working class: the historian, even when confined to one urban location, assumes its chronology and degree at peril.[2]

The birth pains of the middle class in Manchester have been somewhat obscured by the longstanding orthodoxy of the establishment of a Unitarian-liberal hegemony in the city by the 1830s.[3] Although the pioneering accounts of this process by V.A.C. Gatrell stressed that this hegemony emerged out of a sustained period of intra-elite conflict, the security and self-confidence of the liberal elites, and the essentially self-referential nature of their political struggles which he portrayed, has encouraged subsequent studies to take the establishment of bourgeois

---

[1] The most substantial recent studies of the Manchester middle class in this period are two theses, Wach, 'Condition of the Middle Classes', and Gunn, 'The Manchester Middle Class', and a third forthcoming as M.J. Turner, *Respectability and Reform: the making of middle-class liberalism in early 19th-century Manchester*, (forthcoming 1996). Elements of this work have already been published: see H.W. Wach, 'Culture and the Middle Classes: Popular Knowledge in Industrial Manchester', *Journal of British Studies*, 27 (1988), Gunn, 'The "failure" of the Victorian middle class'.

[2] Wahrman, *Imagining the Middle Class*, 1, R.J. Morris, *Class, Sect and Party. The making of the British middle class. Leeds, 1820–1850*, (1990), S. Nenadic, 'The structure, values and influence of the Scottish urban middle class: Glasgow 1800–1870', (PhD thesis, University of Glasgow, 1986), Koditschek, *Class Formation and Urban-Industrial Society*, Trainor, *Black Country Elites*. For a complementary American perspective, see S.M. Blumin, *The emergence of the middle class. Social experience in the American city, 1760–1900*, (1989).

[3] V.A.C. Gatrell, 'Incorporation and the Pursuit of Liberal hegemony in Manchester, 1790–1839', in Fraser, ed., *Municipal reform and the industrial city*.

identity in the 1830s almost as a given, even if they have sought to flesh out its character.[4]

This process cannot be taken for granted in this way. As we have seen, in Manchester the rapid growth of a diversified textile economy created an extremely complex social structure which, even if it provided the building blocks of common class experiences – differential access to resources, a degree of residential segregation, and contrasting patterns of life – was still a long way from creating, in reality, the dichotomous two-class society which was conjured up by the morbid fascination of contemporary observers. Far from the urban environment being conducive to class solidarity, it created deep-rooted problems of leadership and authority, which encouraged a crisis of elite authority and, at least in the early decades of the century, bitter intra-elite conflict. However, out of this conflict had emerged by mid-century a discernible middle-class culture, not the 'curiously rootless' middle class suggested by John Smail, though still one which forcefully illustrates H.L. Malchow's contention that the complex inter-relations of middle-class society in the Victorian period created 'layered identities'.[5]

The crisis of authority

The crisis of authority in Manchester derived essentially from the complexities and inadequacies of its structures of local government and politics.[6] Without borough status, before the 1830s local government and its attendant political processes were vested in a range of overlapping bodies. Legal authority resided in the county magistracy, appointed by the Chancellor of the Duchy of Lancaster. Poor relief, and responsibility for the highways and church fabric, remained in the hands of the vestry, and its churchwardens and overseers. However,

[4] See J. Breuilly, 'Liberalism in mid-Nineteenth Century Hamburg and Manchester', *Labour and Liberalism in Nineteenth Century Europe. Essays in comparative history*, (1992), 197–227.
[5] John Smail, *The Origins of Middle Class Culture. Halifax, Yorkshire, 1660–1780*, (1994), 12, H.L. Malchow, *Gentlemen Capitalists. The Social and Political World of the Victorian Businessman*, (1991), 8.
[6] This has been the subject of a series of studies: the classic account is A. Redford, *The History of Local Government in Manchester*, (3 vols, 1939–40); but see also S.D. Simon, *A Century of City Government in Manchester, 1838–1938*, (1938), Vigier, *Change and Apathy*.

until 1792 the dominant institution was the manorial court leet, comprising jurors nominated by the lord's steward from among the leading inhabitants, who in turn selected the boroughreeve, the constables, and other manorial officers.[7] In 1792 the court leet was supplemented by a Police Commission, a body which in fact rapidly assumed most of the local government responsibilities of the court leet, and was thus the pre-eminent institution of local government in the early nineteenth century.

As became increasingly clear in the years before 1832, these structures were unequal to the task of administering a rapidly growing industrial town. The potential membership of the Police Commission made it too unwieldy a body, and having failed to purchase the manorial rights in 1809, or to obtain control over the town's water supply, its efficacy in developing efficient local administration was severely constrained.[8] Reform in 1829, limiting the number of commissioners to 240, brought little improvement.

The court leet, having proved incapable of providing for even the residual functions which it retained, most significantly that of the local police force, was by the 1830s also finding it difficult to select suitable residents willing to serve as boroughreeve, as evinced by the refusal of William Neild to accept the nomination in 1837.

The deficiencies of these administrative agencies were compounded by the increasingly bitter conflicts which competition for their control engendered in the early decades of the century. Before the 1790s the structures of local government, for all their inadequacies, had been relatively open to the local elite irrespective of political affiliation. However, from the 1790s political conflict intensified, and Liberals, especially Unitarians, found themselves excluded from local office. In the early nineteenth century local government in Manchester, as Gatrell has expressed it, 'became the preserve of an allegedly corrupt, but certainly Tory oligarchy which soon monopolised all significant posts in the town'.[9] During the 1810s and 1820s, the various committees of the Police Commission were dominated by a small, self-perpetuating oligarchy of leading Tories, who resisted firmly efforts to expand the social and political base of local government.[10]

---

[7] Redford, *Local Government in Manchester*, I, chaps 2–4.

[8] Redford, *Local Government*, I, chaps 9–11.

[9] Gatrell, 'Incorporation', 34.

[10] See M.J. Turner, 'Gas, Police and the Struggle for Mastery in Manchester in the 1820s', *Historical Research*, LXVII (1994), 301–17.

The result, as Shena Simon noted some time ago, was '[t]he lack of practically any regulations except those necessary for governing a village or small town'.[11] Paving and drainage were confined to the principal streets and a few of the side streets; most of the back streets, courts and alleys remained unpaved and undrained. There was no system of sanitation, beyond the inadequate supply of infrequently emptied privies, and the result in the oldest of the working-class districts was the degree of wretchedness described by the early commentators discussed in chapter 2, and which formed the breeding ground of the cholera outbreak of 1832, and, in the imaginations of the propertied, of all manner of working-class profligacy and vice.

Little control could be exercised over the working classes. There was no effective system of 'nuisance' inspection, no regulations on building standards. Most significantly, the mechanisms of law and order were frighteningly rudimentary. As late as 1832 there were only 25–30 day police in the city, and as F.C. Mather has demonstrated, the maintenance of law and order rested heavily on the military.[12] In 1812, 1817, and most famously in 1819, the military were deployed to put down rioting. The catastrophe of the 'Peterloo' massacre, when the tory-led yeomanry charged into a largely peaceful crowd of working-class radicals, killing at least eleven people and injuring several hundred, raised in acute form the crisis of control structures in early nineteenth century Manchester, and prompted an ever more vigorous and wide-ranging challenge to the Tory oligarchy by a close-knit band of liberals, predominantly but not exclusively Unitarian, and mostly engaged in the cotton trade, led by Thomas and Richard Potter, supported by propagandists like Archibald Prentice and John E. Taylor, and more substantial men of business like John Shuttleworth, J.B. Smith, Joseph Brotherton and William Harvey.[13] In 1819 Thomas Fleming, the Treasurer of the Police Commissioners, and the dominant figure in the city's local government since 1810, was forced to resign in the face of radical criticism of the financial state of the Commissioners, and the ensuing years saw an extended war of attrition, over issues such as the use of the surpluses from municipal gas

[11] Simon, *Century of City Government*, 20.
[12] Mather, *Public Order in the Age of the Chartists*, 62–75, S.J. Davies, 'Classes and the Police in Manchester, 1829–1880', in A.J. Kidd and K.W. Roberts, eds, *City, Class and Culture*, 26–47.
[13] To these Turner adds F.R. Atkinson (attorney), Edward Baxter (merchant), and Absalom Watkin (calico dealer), 'Before the Manchester School', 217.

production, and the deployment of church rates.[14] The establishment of the moderately reformist *Manchester Guardian* in 1821 provided the liberals with a means to counteract the dominant Tory tone of the local press, and from 1828 it was supplemented by two more radical voices – Prentice's *Manchester Times and Gazette* and the *Manchester and Salford Advertiser* (1830). By 1822 the new manufacturing classes had also formally established the Manchester Chamber of Commerce. Although the Chamber was to be firmly non-political, and elected H.H. Birley as its first president, it steadily evolved into a leading forum for debate on such politically-charged issues as protectionism.

Nevertheless, interim victories notwithstanding, the terms and operation of the revised Police Commission after 1828 attested to a narrow political system still dominated by the Tory elite. Elections generally brought victories for the old ruling party, so much so that Prentice was left comparing the performance and political bias of the new Commission unfavourably with that of the pre-1828 one.

The problem of politics

The centrifugal force of political animosities on the Manchester middle class reached its apogee in the 1830s and early 1840s, commencing with the debates over parliamentary reform before 1832 and the subsequent parliamentary elections of 1832 and 1835, reaching a crescendo in the bitterly contested incorporation campaign of 1837–38 and its long-running legal aftermath, and then being sustained by the campaigns for the repeal of the Corn Laws in the 1840s. These conflicts were fuelled by the violent tone of debate encouraged in the Manchester press, and by the press's vigorous partisanship.

The campaigns for parliamentary reform which preceded the 1832 Reform Act did not encourage the full development of middle-class conflict in Manchester.[15] Most of the reforming party retained very circumscribed aspirations, seeking the representation of Manchester (and other industrial cities and the new wealth they represented), but not the enfranchisement of what was largely seen as a venal and

---

[14] D. Fraser, *Urban Politics in Victorian England. The structure of politics in the Victorian cities*, (1976), 37–8.

[15] See A. Briggs, 'The Background of the Parliamentary Reform Movement in Three English Cities, 1830–1832', *Collected Essays of Asa Briggs. Vol 1*, (1985), 180–213 (original 1948).

dependent working class, and during the debates of the later 1820s the divisions within the reforming party were as wide as any between them and the Tories.[16] In consequence, the reform campaign lacked any institutional unity: the radical-liberal Manchester Political Union, itself challenged from early 1831 by a working-class Political Union which steadfastly opposed limited enfranchisement, was largely an irrelevance to the cross-party consensus that Manchester ought to be represented, and that the franchise ought to exclude the working classes.

The first parliamentary election of 1832 was a different matter. Bitterly contested by five candidates, ranging from Tory churchman to radical Benthamite, it encouraged the coalescence of liberalism around the candidatures of C.P. Thompson, the radical free trader and Mark Philips, a wealthy local cotton merchant, and a looser rival alignment of Tories and working-class radicals, alignments which dominated the conflict over incorporation in the later 1830s. In 1833, led by Prentice, the radicals attempted to capture the office of churchwarden, and although the popular vote at the vestry meeting was reversed on the poll (which was subject to the distortions of the Sturges Bourne system), there were further contests over the church rate itself in 1833 and 1834, and then again over the churchwardens in 1834. In 1835, with the prospect of a further bitter poll contest over the church rate, the churchwardens chose not to call for a poll to reverse their defeat at the vestry meeting, and instead took up the suggestions of Thomas Potter for a voluntary subscription. However, although this reduced tensions over the parochial offices for a couple of years, they were soon to be sucked into the political fray during the incorporation conflict.[17]

The significance of the campaign to incorporate Manchester was that, as illustrated by Richard Cobden's clarion call *Incorporate Your Borough* (1837), it articulated even more sharply the themes of democracy versus privilege, and of the rights and powers of the productive classes against aristocracy and oligarchy, combining these with an increasingly unanswerable call for the reorganisation of local administration. What was different about this campaign was the vastly more efficient organisation achieved by Cobden and his allies. In contrast to previous defeats, the incorporationists were able to carry

[16] See for a detailed account, M.J. Turner, 'Manchester Reformers and the Penryn seats, 1827–28', *Northern History*, XXX (1994), 139–60.
[17] Fraser, *Urban Politics*, 37–41.

their plan at a public meeting in February 1838, and then triumph in the subsequent struggle for signatures to rival petitions.[18] Although the demonstration that over 70% of the signatures on the anti-incorporation petition were invalid won the grant of a charter from the Privy Council in the summer of 1838, this proved to be the beginning, and not the end of the controversy.

Far from accepting defeat, the Tories proceeded to challenge the legality of the charter and refused to recognise the new corporation elected in early December 1838. The new corporation was denied the use of the Town Hall by the Police Commission, still dominated by anti-incorporators; its right to appoint a coroner was disputed; the Manchester township refused to disband its police force to make way for the new borough police; and the churchwardens and overseers refused to levy the borough rate. In the face of this impasse, a government-nominated Police Commissioner, Sir Charles Shaw, was appointed. When he arrived in Manchester in September 1839 he found 'local party animosity carried to an incredible height, the feelings of hatred of each other being so rabid as not even to be exceeded in the civil commotions of Portugal and Spain'.[19] The struggle over the corporation dragged on for several years, and was only finally resolved by a verdict in favour of the Corporation in 1841, followed in 1842 by the confirmation of the Manchester charter by act of Parliament.[20]

Unfortunately, as the conflicts over incorporation were being resolved, so those over the Corn Laws were reaching their peak. As Michael Turner has recently pointed out, it is misleading to portray free trade and laissez-faire attitudes as an established orthodoxy, even amongst liberal Manchester manufacturers and reformers before the 1840s.[21] During the 1820s and early 1830s, although there was a good deal of dissatisfaction with the laws, a broad range of reforming measures was canvassed, no firm lines of demarcation were developed, and the Manchester Chamber of Commerce held back from any blanket endorsement of free trade, much to the frustration of Richard Cobden and the other advanced liberals.[22]

---

[18] For the violence of the placard war which preceded this meeting, see *MC*, 10 February 1838.

[19] Sir C. Shaw, *Replies to Lord Ashley*, 10–11, cited in Simon, *Century of City Government*, 98.

[20] For full details of the war of attrition between the two parties, see Simon, *Century of City Government*, 98–116.

[21] Turner, 'Before the Manchester School', *passim*.

[22] N. Edsall, *Richard Cobden. Independent Radical*, (1986), 42–50.

From 1838 however, clear divisions began to solidify. After the formation of the Manchester Anti-Corn Law Association in September 1838, the advanced liberals were finally able in the following December to obtain a resolution in favour of repeal passed by the Chamber of Commerce. This, and the election in the following February, at the head of a free trade slate, of J.B. Smith as President of the Chamber, ushered in a period of heated controversy. Elections for the Chamber itself were vigorously contested, although the continued emergence of a moderate-liberal stance around the *Manchester Guardian* blurred distinctions somewhat, and it was not until 1845 that the repeated defeats of the conservatives prompted their defection to form the rival Manchester Commercial Association.[23]

Conflicts of culture

Although there might have been a peculiar local intensity to these political conflicts, similar struggles have been identified elsewhere. In Leeds, for example, R.J. Morris has described a middle class deeply divided by religion and politics up to the 1830s. However, Morris has suggested that from the 1830s onwards it is possible to see the tempering of these divisions, and the emergence of a new sense of middle-class identity. While acknowledging this was a complex process, Morris' account of the causes of this process concentrates on cultural practices – the voluntary societies, and their characteristic forms and rituals: 'it was the voluntary society with its distinctive qualities which not only overcame these divisions but allowed the fragmentation of the middle classes to become part of a class project'; they alone 'allowed that variety of patterns of association, participation and action which was essential if a fractured and divided socio-economic group was to act as a class'.[24] 'The most important function of these societies', he argues, 'was to create a neutral area through the "no religion, no politics" rule [which] could then become the basis for class action in cultural and philanthropic matters'.[25]

[23] Turner, 'Before the Manchester School', 239–40; Edsall, *Cobden*, 66–74.
[24] Morris, *Class, Sect and Party*, 167–8; see also *idem*, 'Voluntary Societies and British Urban Elites, 1780–1850', *Historical Journal*, 26,1 (1983), 95–118.
[25] Morris, *Class, Sect and Party*, 277.

Morris' picture of Leeds gives some indication of how protracted this process could be, and the evidence of Manchester amplifies this impression. From the early century into the 1840s, sectarian and party conflicts spilled periodically into the cultural sphere, breaking down the barriers of the proscriptions on politics and religion, and undermining attempts to create a neutral space for the furthering of class collaboration.

In the late eighteenth and early nineteenth centuries, Tory hegemony in Manchester, expressed in its control of the institutions of local government, had rested on the cultural integration of the Tory elite. In addition to attendance at the central Anglican churches, this integration was rooted in the overlapping membership of John Shaw's Club, the Pitt Club, semi-political societies such as the Association for Preserving Constitutional Order, and the first local cultural associations, such as the Manchester Agricultural Society.[26]

Gradually, however, the cultural hegemony of the Tories was also whittled away by the emergence of rival institutional forms and practices. The significance of the most important of these, the Manchester Literary and Philosophical Society, has been fully illuminated by Arnold Thackray, who has demonstrated that the Lit&Phil was dominated by a closely knit, almost dynastic, elite of Unitarian families whose pursuit of natural science marked the ratification of a new economic order and new social groups.[27]

The same individuals were largely responsible in 1833 for the establishment of the Manchester Statistical Society, the first such society, dedicated to social investigation.[28] Indeed, during the 1820s and 1830s this group and its liberal allies were instrumental in the formation of a series of cultural institutions which largely established the shape of middle-class cultural life during the mid-century. The first of these was the Royal Manchester Institution, established in 1823. Here the lead was taken by G.W. Wood, merchant and prominent member of the Lit&Phil, but the society, ruled by an exclusive group

[26] Turner, 'Gas, Police, and the struggle for mastery', 307–8, F.S. Stancliffe, *John Shaw's, 1738–1938*, (1938), A. Thackray, 'Natural Knowledge in Cultural Context: The Manchester Model', *American Historical Review*, 79 (1974), 682–3.

[27] Thackray, 'Natural Knowledge', *passim*; R. Kargon, *Science in Victorian Manchester* (1977), 5–14.

[28] T.S. Ashton, *Economic and Social Investigation in Manchester*, (1934), D. Elesh, 'The Manchester Statistical Society', *Journal of the History of the Behavioural Sciences*, 8 (1972), 280–301, 407–17.

of hereditary, life and annual governors, and closed to non-subscribers, quickly came under conservative influences.[29]

As a consequence, in 1825 Wood, aided by Benjamin Heywood and other leading liberals, established the Manchester Mechanics' Institution, aimed explicitly at the working classes. Despite being governed by a narrow oligarchy of honorary and life members, the MMI prompted the opposition of conservatives uneasy at the offer of knowledge to the lower orders, concerns reiterated in the 1830s when, partly as a response to the breakaway radical 'New Mechanics' Institute', the institute was democratised, and a newspaper reading room introduced.[30]

The cultural tensions over the MMI were magnified in the case of the Manchester Athenaeum. The Athenaeum was launched in 1836 by Manchester liberals, headed by Richard Cobden, as an association for the commercial middle classes in Manchester, and especially young men drawn to Manchester by employment in its mercantile sector.[31] Although individuals from both sides of the political divide had been involved in the preliminary meetings, the Athenaeum, perhaps because of Cobden's involvement, perhaps because the committee chose to open the institution on Sundays, had to struggle from the outset against accusations of liberal bias.[32] At the AGM in 1838 two rival slates for the election of directors were in circulation. One, the 'reform list', contained no Unitarians, and was described as being 'anti-Cobdenite' by one of its supporters.[33] In 1840 a paper on socialism presented to the Athenaeum's essay and discussion society brought renewed attacks on its liberal leanings, and in 1841 some injudicious comments by James Heywood at the AGM provided further ammunition for those wishing to portray it as a stronghold of liberalism.[34] Hindered by this

---

[29] S.D. Cleveland, *The Royal Manchester Institution*, (1931), R.F. Bud, 'The Royal Manchester Institution', in D.S.L. Cardwell, ed., *Artisan to Graduate*, (1974), 119–33, Kargon, *Science in Victorian Manchester*, 16–19.

[30] M. Tylecote, 'The Manchester Mechanics' Institute', in Cardwell, *Artisan to Graduate*, idem, *The Mechanics' Institutes of Lancashire and Yorkshire before 1851*, (1957), Kargon, *Science in Victorian Manchester*, 20–4.

[31] The fullest recent account of the Athenaeum is to be found in Wach, 'The Condition of the Middle Classes', 34–64.

[32] 'BETA', *MC*, 23 January 1836, 'A Subscriber', *MC*, 10 December 1836, 'A Member of the Athenaeum', *MC*, 2 February 1837, 'A Constant Reader', *WMC*, 14 October 1837, editorial and 'Another Constant Reader' *WMC*, 21 October 1837.

[33] *MG*, 3 February 1838, *MC*, 3 February 1838, 'Fair Play', *MC*, 10 February 1838.

[34] Wach, 'Popular Knowledge', *MC*, 22,29 February 1840, 'A Churchman', *MC*, 30 January 1841, *MG*, 13 February 1841, Athenaeum 'Minutes', 25 February 1841,

suspicion, the Athenaeum struggled to remain solvent in the early 1840s, and ultimately it was rescued only by the funds generated by its spectacular annual soirées.

The extent of this cultural conflict is demonstrated by the controversy generated by the lectures of George Dawson and Ralph Waldo Emerson in Manchester from 1845 to 1848.[35] Emerson was one of the foremost platform speakers of the age on either side of the Atlantic; Dawson was less significant as an original thinker, but perhaps more important for British audiences as a populariser and interpreter of Carlylean and transcendental ideas. In both cases their lectures in Manchester prompted a storm of protest. Not merely Anglicans, but conservatives of every religious hue denounced the ultra-liberal and supposedly anti-Christian thrust of the lectures, and claimed clear violation of the neutrality of the platform. Defenders of the two lecturers took their stance on the issue of free speech, and the inability of the managers of cultural institutions to exercise complete control over the utterances of lecturers. Perhaps because of its history of anti-liberal suspicions, the Athenaeum again bore the brunt of campaigns to purify civic cultural life, being subjected to a sustained campaign of public vituperation, private intrigue, and disruption of its annual meetings. Ultimately, it was able to stave off attempts to establish a rival, more conservative, institution, but only at the cost of effectively barring Dawson, and exercising a much tighter control over both lecturers and other activities. The passions roused, and the sense of cultural crisis generated, were sufficient for the confrontation to be remembered as a crucial moment in the cultural history of the city forty years later.

In these circumstances, it was not surprising that the Manchester middle class developed an ingrained sense of cultural cleavage which encompassed not only inter-class divisions, but also intra-class dissension and fragmentation. Although Canon Richard Parkinson's oft-quoted pamphlet *On the Present Condition of the Labouring Poor in Manchester* (1841) concentrated on the gulf that had grown up between rich and poor, Parkinson was nearly as concerned with the extent to which the outmigration of the middle classes had deprived the city of social leadership by severing the bonds within the middle class. 'There is probably no town in the world', he pointed out, 'where men know

M2/1/2, MCLA.

[35] This illuminating engagement is covered in full in my as yet unpublished 'Ralph Waldo Emerson, George Dawson and the control of the lecture platform in mid-nineteenth century Manchester'.

so little of each other, or where it is so difficult to arrive at an accurate knowledge of what is the prevalent feeling on any question, as in Manchester': public meetings were continually undermined by the relative lack of close acquaintance of the participants and their consequent inability to establish a common basis of understanding.[36] In 1840 when Sir Charles Shaw, the government-appointed Police Commissioner, arrived, he found a state of pandemic anarchy, and the resulting air of crisis helped feed middle-class perceptions of social dislocation and crisis.[37]

The resolution of conflict

This sense of scission never entirely departed. Commenting on the huge disparity of opinion over Sunday schools which had been revealed in a controversy in its columns in 1864, the editor of the *Manchester Examiner and Times* lamented 'how little we know of each other. We all move in our own sets and circles; we all grind away at our own habits and notions..never looking over the hedge into our neighbour's sentimental garden'; this 'want of intercourse between people of different opinions', he warned, 'is not favourable to vigorous moral growth'.[38]

If anything, political conflict was reinvigorated in the 1860s by the 1867 Reform Act and the revival of Conservatism, both in parliamentary and municipal politics. Similarly, the celebrations of the bicentenary of the ejection of 1662 in 1862, and the impetus which these provided for the renewal of calls for disestablishment, infused new warmth into religious disputes. Nevertheless, it is possible to see within the middle-class a moderation of tension and the emergence of a more comfortable sense of class identity, putting down roots in the 1830s, and growing more strongly from the 1840s.[39]

This was most readily apparent in local government. Owing to the initial Tory boycott of the municipal elections, after the final rejection of the legal challenge to incorporation in 1841 and the purchase of the rights of the manor in 1846, the liberals were left in almost complete

---

[36] Parkinson, *On the Present Condition of the Labouring Poor in Manchester*, 8.
[37] C. Shaw, *Replies of Sir Charles Shaw to Lord Ashley, regarding the Education and Moral Condition of the Working Class*, (1843), *passim*.
[38] *MX*, 10 September 1864.
[39] Cf. Morris' picture of Leeds, *Class, Sect and Party, passim*.

control of local government in the city. The council, almost by default, was thus established on *de facto* principles of non-party candidacies, and it served the interests of those Conservatives who sought election to maintain these conventions. In consequence, party alignments were not a significant element of municipal politics before the 1870s: instead, as Gunn has expressed it, municipal politics 'derived less from party divisions than from shifting conceptions of the role and scope of local government, as pressures for "economy" alternated with a larger, more grandiose vision of the "civic"'.[40] Although Conservatives never made up more than 30% of the council before 1900, in the 1860s it was possible for J.M. Bennett, timber merchant and prominent Conservative, to be elected mayor virtually without comment.[41] At the same time, despite frequent complaints about the quality of councillors attracted to serve, the councils remained almost exclusively the preserve of middle-class groups, with a strong cadre of manufacturers and merchants, and an increasingly long tail of retailers.[42]

Ultimately, a not dissimilar process occurred in local parliamentary politics. Despite the run of Liberal victories, the early parliamentary elections in Manchester were keenly contested, and the narrowness of the victory margin of R.H. Greg in the 1839 by-election (3421–3156) demonstrated the relative balance of political power. However, the strength of party conflict was subsequently undermined. The selection of Milner Gibson and John Bright as the Liberal candidates for the 1847 election, coupled with the failure of the Conservatives to present a credible candidature, began a process of alienation of the moderate wing of the League party, a process which was brought to a culmination by the unpopularity of their opposition to the Crimean war.[43] The rejection of the League candidates in 1857 in favour of the moderate liberalism of Sir John Potter and John Aspinall Turner represented the constitution of a moderate centrist alignment around support for Palmerston and repudiation of the perceived extremism of the League party.[44] The elections of 1859 and 1865 (which saw the

---

[40] Gunn, 'Manchester Middle Class', 315, 315–22.

[41] Fraser, *Urban Politics*, 120–1, 143–51. For the even more rapid establishment of a non-party consensus in Salford, see Garrard, *Leadership and Power*, 211–13 etc.

[42] Garrard, *Leadership and Power*, 13–37, Howe, *Cotton Masters*, 144–5, 148–9.

[43] For an analysis of the divisions which opened up in Manchester liberalism in the aftermath of the repeal of the Corn Laws, see John Skinner, 'The Liberal Nomination Controversy in Manchester, 1847', *Bulletin of the Institute of Historical Research*, LV (1982), 215–18.

[44] The disruption of the natural alignments is indicated by the amount of Conservative

election of the ultra-Palmerstonian, Edward James) demonstrated that electoral politics in Manchester had become a matter of selecting that shade of reformism most acceptable to the majority.

Indeed, after 1857 party structures in Manchester collapsed almost entirely. Although a Conservative Association was established in 1858, the limit of its ambitions was to exert sufficient influence in the borough to promote the return of moderate Liberal candidates.[45] Likewise, in 1859 the Liberal party in Manchester was 'disorganised' and 'demoralised', and had been for the previous two years: '[w]e cannot', regretted one party activist, 'get a dozen people to walk across the street to save the Liberal party'.[46]

Even in those areas where there was no legislative removal of the fulcrums of dispute, the mellowing of conflict is apparent. In education, for example, the mid-1850s saw a reconciliation between many of the supporters of the rival schemes of 1850–51, flowering into a widespread (although not universal) consensus around the efforts of the Manchester Education Aid Society, established in 1864 with the aim of furthering the education of the poor, and testing the potential of the voluntary system, by providing grants to cover the school fees of destitute parents.[47]

At the same time, it is possible to see the emergence of a wide subscription to a series of shared values.[48] There was a general acceptance of the economic status quo. Although an undercurrent of anti-industrialism, especially among the Anglican clergy, is never entirely absent, the fortunes of Manchester at mid-century were so visibly tied to the expansion of old and new industries that there was little challenge to their validity.[49] Instead, the progress of the city

correspondence in the Manchester press in 1850s and 1860s signed with names such as 'A Reformer of 1832' or 'An Old Member of the League'; see also Breuilly, 'Liberalism', 204–9.

[45] John Ludlow to Joliffe (Conservative Chief Whip), 23 June 1858, Hylton Manuscripts, Somerset Record Office, cited by R. Stewart, *The Foundation of the Conservative Party*, (1978), 333.

[46] Thomas Ashton to George Melly, 13 May 1859, Melly Papers, I, 338, 920 MEL, Liverpool Record Office.

[47] S.E. Maltby, *Manchester and the Movement for National Elementary Education, 1800-1870*, (1918), 90–2; for the operations of the Education Aid Society see its *Annual Reports*, (1864–70), and E. Brotherton, *Popular Education and Political Economy. Six Letters by 'E.B.' reprinted from the Manchester Guardian, January 5th to January 27th 1864*, (1864).

[48] I acknowledge the changes of reductionism and over-simplification inherent in a short précis of this sort.

[49] For the reconciliation of Anglicanism to industrial progress, see Jane Garnett and A.C.

constantly affirmed a typical rejoicing in the virtues of progress. In parallel, few questioned the legitimacy of industrial wealth or the control which the middle classes sought to exercise in warehouse or factory. This in itself was part of the wider acceptance of the tenets of the political economists. For some, the old attitudes of paternalism (as distinct from the utilitarian industrial paternalism of Joyce) died hard, and the allocative function of the market was intermittently questioned by groups like the Christian Socialists, or individuals like the Congregational minister T.G. Lee, but for the most part the iron law of supply and demand was the beginning (and for many the end) of their economic assumptions.[50] Hence the reluctance to accept extensions of state intervention, and the persistent opposition to unionism (except in those few sectors where they could be institutionalised and used to facilitate management).[51]

Personal and community experience, as well as the teachings of the intellectuals, invested individualism with the honours for this advance. Here the core of the consensus touched roots in evangelicalism. As several historians have demonstrated, evangelicalism dominated the attitudes of all Victorians, even those who would have spurned the label evangelical.[52] The Manchester middle classes inhabited an intellectual world in which man was corrupted, a constant prey to evil influences and desires, capable of restraint and virtue only by the constant and minute attention to the details of everyday life. From such a stance, social disorder or deprivation was a problem of self-control; for Canon Charles Richson drunkenness was 'the result of the corrupt propensities of our carnal nature, unrestrained by the pure influences of pure and undefiled religion'.[53] As a result it was necessary 'to form the mind, to mould the character, to train the habits, to regulate the feelings and

Howe, 'Churchmen and Cotton Masters in Victorian England', in D.J. Jeremy, ed., *Business and Religion in Britain*, (1988), 72–94.

[50] T.G. Lee, *A plea for the English operatives, in which the means of elevating the working classes are humbly suggested*, ([1850]); see also H. Stowell, *A Plea for the Working Man. Do not lower his wages, addressed to employers*, (1848); there are numerous quotations, however, which illuminate the general orthodoxy in Finn, *After Chartism*, 73–81, 148–59.

[51] Howe, *Cotton Masters*, 163–93, G.R. Searle, *Entrepreneurial Politics in Mid-Victorian Britain*, (1993), 271–89.

[52] Morris, *Class, Sect and Party*, 321, Callum C. Brown, *The Social History of Religion in Scotland since 1730*, (1987), 136–43; cf. W. Houghton, *The Victorian Frame of Mind*, (1957), R.D. Altick, *Victorian People and Ideas*, (1974).

[53] Charles Richson, *'Drunkenness and other moral and social evils', Sermons to the working classes, preached in St Philip's Church, Salford, on Wednesday evening, February 24th, 1858*, (1858), 9.

motives' of the working classes.[54] In particular, it was necessary to inculcate the values of thrift, frugality, sobriety, industriousness, and above all, self-help.

These virtues comprised a constantly reiterated canon of middle-class behavioural morality, and the dangers of idleness its equally common refrain. Behind them lay the often explicit assumption that individual circumstances were a function almost entirely of moral standards and personal conduct. So universal were such assumptions that even John Ashton Nicholls, a unitarian cotton master and popular lecturer to the working classes, told an audience in 1856 that the sole cause of working-class problems was their 'extravagant and thriftless habits', and their intemperance.[55] Those unitarians who had a less all-encompassing notion of original sin apart, it was accepted that religion provided the only effective shield against human weakness.

Much of the coherence of middle-class values derived from the degree to which they were perceived in opposition to the values (or even lack of them) of the working classes.[56] The latent conservatism of the bulk of the middle classes was rooted in their perception of the working classes as the antithesis of morality. Their poverty was caused by profligacy or idleness. Their leisure activities involved little more than abandonment to sensual pleasures, beginning with drink and likely to end in all manner of suspected sexual excesses. Their neglect of organised religion left them undefended against the allurements of vice in all its forms. The ignorance which resulted from their inattention to education left them vulnerable to the misleading murmurings of every disreputable agitator. Their poverty would lead them to use political power to help themselves to the property of others. And even if there is a good deal of evidence of a more balanced picture of the working classes emerging from mid-century, the absolute condemnation of working-class character remained a common rhetorical strategy in the manual of middle-class self-affirmation. Hence the characteristic comment of one speaker at a public meeting in Rusholme in 1866 that

---

[54] J.P. Lee, Bishop of Manchester, cited by Charles Richson, *A Sketch of some of the causes which induced the abandonment of the voluntary system in the support of schools, and the introduction of the Manchester and Salford Education Bill*, (1851), 43–4.

[55] J.A. Nicholls, *A Lecture on Strikes*, (1856), 20.

[56] For a forceful analysis of this point see Smail, *Origins of Middle Class Culture*, 193–221.

'the working man was a machine for burning tobacco and swallowing beer, and devouring such literature as *Bell's Life*'.[57]

Until the discovery in the mid-1860s of the moral sense of at least sections of the working class, such beliefs underpinned marked middle-class suspicion of any substantial measure of franchise extension to the working classes. Miles Taylor has recently demonstrated that middle-class reformism had always been a mechanism primarily for increasing the accountability of the executive to the House of Commons, by the augmentation of the number of independent MPs, rather than a crusade to extend the social compass of the franchise. This is clearly reflected among the Manchester middle class, where even the League radicals showed scant enthusiasm for further franchise extension after 1832, settling, if they sought further parliamentary reform at all, for the ballot or redistribution.[58]

Sources of middle-class identity

What were the roots of this emerging consensus, and strengthening sense of middle-class identity?

In the first place the process of integration was eased by the fact that for all the fissures of religion and party, there was little in economic policy to divide the Manchester middle class. For all the split of the Chamber of Commerce in the 1840s, and the establishment of a rival Commercial Association, divisions even over Repeal had been as much ones of tone as of substance, and with the collapse of protectionism as practical politics in the wake of 1846, only personal grievances kept the two associations separate for so long. The appeal to both conservatives and liberals of the foreign policy of Palmerston brought this identity to the forefront.[59] The Chamber of Commerce and the Commercial Association were reunited in 1857, and the identity of interest of much of the commercial and industrial middle classes was confirmed in the ensuing years by concerns over the world supply of raw cotton, which

[57] *MCN*, 27 January 1866.
[58] For one illuminating case study, see R.J. Helmstadter, 'W.R. Greg: A Manchester Creed', in R.J. Helmstadter and B. Lightman, eds, *Victorian Faith in Crisis. Essays on Continuity and Change in Nineteenth Century Religious Belief*, (1990), 187–222, esp. 212–14; see also Searle, *Entrepreneurial Politics*, 202–35.
[59] See Kidd, 'The Middle Class', 6–7, R. Lloyd-Jones and Lewis, *Manchester and the Age of the Factory*, *passim*. The appeal of Palmerstonianism to the Manchester middle class was established in Gatrell, 'The commercial middle class'.

prompted the formation of the Cotton Supply Association, and ultimately, to the all-encompassing relief efforts of the 'Cotton Famine' years.[60]

In this sense the conflicts over reform in the 1830s and 1840s effected a temporary and unnatural division of the middle classes, and as each of these issues reached a legislative settlement, so the bitterness of political strife declined. Many natural Conservatives, who had been brought into the Liberal camp by support for moderate parliamentary reform or repeal of the Corn Laws, reverted to conservatism. The state gradually lost its tarnish of aristocratic dominance, and as the key issues in politics appeared to be resolved increasingly into the question of the degree of further parliamentary reform needed to fulfil the aims of the Reform Act of 1832, many one-time reformers, comfortable in their enfranchisement and local influence, predictably found themselves adopting a conservative, whiggish, stance; '[y]ou are frightening us all into Conservatism', wrote Benjamin Heywood to Henry Brougham in 1838, 'We are all tired of agitation, & want to be quiet & mind our own business'.[61]

The cooling of political partisanship also reflected, and contributed to, the settling of religious animosities.[62] In large part this derived from national circumstances: the removal of many of the disabilities of Dissent during the 1830s, the encouragements given to a new protestant identity by the combined threats of Papal aggression and the Oxford movement, the workable compromise over education which had apparently been established by the early 1850s, and developments within the city built on these processes.[63] There had never been a clear division of economic groups on the grounds of religion, and the struggles to effect a reform of religious provision for the parish of Manchester (which produced the 1850 Rectory Division Act, splitting the original parish of Manchester, and applying the surplus funds of the Collegiate Church to pastoral care within the new parishes), brought

---

[60] See P. Harnetty, *Imperialism and Free Trade: Lancashire and India in the mid-Nineteenth Century*, (1972), esp. 36-58.

[61] B. Heywood to Brougham, 3 January 1838, # 14362, Brougham Papers, University College, London. This was Cobden's well-known opinion, but one shared by many others in Manchester: see James E. Nelson to George Wilson, 25 June 1865, Wilson Papers, MCLA. For more general analyses see Searle, *Entrepreneurial Politics*, 129-32.

[62] For the extent to which 'religion cut both ways, playing a part in middle class culture that was simultaneously competitive and consensual', see Gunn, 'Manchester Middle Class', 256-300, on which the following paragraphs draw heavily.

[63] For a useful summary, see Parry, *Rise and Fall of Liberal Government*, 199-207.

into co-operation evangelicals from across the Anglican-Dissent divide.[64] Without gaining the cross-denominational popularity of his successor, James Prince Lee, first Bishop of Manchester, did much to encourage the sense of shared Protestant identity, itself feeding on the tensions inevitable in a city with the large Irish Catholic population of Manchester.

Although denomination still divided the middle class, the sense of a religious commitment markedly different from that of the working classes below (a sense heightened immeasurably by the results of the 1851 census), and the universal cultural forms of congregational life, provided plentiful bonds of shared experience.[65] Church and chapel functioned as mechanisms of recruitment for the middle class, integrating in-migrants and the upwardly mobile, and opened up opportunities for public activity for middle-class women. Religious affiliation continued to exercise a dominant influence over the choice of marriage partners, but interdenominational marriage increased markedly after 1850, and, as Howe has pointed out, marriage among the middle class 'reveal[ed] much social and occupational solidarity'.[66]

In the same way, social and religious distinctions of educational experience and background among the middle class declined steadily as the period progressed.[67] Despite its institutional variety, the education of the competing elites of the early nineteenth century had been sharply divided. For the Tory middle class the natural progression was from Manchester Grammar School to Oxford, although of course the association of a university education with the clerical profession, and the frequent use of private tutors meant this was a far from universal experience. However, the alumni of the Manchester Grammar School, the Wanklyns, Westheads, Peels, and Sowlers, constituted the Tory leadership of Manchester into the 1860s. Conversely, the Dissenting Academies, especially Manchester New College (Darbyshires, Philips, Woods, Taylors) or Ackworth School (the Ashworths), and the various provincial Grammar Schools, occasionally supplemented by University College London or a Scottish or continental university, educated many of the city's Liberal leaders.

---

[64] Howe, *Cotton Masters*, 61–72.
[65] See H. Meller, *Leisure and the Changing City, 1870-1914*, (1976), 78–85.
[66] Howe refers in particular to the textile elite, *Cotton Masters*, 78, but see also figures in Gunn, 'Manchester Middle Class', 229–32.
[67]Once again, this section relies heavily on Simon Gunn's work: see 'Manchester Middle Class', 111–25.

While educational experiences remained heterogeneous, there were various shifts towards a less bifurcated pattern from the 1840s. As the commercial economy reached maturity, of course, the most significant education of many members of the middle class was obtained within the warehouse or counting house. Concern at the deficiencies of 'middle-class education', itself a term pregnant with a more coherent sense of class identity, brought reforms to the Grammar School, establishing Nonconformist representation on the board of trustees, and tilting the balance of provision away from boarders and towards, it was hoped, the local middle classes. Other overtly middle-class schools joined the Grammar School in its reforms, including the Manchester Commercial Schools, Chorlton High School, and, at a more lowly level, the schools and classes of the Manchester Mechanics' Institution, the Athenaeum and the YMCA.[68] And at their apex was Owen's College, founded in 1851, with pretensions to be the pinnacle of local middle-class education, on the model of the Scottish universities. Owen's, indeed, despite its early difficulties, testifies to the strength of local identity among Manchester's elite: the response of the *Saturday Review* was that '[a]nyone educated in Manchester would certainly be dull and probably vicious'.[69]

This was a typical piece of metropolitan prejudice. In fact, middle-class society in Manchester established the same forms of cultural expression as the new elites of the other provincial cities. The bedrock of this culture remained the sphere of middle-class domesticity: the well-ordered household, with its dinners, visits, and family gatherings. The private gulf between the parlour or the drawing room, and the cellar or the two-up, two-down house, spoke eloquently of social distinctions, and the middle-class home was the icon of the public apartheid which divided rented pews from free benches, reserved shilling seats from the penny gallery, first and second class ticket holders from the occupants of the third class carriages.[70]

Of course, identities of education, religion, and domestic culture were only elements of an emerging middle-class culture. Ultimately,

[68] For parallel processes in Sheffield and Birmingham, see Smith, *Conflict and Compromise*, 106–140, 176–82.

[69] P.J. Waller, *Town, City and Nation. England 1850–1914*, (1983), 83.

[70] There is no space here to develop the significant insights into the domestic or 'private' determinants of middle-class cultural identity which have emerged in the wake of the seminal work, L. Davidoff and C. Hall, *Family Fortunes: men and women of the English middle class, 1780-1850*, (1981).

they were in turn meshed together by the ritual platitudes of the mid-Victorian public platform, the general meeting, and the annual dinner, their differences transcended by the integrating force of a broad range of philanthropic and cultural institutions designed to develop and sustain class identity. Although, as we have seen, the creation of a neutral public space within which the rival middle-class elites could forge bonds of unity was a difficult and long-drawn out process, it is noticeable that from the 1820s and 1830s, just as the geographic dispersal of the bourgeoisie was gathering pace, and its political battles were at their most intense, there was an acceleration in the creation of cultural institutions for the middle classes.

The proliferation of musical societies provides one illustration of such trends. The Concert Hall and the Manchester Assembly Rooms were central to the social constitution of the city's middle class from the later eighteenth century, and by the 1840s they functioned increasingly not so much to provide music as a place for upper-middle-class social intercourse, and to define membership of Manchester 'society'.[71] From 1830 these were supplemented by countless informal and local musical societies, and several with grander, city-wide pretensions, including the Gentlemen's Glee Club (1830), the Choral Society (1835), the Madrigal Society (1840), the Hargreaves Choral Society (1841), and the Harmonic Society (1843).[72]

With the partial exception of the Hargreaves Choral Society, these were self-consciously (and highly socially exclusive) middle-class associations with little didactic purpose, and in this they followed a more general pattern. Many of the new societies of this period, including the Manchester Medical Society (1834), the Manchester Architectural Society (1837), and the Manchester Incorporated Law Association (1847), involved the creation of a sense of occupational identity for sections of the professional middle classes. Others, and in particular the Natural History Society (1821), the Botanical and Horticultural Society (1828), the Phrenological Society (1829), the Geological Society (1838), the Victoria Institute (1840), and Chetham's Society (1843), supplemented the grander institutions of liberal culture, the Lit&Phil, the RMI and the Athenaeum, while being structured and priced in such a way as to sustain a comfortably middle-class

---

[71] 'A Member of the Concert Hall', *MG*, 12 January 1853, *MG*, 4 January 1851.

[72] For a general account of musical societies in Manchester see *Freelance*, III (1868), 117-19; for the early history of the Manchester Gentlemen's Glee Club see *MC*, 8 October 1859; for the Hargreaves Choral Society see *MCN*, 12 April, 17 May 1879.

membership and hence avoid the sensitivities associated with inter-class initiatives.[73]

However, as Morris has argued, middle-class identity was forged at least as much in the attempts to define its relationships with other social groups, and assert its leadership of the community as a whole; as such the significance of these exclusively middle-class institutions was that they provided essential foundations for the rapidly multiplying range of religious, cultural and philanthropic associations which formed the larger part of the associational life of mid-century Manchester, and whose collective operations embodied what can be described as middle-class 'moral imperialism'.[74]

The contours of 'moral imperialism'

The institutions of 'moral imperialism' were neither mutually exclusive, nor organisationally or chronologically discrete. Nevertheless, there is a broad sequence which can be identified. At the outset the primary appeal was made to religion as the means of sustaining social stability, both through church and chapel, and also the associated educational and missionary institutions. However, the opinion gained ground steadily in the 1830s and 1840s that religion needed to be at least supplemented with a more conscious effort to inculcate correct principles and knowledge, first of social and economic dynamics, and then eventually of politics. In turn, although this ideal was never abandoned, the tenor of middle-class efforts, from undercurrents of activity in the 1830s through to the full thrust of endeavours in the 1860s, gradually shifted away from didacticism towards the shaping more generally of working-class culture and mores by the encouragement of wholesome and improving styles of life.

Particularly for Conservatives, and hence most clearly associated with Anglican initiative, religious instruction was the cornerstone of any effective campaign to restore social integration, and strenuous resistance was offered to any rival suggestion. As Benjamin Love wrote in 1843, 'morality is not the offspring of mental education, but rather is the fruit of religious training', whilst Parkinson looked for the

---

[73] For brief details of these societies see *Love and Barton's Manchester Handbook*, (1842), 208–9, 245–8, Kargon, *Science in Victorian Manchester*, 14–16, 24–7.
[74] Morris, *Class, Sect and Party*, 232 etc.

'infusion' of religious principles to solve the problems he identified in 1843.[75] But more liberal opinion often sounded very much the same. Layhe stated clearly in 1841 that any comprehensive schemes of educational improvement 'that are not based upon the great and commanding truths of morality and revealed religion, [would be] essentially defective, and likely in their practical application to do the nation more harm than good'.[76]

For Anglicans, the church was particularly suited from its parochial structure and distribution of clergymen to assume the functions of moral mentor of the new working-class communities. The results in the 1830s included a substantial impetus towards church building, particularly in the Church of England; renewed enthusiasm for Sunday school education, coupled with a new concern for the more extended standards which could be obtained only from regular day school attendance, and which in turn led to the emergence of national education campaigns; and a particular concern with the missionary and domestic visiting arms of religious institutions, symbolised in Manchester by the formation in 1833 of the Manchester and Salford Town Mission (later the Manchester City Mission).

Of course, in many cases such institutions were concerned not simply with inculcating a value system, but with providing the working classes with knowledge. The middle-class caricature of the working man was of a largely ignorant individual whose lack of knowledge left him vulnerable to the persuasive rhetoric of the unprincipled demagogue: as Layhe pictured them, 'Without any solid basis of education in their youth – without any permanent connexion with our schools and Mechanics' Institutes in their maturer years – without any comprehensive and well-arranged plan of self-improvement before them, they are thrown upon some popular demagogue, or worthless oracle of a newspaper, for guidance'.[77]

In the early nineteenth century the dominant response to this analysis had been the attempt to isolate the working classes from political information, suppress the channels of its distribution and coerce aspiring radicals. Although such attitudes survived into the 1830s (and

[75] B. Love, *Chapters on Working People: How to Elevate their morals and to Improve their social condition*, (1843), 6, *MC*, 9 September 1843.
[76] *MTPAR*, (1841), 42. Of course there was a minority secular education lobby which believed, as J.A. Nicholls put it, 'that even without direct theological instruction, an educated people will finally became a religious people', 'Nicholls', *MG*, 12 August 1846.
[77] *MTPAR*, (1848), 18.

the comments above in part reflect them), the fact that the working classes could gain access to political information, and the realisation that 'warmth and bitterness of feeling are...even more likely to be excited by incidental allusions than in occasional discussions of those topics in which the pros and cons are fully gone into', encouraged the development of initiatives which attempted more directly to propagate 'correct' (or 'useful') information, and challenge wrong-headedness.[78]

By the 1850s the discussion of politics had been sold to the Conservatives as the best way, as Robert Rumney put it, 'to remove all this ignorance upon questions of politics and their application to political economy and kindred subjects'.[79] Indeed this project struck a readier chord with many liberals who had never thought that the main need was to restrain the corrupt tendencies of all, but who saw the problem more in terms of the necessity to provide appropriate skills and values within which individuals could work out their own destiny, and of correcting, in the term of T.G. Lee, the distorted 'optics', not necessarily through the imposition of beliefs, but at least in the provision of an educational lens to correct working-class myopia.[80] With the religious and educational institutions apparently unsuitable for this purpose, the result was initiatives beginning with the mechanics' institutes of the 1830s and the lyceums of the 1840s, stretching through to the various night schools and lecturing venues which were established by the 1860s.

In fact, as many of these institutions developed, they tended to put more and more emphasis not on the promulgation of correct knowledge, but on the third major motif of middle-class moral imperialism, the overriding need to establish appropriate habits and patterns of leisure, both as an end in themselves, and as a vital prerequisite to any successful move to either education or conversion. 'It was', according to George Jackson, one of the pioneers of the Salford Mechanics' Institution, 'not in the well occupied hour that men thought of evil, it was when their hands were idle and their minds unfurnished'.[81] The difficulties of attempting to educate or convert those suffering from destitution or deprivation were also recognised, as was the fact that some of the worst features of the economic and urban

[78] *Report of the Manchester District Association of Literary and Scientific Institutions*, (1840), 11.
[79] Manchester Mechanics' Institute, *Annual Report*, (1856), 32.
[80] T.G. Lee, *A Plea for the English Operatives*, 15.
[81] *MG*, 1 June 1839.

structures could be softened by provision for 'innocent' amusements of various sorts, along with the encouragement of that frugality and sobriety the middle classes admired so much in their own self-image.[82] Such ideas had been a feature of the mechanics' institutes and their offsprings, but they found fuller expression in the provision of recreational facilities such as public parks in the mid-1840s, the Free Library in 1851, the various working men's clubs and penny readings of the 1860s, and in middle-class encouragement of temperance and provident institutions which were active among the working classes.

Unfortunately, the achievement of a relatively stable consensus on these desiderata was rarely matched by similar consensus on either their relative priority or importance, or the methods by which they could be implemented. Tensions over the emphasis placed on broader cultural change, direct education, or the centrality of religion, continually strained middle-class cohesion, and produced discontinuities, divisions and rivalries which undermined the projects of moral imperialism. The vexed issues of religion plagued education to the extent that considerably more effort was often exerted in controversies over rival schemes than was actually applied to the practical extension of schooling. Likewise education at the national level and many local initiatives that came under the auspices of municipal government, including the parks and the Free Library, were constrained by that mixture of economism and individualism which resisted every expenditure that could be attacked as something which individuals should provide for themselves. And the same sense of social distinction that impelled middle-class moral imperialism in the first place, also encouraged the sorts of social exclusivity which inhibited the use, within the sweep of efforts of improvement, of the original middle-class cultural institutions, such as the Natural History Museum. Ultimately, therefore, acceptance of the role of the middle class *qua* class does not mean that we can underrate the importance of the strains within that class.

[82] The stress on habits of course had a long pedigree: see the various speeches at the meeting to establish the District Provident Society, *MSA*, 23 March 1833.

Conclusion

Despite the ferocity of the antagonisms created in the early decades of the century around the inadequate structures of local government and their Tory incumbents, antagonisms which spilled over into almost all areas of middle-class activity, it is clear that in Manchester, as in other industrial towns and cities, commencing in the 1830s and flowering in the later 1840s and 1850s, it is possible to see the successful construction of a sense of middle-class identity, and of a new cultural coherence. The removal or softening of key sources of tension, and the diaspora of the middle classes in the 1830s and 1840s, prompted the creation of a comprehensive matrix of political, cultural, religious and philanthropic organisations. In turn this class consciousness prompted the implementation of a broad programme, with arguably a rough three-way division, of moral imperialism, designed to restore and maintain social stability and middle-class authority.

Chapter Four

The rejection of religion

Organised religion was the engine-room of middle-class moral imperialism. As the core of the middle-class world view, religious belief provided the norms it was anxious to universalise, and can be identified in almost all its moral imperialism. At its heart, particularly in the early part of the period, was an interlocking group of institutions in which religion remained paramount: the churches and chapels, day and Sunday schools, and missionary organisations.

The status of religion in the mid-Victorian city is currently much debated. The traditional picture has long suggested that organised religion fought a losing battle with rapid urban growth, the traditional mechanisms of parish and congregation being overwhelmed by the scale of the problems presented by rapid demographic change. More recently, however, the balance of argument has shifted towards a more positive evaluation, suggesting that despite the obstacles it faced, urban religion adapted with some success to its challenges, and played an important role in the effective propagation of bourgeois values amongst at least a section of the working classes.[1] The history of Manchester suggests, however, that although the institutions of organised religion were not unsuccessful in developing to meet the expanding demands of the city, their successful institutional response masked a deeper failure to impose themselves on the city and its working-class population.

The religion of church and chapel

In 1832 organised religion was only beginning to come to terms with Manchester's rapid social transformation. Anglican organisation was still based on the single parish of Manchester, which covered all the industrial town and some of the surrounding villages, and was itself part of the over-large and poor diocese of Chester. Although there had been some church building, progress had been slow, and new churches had not been assigned specific districts. Tension was growing between

---

[1] For a resumé of the debate see H. McLeod, 'Introduction', *Religion in the Age of the Great City*, (1995); the clearest statement of the 'revisionist' position remains C.G. Brown, 'Did urbanization secularize Britain?', *Urban History Yearbook*, 15 (1988), 1–14.

the canons of the Collegiate Church (the parish church) and an emerging evangelical party under the rector of Christ Church, Salford, Canon Hugh Stowell.[2] Unburdened by the Anglican Church's claims to universality, Dissent, although growing, had also done little to accommodate a rapidly expanding population, and in 1830 Catholicism was a minor presence with only three churches. The obvious consequence of this was a working class population who lived largely beyond the influence of religion.

The Anglican response was a determined drive to build new churches in unprovided working-class districts, first through the Manchester and Eccles Church Building Society which built two churches between 1836 and 1840, and then the rival Ten Churches Association (evangelical), after whose establishment in 1841 and the New Parishes Act of 1843, mutual rivalry brought a spate of new churches.[3] Unfortunately, the weight of debt which resulted forced a period of consolidation in the late 1840s, and the formation of the new diocesan building society in 1851 diverted energies to the out-townships.[4] Among the other denominations, only the Catholics showed a parallel determination to expand church provision: the influx of Irish Catholics and the establishment in 1851 of the diocese of Salford facilitated an increase of churches from three in 1830 to twelve in 1872.[5] For the rest, apart from the Unitarian Ministry to the Poor, Dissent showed itself relatively unconcerned with church extension in this period. It was not until 1868 that the Lancashire and Cheshire Chapel and School Building Society appeared; the burst of activity occasioned by the 1662 Commemoration cannot hide the undynamic nature of Manchester Congregationalism in this period.[6] During the 1830s and 1840s Methodism in Manchester suffered from the national conflict between its tory and liberal wings and was much weakened by the subsequent secessions, and the Presbyterians and Baptists both largely stagnated.[7]

---

[2] For Stowell see J.B. Marsden, *Memoirs of the Reverend Hugh Stowell*, (1868).

[3] W.R. Ward, 'Church and Society in the First Half of the Nineteenth Century', in R. Davies, et al., eds, *A History of the Methodist Church in Great Britain*, (1978), 69–70.

[4] W.R. Ward, 'The Cost of Establishment: Some Reflections on Church Building in Manchester', in C.J. Cumming, ed., *Studies in Church History*, III, (1966), 277–89.

[5] G.P. Connolly, 'The Transubstantiation of Myth: towards a New Popular History of Nineteenth Century Catholicism in England', *Journal of Ecclesiastical History*, 35,1 (January 1984), 78–104; *Nonconformist*, 23 October 1872 (Supplement).

[6] W.G. Robinson, *A History of the Lancashire Congregational Union, 1806–1956*, ([1955]), 56–7.

[7] D.A. Gowland, *Methodist Secessions. The Origins of Free Methodism in Three Lancashire towns: Manchester, Rochdale, Liverpool*, (1979).

Table 4.1 Church accommodation in Manchester, 1836-71[8]

	1836	1851	1871
Population	218,556	303,882	355,665
Sittings (Anglican)	29,400	38,120	50,770
Sittings (Dissent etc.)	37,450	57,809	70,716
% population provided for	32	32	34

In consequence, little impression was made on the shortfall of church provision apparent in 1832. The spasmodic effort allowed the churches to keep pace with decelerating population growth, but failed to narrow the gap which had already opened up. Taking contemporaries' measure of the ratio of sittings to population, accommodation in Manchester failed to rise much above half the 60% of total population level which was deemed optimal (see Table 4.1).

Even this picture is optimistic. The reliance of ministers of all denominations (bar the Catholics) on pew rents left only a fraction of the total available for those unable or unwilling to pay. Indeed, as the new St Matthews in the working-class district of Campfield amply demonstrated, the inadequate endowments of many of the churches built in the 1840s had left them with more rented pews and even fewer free sittings than had previously been normal.[9] In 1856 apart from 150 free seats in St John's, only the free seats in the Cathedral prevented the poor of the whole central region of the city being entirely unprovided for by the Church of England.[10]

Such problems of geographical distribution remained hidden by the aggregate figures, which disguised the concentration of provision in more prosperous suburbs, to the neglect of large working-class districts where they were most needed. This was particularly so given the drift of many Dissenting congregations to the suburbs, exemplified by the movement of the prosperous Mosley Street and Cannot Street congregations to Stretford Road and Brooks Bar, 'to be near the mansions and villas of the merchant', as one critic put it.[11] Congregations in working-class districts were sometimes left to collapse, and it was not until the 1870s that the widespread adoption of missions and mission halls marked a general acceptance by Dissent of congregational responsibilities to take religion to the working

[8] Report of W.J. Kidd, *MG*, 16 November 1836; *Nonconformist*, 23 October 1872 (Supplement), 1095.
[9] Ward, 'Cost of Establishment', 286–7.
[10] 'A Crotchetty Man', *Church of the People*, n.s. I (1856), 12.
[11] *MX*, 10 May 1860.

classes.[12] The Catholic Church, although expanding, had no greater pretensions to comprehensiveness. This left the burden of serving working-class districts largely on the Church of England parochial system, and it could not cope.

When, as late as 1870, the Rev. C.B. Holder of All Souls, Ancoats, spoke of his parish's 'utter inability to cope with the claims of our large population' (of 11,000), and of the resulting 'low tone of morals, which has rendered this & some contiguous parishes almost proverbial', he was, albeit in the pursuit of central handouts, articulating an almost universal complaint among Anglican clergy.[13] The difficulties of the Church of England left large areas of the city almost wholly without formal religious provision. In the Bennett Street area of Ancoats, for example, the collapse of efforts to build a new church for the district in 1854 left a population of 40,000 served by only one church and three dissenting chapels.[14] Generally, parishes in working-class areas remained very large: in 1847 St George's with 1500 sittings was the only Anglican church for a district which in 1841 had contained 40,000 people, and even after sub-division still contained over 20,000 inhabitants.[15]

Moreover, the large city parishes often laboured under a variety of obstacles to their sustained efficiency. The history of the parish of St Andrew's in Ancoats graphically illustrates the difficulties faced. The church was erected in 1829 (and consecrated in 1831), out of the Ecclesiastical Commissioners' funds, in a district which subsequently provided ten further parishes as population grew. It had no initial endowment, but with not more than a third of the sittings free, it had been hoped that the pew rents of the rest would provide a stable, if modest income to the incumbent. However, as the parish steadily became almost exclusively working class in character, income from pew rents fell steadily, and the income of the parish was never really adequate for its expenses. Even after the manifestly inadequate sum of £26 was granted by the Commissioners in 1842, the parish remained chronically underfunded, and in 1845 the total income of the incumbent was only £150 p.a.

Although the aid of a curate from 1839 enabled the parish priest, George Dugard, to begin developing various congregational societies,

[12] B. Nightingale, *Lancashire Non-conformity*, (1890–93), V, 132, 178.
[13] Rev. C.B. Holder – National Society, 9 December 1870, All Souls Ancoats file, National Schools Archive, Church of England Record Office.
[14] 'A Subscriber of St Paul's Day and Sunday Schools', *MX*, 6 May 1854.
[15] See statistics of church accommodation and population, *MG*, 7 July 1847, 9 November 1861.

this could often be done only by providing the funds from his own pocket, and eventually declining income, despite an increase in the number of rented pews, drove him to resign. Over the ensuing years the parish rapidly had four more incumbents, and on at least one occasion was forced to close for want of a replacement. Despite the opening of day schools in 1846 (with the aid of the Church Education Society), it was not until 1851 when, under the arrangements for the reform of the parish of Manchester, the district was allocated to Charles Richson, one of the Collegiate Church canons, that any stability was achieved.

By that stage the parish had all but disintegrated, the congregation numbering barely 40. The areas of free seating in the church were 'so mean and dirty in their appearance as to present an almost insuperable objection to any decent mechanic using them', the school rooms were unsanitary and dilapidated, and parochial associations virtually non-existent.[16] Under Richson the efficiency of the parish steadily improved, but even with three curates (whose stipends alone amounted to one and half times the income of the parish), resources were completely inadequate for a population in 1861 of over 16,000, of whom between a half and two thirds claimed at least nominal Anglicanism, in a district virtually bereft of dissenting places of worship. Although Richson had begun holding services in a room in one of the outlying parts of the parish by the early 1860s, he was unsuccessful in an attempt to raise the money necessary to buy a building as a school and church room there. By 1871, with Richson ageing and increasingly inactive, the state of the parish was once again coming under criticism.[17]

Such difficulties weighed particularly heavily because the traditional rituals of organised religion appeared almost designed to alienate the

---

[16] St Andrew's, Ancoats, Contributions and Expenditure [in the five years from March 1855], 3, in Archdeacon Rushton's Visitation Returns, Vol 40, msf 942.72 R121, MCLA.

[17] The story of St Andrew's can only be pieced together from a wide range of sources: [John Henry Sicot], *St Andrew's Church, Travis St Ancoats...A commemorative booklet for the centenary*, (1931), *passim*, J.Y. Caw, *The duty of increasing the stipends of the Manchester clergy, stated and proved, by a practical example*, (1852), *Plan for the Endowment of the Church of St Andrew's, Ancoats, Manchester*, (1846), miscellaneous material on St Andrew's Church Endowment Society in MCL at 283 M17, as well as the material in the entry on St Andrew's in Archdeacon Rushton's Visitation Returns, *op. cit.*, and correspondence of George Dugard with the National Society, St Andrew's Ancoats file, National Society Archive, Church of England Record Office. See also Church Education Society, *Annual Report*, (1847), 16, *MG*, 24 March 1841, *WMC*, 24 August 1844, *MG*, 8 December 1849, *MC*, 12 February, 14 June 1859, *MX*, 25 June 1864, *Sphinx*, IV (1871), 343.

working classes. Their sheer length was intimidating: perhaps three Sunday services, the morning one often two hours long, comprising long litanies of prayers and often longer sermons (J.R. Beard, minister of Strangeways Unitarian Chapel, considered one and a quarter hours normal and spoke on occasion for more than three!).[18] Prayers and sermons were often delivered in a dreary monotone, amid an atmosphere characterised by one visitor to the Collegiate Church in 1847 as 'heavy inattentive decency'.[19] The subject matter was often doctrinal, metaphysical and convoluted.[20] For most of the working classes, as Edward Brotherton put it, 'the sermon can be attended to only with a dull stare and a sense of darkness and degradation which must make the forms of service distasteful'.[21] While all denominations had their popular pulpit performers, these were the exception. Hence among Manchester Congregationalism too the 1850s brought complaints at the 'easy self-complaceny' of the ministry and the 'sheer lack of life' of the services.[22] The consequence was, as the Rev. J.L. Poore, a Salford Congregational minister, pointed out in 1848, '[t]he working millions will not enter our houses of prayer, or, if they come, being ignorant of our phraseology, the pulpit teachings are not understood, and failing to meet what they want, they grow weary and retire'.[23]

The message of the pulpit was also often couched in terms which the working classes would have found anathema. The Anglican clergy especially were often staunchly tory: Stowell was accused in 1837 of having transformed his pulpit 'into the rostrum of a political club'.[24] Conversely the Manchester liberalism of many Dissenting clergy, with their opposition to legislative protection and trade unionism, was unlikely to endear them to the working classes. Politics apart, outspoken opposition to Owenism, the National Public Schools Association, and to the opening of public institutions on Sundays all helped fuel working-class suspicion of the clergy in general.[25]

For organised religion to appeal successfully to the working classes it was thus vital that the regular services be supplemented by forms of

---

[18] H. McLachlan, *Records of a Family, 1800–1935*, (1935), 14, 24.

[19] Hugh Miller in the *Scotsman*, extracted in *MG*, 1 May 1847.

[20] Joseph Booth, 'Our Working Classes', *Manchester Papers*, I (1856), 300.

[21] *EASAR*, (1865), 10.

[22] *Christian Reformer*, (1854), 55, citing *A Letter to the Congregational Churches of Manchester*, and *A Letter to the Author of a Pamphlet entitled 'Congregational Reform etc'*, (by P.Q.R., another Manchester Congregationalist).

[23] J. Corbin, *Ever Working, Never Resting: a memoir of John Legge Poore*, (1874), 440.

[24] 'A Churchman', *MG*, 19 July 1837.

[25] For an example of the depth of the suspicion see the tale of E.B. Chalmers, *SWN*, 10 December 1859.

religion and mechanisms of support tailored more specifically to working-class tastes and needs. One of these was the organisation of religious lectures specifically for the working classes. Both general and specifically congregational lecture courses were staged by Anglican clergy, but this practice was perhaps more common among Dissent, where there are cases of ministers making a determined effort to sustain special working-class lectures over a long period, although in general activity tended to be irregular.[26] The most prominent example was Arthur Mursell, a Baptist minister who delivered winter Sunday afternoon lectures for the working classes in the Free Trade Hall, from 1857 to 1864, often attracting large audiences. Yet Mursell's lectures and the considerable controversy they provoked, most particularly because of the racy style he adopted, and the populist anti-rich tone which infused his comments, demonstrated the ambivalence of middle-class commitment to providing a style of religion which might attract the working classes.[27] The various revivalist services which became common in the 1860s were greeted with similar suspicion, summed up by a writer in the Grosvenor Street Chapel magazine, *Our Magazine*, who expressed his 'profound pity for the poor, ignorant people who are so vilely caricaturing our holy religion by such disgusting and abominable exhibitions'.[28]

Religion in schooling

Attendance figures give a misleading picture of the contact which organised religion had with the working classes, because many who rarely if ever attended religious services came into contact with religion through its educational activities. Moreover, as the contemporary wisdom came to accept, in comparison to an adult population stubbornly set in its ways, the mind of the child was malleable, and hence provided a 'golden opportunity of raising the general standard of society'.[29]

[26] T.G. Lee, *The Dignity, the Objects, the Rewards, and the Triumphs of Labour, discussed in 4 lectures at the Pendleton Mechanics' Institution, in November 1860*, (1860), iv.
[27] A. Mursell, *Lectures to Working Men, delivered in the Free Trade Hall, Manchester*, ([1858-64]); see also my 'Popular Platform Religion: Arthur Mursell at the Free Trade Hall, 1856–65', *Manchester Region History Review*, (forthcoming 1996).
[28] Anon., *Our Magazine*, (1866), 16.
[29] 'A Manchester Man' [J.R. Wilkinson], *MX*, 24 January 1864.

In the early nineteenth century the churches in Manchester had concentrated educational effort on the Sunday schools. Initially attempts had been made to provide umbrella organisations in which resources could be directed to cases of want, but by the 1830s only fragments remained. There was no effective co-ordinating body for the 33 Anglican Sunday schools.[30] The schools of eight of the evangelical dissenting denominations were organised under the Manchester Sunday School Union (established 1824) with 37 schools by 1842.[31] In 1834 the Catholic Schools Society presided over 12 schools.[32] At this stage the remaining schools were organised in the 'Sunday Schools of All Denominations', but after they split in 1835, the Wesleyan Methodist Schools, the reformed schools of all denominations (with only three schools affiliated) and the schools of those bodies like the Unitarians who found no home in local associations, completed the mosaic of Sunday school organisations.[33]

In the 1830s and 1840s the Sunday schools were generally accepted as 'the school for secular as well as religious education'.[34] There were no Catholic day schools until the late 1840s and in 1841 there were three times as many children in Anglican Sunday schools as in their day schools.[35] Although day schooling expanded, the tendency to concentrate on Sunday schools to the neglect of day schools remained a common one into the 1860s.[36]

Despite this, the development of Sunday schooling in the 1840s and 1850s was uneven. The unions, unlike the earlier Anglican Sunday School Union, were loose federations which did little to channel funds to those areas most in need, and instead made desultory provision of services such as libraries, normal classes, and lectures.[37] The 1856 canvas movement notwithstanding, there was little sustained pressure for expansion, and while the more prosperous parishes and congregations built up flourishing schools, there was little impetus before the 1860s towards any comprehensive extension of Sunday

[30] The schools had 12,966 scholars; see Ward, *Religion and Society in England, 1780-1850*, (1972), 40-2; Manchester Statistical Society, *Report...on the State of Education in the Borough of Manchester in 1834*, (1837), 37, idem, *Report...on the State of Education in the Borough of Salford in 1835*, (1836), 37.

[31] *MC*, 21 May 1842.

[32] *MSA*, 27 December 1834, *Report of the proceedings of the meeting...presenting an address from the Catholic Sunday school teachers to Thomas Wyse*, ([1837]).

[33] *MG*, 13 February 1836, *MSA*, 5,12 March 1836, 14 February 1846.

[34] *PP*, (1845) XXXV [622], 214.

[35] *MSA*, 27 December 1834, *MC*, 4 December 1841.

[36] Brotherton 'Scrapbook', #124, M98, MCLA, *MCN*, 31 March 1866.

[37] *MX*, 22 December 1855.

schools in working-class districts.[38] It is significant that the most dynamic development of Sunday schooling came from outside the regular denominational structure in the form of the Sunday Evening Ragged Schools set up in the late 1850s initially under the auspices of the Manchester and Salford Sunday Ragged School Union (1858).[39]

Nevertheless, the numbers in Sunday schools did expand considerably during this period. Fragmentation and the intense rivalry for scholars makes precise enumeration difficult. The educational census of 1851, James Kay-Shuttleworth's 1861 survey, and the various computations made during the 1860s all suffer, like those for day schooling considered below, from a number of defects. Statistics were collected by participants in heated educational debate, in an attempt to bolster largely predetermined positions. Figures for scholars registered or 'on the books', like Whit figures swelled by seasonal entertainments, overstated regular attendance, while figures of actual or average attendance underestimated the numbers in frequent attendance. Surveys were rarely comprehensive, and tended to omit schools outside denominational control (a particular drawback for day school surveys), and the areas of surveys were usually not compatible with previous ones. In consequence, the conclusions of the following discussion must be treated with restraint.

In aggregate, the picture is one of substantial expansion throughout the period. In the mid-1830s Statistical Society figures suggest an average attendance at Sunday schools in Manchester of 31,501; Kay-Shuttleworth's figures for 1861 give an average attendance of 59,041.[40] Various figures from the early 1850s, including the educational census, suggest a figure of around 40,000 for 1851, implying that growth was more rapid in the 1850s than it was in the 1830s and 1840s.[41] Figures of scholars on the books tend to be 50% higher than these figures, and even allowing for exaggerations, it can be estimated that about 35,000 children were attending Sunday school in the mid-1830s, rising to over 70,000 by the early 1860s. The Church of England was most active, improving its position from providing less

[38] For the canvas movement see *MX*, 29 April 1856.

[39] See I. Wallace, 'A History of the Manchester and Salford Shaftesbury Society', (ts, nd), MCL. The national context is given by H.W. Schupf, 'Education for the Neglected: Ragged Schools in Nineteenth Century England', *History of Education Quarterly*, XII (1972), 162–83.

[40] Manchester Statistical Society, *op. cit.*, (note 4), J.P. Kay-Shuttleworth, *Sketch of the Progress of Manchester in Thirty Years from 1832–62*, (1862), 110.

[41] *PP*, (1852–53) LXXIX (514), 8–9, C. Richson, *Educational Facts and Statistics of Manchester*, [1853].

Table 4.2 Sunday school provision in Manchester and Salford by denomination[42]

	1834/5	1851	1865
Church of England	10363 (26)	16369 (30)	27000 (36)
Methodist	15677 (40)	13391 (25)	19417 (26)
Independent	5546 (14)	9544 (18)	14380 (19)
Catholic	4493 (11)	10800 (20)	5030 (7)
Baptist	1563 (4)	1750 (3)	2540 (3)
Unitarian	403 (1)	784 (1)	1977 (3)
Ragged			3149 (4)
Miscellaneous	1217 (3)	1691 (3)	2208 (3)

than 30% of Sunday scholars in the mid-1830s to 36% in the mid-1860s (see Table 4.2). The crisis of Methodism was reflected in an erosion of the primacy it had held at the start of the period; likewise, although Congregationalism increased its provision, the actual attendances failed to keep pace with the rising population, and after a burst at mid-century, the diversion of Catholic attention to day schooling caused a considerable falling off in Sunday school scholars. Although all the denominations managed to increase their numbers in absolute terms, relative growth was found only among the Unitarians (who had had very few scholars in the 1830s) and in the emerging non-denominational Sunday Ragged Schools.

The impact of this effort was fiercely debated. Supporters of the voluntary system argued that the schools had 'a vast moral influence in producing that quiet and good order which so extensively prevails among our operative classes'.[43] However, by the late 1840s the tide of opinion had swung in favour of those who saw the schools as, in Rev. J.L. Poore's words, little more than 'institutions for teaching poor children to read the scriptures and for keeping them out of harm's way during a certain portion of the Sabbath', which might be auxiliaries to, but could not be substitutes for day schooling.[44] As a result, the thrust of educational endeavour in Manchester from the late 1830s onwards was increasingly directed towards the expansion of day schooling. The

---

[42] Manchester Statistical Society, *Education in Manchester*, 37, idem, *Education in Salford*, 37, *PP*, (1852) XI (499), 293; Brotherton Scrapbook, #158, M98, MCLA.
[43] James Adshead, *PP*, (1852) XI (499), 302; cf. Robert Lamb, *Free Thoughts*, (1866), I, 66.
[44] Corbin, *Ever Working*, 433; cf. Stowell's *Letter to Peel*, cited in Marsden, *Memoir*, 184.

obstacles were enormous. Population growth had swamped the remnants of the educational establishments of the later middle ages and the limited denominational provision. Even allowing for the activity of the recently rehabilitated private 'dame' schools, and despite the educational clauses of the 1833 Factory Act, the inquiries of Kay[-Shuttleworth] and the Manchester Statistical Society demonstrated both the overall shortage of educational provision in the district and the generally low quality of education provided.[45]

Although the evidence collected in the 1830s, and the considerable social unrest of the chartist period, provided fresh impetus to the expansion of the education system, the effectiveness of educational reform was hampered by the deep divisions which emerged over the nature of the system it was desirable to create. The result was a long-running battle of local pressure groups representing rival national educational schemes, including the Manchester Society for Promoting National Education (1837–42) and the Lancashire (National) Public Schools Association (1847–57) for the Radicals-secularists; the Chester Diocesan Board of Education, the Manchester Church Education Society (1844–52) and the Manchester and Salford Committee on Education for the Anglicans and Wesleyans; the Manchester and Salford Auxiliary to the Sunday School Union used by the voluntaryist dissenters; and cross-party bodies like the General Committee on Education (1857) and the Education Aid Society (1864). The energies of these bodies were not engrossed entirely by political battles, and several engaged in at least some practical work. Nevertheless, their focus represented a diversion of resources from the practical extension of education in Manchester through local effort.[46]

This did not, of course, preclude progress. In the 1830s and 1840s the Anglicans led the way: from one national school in Manchester in 1831, by 1847 there were 22.[47] Before the early 1840s dissenting endeavour was less noticeable. The independents had done little prior to the establishment of a central education board in 1843, and despite

[45] P. Gardner, *The Lost Elementary Schools of Victorian England*, (1986); Kay[-Shuttleworth], *The Physical and Moral Condition*, Manchester Statistical Society, *Education in Manchester*, 5–18. For the impact of the 1833 act see *PP*, (1837) XXXI, 4, 7–11, and C.M. Brown, 'Lancashire Industrialists and their schools, 1833–1902', *Journal of Educational Administration and History*, XV,1 (1983), 10–21.
[46] See Maltby, *Manchester and National Elementary Education, passim.*
[47] M.A. Cruikshank, 'The Anglican Revival and Education: a study of school expansion in the cotton Manufacturing areas of North-West England, 1840–50', *Northern History*, 15 (1979), 178, 188, Richson, *Sketch, passim.*

Table 4.3 School attendance in Manchester and Salford, 1830–70[48]

Date	Total average attendance	% of 5–14 year olds (estimated)
1836	24,365	40%
1851	29,245	34%
1864	35,200	35%
1865	38,038	38%

good intentions this soon collapsed in the face of the unwillingness of individual congregations to subscribe to a central fund.[49] Before 1850 both the Methodists and Catholics also concentrated on Sunday schools and remained backward in day school provision, although after the establishment of the Salford diocese in 1851, the Catholics began to pay more attention to the extension of day schools.[50] This pattern of activity was reflected in the results of John Watts' survey of education in two Manchester wards in 1851, which revealed that over 40% of day scholars were in Anglican day schools, 24% in Catholic Schools, and only 14% in the various Chapel, Lancastrian and Dissenting Schools.[51] Despite occasional bursts of activity, Dissent was unable to sustain any impetus towards educational expansion, and if anything there were signs of contraction: for example the prosperous Cavendish Street Chapel had to abandon its associated Mather Street school in 1853, and kept its own day school going only by subsidisation from the Sunday school.[52] Even where schools were maintained, the expectation that they should be self-supporting meant that the schools of the Independents charged fees which took them out of the reach of the bulk of the working classes. Although claims as to the number of schools varied, it was clear by the mid-1860s that there were only a handful of Independent schools in Manchester, despite the existence of nearly 30 wealthy congregations, and that these were providing essentially

---

[48] Figures from Manchester Statistical Society, *Report on the State of Education in Manchester*, vii, Richson, *Educational Facts*, 4, *EASAR*, (1867), 13.

[49] 'Observer', *MG*, 2 September 1843, 'Nonconformist', *MG*, 6 September 1843; 'A Dissenter', *MG*, 29 August 1846.

[50] *PP*, (1852–53) LXXX [1624], 719.

[51] John Watts, *Report of a statistical enquiry of the Executive Committee of the N.P.S.A.*, (1853), figures from tables 5 and 14 combined.

[52] *MX*, 15 May 1849, 30 October 1852, 'One of the Congregation', *MX*, 4 May 1853.

middle-class education.[53] Similarly, the Methodists made little progress before the mid-60s. In 1865 it was noted that although there were over 30 Methodist chapels in and around Manchester, there were only seven schools, three very recently established, and only one, with accommodation for scarcely more than 100 scholars, in central Manchester itself.[54] By 1871, while the Church of England provided 56 day schools catering for the working classes, and the Catholics 17, the British and Foreign School Society and the various dissenting congregations provided only 24.[55]

Not surprisingly, the result of this patchy endeavour was a pattern of education which deeply dissatisfied educational reformers. Much comment focused on the inadequacy of the amount of education which the working classes received. Of course, educational reformers had erected an unrealistic and ambitious ideal. Direct interpretation of the evidence of the density of education in Manchester in 1834, 1851 and 1865 (see Table 4.3) suggests that on average each child in Manchester received just about four years of day school education in 1834, declining to below three and a half years in 1851 and advancing only marginally by 1871. Given that such figures undoubtedly underestimated the survival of independent working-class schools (see below, pages 107-8) and included some measure of undercounting, this represents the most pessimistic assessment. When the Lancashire Public Schools Association surveyed the educational history of 13–14 year olds in 1851 it found only 10.3% who had never attended any school, and a median length of attendance for those who attended day school at between 5 and 6 years.[56]

Given that such figures were likely to have improved in the 1850s and 1860s, it would thus be misleading to suggest that the working class of mid-nineteenth century Manchester was uneducated. What particularly concerned the middle-class educationalists was the nature of the education which they received. In part, the problem was not so much the time spent at school, as its irregular pattern. It was quite normal for working-class children to lose Monday to shopping, Friday to cleaning, and to be withdrawn from school for any domestic chore which might come up, such as the taking of lunch to working

---

[53] *MG*, 3 June 1865.
[54] *Ibid*.
[55] *PP*, (1870) LIV (91), 13 (table 12).
[56] Watts, *Report, passim*.

fathers.[57] The Newcastle Commission found that more than one in six children attended at school for less than 50 days in the year, and 38.3% for less than 100; throughout the period average attendance, even where the roll was kept up to date, was only 70–75% of registered scholars.[58] Education was likely to be episodic rather than permanent, disrupted by withdrawal to take up jobs, because the household could no longer afford the cost, or because of the migratory habits of the working class. Hugh Stowell estimated that a third of his population moved each year, and in 1847 the average length of attendance at Granby Road National Schools was only five months.[59] For middle-class educationalists such irregularity created two problems. It undercut the impact which education could have, allowing children to attend school for several years without either learning to read, or imbibing basic religious truths. As the Education Aid Society acknowledged gloomily in 1867, even where children accumulated four or five years education, 'most such children attend only by fits and starts [and] the result is as might be expected. The sum of this broken education amounts to nothing'.[60] What Richson described as 'the habit of capriciously changing schools', allowed changing of schools to be used as a parental sanction against unwelcome aspects of schooling, and undermined the authority of the school and its teachers.[61] As the master of the Ancoats Lyceum school confessed, as a result, he 'had great difficulty in instilling anything like moral sense into the children'.[62]

The denominational system, both day and Sunday, was also ineffective because of the nature of its teaching and curricula. By 1832 all Manchester Sunday school teachers were volunteers, and tended to be elder scholars with little qualification beyond seniority for their position, and a wavering commitment to their task. Even well organised schools had difficulty in retaining enough teachers to cover for all their classes, and once classes were left without teachers, attendance usually

[57] *PP*, (1852–53) XXIV (571), 267; cf. Mosley Street Schools, *Annual Report*, (1867), 8.
[58] *PP*, (1861) XII [2794-I], 172.
[59] *PP*, (1845) XXXV (84), 131, *PP*, (1847) XLV [787], 226.
[60] *EASAR*, (1867), 14, 'E.B.', *MC*, 28 December 1865.
[61] *PP*, (1852) XI (499), 58, *PP*, (1870) LIV (91), 133; hence the withdrawal of children from Granby Road Boys school because of frequent ill-treatment by the pupil teachers. 9 November 1864, Log Book, Granby Road School, M66/30/1/1, MCLA.
[62] P.E. Razell and R.W. Wainwright, *The Victorian Working Class. Selections from letters to the Morning Chronicle*, (1973), 174–5.

dropped away steadily.[63] The use of volunteers also meant that, especially in the 1830s and 1840s before the successful Early Closing campaigns, most of the teachers were themselves working class, and their own fragile religious commitment and rudimentary education made them far from effective, particularly as religious teachers.[64] Similar difficulties faced efforts to develop a cadre of vocationally-trained day school teachers. As late as 1847 only one in three teachers in the national schools had any training for being a teacher, and despite the formation of several mutual improvement classes for teachers in the 1830s and 1840s, when the Privy Council introduced its scheme of certification in the late 1840s, the Manchester Church of England schools found the standard too high for its teachers.[65] Despite the potential of the pupil-teacher scheme of 1846, in the short term many pupil-teachers were used in ways analogous to the old monitors, bearing the brunt of the teaching effort. Later government restrictions on the numbers of pupil-teachers any one master could have, did not stem the considerable demoralisation of teachers in Manchester which came with the 1862 Revised Code.[66]

The upshot, according to Benjamin Templar, the widely-respected teacher of the Jackson Row Secular School, was that many teachers were unable to make their teaching either attractive or effective, providing only a narrow, unstimulating education which emphasised rote learning at the expense of any wider understanding and intellectual development.[67] In many, even the more sophisticated schools such as the Cavendish Street Schools, differential fee structures, which increased the cost of education beyond reading and writing and perhaps (but by no means always) arithmetic, effectively restricted the curriculum, even if a wide range of subjects was nominally offered.[68] In some denominational schools so basic was the education provided that even writing was not always part of the curriculum, and with schools rarely financially secure enough to provide copy-books to their

[63] Mosley Street Schools, *Annual Report*, (1854), 9–10, *ibid*, (1865), 12.
[64] R.B. Grindrod, *The Wrongs of our Youth*, (1843). For the limitations of Sunday School teachers see *MX*, 11 July 1856, *SWN*, 21 January 1860, 'W.B.', *MX*, 27 August 1864.
[65] *PP*, (1847) XLV [787], 211, Manchester Church Education Society, *Annual Report*, (1848), 18.
[66] The dissolution of the Schoolmasters Association was merely one example of this, *PP*, (1867–68) XXV [4051], 169.
[67] 'B.T.' [Templar], #16, Brotherton Scrapbook, M98, MCLA.
[68] 'Minutes of the Cavendish St School Committee', 2 April 1849, Box 47, M136, MCLA.

pupils, much of the writing teaching which ostensibly went on was probably of little worth.[69]

Moreover, the extent to which the denominational schools provided religious training is also unclear, wrapped up as it is in wider educational controversies. For supporters of nonsectarian education such as Thomas Bazley, 'the Scriptures [were] merely introduced as so many qualifications for the council's grants' and 'the duty [was] often performed in the most ineffectual manner'.[70] The constant use of the Bible as a class book, it was pointed out, 'induc[ed] a familiarity that often resulted in something worse than mere indifference – in positive dislike and contempt'.[71] The success of the LPSA in gathering amongst its supporters a strong body of religious ministers and religiously-committed lay people bore witness to the widespread agreement with the opinion of Rev. Samuel Davidson, of the Lancashire Independent College, that 'the day school is not a place for the seed of religious truth to germinate in the heart'.[72]

Moreover, despite the best efforts of middle-class educationalists, the working classes continued to send their children to non-denominational schools.[73] The claims of the educationalists that these schools were being rapidly superseded by the early 1850s must be treated cautiously: in the various surveys of this period many private schools using Sunday school buildings, but without denominational control or religious content, and providing education which bore little resemblance to that desired by educational reformers, were included as denominational.[74] Moreover, although the evidence is sketchy, it is clear that many private schools simply fell through the nets of educational surveyors, except on the rare occasion when a very thorough survey of a small area was undertaken. Thus, for example, when the St George's district of Manchester was surveyed by D.R. Fearon for the 1870 Select Committee on Schools for the Poorer Classes, he found thirteen private

---

[69] *PP*, (1850) XLII [1215], 180.

[70] T. Bazley, *National Education. What should it be?*, (1857), 7.

[71] *PP*, (1846) XXII [741], 323, B. Templar, *The Religious Difficulty in National Education*, (1858), 7.

[72] S. Davidson, *The Present Aspect of the Education Question*, [1851], 11, in M136/3/9/234, MCLA.

[73] The pervasiveness of these schools before 1870 has been persuasively demonstrated by Gardner, *Lost Elementary Schools*.

[74] See comments of Richson, *PP*, (1852) XI (499), 360–1, and Watts, *PP*, (1852–53) XXIV (571), 101; cf. comments of Fearon on one reputedly public church school which had 44 children from 3 to 14 in one class, and exhibited 'a great want of order, method, and school materials', *PP*, (1870) LIV (91), 130.

day schools; when the same area was surveyed by the newly established Manchester School Board in 1871 it also found thirteen private schools.[75] Yet in between these two surveys, a more detailed inquiry by an investigator for the Manchester School Board found 25 private adventure schools, only six of which he described as superior, and at least twelve of which were being held in private houses. Although unfortunately no attendance figures were given for these schools, one boasted almost 80 pupils.[76] This sort of undercounting was probably endemic in the surveys of these years. The survival of the private schools is important, because they thrived on a responsiveness to parental priorities and control which the denominational schools clearly could not. Hence their longevity represents a further weakness in the ability of the day school system to inculcate appropriate religious values.

Unfortunately, it was not clear that the Sunday school was more efficient: Thomas Laqueur has dissected in detail the tension between the image of the Sunday school as 'a remarkably successful agency of bourgeois moral imperialism', and the extent to which the schools were staffed and run by the working classes, and predominantly reflected in practice working-class concerns and preoccupations.[77] Despite the presence of clergy and superintendents conscious of their task of, according to one superintendent, 'inculcating good principles against the too prevalent scepticism and discontent of the working classes with all established institutions', clerical control was often attenuated. In asserting in his 1871 handbook for Sunday schools that the governance of such schools should be 'monarchical', Robert Adams, Rector of St Stephen's, Hulme, was upholding a model rarely maintained.[78] Notwithstanding that in some Dissenting schools the formal self-governance of the teachers only thinly masked the dominant influence of a minister, there was constant pressure throughout the period, as evinced by the various public conflicts over control, for greater autonomy for teachers and senior scholars.[79]

---

[75] *PP*, (1870) LIV (91), 140–2; Manchester School Board, 'Minutes', 147, M65/1/1/1, MCLA.

[76] Manchester School Board, 'Minutes', 70, M65/1/1/1, MCLA.

[77] Laqueur, *Religion and Respectability*, 170, 189 and *passim*; for a Manchester example see J. Hassall, 'The Bennett Street Sunday School, Manchester. A study in nineteenth century Educational and Social Improvement', (PhD thesis, University of Manchester, 1986), especially chapter 9.

[78] R. Adams, *Handbook for the Sunday School: A Manual of Suggestions*, (1871), 10.

[79] See, for example, 'A Late Teacher', *MWA*, 3 September 1859, 'A Father', *MWA*, 17

Even where working-class children did attend tightly regulated
Sunday schools, the long services, addresses and prayers which the
young scholars were forced to endure, and the rigidly disciplined
routine of most schools, all undermined their impact.[80] Moreover, it
is clear that both parents and pupils looked upon the Sunday schools as
places to learn basic literacy skills, initially both reading and writing,
and even after writing was banished to weekday evenings then still
reading. The background and experience of most teachers meant that
the development of reading skills, even if based on religious texts, was
the essence of teaching, and it was not until the late 1850s that there
was any real attempt to downplay the role of reading and emphasise
instead more directly religious education.[81] Visiting the Mosley Street
Sunday School in 1857 J.C. Street found that 'the lads are able to read
and write better upon the average than any class I ever met with; but
I regret to say that their misconduct and wilfulness is such as to
neutralize to a great extent their advantages'.[82] The tiny numbers of
Sunday school scholars who remained attached to churches and chapels
in adulthood prompted an enduring debate in the early 1860s on the
failures of the Sunday school system in Manchester.[83]

Not surprisingly, middle-class reformers were repeatedly
disheartened by the difficulties faced by schools in Manchester.
Attendance at denominational schools persistently fell short of even the
most modest expectations. Even for those who did attend, the results
appeared to be negligible. As Edward Birley told the Newcastle
Commission in 1861, '[t]he state of education in this district is
lamentably deficient', both from the want of schools, and the fact that
in the existing ones, the 'children are taught but little'.[84] Nor was

September 1859, 'W.M.', *MC*, 11 June 1859, 'A Teacher', *MC*, 17 March 1860, 'E.E.',
MX, 5 September 1864. The continuities of these later incidents with an earlier one
detailed in *An Account of the Extraordinary, Arbitrary and Illegal Proceedings of the
Wesleyan Sunday School Committee, Manchester South Circuit, in the expulsion of
conductors and consequent resignation of the teachers in Chancery Lane Sunday School*,
(1835), is clear.

[80] T. Kirkham, *A History of German St. Church of England Sunday School, St. Martins*,
(1876), 24–5, 'W.J.', *MX*, 31 August 1864.

[81] For example, H. Rawson, 'English Teaching in our Sunday Schools', *XR*, (1856), 345;
for the decline of reading teaching see 'John B. Marsh', *MG*, 6 December 1864.

[82] J.C. Street, 'Diary', 8 February 1857, Unit. MSS. MJRL.

[83] See, for example, 'W.B.', *MX*, 27 August 1864, 'W.S.A.' and 'W.J.', *MX*, 31 August
1864, 'A Parish Priest', *MX*, 1 September 1864, 'H.O.', 'J.B.' and 'J.A.', *MX*, 2
September 1864, 'E.E.', *MX*, 5 September 1864, etc.

[84] *PP*, (1861) XXI [2794–V], 106.

there much hope that the basis had been laid for future progress: looking at the adolescents leaving his schools, John Layhe regretted that, '[t]he majority, I fear, leave the school without having laid a satisfactory foundation for future attainments, or having acquired the habits of self-culture'.[85]

The root of the problem, it was realised, was the position of religious education outside the everyday life of the working-class community: in the struggle between school and community, school rarely emerged victorious. The partial and irregular nature of school attendance undermined the authority and standing of the teacher and the values he or she represented, *vis á vis* the home and the very different values of the working-class community. Periods of absence from school re-immersed children into a street and community culture whose visible values contradicted much of what teachers were attempting to instil in them. The rapidity with which such environmental factors could destroy the impact of school during the week was increasingly recognised in the 1850s and 1860s. The solution by the later 1860s was more and more seen as compulsory state education, and certainly Forster's 1870 Education Act, and the subsequent amplifications, made for a very different educational economy. However, in the 1832–67 period, the ultimate resource was to take religion to the working classes.

Religion in the community

The result was a range of organisations of an explicitly 'missionary' character. The more overtly religious of these ranged from the interdenominational city-wide Manchester and Salford Town Mission (later Manchester City Mission) (1837), general denominational associations such as the Church of England Evening Visiting Association (1857), congregational visiting, both lay and clerical, and specific outreach projects such as the Unitarian Ministry to the Poor (1833). There were also non-religious organisations like the District Provident Society (1833) and the Manchester and Salford Sanitary Association (1852) whose activities will be considered in chapter 6. Taken as a whole, they mark the most direct attempt by mid-Victorian society to confront and neutralise the 'dangerous classes'.[86] Domestic

---

[85] *MTPAR*, (1846), 11.
[86] For the urban mission to the working classes, see especially D.M. Lewis, *Lighten*

visitation had of course an established pedigree. What emerged in the years around 1830 was a realisation that the new problems caused by massive urbanisation necessitated a much greater systemisation of the traditional mechanisms of parochial and congregational support, and a move towards more aggressive and missionary activity among those who stood beyond them.[87]

Traditionally, domestic visiting had formed an important part of the role of the cleric, but in Manchester as elsewhere, the burdens of large parishes meant that even for the Church of England, it was an ideal honoured more in the breach than the observance: at St Andrew's in the 1830s, George Dugard could do little more than visit the sick.[88] The recognition of constraints like this had been instrumental in undermining enthusiasm for church building schemes in the 1840s, diverting attention to the more general provision of pastoral care, and raising the question of reform of the Manchester parish. Dissatisfaction with the monopoly of parochial revenues enjoyed by the canons of the Collegiate Church, coupled with their refusal to acknowledge anything beyond the most rudimentary responsibility for the care of souls, culminated in the Manchester Rectory Division Act (1850) which forced the canons to assume parochial duties, and ensured a minimum income of £270 per parish.[89] It also prompted greater interest in the Church Pastoral Aid Society and the Additional Curates Society: by the late 1850s between them these societies were supporting 20 incumbents, 27 curates and 19 lay assistants.[90] The Diocesan Church Building Society also helped support incumbents from the mid-1850s.[91]

The availability of curates and lay assistants greatly increased the practice of congregational visitation. It also enabled the holding of local

Their Darkness: The Evangelical Mission to Working Class London, 1828–60, (1986), D. Englander, 'The Word and the World: Evangelicalism in the Victorian City', in G. Parsons, ed., *Religion in Victorian Britain. II Controversies*, (1988), F. Prochaska, *Women and Philanthropy in Nineteenth Century England*, (1980). The origins of the visiting societies are dealt with in greater detail in H.D. Rack, 'Domestic Visiting: a chapter in early nineteenth century English evangelicalism', *Journal of Ecclesiastical History*, XXIV (1973), 357–76. Fuller consideration of the Manchester experience than is possible here is given in M. Hewitt, 'The travails of domestic visiting: Manchester, 1830–1870', *Historical Research*, (forthcoming).

[87] *District Visitor's Record*, (January 1836), 2; see John Seed, 'Unitarianism, political economy and the antinomies of liberal culture in Manchester, 1830-1850', *Social History*, 7,1 (1982), 1–25.

[88] *MC*, 13 April 1839.

[89] Ward, *Religion and Society*, 220–32.

[90] Church Pastoral Aid Society, *Occasional Paper*, LIII (1858), 6.

[91] *MG*, 17 April 1857, *MX*, 5 April 1861.

cottage meetings, providing addresses and simple services in environments within which the working classes did not feel out of place, and where there was no difficulty of having to appeal both to middle-class and working-class members of the congregation. Likewise it did provide some of the resources necessary to establish and maintain district mass or mission rooms in larger parishes, and helped to further the sub-division of larger parishes.

Nevertheless, the practice of ministerial visitation was still far from universal. There remained those who considered the primary task of the clergyman 'to feed his flock when he gets them all together, not to look after them in their homes'.[92] There were dark mutterings from some Anglicans that the 1850 Rectory Division Act had done little to encourage industriousness among the Anglican clergy, and the attitude was prevalent among Dissent.[93] Rev. Joseph Parker took up his position at Cavendish Street Chapel only on condition that he would not be expected to do any visiting, and the Rev. Alexander Thompson of Rusholme Road Chapel concentrated entirely on his preaching, spending so much of his week in the Portico Library that he was reputed to have read virtually the entire stock of contemporary literature, theology and travel.[94] Other ministers were more conscientious, and the image of the strictly preaching Dissenting minister assiduously propagated by Anglican controversialists was never strictly accurate. Nevertheless, the emphasis in Dissent was much more clearly on the establishment of an extensive network of auxiliary clubs and visiting societies.

Concern with the dislocating impact of urban growth developed nationally in the 1820s, and was marked by the formation in 1828 of the London-based General Society for Promoting District Visiting. By the early 1830s, Anglican activity in Manchester was gaining impetus from the enthusiastic espousal of both J.B. Sumner, Bishop of Chester, and Hugh Stowell, who looked to increased voluntary visitation by private individuals as part of a restoration of the social ties which the city threatened to destroy entirely.[95] Elsewhere, American precedents

[92] *MX*, 27 August 1864.

[93] 'A Parishioner', *MX*, 29 July 1864.

[94] T.T. James, *Cavendish Street Chapel 1848–1948*, [1948], 13, J. Radford Thompson, *Sermons by the late Rev Patrick Thompson, M.A., edited and prefaced with a brief memoir*, (1872), 15–16.

[95] J.B. Sumner, *District Visiting Societies Recommended*, (1832); *District Visitor's Record*, (July 1836), 58; Sumner was later Archbishop of Canterbury and a leading Evangelical who saw religion as a key element in social disciplining, see G. Parsons,

inspired Manchester Unitarians led by J.R. Beard to establish a Ministry to the Poor in the Miles Platting area of the city.[96] The initial model of missionary activity was the maintenance of social intercourse between the classes through voluntary visitation of the poor by the rich. When this proved difficult, the use of full-time missionary agents was instituted. The Manchester City Mission was the most important institution of this type. Professional missionaries demanded considerable finance, and much of the history of the MCM revolved around its efforts to raise the finance to fund the increasing number of missionaries which Manchester required. The MCM lived a life of endemic financial difficulty. In the 1840s it could afford only half the 80 missionaries it needed, and although the numbers increased steadily during the 1840s and 1850s, when, in 1853, the MCM, realising that its districts were too large for effective visitation, sub-divided them, the short-term result was merely to leave 32 out of 94 districts unoccupied. Although the new notional optimum of a hundred in 1861, by 1866 the number of missionaries had dropped back to 80.[97] The supplementation of the work of the city missionaries by missionaries employed by private individuals, such as James Bembridge, who was employed by T.C. Worsley to visit in Ancoats, did little to make up the shortfall.[98]

The suspicion of the Anglican clergy of the non-denominational evangelicalism of the city mission, and their possession, in the parochial system, of a parallel framework, meant that here considerable effort continued to be directed towards the development of effective parish-based organisations which could combine full-time and volunteer missionaries. At St Andrew's, George Dugard and W.E.N. Molesworth his successor established a well supported visiting society and in Salford, Hugh Stowell, fired by his strident evangelicalism and anti-popery, created and maintained a highly regimented cadre of scripture readers, lay visitors and tract distributors, as well as encouraging the tract distributors and scripture readers of the Operative Protestant Association.[99] By the mid-1840s a District Visiting Society

ed., *Religion in Victorian Britain. I Traditions*, (1988), 27.
[96] 'Introduction' to J.R. Beard, ed., *The Visitor of the Poor*, (1832), *MTPAR*, (1833).
[97] *MCMAR*, (1837-67), *passim*.
[98] For Bembridge see his 'Journals', BR ms 259.B1, MCLA.
[99] *MC*, 18 May, 23 November 1839, 13 April 1844. Marsden, *Hugh Stowell*, 47, 283–4, 397; this activity is put into context by D.G. Paz, *Popular Anti-Catholicism in Mid-Victorian England*, (1992), and J.R. Wolffe, *The Protestant Crusade in Great Britain, 1828–60*, (1991).

was accepted as one of the normal pieces of parochial machinery. This did not mean that it was always possible to maintain one: without paid assistance many parish clergy found regular district visiting almost impossible, and even with improvements in funding, expanding population, discontinuities between incumbents and the alienation of visitors all took their toll. When Rev. John Garrett was appointed to Christ Church, Moss Side, Hulme, in 1864, he found himself 'destitute of any ordinary machinery – no tract distributors, no district visitors, no day scholars, no scripture readers...'.[100] One response to this was the establishment at the beginning of 1858 of an over-arching Church of England Evening Visiting Society (later the Church Visiting Society). By 1862 this society was financing eighteen visitors in various working-class parishes who held full-time jobs, but who were employed to converse with working men in their homes for a few hours each evening.[101] The combined efforts of the local hierarchy and the national societies considerably strengthened the resources of most parishes: large working-class parishes like that of E.B. Chalmers at St Matthias' Salford, could expect by the end of the 1850s to have a growing band of curates, lay agents, scripture readers and evening missionaries.[102]

Dissenting efforts were channelled primarily into the MCM, but some congregations also organised visitation and tract distribution over a wide area. For example, Cavendish Street Chapel had 24 visitors for twelve districts close to the chapel and 41 tract distributors covering a wider area.[103] Day and Sunday schools endeavoured to keep scholars in attendance, and even attract new ones through visitation by teachers and senior scholars, or by specially-organised bands of visitors.[104] The upshot was numerous congregational workers like the Unitarian Travers Madge, whose multiple responsibilities included tract distribution and visitation.[105] In the 1840s the various Wesleyan congregations supported a tract society with 200 distributors, and the Catholic hierarchy also had a vigorous system of tract distribution, as

---

[100] Christ Church, Moss Side, *Parish Magazine*, November 1864, 38; cf. comment of Rev. W.A. O'Connor of St Simon's and St Jude's, *MC*, 12 January 1861.

[101] *MG*, 27 November 1861, *SWN*, 6 December 1862, *MX*, 3 May 1866.

[102] Rev. E.B. Chalmers, *The Parson, the Parish and the Working Men*, (1859), 6–7.

[103] James, *Cavendish Street Chapel*, 14.

[104] For example the female missionary employed by the Great Bridgewater Street Ragged School, 'Richard Heap', *MX*, 26 November 1862.

[105] Brooke Herford, ed., *Travers Madge. Memoirs*, (1867).

well as an expanding body of religious visitors, such as the Sisters of
the Cross and Passion.[106] As a result of the unco-ordinated efforts of
the various religious bodies, it was possible for some districts to have
as many as four different sets of visitors, while other areas received
none at all.[107] But like all visitation the practice was difficult to
sustain: in 1843 Bembridge came across a man in Ancoats who had
been living in the district for seven years and had never been left a
single tract.[108] Visitation was by no means universal even in the
1860s.[109]

The amount of social intercourse which these activities involved
varied. Although tract distribution allowed for the circulation of ideas
within the tracts, it often involved little personal proselytism, and much
missionary activity remained at this level. More significant were those
visitors who attempted to engage in conversation and discussion. For
'scripture readers' this could be structured by the relevant Bible texts
used, and it was only infrequently, particularly by the MCM
missionaries, that visitation was conceived as an unstructured
interchange of ideas and a direct attempt at conversion. Nevertheless,
missionary activity constituted a major attempt to overcome the
drawbacks of the essentially passive structures of education and
traditional religious organisation.

The success they met with is less clear. Rev. W.J. Kidd of St
Matthew's Campfield claimed that his district visiting society had
'produced an evident change in the order and regularity of the poor in
this district', and in the self-congratulatory reports of the City Mission,
contemporaries were often enthusiastic about the achievements of
missionary activity.[110] In contrast, Travers Madge noted that '...there
is a great deal of idle visiting mixed up with it all – a great many hearts
I never see into – a great many persons with whom I have no more or
better intercourse than with any stray passenger I might speak to by the
way'.[111] Layhe commented in 1846 that he had '...never had the

---

[106] *MSA*, 27 November 1841, 'De Facto', *MC*, 5 December 1846, E. Hamer, *Elizabeth Prout 1820–64: A Religious Life for Industrial England*, (1994).

[107] *MCMM*, February 1853, 6.

[108] Bembridge, 'Journal', 27 February 1843.

[109] [Brotherton], *Popular Education and Political Economy*, 18–23.

[110] *MC*, 29 April 1837; Kidd was perpetual curate of St Matthew's 1836–42, before being presented to the living of Didsbury, *MCN*, 24 December 1880.

[111] Herford, *Travers Madge*, 59.

satisfaction of reclaiming a profligate character', and this after five years' full-time labour.[112]

There were many difficulties. The problem of finance and the demands of an ever-growing population have been noted. Effective missionary activity was also restricted by the response of the working classes themselves. Domestic visitors continued to face considerable hostility derived from the general antagonism to organised religion. At times this could make whole areas impenetrable even to missionary activity. In 1854, Rev. Charles Burton, incumbent of All Saints, confessed that six or seven of the 20 districts of his parish to which he had previously appointed agents, had been abandoned as 'unvisitable' because of the strength of rejection by the population.[113] Even within districts with missionaries, it was possible for as many as 20% of the houses to be deemed unvisitable, and the MCM estimated that it could gain even minimal access to only half the Catholic households in the city; hence it was admitted in the 1850s that in Angel Meadow 'and other districts in which are included large masses of the lowest orders of society...their success has been comparatively limited in proportion to the efforts they have made'.[114] The neglect of 'unvisitable' households represented the abandonment of just those elements of the working classes most thoroughly at odds with middle-class values.

Even with their load thus lightened, missionary visits were usually infrequent: the city missionaries expected to repeat visits every six to eight weeks. Such a long gap was far from conducive to the support and maintenance of any impact the missionaries were able to make, for as the missionaries themselves were quick to point out with reference to the activities of street preachers, revivalists, and other brief visitors to the city, the initial emotional response which missionary activity, especially of a religious kind, could often evoke needed to be nurtured by constant support and attention if it were not to be choked by the weeds of environmental considerations and peer group pressure.[115] Moreover, daytime visits, while allowing ready access to the old, the sick and the unemployed, failed to provide access to employed adults, (except domestic outworkers). Even when men were found at home there is evidence that they left dealing with the missionary to the

[112] *MTPAR*, (1846), 17.
[113] 'Rev. Charles Burton', *MX*, 15 March 1854.
[114] *MCMM*, February 1853, 1, '???' *MG*, 19 July 1854.
[115] *MCMM*, May 1853, 16, March 1862, 6.

wife.[116] By 1856 the MCM was concerned enough by the statistic that only 19% of the people visited by the missionaries were men (as against 66% women and 15% children) to introduce Sunday visiting, which doubled the number of men spoken to by the missionaries, but which in turn only served to emphasise the difficulties of gaining access to them. The MCM rejected the idea of evening visiting because of the problem of interrupting the dinners of those visited, and although parochial societies did concentrate on this period, even they found themselves dealing predominantly with women.[117]

Problems of access were compounded by weaknesses of the process of visitation itself. Despite the volume of effort involved, the returns from tract distribution were uncertain. The tracts did have some impact, particularly for those for whom reading matter was in short supply, although it was often only the gently moralistic tale which was acceptable: Bembridge talks of one woman who looked forward to his tracts as 'something fresh to read'.[118] They were a vital resource for those looking for controversial material to support their religious or political beliefs in the face of strong challenge by peers or other proselytisers.[119] But in general Bembridge's experience was of tracts being lost or damaged, and treated with indifference, and he came to realise that although most households would accept tracts, it was of little use pressing them on even the slightly reluctant because they would not be read.[120] Despite the huge numbers of tracts which were printed by the various national religious and philanthropic societies, these were frequently found to be inappropriate by the distributors.[121] Ultimately they suffered from the very disadvantage that missionary activity was designed to avoid: they required active participative effort on the part of those with whom they were left.

In consequence, the heart of missionary endeavour was always the interaction, whether brief or extensive, of visitor and visited. The nexus of this interaction was the missionary himself (and later herself), and it was the missionary who was the weak link in the chain. The life of

---

[116] *MCMM*, May 1849, 22.
[117] *MCMM*, January 1858, 4–5, January 1859, 3–7; the figures for the evening visiting society of St Matthias' Salford were 39% men, 61% women, Chalmers, *The Parson*, 7.
[118] Bembridge, 'Journal', 15 November 1841.
[119] See, for example, the comments of Cosgrove, *Manchester Illuminator and General Catholic Record*, 29 December 1849.
[120] Bembridge, 'Journal', 11 June 1842, 20 June 1843.
[121] Herford, *Travers Madge*, 161.

a city missionary was not a particularly attractive one; the pay was low, the conditions of work often unpleasant and unwholesome, and missionaries were usually tightly controlled by an overseeing committee.[122] The belief was also prevalent that the job was most effectively done by those from a similar social and educational background to those being visited, and consequently missionaries tended to be men of restricted intellectual attainments and a certain narrow dogmatism.[123] As a result, their approaches were often counter-productively direct: in the early 1860s one prominent ragged school worker 'deprecated the abrupt manner in which many well-meaning persons attempted to storm the hearts of those whom they visited'.[124] Lack of imagination and the strict regulations often laid down to govern interviews meant that all too often missionaries were forced to retreat from confrontations with opponents into the insistent repetition of simple scriptural texts.

The religious bodies and missionary organisations developed three strategies to try to overcome the various deficiencies of traditional domestic visiting. The most novel of these was workplace visiting. Beginning in the late 1850s with railway and public service workers including the nightsoil carriers and railway porters, and extending in the early 1860s to include a wide range of industrial workers, by 1865 the MCM was holding workmen's meetings in 68 different venues.[125] Unfortunately concern about the justice as well as the advisability of forcing the ministrations of missionaries on working men in this way, and the reluctance of many employers (in the cotton factories for example) to have their work routines disrupted, meant that such meetings could only scratch the surface of the problem.[126]

Secondly, and along more traditional lines, was a reversion to open air preaching, for a long time a common practice of many religious groups, but by the 1830s regarded rather ambivalently by most resident ministers, leaving those like Rev. T.G. Lee who attempted to maintain a regular practice of street preaching in the minority. Street preaching became a prominent sword in the armoury both of the MCM and more

---

[122] 'A Friend to the City Mission', *MX*, 26 May 1852.
[123] *MTPAR*, (1858), 16.
[124] *SWN*, 23 April 1864.
[125] *MCMAR*, (1865), 4, (1861), 4.
[126] See, for example, the controversy over MCM meetings with the Manchester police, *WCM*, 14 December 1865, *MX*, 20,22,24,27 November, 7,9 December 1865, *MCN*, 9 December 1865.

especially of the 'missionaries' who periodically descended on Manchester from outside. In the 1830s and 1840s efforts had been concentrated on specific activities such as confronting the Socialists outside the Hall of Science, or events like Knott Mill Fair, but by the 1850s, more general street preaching, at public places like the entrances to the parks, or in the back streets where the most destitute of the working classes could be found, was being adopted.[127]

A more wide-ranging response to the weakness of missionary activity on its own, was the attempt to integrate this activity into a more comprehensive network of church and chapel based associations. Both street preaching and the wider associational drive represented one consequence of the continued pre-occupation of the missionaries with working-class culture as a formidable barrier to effective religious proselytism, and to the associated inculcation of desirable styles of life, subjects considered more fully in chapter 6.

The nature of working-class religion

To argue that the religious institutions of middle-class moral imperialism failed is not to suggest that the working classes remained untouched by religion. On the contrary, it is increasingly becoming a commonplace that religion was a vital part of Victorian working-class life.[128] Even at the height of Manchester Owenism in the 1840s, the numbers of the working class who embraced infidelity was small, and by the early 1850s city missionaries were happily reporting that only a handful remained. The occasional local and parochial surveys which were carried out confirm this picture. A survey of St James' parish in 1837 found only 43 out of about 10,000 families who insisted they had no religion, and a similar survey of St Andrew's, Ancoats in 1860 listed 277 of 14,470 likewise.[129] The evidence of the missionaries and the willing hearing they often obtained, the popular fervour demonstrated in the perennial conflicts between anti-Catholic and Catholic lecturers, and the richly religious rhetoric of working-class

[127] *MCMM*, November 1857, 32–5.
[128] H. McLeod, *Class and Religion in the Late Victorian City*, (1974), G. Parsons, 'A Question of Meaning: Religion and Working Class Life', in *idem*, *Religion in Victorian Britain*, I, 63–87.
[129] *MC*, 25 November 1837, *MG*, 11 April 1861; there was an early survey of St Andrew's parish in 1855, which gave similar results, see *MC*, 12 May 1860.

political movements, all help confirm the extent to which working-class life in Manchester was impregnated with religion.

The problem for the middle classes was that working-class religion was of a quite different nature to the religion which they wished to spread: it was a diffuse sense of belief which helped underpin working-class morality and inform its world view, rather than a code of practice and behaviour.[130] In most cases it involved little regular contact with the institutions of organised religion. The results of local inquiries suggest that 15–20% of the population (and hence a smaller percentage of the working classes) could be described as regular attenders at church or chapel, perhaps another 30% attended irregularly, and the rest were likely to appear only for the lifecycle events of birth, marriage and death.[131] Instead, organised religion was treated with considerable suspicion. Although the virulence of this suspicion may have declined over the period, anti-clericalism was rife; little or no interest was shown in the theological and doctrinal niceties which were central to many of the observances of organised religion; the sense of personal sin and complete reliance on the saving grace of God, as mediated by the churches, was largely absent. Rather working-class religion was a mixture of 'commonsense morality' and the 'simple religion of Christ'.[132]

As a result, working-class religiosity brought neither the discipline of manners nor the political quietism for which the middle classes looked. The advantage of diffuse religion for the working classes was that it remained completely compatible with rough as well as respectable culture: missionaries found to their cost that the deeply religious listener one day could easily become the street brawler, the drunkard, or the music hall entertainer, the next.[133] As Layhe commented, religion was 'an affair of time and circumstances, good on occasions of special trial or danger,…an outward thing, which, like their Bibles, they can take up, lay down, and put on the shelf at their pleasure'.[134] Similarly, deprived of the status of interpreter and guide

[130] For evidence of the nature of working-class religion on which much of the following is based, see *MCMAR*, *MCMM* and *MTPAR*, *passim*.
[131] *MCMM*, May 1853, 16–17, *MX*, 16 October 1860, *MG*, 4 July 1864.
[132] *MTPAR*, (1840), 13–14.
[133] For a good example, see *MCMM*, November 1854, 158.
[134] *MTPAR*, (1851), 38.

for the working classes, which only more widespread church membership would have given, ministers and missionaries were unable to inhibit the flourishing of distinctly working-class interpretations of religious truths, which emphasised the anti-wealth communalism of scriptural christianity rather than the obedience and worldly satisfaction which organised religion proclaimed.

Conclusion

Religious conceptions were never far from the surface of nearly all middle-class moral imperialism during the mid-century period. Nevertheless, the most sustained efforts of religious proselytism developed directly from church and chapel and the educational, missionary and parochial institutions which they fostered. Particularly in the 1830s and 1840s they represented the vanguard of middle-class attempts to overcome the problems of social dislocation created by the rapid growth of Manchester, and establish effective social control over the working classes.

Close examination of the histories of these endeavours, however, demonstrates how ineffectually they struggled with the obstacles which had emerged to the effective re-establishment of religious ties. Organised religion never overcame the disadvantages presented by the alien face which its rituals and liturgies presented to the working classes, or the excluding effects of restricted provision of churches and chapels. Likewise initiatives in education were stalled not only by squabbling within the middle classes, but also by the clear repudiation of middle-class priorities by working-class parents and their children. The attempt to overcome these difficulties by taking religion to the people ultimately suffered in much the same way.

The consequence was not an irreligious working class, but a working class antipathetic to the codified, doctrinal, all-encompassing religion of the middle classes. Faced with the persistence of religious attitudes rooted in the practicalities of daily living, and a suspicion of organised religion derived largely from political perceptions of its role in supporting the status quo, the middle classes were forced to supplement their continuing religious endeavours with initiatives designed both to spread the kind of economic and political beliefs within which it might be possible for religious beliefs to develop, and to shape the contours of working-class cultural life into paths more amenable to correct religious practices.

Chapter Five

The repudiation of useful knowledge

Attempts to influence working-class consciousness across a broader spectrum did not abandon the institutions of religion: indeed parochial and congregational organisations, particularly schools and schoolrooms, provided the core of many of the more secular intellectual initiatives. Nevertheless, these represented merely a small part of the multiplicity of cultural institutions which emerged as the middle classes sought to widen the scope of their moral imperialism. Indeed, as John Garrard has commented, '[t]here seem...to have been few institutions or activities in the Victorian industrial town which do not have the transmission of appropriate values as part of their intended or hoped-for function'.[1]

However, if the impetus for the establishment of these associations was the belief that they could overcome the deficiencies of the purely religious institutions and, in Brian Simon's words, 'instil their own doctrines' into the working classes, the extent to which they succeeded in this was another matter.[2] It was not, as some contemporaries argued, that the working classes remained untouched by such initiatives, because taken as a whole, their participation in such institutions was considerable. Rather it was that far from imposing ideologies, the institutions of useful knowledge created an arena of cultural contest and inter-class bargaining. In Leeds, R.J. Morris has argued, substantiating their claims to social and cultural leadership through the forms and ceremonies of the voluntary society, the middle classes were able to establish an hegemony which although 'neither total nor immune from compromise' nevertheless structured inter-class relationships and was central to social stability.[3] The evidence of Manchester suggests that despite the conclusions of Gatrell and Seed,

---

[1] Garrard, *Leadership and Power*, 48-9.

[2] B. Simon, *Studies in the History of Education*, (1960), 216.

[3] Morris, *Class, Sect and Party*, 241 and *passim*; similarly Dennis Smith portrays the working classes of Birmingham and Sheffield being tied into 'a complex network of institutions through which inter-class control and intra-class bargaining took place', *Conflict and Compromise*, 106.

the process of accommodation was much more evenly contested than Morris argues. Indeed the breadth of popular participation suggests that middle-class initiatives were unable to withstand working-class pressure, which gradually transformed the cutting edge of moral imperialism into innocuous institutions of rational recreation. If successive initiatives in these fields and the individual and institutional responses of the working classes created a cultural battleground, then the tally of victories and defeats goes a long way towards illuminating the fate of middle-class moral imperialism.

The shape of intellectual life

The middle-class cultural associations which were established in the 1820s and 1830s were socially exclusive and possessed no real sense of mission. Rather, middle-class concern for the working classes was channelled into institutions designed specifically for them, such as the Manchester Mechanics' Institute.[4] The MMI was joined gradually by other local institutes, both within the municipalities of Manchester and Salford, at Miles Platting (1836), Salford (1838), Chorlton-upon-Medlock (1848), Pendleton (1852), and in the immediate vicinity, at Harpurhey, Blackley (1847), Middleton, Lower Crumpsall (1850), and Longsight (1855). In general, these institutions followed the traditional pattern, a mixed preoccupation with technical education and morally-improving general learning, their activities focusing initially on a library and courses of scientific lectures, the latter gradually being replaced by classes.[5]

Concern for technical education apart, this formula was far from unique to the institutes. After the rapid passing of the first crude attempts at direct ideological indoctrination, like the Pendleton Society for the Promotion of the Cultivation of Useful Knowledge, the Salford Society for the Diffusion of Literature, and the Society for the Diffusion of Useful Knowledge to the Welsh People, all active in the

---

[4] For a forthright articulation of the middle-class reforming inspirations of the MMI see B. Heywood to Henry Brougham, Brougham Papers, #30456, University College, London; Cardwell, *Artisan to Graduate*, M. Tylecote, *The Mechanics' Institutes of Lancashire and Yorkshire before 1851*, (1957).
[5] The best documented of these is the Miles Platting Mechanics' Institute, another initiative of Heywood, see E. and T. Kelly, *A Schoolmaster's Notebook*, (1957).

mid-1830s, the model was quite widely aped.[6] By 1838, concerns about the limited success of the larger institutions for the working classes had prompted the establishment, largely on the initiative of a young liberal-Anglican, Edward Herford, of 'Lyceums', mechanics'-institute-like organisations whose distinctiveness lay in their considerably lower membership fees, more stridently democratic ethos, and provision of newsrooms. The first of these, the Ancoats Lyceum, was instituted in the autumn of 1838, quickly followed by others at Chorlton-on-Medlock, Salford, and later at Pendleton. Contemporaneously, concern in religious circles at the spread of Owenism and chartism, and at the determination of the Lyceums' members to have them open on Sundays, resulted in the appearance of religious institutes. These included the 'Christian Institute' established in the Conservative interest in Chorlton in direct competition with the Lyceum there; Stowell's Christ Church Institute in Salford; the Bennett Street Institute, associated with the Bennett Street Sunday Schools; and the West Manchester Institute in connection with W.J. Kidd's congregation at St Matthew's, Campfield.[7] Although their history is often obscured by their purely parochial appeal, it is clear that these associations attempted where possible to provide the full range of facilities to be expected of a mechanics' institute, along with a religious bias which meant that although science still featured prominently, the element of moralism was stronger than elsewhere.[8]

Many of these institutions did not survive long, suffering from the drawbacks of the larger mechanics' institutes without having the prestige to attract the more status-conscious clerks on whom the institutes relied in the 1840s. There was nevertheless a steady turnover of similar institutions throughout the 1840s and 1850s. Some, such as the Red Bank Institute, at St Thomas' (Red Bank), grew to rival the suburban mechanics' institutes in longevity and range of activities. Even where separate institutes were not themselves established, other

---

[6] *WMC*, 28 January 1832, *MSA*, 4 October 1834, 16 January 1836, *WMC*, 10 June 1837.
[7] For the conflict over the Lyceums, and their links with Owenism, see *NMW*, VIII (1840), 360. For the early parochial institutions see *MC*, 30 November 1839, *MG*, 10 October 1840.
[8] A good example of the wide range of facilities which could be offered is given by the handbill of the Bennett Street Institution for autumn 1839, which promised a library of 2000 volumes, reading room, lectures (both religious, and literary and scientific), and classes in writing, maths, grammar, geography, needlework and vocal music, M38/4/2/1, MCLA. For a picture of the range of such institutions see I. Inkster, ed., *The Steam Intellect Societies: essays on culture, education and industry, c.1820–1914*, (1985), 8–14.

bodies, particularly Sunday schools, attempted to fulfil the same function; despite the collapse of its Institute, in 1851 the *Annual Report* of the Bennett Street Sunday schools claimed that it provided 'every advantage of a mechanics' institute'.[9] Similar associations, such as the Cavendish Street Literary and Scientific Society (1849) and the Gaythorn Christian Institute (1859), were also found among Dissent, but here the primary congregational focus encouraged the popularity of the Young Men's Mutual Improvement Society format, pioneered in Manchester by the Scottish Presbyterians. A large number were established from the late 1840s. Of course, the mutual improvement format was itself nothing new: by the end of the 1830s it had become an accepted element of the mechanics' institute offerings, been widely adopted in temperance and working-class contexts, and occasionally by Sunday school teachers.[10] But it was in the congregational setting that the mutual improvement format was most widely adopted, usually drawing together between ten and twenty-five young men for study, discussion and social intercourse under the watchful eye of the minister.[11]

Indeed the growing taste of the working classes for lectures in the 1850s provided a new lease of life for various parochial institutes which were able to maintain their existence around an annual popular lecture course.[12] The renewed popularity of lectures also helped maintain the more overtly religious central institutions which emerged around mid-century, such as the YMCA, founded in 1844. Initially a sickly growth, endemically in debt, and without a permanent home until the former Natural History Museum in Peter Street was purchased for it in 1872, between 1844 and 1867 the YMCA was sustained only by its annual lecture course, although by the early 1860s scriptural and devotional classes and lessons in Greek, French and German were also offered. As this suggests, the YMCA was primarily conceived as catering to young clerks, but by means of distributing reduced-rate

---

[9] Bennett Street Schools, *Annual Report*, (1851), 3.

[10] See C.J. Radcliffe, 'Mutual Improvement Societies in the West Riding of Yorkshire, 1835–1900', *Journal of Educational and Administrative History*, 18,2 (1986), 1–16, M.I. Watson, 'Mutual Improvement Societies in nineteenth century Lancashire', *Journal of Educational and Administrative History*, 21,2 (1989), 8–17.

[11] The earliest of these societies seems to have been at St Peter's (the Scotch Church) in 1833, then at St Andrew's Free Church (1846) and William McKerrow's Lloyd Street Chapel (1848); outside the Scotch churches the earliest establishment appears to be at Rusholme Road Chapel (1843). After 1848 there is evidence of a wave of new societies.

[12] *MG*, 6 January 1855, *MX*, 23 October 1856.

tickets to senior scholars of Sunday schools, and later making its lectures free, it also attempted to play a wider role.[13] Likewise lectures continued to feature prominently in the activities of the spate of work-based associations appearing from the mid-1840s, which often sought to attract members from beyond the specific company within which they were established: a good example of these is the Hulme Operative Institute, established in 1845 with the strong support of the Pooleys of John Pooley and Co., weavers.[14] During the 1850s, the provision of such facilities became an increasingly common practice for those larger companies who attempted to take the practice of industrial paternalism beyond the annual workingmen's treat.[15]

In this way, although individual institutes might suffer difficulties and even collapse, the institutes' broad ideal continued to attract support into the early 1860s. As a vision of widespread popular education it was only finally destroyed by the failures of the Working Men's Colleges movement in Manchester. In 1857–58 Working Men's Colleges were established in Ancoats (where Charles Richson took the lead), Manchester itself (using the Manchester Mechanics' Institute) and Salford. Although departing from the institute model in eschewing lectures, the colleges significantly resisted other contemporary trends by emphasising a strictly educational purpose, and following the initial practice of the institutes in proscribing distractions like newsrooms.[16]

Unfortunately, the career of the colleges was entirely predictable. The Ancoats College, despite being staffed largely by an existing thriving working-class institution, the Phonetic Sunday School, never really established itself; by 1861 the Manchester College had only partially covered its collapse by merging into the evening classes of Owen's College, and although the Salford College prospered briefly, by 1867 it too was faltering badly.[17]

[13] *MC*, 22 January, 27 December 1848, *MX*, 11 November 1854, *MG*, 8 January 1862.
[14] *MG*, 2 April 1845. For other examples see the Chorlton New Mills Mutual Improvement Society, established in 1845 with classes, library and newsroom, and the libraries and newsrooms established at Fir Mills, Failsworth, *MX*, 9 January 1849, Mayfield Print Works, *MX*, 20 October 1849, J. & J. Lockett's Engraving Works, Strangeways, *MX*, 4 May 1853.
[15] For a good example of this see the Gorton Institute, formed in 1856 for the employees of the Manchester, Sheffield and Lincolnshire Railway, beginning with a library, reading room and school, and soon adding lectures, table games, and a brass band, *MG*, 10 January 1857, *MX*, 9 March 1858.
[16] 'Fiat Justitia', *SWN*, 7 December 1861. For details of the early history of these colleges see the *Working Men's Colleges Magazine*.
[17] *MC*, 18,22 October, 1859, 'I.T.K.', *MX*, 1 October 1861. For an account of the more

Pontificating middle-class commentators sometimes insisted that the failure of the institutes was an indication of the complete rejection by the working classes of educational associations. In fact, careful trawling of the available sources suggests that, largely obscured by their humble inspirations and unwillingness to court publicity, informal or semi-formal organisations and classes, often growing out of the very associations which were supposed to be being neglected, were proliferating. Most dropped the word 'mechanics" but described themselves as 'institutes', and they can be collectively described as 'working men's institutes'. From the late 1840s onwards, it is possible to perceive a steady growth, fed by several distinct sources, in such institutions.

Occasionally, scattered groups of working men began to form themselves into informal educational associations, perhaps hiring a small room, establishing a library and organising classes. The history of these institutions is largely obscured by their relatively rapid turnover and the lack of surviving records. However, there was clearly a considerable tradition of this type of activity, operating at a semi-formal level, and evolving in different directions in constantly shifting patterns.[18] The most ambitious of these was the People's College, established in Manchester at the start of 1850, with Hugh McLeod, a journeyman painter, as president, which attempted to provide classes on weekday mornings as well as evenings and Sundays.[19] But perhaps more typical was the mutual improvement society established by workmen in an emery mill in Newton Heath, which later grew into the Miles Platting Working Men's Institute.[20]

In many cases these working men were brought together by a shared interest. One was temperance. As early as the 1830s, several of the Temperance Hotels had associated mutual improvement societies.[21] In

successful career of the mother-institution, see J.F.C. Harrison, *A History of the London Working Men's College, 1854–1954*, (1954).

[18] See, for example, the Utility Society of the co-operator E.T. Craig, which flourished in the late 1820s, the 'Mechanics' Mutual Improvement Society', established by the Journeymen Steam-engine and Machine Makers Society in 1841, *MSA*, 3 April 1841, or the 'Intellectual Discussion Society' associated with the Countess of Wilton Lodge in Manchester, of the Manchester Unity, Independent Order of Oddfellows, *The Oddfellow's Magazine*, (1844), 161. A similar picture is given by Kate Tiller, 'Working Class Attitudes and Organisation in Three Industrial Towns 1850–1875', (PhD thesis, University of Birmingham, 1975), 160–6.

[19] *MX*, 9,13 February 1850. It does not seem to have existed for long.

[20] *MX*, 23 February, James Dalton, *MX*, 3 March 1863.

[21] By September 1836 there was one in Dewsnup's, and a similar society was quick

many cases these grew into more formal institutes. Pendleton Mechanics' Institute had its origin in a small mutual improvement institute established by a group of total abstainers who contributed 4d a week for rent of a room and some periodicals, and whose expanding membership and increasingly formalised classes led it to adopt the title 'mechanics' institute' in 1853.[22] When it applied for membership of the umbrella advocates' society in 1850, the Lower Mosley Street society had a reading room, a library of 1300 volumes, a savings bank and elementary, mutual improvement, and singing classes, for 5d a month.[23] The adoption of the title 'institute' by several of the other local societies during the 1850s bears witness to their similar activities; the Salford Athenaeum and Temperance Hall, and the Chorlton-upon-Medlock Temperance Hall and Mechanics' Institute were merely the grandest of many similar institutions.[24]

Another bond was radicalism. Working-class political activity, with its network of local political associations sustained by newspapers and political meetings, lent itself to this form of association. One example was the informal circle of radical autodidacts who formed the impressively-titled, but in reality rather modest, Hulme Philosophical Institute, which later became the Christ Church Institute.[25] Another was the Universal Debating Society which met at the Temperance Hotel run by William Dixon, the ex-*Northern Star* reporter, and which evolved into the People's Institute in Heyrod Street Ancoats, Manchester's chartist hall.[26] Opened in 1846, it aimed to provide lectures, classes and discussions on a range of scientific and political topics, as well as a venue for working-class societies and public meetings.[27] Although a useful venue for working-class activities

established in Stanley's, *Manchester and Salford Temperance Journal*, 17 September, 1 October 1836.

[22] *MG*, 1 September 1856; the use of the nomenclature of the mechanics' institutes was undoubtedly prompted more by a desire to tap middle-class patronage than any whole-hearted commitment to the ideals of the early institutes.

[23] *MX*, 11 September 1850.

[24] Indeed, in recognition of this, the latter body had adopted the less grand title of 'Grosvenor Street Institute' by 1860; for others see the Henrietta Street Working Men's Room, *Alliance News*, 20 February 1864 and the Naylor Street Working Men's Room, *Alliance News*, 7 May 1864.

[25] The Hulme Philosophical Institute/Christ Church Institute was unusual in that it could trace a continuous history throughout the 1832–67 period: see the brief history in *MCN*, 12 November 1878.

[26] *NS*, 26 December 1846.

[27] Manchester People's Institute Association, *Laws of the Manchester People's Institute Association*, (1844), *MG*, 25 September 1847.

throughout the late 1840s and 1850s, it never really established itself as an associational focus, and was gradually taken over by middle-class missionaries from within the Manchester City Mission, ultimately becoming home to the Heyrod Street Ragged School.[28]

Indeed, the Sunday and Ragged schools were the third common organisational base for the working men's institutes. In some cases the schools provided little more than convenient accommodation.[29] More often they provided the impetus for separate organisations, such as the Angel Meadow Working Men's Association, based on the Sharp Street Ragged School, in the heart of one of the most poverty-stricken working-class districts. The association offered a newsroom and a library, along with classes in writing, arithmetic, geography, history, phonography, algebra and music, for 1d a week.[30] Elsewhere, as Sunday and Ragged school managers realised the breadth of demand for basic adult education, distinct from the existing weekday evening classes provided for the Sunday school scholars themselves, many threw their institutions whole-heartedly into the business. Not surprisingly, working-class bodies led the way: the non-sectarian Phonetic Sunday School established in Tame Street Ancoats in 1850 had in response to the demand expanded into the Working Men's Educational Institute and Phonetic Sunday School, with classes concentrating on reading (using the phonetic method pioneered by A.J. Ellis), writing, maths and geography.[31] As the ragged schools spread, they were seized upon by scholars seeking basic education, and by the end of the decade most of the 30 or so Sunday schools in the Ragged School Union had weekday classes, and several developed these into fully-fledged working men's institutes, such as the Chorlton-upon-Medlock Working Men's Institute (based on London Road Ragged School) and the Gaythorn Christian Institute (based on the Hewitt Street Ragged School).[32] By the early 1860s Manchester was also at the forefront of the parallel drive towards the establishment of night schools in association with the existing religious day schools.[33] The result was

---

[28] *MWT*, 10 January 1863, Robert Lee, *Missionary Miniatures*, (1937), 15, *Ragged School Union Magazine*, XX (1868), 9.

[29] For example, the Chorlton-upon-Medlock Institute, see *MX*, 2 December 1862.

[30] *MSp*, 11 October 1856, *MWA*, 13 June 1857.

[31] *MX*, 10 December 1856.

[32] *MG*, 12 December 1866, 30 March 1859, *PP*, (1870) LIV (19), 171-2, *MC*, 6 December 1862, *MCN*, 6 March 1875.

[33] *PP*, (1859) XXI(i) [2510], 90-1.

a confusing profusion of activity without clear delineation, and within which even the names applied to associations seemed to owe more to whim than to activity: as James Kay-Shuttleworth explained in 1861, in the manufacturing districts of Lancashire, 'the night schools which exist have for the most part, the name of literary institutions, or mutual improvement societies, or some similar name'.[34]

The cash nexus

The inglorious performance of the Working Men's Colleges finally laid to rest the institute blueprint. But for their enduring optimism the middle classes would have conceded failure considerably earlier. The weaknesses had been there for all to see. Despite considerable amounts of middle-class patronage, few attained financial solvency for any length of time. The costs of even the small parochial institutes were considerable (the Christ Church Scientific Institute spent £162 in 1846), and they quickly multiplied for those faced with their own building: erection costs apart, the Chorlton-upon-Medlock Temperance Hall and Mechanics' Institute cost £230 just to fit out, and the institute began £550 in debt.[35] Accommodation, books, lecturers, efficient teachers, were all scarce or expensive, and often both. The situation was exacerbated by the fragmentation of endeavour and duplication of facilities which sprang out of the reluctance to countenance any strong federated structure of associations, and the differences of purpose and emphasis of rival institutions. While R.J. Morris has advanced the notion of the 'hegemony of the annual accounts' as a mechanism by which the upper middle class was able to enforce its leadership over the class as a whole, it could equally be argued that the institutional proliferation of these years demonstrates the counter-hegemony of the cash nexus.[36]

---

[34] *PP*, (1861) XXI [2794–iv], 381.
[35] *MC*, 8 April 1846, *Report of the Trustees of the Temperance Hall and Mechanics' Institute, Grosvenor-st, Chorlton-upon-Medlock*, (1851), 3.
[36] Morris, *Class, Sect and Party*, 280–317. Morris' framework certainly helps explain the collapse in the early 1830s of the short-lived New Mechanics' Institute, founded as a rival to the Manchester Mechanics' Institute, and also the failures of the Hall of Science and the People's Institute. What, perhaps, it cannot so easily encompass is the continued vitality and turnover of unassuming working-class associations, and middle-class sponsored societies.

In part the multiplication of institutes in the late 1830s and 1840s was a necessary response to the size of the city Not only were residents of Salford unwilling to see their separate community identity swallowed up in exclusively Manchester-based institutions, but local associations were promoted as more convenient and more responsive than the grander city-wide bodies.

However, ultimately the appearance of new institutes rested more on rivalries within the middle classes. Politics played a part: Manchester Mechanics' Institute, the Athenaeum and the Lyceums all suffered from association, which they worked tirelessly but not always successfully to dispel, with the Liberal-Radical interest. More pervasively, particularly within the Church of England, suspicions remained of educational institutions which resisted religious conformity. The issue of Sunday opening constantly poisoned relations between churches and working-class institutions: although some were prepared to take the stand of William McKerrow, disagreeing with the practice, but not letting this disagreement stand in the way of important work, many more campaigned assiduously to prevent Sunday opening and to undermine the position of those associations which persisted in the practice.[37] All that was achieved was the division of middle-class effort through the formation of directly competing institutions, and the alienation of working-class members, who resented being deprived of the facilities which were still offered by exclusively middle-class associations.

The history of the Lyceum movement in Manchester illustrates the difficulties graphically.[38] Despite the clear failure of the mechanics' institutes to attract more than a handful of working-class members, the establishment of the Lyceums prompted considerable hostility from their supporters. In Chorlton, the liberal principles and support for Sunday opening of the Lyceum prompted the establishment of the strictly sabbatarian Christian Institute. By 1844 both had collapsed.[39] At the other extreme, the Lyceums also met with hostility from the leadership of the temperance movement, which proceeded to launch

---

[37] *MG*, 26 February 1840.

[38] For the most graphic account of the Lyceum experiment see the letters of Edward Herford to the Society for the Diffusion of Useful Knowledge, including Herford to Brougham, 9 August, 29 November 1838, SDUK/35, Herford to Thomas Coates, 18 April, 29 June 1840, SDUK/37, SDUK Papers, University College, London.

[39] *MG*, 7 June 1843, 10 July 1844.

their own version, the Parthenon, which survived only long enough to hinder the vital early fund-raising efforts of the Lyceums.[40]

In Salford, resort to the Lyceum model again only created two precarious institutions where there had previously been one. The natural solution was some form of co-operation, but the unwillingness of the Institute directors (fearful of Sunday opening) to accept that the rules of the combined association should be drawn up and approved by its combined membership sabotaged any union. When ultimately the Mechanics' Institute was wound up in 1843, the Lyceum took the chance to buy up much of its library and rechristen itself the Salford Literary and Mechanics' Institute, only to be faced almost immediately with the reformation of a Salford Mechanics' Institute by the recalcitrant rump of the former directorate.[41] Although this institution faded away in its turn in 1846, the whole saga was repeated in 1851 when attempts were made to amalgamate the Literary and Mechanics' Institute with a projected Temperance Hall and Athenaeum. Such rivalry produced duplication, waste of resources, and the fragmentation of middle-class patronage and support. As such, it weakened all cultural associations.

The situation would have been much improved if it had been possible to establish strong bonds of co-operation between the various local associations. This had been one of the aims of Edward Herford, and the early careers of the Lyceums did demonstrate the potential advantages, both in fund-raising and in the provision of lectures. However, even here tensions emerged (the Ancoats institution withdrew from the collective for a while), and attempts to create a more comprehensive union of intellectual associations never prospered. The Manchester and District Association of Popular Literary and Scientific Institutions was undermined by a general unwillingness to sacrifice any element of independence, or make any real financial commitment, particularly among the more established institutions.[42] Although it struggled on under a series of names, the Manchester District Association, and from 1847 the Lancashire and Cheshire Union of Mechanics' Institutes (LCUMI), it did little more than provide itinerating library boxes and

[40] For the Parthenon see *MG*, 3 October 1838, *MC*, 8 December 1838; the fact that a December 1839 report on Manchester associations for the SDUK by Coates does not mention the Parthenon suggests that it had effectively collapsed within 12 months, *MG*, 11 December 1839.

[41] *MG*, 6,10,13,17 May 1843.

[42] E. Herford to T. Coates, 21 September 1843, SDUK/40, UCL.

make half-hearted attempts to establish registers of voluntary lecturers and a library of manuscript lectures.[43] Although the supervision of local examinations from 1856 opened up opportunities for a considerable strengthening of the institute model, by 1860 the Union had degenerated into an exclusive oligarchy, financed largely by the receipts of the popular annual prize-giving soirées at which a leading literary or political figure presided. After considerable public controversy it was reorganised in 1863.[44] But even after this, the subsequent provision of an itinerate teacher paid from central funds, and closer inspection and advice, the LCUMI seems to have remained as much a campaigning body as an effective provider of services for member institutes.[45]

The failure to achieve any integration between the expanding range of cultural institutions produced a formless jumbling of different types of association, often short-lived and unstable, many leaving few marks on the historical records of the city. While the central institutions, such as the MMI and the Athenaeum could rely to a certain extent on the patronage of the middle classes anxious to sustain such monuments to civic culture, and hence maintain at least a shabby gentility, the rest were ultimately reliant on membership receipts. This created obvious difficulties: not only was their intended constituency unable and unwilling to pay the level of subscriptions which could have ensured solvency, but the uncertain and often irregular nature of working-class employment meant that it was difficult to establish a stable membership, and that economic downturn was likely to bring a severe reduction in receipts. Membership tended to be highly unstable, with an average length of only six months, lapsing and then being renewed according to the season, personal circumstances and the attractions offered. In such circumstances, a difficult balance had to be achieved between lowness of subscription rates and a suitably attractive range of facilities. And perhaps herein lies the real significance of the financial position of the institutes. Reliance on subscriptions left these institutes prey to the exigencies of the market: to survive they needed to attract the working classes, to attract the working classes they needed to respond to working-class demands, and this imperative increasingly sapped their

---

[43] *MG*, 24 March, 20 October 1847, *MX*, 20 March 1849.
[44] [John Watts], *The Associated Mechanics' etc Institutes of Lancashire and Cheshire*, (1862).
[45] *MX*, 4 August, 24 October 1863, *MG*, 11 August 1865.

ability to function effectively as channels of middle-class moral imperialism.

The control of intellectual life

Pressure was applied to the institutions of middle-class moral imperialism across a broad front. At its most blatant it evolved into conflicts over the control of institutions. The model of government established by the MMI engrossed effective control in the hands of a narrow liberal-Dissenting elite. The rationale behind this arrangement was clear: the directorate, insulated from the pressure of its membership, could keep the institute true to its moralising mission. The membership resented this lack of democratic control, and by 1832 internal disputes had already prompted a schism and the establishment of the New Mechanics' Institute, which took its stance on the principle of a true working-class ethos and complete control by the membership.[46] Although the damage which this did to the membership of the Mechanics' Institute quickly prompted it to liberalise its internal government, middle-class control was effectually maintained; of the eighteen directors elected for 1836, only one, an overlooker, could reasonably have been termed a working man, and several were prosperous middle-class figures.[47] The persistence of this control can be illustrated by the heated controversy over its internal government (and in particular relations between the teachers, as the active workers in the Institute, and the directors) which engulfed the Institute in 1867, prompting the election of a 'reform' list of directors, and the subsequent public withdrawal of patronage by several leading supporters.[48]

Even if the reins of control could usually be more lightly held, this was not a state of affairs which working-class members or potential members were prepared to accept, and the importance of control by a clearly working-class electorate was one of the central features of the

---

[46] For a detailed account of this episode and the career of the New Mechanics' Institute, see R.G. Kirby, 'An early experiment in workers' self-education: the Manchester New Mechanics' Institution, 1829–35', in Cardwell, *Artisan to Graduate*, 87–98.

[47] *MG*, 28 December 1835.

[48] *MG*, 23 May 1867, 'Thomas Marshall', *MG*, 24 December 1867, *MX*, 25 February 1867, 'Samuel Cottam', *MX*, 24 April 1867, 'LM', *MCN*, 11 May 1867, 'John Angell', *MCN*, 1 June 1867.

revised blueprint implemented by the promoters of the Lyceum movement in 1839. At the same time, the Lyceums remained associations designed for the working classes rather than by them, and Herford obtained a seat on the various boards of directors, with every expectation of having a large say in the way in which they were run. The resentment which even the influence of a relatively liberal individual like Herford caused, in the case of the Ancoats Lyceum stretching as far as plots to exclude him from the board, emphasises the extent to which the working classes expected their control to be real as well as formal.[49]

Promoters of subsequent intellectual institutions were alive to the dangers. Rev. E.B. Chalmers, rector of St Matthias' Salford, and one of the local pioneers of the Club and Institute movement, took great pains to ensure that although some safeguards existed to ensure a continued connection to the parish within which clubs and institutes had developed, the predominance of the working-class element in their direction should be well advertised.[50] Likewise strenuous efforts were made to ensure that the local Working Men's Colleges would not be tarred with the brush of exclusive management: as George Parry reminded the preliminary meeting of the Salford Working Men's College, one of the main reasons for the failure of local mechanics' institutes had been that 'the working man did not like to be managed'.[51]

In particular, the working men's institutes and clubs epitomised the numerous self-consciously working-class initiatives, firmly committed to working-class control, which appeared in the 1840s and 1850s. The Hall of Science, the Carpenters' Hall and the People's Institute were merely the most visible of innumerable working-class attempts to assert their self-reliance. The leaders of the Angel Meadow Working Men's Association made great play of their independence, with one member even going so far as to comment that he 'wish[ed] that working men should do more for themselves and depend less upon gentlemen to help them'.[52]

---

[49] For Herford's comments on these events see his 'Diary' (especially December 1838), Ms923.4 H32, MCLA.

[50] Chalmers, *MG*, 27 October 1860; cf. the comments on Charlestown New Institute, *SWN*, 29 November 1862.

[51] *MX*, 19 May 1858.

[52] *MX*, 12 May 1856, 'A Member of the Angel Meadow Working Men's Reading Room', *MX*, 8 December 1856. See also the preoccupation with independence of the Working Men's Institute in the Holland Street Ragged School in the early 1860s, 'Thomas Bright',

Unfortunately, the appearance of these institutes in the press was often caused by their reluctant appeal to middle-class sympathisers for funds. Thomas Bright, the spokesman of one such institute, argued that while reliance on aid of this kind was undesirable, in the early years of such institutions it was almost inevitable to avoid failure. Hence even the humble Hulme Working Men's Institute, founded in 1860, acquired the usual paraphernalia of elite patronage, including the Hon. Algernon Egerton as President.[53] The crux of the matter was often satisfactory accommodation. While it was a relatively simple matter to hire a small garret or room, and fit it out as a reading room for a small group, this provided little or no scope for the provision of other facilities such as classes, or the ability to raise funds by attracting entrance-paying non-members. Just as the New Mechanics' Institute in the 1830s had been fatally constricted by its accommodation, so, as it expanded, the embryo of the Pendleton Mechanics' Institute had to move several times in the space of two years to find accommodation to meet its growing needs, before ultimately being forced into attempting to raise the money to build its own hall.[54]

Repeated experience demonstrated that the expenses of establishment, or of transformation from a small company of mutual improvers to a fully-fledged institute or club, were usually beyond the unaided resources of working-class groups. The Hall of Science, Carpenters' Hall and People's Institutes were all lost to their working-class promoters after a relatively brief period of operation.[55] Given the costs of new buildings, it was not surprising that existing Ragged and Sunday schools became the most popular venue for working men's institutes; but of course, access to these buildings was mediated by the concerns of trustees and interested ministers, and almost certainly involved subtle forms of influence. The alternative, the erection of a society's own hall, generally brought the firm control of middle-class patrons, as the positions achieved by David Morris at the Chorlton Temperance Hall and Mechanics' Institute, and John Ashworth at the Pendleton Mechanics' Institute illustrate.

MX, 8, 20 February 1864.

[53] *MC*, 1 February 1862, 1 February 1864

[54] *MG*, 1 September 1856.

[55] The Carpenters' Hall was built in 1837–38 by the Carpenters and Joiners union as a direct response to middle-class control of other public venues; capable of holding 5000 people, from the late 1840s it seems to have been leased out for a variety of purposes, although intermittently it was available for working-class meetings throughout this period.

Nor was the problem simply one of accommodation. The middle classes also possessed various skills which were highly desirable for the successful operation of cultural institutions, as teachers, and most noticeably as popular lecturers. Even the proudly independent Angel Meadow Working Men's Association benefited from the interest taken in its activities by several middle-class figures, and its lecture course was sustained by clerical lecturers.[56] Indeed by 1857 it would seem that Rev. Arthur Mursell and Rev. J.A. Picton had conjointly assumed directing roles in the association's affairs.[57] The working classes were well aware of the danger: in 1859 Samuel Bamford warned the Chadderton and Tonge Mechanics' Institute, that 'the favoured party cannot help foregoing one small condition of self-will, and then another, until in the end, he is completely enmeshed in the influences of his rich friend, his original character obliterated, and his manly independence gone'.[58] However, while the annual lecture course played a vital role in the activities of many institutes, and audiences became increasingly sophisticated, few could afford to take their independent stance to the lengths of alienating middle-class opinion.

The result was not the capitulation of working-class independence, any more than the failure of the initial institutes had produced the resignation of the middle classes. Instead, what emerged was a compromise. The middle classes realised that they could not maintain the autocratic paternalism which had characterised many early institutes. The working classes accepted that democratic government, self-reliance and independence had to be tempered by the demands of stability. Of course, the issue of dependence or independence was not simply an abstract one, but related in turn to the ability to mould the shape and content of institute activities. The balance of their diverging demands was adjusted institution by institution, and it is to this adjustment that it is necessary now to turn.

[56] *MX*, 12 May 1856, 'A Member of the Angel Meadow Working Men's Reading Room', *MX*, 8 December 1856, 'A Mill Operative', *MX*, 11 December 1856.
[57] 'A Mill Operative', *MX*, 11 December 1856.
[58] S. Bamford, 'Diary', 28 October 1859, MS 923.2 B99, MCLA.

The content of intellectual life

The move to functional education: classes

The collapse of the institute pattern was the result of wholesale working-class rejection of the content of the intellectual culture which they offered. Nowhere was this more obvious than in the replacement of lectures by classes, and science by elementary education. Institute promoters had intended to provide both theoretical and practical science lectures, assuming that working men would be anxious for education in their various occupations.[59] Even if the initial long science courses were quickly abandoned, the MMI persisted in concentrating on science lecturing into the 1840s. By the early 1850s, however, lecturing had largely been replaced in the priorities of the Institute by a day school and an expanding portfolio of evening classes. Eschewing the reliance on miscellaneous lecturing so common elsewhere, the MMI stance can be summed up by the comment of its secretary (in 1860), Thomas Marshall, that the development of a sound system of class education was 'the most, if not the only, legitimate work of every well-regulated mechanics' institute'.[60]

The difficulty was that even in the MMI the initial choice of subjects was often inappropriate. Along with science, the institute stressed the higher branches of mathematics, and Latin and Greek. In fact, the practical difficulty of giving such teaching apart, it was soon apparent that there was little demand for it.[61] What the working classes wanted, it gradually became clear, was the acquisition of the basic writing and even reading skills which interrupted or non-existent education had denied them. As the editor of the *Monthly Literary and Scientific Lecturer* commented in 1853, 'the desire for knowledge had not been sufficiently excited by elementary teaching'.[62] The history of the class-based education offered by the cultural associations was a steady progress towards catering for this demand.

Although the Lyceums and the Parthenon were responding as early as 1839 to this need, their failure for other reasons meant that much of this process took place within the working men's institutes and the Sunday schools. Any attempt to trace the history of this process faces

---

[59] See the prospectuses of the Manchester and Salford Mechanics' Institutes.
[60] 'Thomas Marshall', *Journal of the Society of Arts*, VIII (1859–60), 854.
[61] See Tylecote, *Mechanics' Institutes*, 107–11.
[62] *Monthly Literary and Scientific Lecturer*, IV (1853), iv.

a series of difficulties. Most particularly, it is often impossible to distinguish between the long-established night schools which catered for young adolescents whose work prevented them from pursuing education during the day, and more specifically adult education classes; not least, of course, because there was little clear demarcation between the two in practice. To increase the difficulties, much of this activity took place in small local associations the histories of which it is impossible to uncover.

Evening classes had long been an important element of the educational system in Manchester. The dominance of Sunday schools reluctant to teach secular subjects had spawned a large number of evening classes. The Manchester Statistical Society surveys of 1834 recorded over 150 evening schools in Manchester and Salford, catering for nearly five thousand students.[63] By 1851, although estimates varied, this could have expanded to as many as six or seven thousand.[64] After this, figures become more unreliable: the report of 1869 suggested there were 40 night schools of this class in Manchester, but these tended to be of the type of the school associated with the Ministry to the Poor, which catered for around 650 students, mostly factory hands.[65] In the 1830s and 1840s these were largely schools for children, but by the early 1860s those attending night schools could be divided much more equally into three groups: children using them as an alternative to day school education; young adults up to 25 using them to continue their day school education; and finally a wider range of adults seeking to make up for their neglected education and looking for elementary reading, writing and arithmetic classes.[66]

The rudimentary skill-based education provided in such classes had initially led the middle classes to dismiss them. Richson, although he was very much aware of the potential of evening schools, commented in 1851 that they were 'in some cases little more than reading schools', and viewing them from within the context of juvenile education, was concerned that, in attracting older pupils, they were less advantageously placed than day schools for effecting a thorough-going moral

[63] Manchester Statistical Society, *Education in Manchester*, (1837), vii.
[64] *PP*, (1852) XI (499), 30; disputed by Edward Baines who suggested only 6–7000, *ibid*, 219.
[65] *PP*, (1870) LIV (91), 3, 171.
[66] See the comments of Kennedy, *PP*, (1861) XLIX [2828], 93–5; though note the comments of D.R. Fearon that he could find no evening school in Manchester which was really attempting to provide education continuing from school, *PP*, (1870) LIV (91), 172.

education.[67] As a result, calls were made to make good some of the deficiencies of the institutes by establishing evening schools for elementary education. Plans were drawn up by the Manchester Education Society, which established a couple of night schools in the early 1840s. However, there was no concerted widely-supported campaign and by the end of the 1840s little had apparently been achieved.[68]

The emergence of working men's institutes changed this. The middle classes gradually threw their weight behind these organisations in the realisation that they were responding to a widely felt desire among the working classes, and that they attracted the illiterate and semi-literate working classes for whom the mechanics' institutes had offered little. The Hulme Working Men's Institute was not untypical in this respect: according to its secretary, of its membership 'some cannot read at all, and others very imperfectly; there are many who cannot write'.[69] In 1862 it had over 600 members and eight classes nightly.[70] The difficulty for these institutions was not attracting new members, but finding teachers able and willing to take classes, and rooms in which to accommodate them: the Hulme institute suffered a falling membership in 1863 before an improvement in the supply of teachers allowed it to increase its number of classes to ten in 1865.[71] Within such classes, it was accepted that the scope for moral or religious education had been considerably reduced: Fearon commented that those who attended these schools did so 'to learn the merest elements': they sought practical skills rather than improving knowledge.[72]

The move to political education: reading rooms and mutual improvement societies
It was not only in their concentration on science that the institutes proved unattractive to the working classes. Of equal importance, particularly in the context of the 1830s and 1840s, was their determination to avoid politics. In part this was merely the natural

---

[67] *PP*, (1852) XI (499), 362.
[68] See the calls of John Watts and others, *MC*, 5,12,19,25 September, 10 October 1846. For example, despite plans nothing had been done to establish night classes in the Manchester National Schools, Manchester Church Education Society, *Annual Report*, (1849), 17.
[69] *MG*, 25 November 1861.
[70] *MG*, 19 March 1862.
[71] *MX*, 30 October 1863, 28 January 1865.
[72] *PP*, (1870) LIV (91), 145.

desire to avoid embroiling cultural institutes in the often bitter party disputes which divided the city in this period. The problems which the Athenaeum faced in the late 1830s and 1840s in overcoming suggestions that it was a Liberal forcing-ground demonstrated, if demonstration were needed, the potential for disruption which this danger held. In addition, however, it was also a reflection of middle-class suspicions that working-class politics was likely to mean ultra-radical politics, precisely the kind of beliefs which the institutes, with their concentration on science and moral improvement, were designed to avoid. As in the case of science, however, the middle classes were ultimately forced to concede to working-class desires, first for newsrooms and then for politically-oriented discussion societies.

The MMI, with Benjamin Heywood at the fore, resisted pressure from the existing membership for the provision of a newsroom throughout the 1830s.[73] But by the end of the decade even Heywood accepted that any institution which sought to appeal to the bulk of the working classes would have to concede this point, and it was with his concurrence that the Lyceums provided newsrooms, and a wide selection of London and local papers. By the end of the 1840s it had been accepted that the focal point of any successful working-class cultural association had to be a newsroom: 'That men should live together in this country and at this time, without taking an interest in politics, is altogether impossible', stated the Unitarian *Christian Reformer* in 1848, and rather than leave them to the 'one-sided and violent' paper of the public house, it recommended the use of newsrooms 'where they can read the best papers and periodicals on every side, and where they are directly brought into connection and conversation with those whose deepest interests are engaged in the progress not only of political reform, but of inward and practical religion'.[74] The provision of newsrooms was often the genesis of many of the institutes of the 1850s. The working men's clubs of the 1860s merely confirm this transition: it was the newsroom which was the unifying feature of the clubs.[75]

At the start of the 1830s, mutual improvement or discussion societies were similarly frowned upon, not least because of expectation that they would become preoccupied with political debates which would spill

---

[73] See his comments at the 1837 AGM, *MG*, 1 July 1837.
[74] *XR*, n.s. IV (1848), 518.
[75] *MX*, 31 October 1865.

over into the rest of institute activities, and when permission was given for the formation of such societies in the 1830s, this was often with the proviso that directorial control would be maintained, and political debates prohibited. The Athenaeum directors had to engage in a running battle with the mutual improvement society there, ultimately allowing its transformation into the Parliamentary and Debating Society, justifying the change on the ground that such societies were 'probably the most efficient means of inculcating sound principles of political economy'.[76] Likewise, in the various congregational and Sunday school mutual improvement societies, a combination of official proscription and self-censorship acted to restrict the discussion of sensitive topics; instead, historical and moral subjects predominated. Yet even in these societies some relaxation is apparent by the 1850s. The group associated with the congregation of advanced-Liberal J.R. Beard at Greengate Chapel, Strangeways, was, by the early 1850s, beginning to discuss contemporary issues like productive employment of paupers, and the desirability of extending political power to the working classes (although 'socialism' as a subject was still rejected), and by the end of the decade, similar topics were even being broached by Anglican Sunday-school-based societies.[77]

This process of relaxation was even more defined in the case of specifically working-class associations. Once again the Lyceums pointed the way, providing discussion classes along with their newsrooms. The popularity of the formula led to its aping by the middle classes, for example in the weekly Sunday debates on contemporary issues organised in the Union Chambers by a group of Liberals including hosiery merchant J.E. Nelson, together with working-class leaders like Edward Hooson, or in the debates of held at the Cobden Coffee House in Port Street, and other similar venues.[78] By 1861 the Salford

---

[76] See Athenaeum Minutes, 7 November 1839, M2/1/1, 5 February 1852, M2/1/4, MCLA; Athenaeum, *Annual Report*, (1853), 11.

[77] Strangeways Mutual Improvement Society, 'Minutes', Box 22, M43, MCLA; St Paul's Mutual Improvement Society, 'Minutes', M38, MCLA; All Saints, Chorlton-upon-Medlock Mutual Improvement Society, 'Minutes', MS283.42, MCLA.

[78] The fullest account of the Union Chambers meetings is in J. Johnson, *People I have Met*, (1906), 98–103; but see also 'Henry Fletcher', *MX*, 22 June 1857, *MG*, 14 January 1858. For radical use of the Union Chambers group see 'James Robertson', *MX*, 16 November 1858. For an interesting account of a meeting see *Alliance News*, 2 April 1864; from 1865 this was called the 'Manchester Discussion Forum', see the later account in *Freelance*, I (1866–67), 50–1. For a later reminiscence of the Cobden Coffee House and this debating culture see F. Hall, *A Northern Pioneer: The Story of J.R. Lancashire*, (1927), 183-6.

Mechanics' Institute was attempting to raise its profile by holding series of what it termed 'free mutual improvement soirées'.[79] The clubs, which already generally provided smoking rooms designed to replicate the pub, where political debate was common, took this one stage further. According to a report on St Matthias', '[s]tirring topics [were] chosen for lectures and conversational discussion, social and political questions having prominence given to them, and the members generally being invited to express their opinions freely'.[80]

The dilution of middle-class ideology: lectures

Lectures were undoubtedly the most conspicuous and enduring feature of the cultural life of the mid-nineteenth century city, and despite frequent reports of their demise, they were delivered, if anything, with increasing frequency in the 1850s and 1860s.[81] But as before, the popular lecture of the 1860s bore little resemblance to the ideals of institute promoters in the 1830s. Popular pressure was able to undermine the narrow-minded evangelicalism of the 1830s, so that by the 1860s propagandists were producing an innocuous mix of middle-class moralism heavily diluted with working-class flattery.

Lectures in the early institutes followed very much the style laid down by the Royal Manchester Institution (RMI): multi-lecture courses (sometimes as many as twelve in a course) on predominantly scientific subjects, shared between local scientific men and professional itinerants. From the outset it was accepted that only lavish and frequent experiments were likely to compensate for the dry technicalities of the subject matter, and these were extensively indulged in.[82] Even with this aid, however, science lectures were never capable of holding the attention of working men, even if in the early 1830s those working-class leaders who directed the New Mechanics' Institute followed a very similar pattern. There was a sudden burst of enthusiasm in the

---

[79] *MSp*, 1 November 1856.

[80] *Occasional Papers of the Working Men's Club and Institute Union*, (March 1863), 4.

[81] There is no adequate study of public lecturing in Britain in this period, although for useful material see Inkster, *Steam Intellect Societies*, and *idem*, 'The Public Lecture as an instrument of Science Education for Adults - the case of Great Britain, 1750–1850', *Paedagogica Historica*, 20 (1981), 85–111.

[82] Tylecote, 'The Manchester Mechanics' Institution, 1824–1850', in Cardwell, *Artisan to Graduate*, 60–5. In a different context I have argued for the need to interpret such experiments in the light of popular demand for spectacle rather than the educational demands with which the lecturers themselves often justified this practice: see M. Hewitt, 'Science as Spectacle: Popular Science Culture in Saint John, New Brunswick, 1830–50', *Acadiensis*, XVIII,1 (1988), 91–119.

mid-1830s: soon after its establishment, the Athenaeum was being given lectures on three nights a week, and there were four concurrent lecture courses in Manchester.[83] Even the RMI was troubled by non-subscribers gatecrashing its lectures.[84] But this was almost entirely a middle-class phenomenon, and by the early 1840s, despite the impetus provided by the mesmerism craze, there were already signs that enthusiasm was beginning to wane. By 1843 the RMI was already reducing the number of lectures it offered. Although popular lecturers like George Dawson and Ralph Waldo Emerson could still generate considerable enthusiasm, middle-class interest in lectures continued to ebb away, and by the end of the decade the general apathy shown towards them was a commonplace. The institutes moved swiftly away from them: the Athenaeum presented only three lectures throughout 1850, and its report remarked on the continuing 'distaste for lectures both on the part of the members and the public'.[85] They were entirely abandoned at Salford as early as 1852, although the MMI persevered until 1857. At the end of 1853 Henry Pitman, journalist with the *Manchester Courier*, social and educational reformer, and brother of Isaac Pitman, the pioneer of phonography, who since 1850 had been producing a little periodical entitled the *Monthly Literary and Scientific Lecturer*, ceased publication in response to the collapse in demand which had accompanied the falling popularity of lectures.[86]

Yet despite all this pessimism, the 1850s saw a renewed interest in lecturing. Just at the time the larger institutes were abandoning them, lectures and lecture courses in connection with the parochial institutes and the working men's associations began to multiply, and the Manchester and Salford Sanitary Association was able to attract large numbers of the working classes to its sanitary lectures, an estimated 12,000 to the lectures in the 1855 courses.[87] In the late 1850s those to the Angel Meadow Working Men's Association were packed to overflowing, and it was possible for Arthur Mursell to attract several thousand at a time to his Sunday afternoon lectures at the Free Trade

---

[83] The *MG* commented in May 1836 that it could 'remember the time when lectures, whether of a literary or a scientific character were considered a great bore...', 21 May 1836.

[84] 'A Governor', *MG*, 4 January 1840.

[85] Athenaeum, *Annual Report*, (1851), 9.

[86] *Monthly Literary and Scientific Lecturer*, IV (1853), iv. For Pitman see *Dictionary of Labour Biography*, I, 271-3.

[87] Manchester and Salford Sanitary Association, *Annual Report*, (1855), 18.

Hall.[88] Indeed, although lecturing was by no means integral to the activities of the working men's clubs, most gave lectures at least intermittently, and there was little sign of any significant reduction in interest in lectures at this level before 1867.[89]

The reasons for this paradox are threefold. Popular lecturing expanded firstly because lecturers abandoned pure science for a miscellaneous mix of history, literature, travel and popularised science, heavily shot through with practical lessons for working-class living. This mélange is perhaps best epitomised by the address of Dr Unger, announced in January 1860 as a lecture on 'Chemistry' in the course at St Simon's schools, Salford, which included both a discourse on the laws of the admixture of gases, and an examination of the means by which the adulteration of food by tradesmen could be discovered.[90] Of course this kind of lecture could (and often did) degenerate into straightforward patronising moralism: under cover of deliberately vague, if not downright misleading, titles, audiences were still confronted by clerical lecturers, telling them what to read, subjecting them to long calls to become religious, and advising them at length as to their social duties.

What redeemed much of this moralism was the extent to which the tone of lecturing had been transformed by the end of the 1850s. The lecturers who successfully attracted audiences in the late 1850s and 1860s were those who rejected the narrow-minded puritanism which had previously characterised much middle-class propaganda, and who attacked it vigorously on the lecturer's platform. The Rev. T.W. Marriott's lecture 'Some Real Wants of the Working Classes' was a good example of this, holding up to scorn the double standards of those who enjoined temperance on the working classes while tippling at home, who complained bitterly about children playing in the streets without making any attempt to provide them with alternative facilities for healthy exercise, and who confined their desire to improve the working classes almost entirely to their moral rather than material welfare, being concerned that the working classes remained in their station.[91] In this way, lessons of middle-class moral imperialism had

---

[88] For the Mursell episode, see my 'Popular Platform Religion: Arthur Mursell at the Free Trade Hall, 1856–65', *Manchester Region History Review*, (forthcoming, 1996).
[89] See the comment of Solly in the *Workingman*, 17 March 1866.
[90] *SWN*, 21 January 1860.
[91] Rev. William Thackeray Marriott, *Some Real Wants and Some Legitimate Claims of the Working Classes*, (1860).

to be increasingly diluted with working-class perceptions of their own moral equality.

Although for some lecturers such statements were mere cosmetic rhetoric, a sweetener to dupe audiences into swallowing the unchanged pill of middle-class moralising, the change in tone cannot simply be so dismissed. Rather (and this is the second cause), the discipline of popular attraction was clearly able to shape the substance as well as the rhetoric of lectures. The most striking evidence of this is provided by two contrasting publications produced by J.A. Nicholls, Liberal cotton master, one-time president of the Ancoats Lyceum, and frequent lecturer to working-class audiences: *The Strike, by a Lancashire Man*, (1853) and *A Lecture on Strikes*, (1856).[92] As the titles suggest, both are on labour relations, but the first was published as an anonymous pamphlet, while the second was the text of a public lecture. They were published close enough together to discount any major change of opinion, and in any case their implicit assumptions are clearly the same; but the two are remarkably different. In the pamphlet Nicholls emphasised the need for working men to bow to the superior education and judgement of their masters, vigorously asserted the right of the masters to do what they would with their own, and stated categorically that with the forces of supply and demand paramount, the workers had to submit to their dictates, or see capital being driven overseas. His attitude was virulently anti-trade union, dismissing union leaders as merely designing men, and declaring that although strikes might be defensible in theory, in practice they were always attended with deeds which made them unjustifiable. By contrast, his lecture, although it contained the same reliance on supply and demand, and rejected the claims of the workers to some share of profits, entirely abandoned the position of dictation from superior knowledge which the pamphlet had adopted, and retreated considerably from its naked individualism, stressing a wider middle-class obligation to the workers expressed in the library and the public parks, as well as the 'right and proper' feelings which would prevent masters unjustly taking advantage of their men, and prompt them to contribute in other ways to the welfare of their employees, particularly by reducing their wages only reluctantly and at the last moment. Nicholls was popular with working men, but his popularity rested on the degree to which when addressing them

---

[92] [J.A. Nicholls], *The Strike, by a Lancashire Man. A Letter to the Working Classes on their present position and Movement*, (1853), idem, *A Lecture on Strikes*, (1856).

without the shield of anonymity he was prepared to contort his beliefs into a shape acceptable to his audience.

The third cause of the continued popularity of lecturing was the extent to which it catered for popular demands for entertainment and excitement, and this leads us into the issue of recreation, the final nail in the coffin of middle-class moral imperialism. At the outset, the institute ethos stressed learning; the emphasis was on the acquisition of 'useful knowledge', and while, as the use of extravagant experiments in science lectures demonstrated, it was recognised that the more entertaining they could make education the more readily it was likely to be absorbed, the emphasis was on entertaining education not educative recreation. This was not a formula which the artisan or factory operative, attending the institutes after a hard working day, found generally congenial.[93] As a result, grandiose ideas of the 'diffusion' of useful knowledge, or the inculcation of religion and morals had to abandoned in favour of a re-orientation of existing activities and the addition of new ones which produced a range of recreations which were, in the words of John Watts, 'innocent, even if not improving'.[94]

In the case of lectures, popular audiences looked for not only practical help which sought to advise rather than moralise, delivered by lecturers whose sympathies and attitudes lay with them, but also recreation. And while figures like the Rev. Sam Coley, a popular Methodist lecturer in the mid-1860s, were able to satisfy audiences with a fluent delivery, a wealth of interesting anecdotes, and a clever turn of phrase, what succeeded most of all with popular lecture audiences was excitement, and increasingly this is what lecturers attempted to offer.[95] As early as 1855 A.J. Scott, the principal of Owen's College, commented that the more sensationalist style adopted by lecturers, in an attempt to appeal to the working classes, had contributed much to the collapse of the popularity of lecturing among the middle classes.[96] Although it is difficult to provide an illustration of this trend, its momentum was clearly recognised. The process of choosing 'stirring topics' took the lecture far away from its initial aspiration to elevate the working classes, and towards a role which differed little from any other

[93] See, for example, the comments of 'J', *MG*, 18 April 1838.
[94] *MX*, 31 October 1865.
[95] *Freelance*, II (1867), 49–50.
[96] *PPL*, I (1855), v–vi.

traditional working-class leisure activity: lecturing had become merely 'a little intellectual cock-fighting or rat-worrying' according to one Manchester secularist writing at the end of 1864.[97]

As such, lecturing was eventually subsumed into those middle-class initiatives that abandoned direct didacticism for a more diffuse pressure to alter working-class lifestyles which will be discussed in the next chapter. Before this, however, it is necessary to consider the impact of the processes of negotiation on the functioning of the institutions of useful knowledge as propagators of ideology and belief.

The impact of intellectual life

The institutions of useful knowledge were not marginal to working-class experience. Edward Royle has long since established the confusion of contemporary complaints and their concentration rather on those who stayed away than those who attended.[98] He might have gone on to say that it also focused unduly on the mechanics' institutes and other bodies in the institute pattern. The overwhelming concentration of the working men's associations on elementary education, even reading, suggests that they drew their clientele from below the ranks of any aristocracy of labour, and the extent to which they struggled against inadequate accommodation and teacher shortages to run large numbers of classes gives no indication of a reluctance to become involved. While at any one time only a fraction of the working classes could have claimed membership of any of the various cultural organisations, the constant flux of membership (the result less of apathy than of the disruptiveness of frequent migrations, the uncertainty of income, changing family circumstances, and the specific-goal nature of much working-class membership), and the participation of many who did not become members but who attended lectures and discussions, meant that the number who flitted in and out of direct involvement was much greater. The activities of the intellectual associations were not simply alternatives to the 'rough' culture of the beerhouse, but an experience which, although perhaps concentrated in the 16–30 age-group, was

---

[97] *NR*, 5 November 1864.
[98] E. Royle, 'The Mechanics' Institutes and the Working Classes, 1840–60', *Historical Journal*, 14 (1971), 305–21.

shared by most of the male (and increasing numbers of the female) mid-nineteenth century working class.

In this respect the intellectual associations were an important element of the intellectual morphology of mid-nineteenth century Manchester, and served as part of the arena of attitude-formation, reinforcement and mobilisation, as well as supporting lifestyles which reinforced the ideological assumptions which went with them.

Lectures stood at the forefront of middle-class attempts at effective propagation. Addressing the Athenaeum in 1836 James Heywood described them as 'the most certain means of communicating useful knowledge'.[99] And there is enough evidence to demonstrate that those who argued that the lecturer's stand, with its opportunities to capitalise on the emotive power of voice, expression and gesture, had potential for persuasiveness that books could never match, were not entirely mistaken.[100] The upsurge of interest in phrenology and homeopathy caused by courses of lectures by Combe and Epps respectively, or the considerable excitement and local following generated by Owenite lecturing during the late 1830s confirms this.[101] Indeed the period is studded by lecturers, sometimes local, but more often outsiders, like George Dawson or Emerson, who created both temporary stirs and lasting impressions on Manchester audiences. After listening to Emerson, Edwin Waugh found 'Emerson's lecture taking root in my whole mind and demeanour as I walk about the streets…turning upside down my schemes and remodelling my plans for life'.[102]

Unfortunately, neither intense interest, nor the kind of conversion experience which Waugh went through, necessarily created permanent results, and in any case, lecturers of the skills of Combe, Epps, or Emerson were relatively few. As the period progressed it was generally accepted that lectures were an ineffective channel for middle-class didacticism. 'Occasional lectures on a variety of subjects are an innocent, and to a certain extent, a useful amusement; but they can never give sound practical instruction', was Francis Horner's verdict

---

[99] James Heywood, *Address to the Members of the Manchester Athenaeum*, (1836), 11–12.
[100] For such an argument see H. Rawson, 'Mutual Improvement Societies', *PPL*, II (1856), 248; see Vernon, *Politics and the People*, 117–131.
[101] Mrs John Epps, *Diary of the late John Epps, M.D., embracing autobiographical records [etc.]*, [1870], 365, *NEM*, October 1842, 562–3; for Combe see *MC*, 6 May 1837.
[102] Waugh, 'Diary', 22, 23 November 1847, MSQ 928.28 W87, MCLA.

in 1861.[103] The persistence of popular lecturing into the 1860s owed much, as Henry Pitman pointed out, to a more realistic appraisal of the role the lecture could play, 'the summarising of knowledge as a guide and incentive to further study'.[104] For those like R.W. Smiles, who retained higher didactic hopes, the lecture was little more than 'seed...sown in faith'.[105]

The advantage of the lecturer was the status of expert and teacher. But this was a fragile position. Often, and especially for more political lectures, it was undermined by the association of a lecturer with a clear position, or by knowledge that he was being paid for his advocacy.[106] The controversy caused in the 1860s by the activities of Thomas Evans, a one-time weaver and smallware salesman, who was taken into the pay of the Anti-Corn Law League party as a speaker and lecturer is illuminating in this respect.[107] In 1866 Evans took a prominent part in advancing the anti-union position in a long-running public debate on the role and efficacy of trade unions, until the exposure of the fact that his activities had been secretly funded by George Wilson and the League party.[108] When, in November 1867, Evans attempted to dispute the arguments of Ernest Jones at his lecture on trade unions in the Free Trade Hall, he was drowned by hostile cries, Malcolm McLeod, one of the leading union politicians in the city, proclaiming that it must 'once and for all go forth that Manchester working men would not listen to men who were in the pay of their opponents, even though a doctor should be the paymaster, and a powerful employers' association should find the funds'.[109]

Even voluntary lecturers had to be careful how much they presumed on their right to 'lecture' their audience, and as has already been suggested, it was only because they presumed less and less that popular lecturing remained popular. Some lecturers went as far as to abandon

---

[103] *PP*, (1861) XXI [2794-V], 263.

[104] *PPL*, III (1857), iii.

[105] R.W. Smiles to J.R. Beard, 20 April 1852, Unitarian Mss., A.2.1., MJRL.

[106] W.B. Hodgson to Combe, 19 October 1850, ff119-122, 7308, Combe Papers, National Library of Scotland; cf. the sharp attacks on professional itinerants who 'get up' a lecture merely for profit, in the Bennett Street School, Mutual Improvement Society, 'Minutes', 11 February 1859, M12/8/1, MCLA.

[107] For Evans see Evans to George Wilson, 14 July 1862, Wilson Papers, MCLA, 'Open Letter of Thomas Evans', Broadside F1865/1e, MCL.

[108] *MX*, 19,20 November 1866, *MCN*, 24 November, 1 December 1866, *BH*, 22 December 1866.

[109] *MCN*, 2 November 1867; for further details of this long-running debate see below, pages 218-21.

their privileged status entirely: Rev. Robert Steel, for example, told the audiences that listened to his lecture 'The Literature of Labour', that they should treat lectures as 'an intellectual grindstone for the sharpening of [their] wits', urging that 'although it may take ill with the author, yet I hold it eminently advantageous to you that you take the discourse to pieces'.[110]

The status of lecturer as teacher was also undermined by the prevalence of controversial lectures and structured debates, and by the development of discussions from brief post-lecture exchanges to an activity in their own right. Along with mutual improvement societies, these acted to formalise the introduction of rival interpretations, which left audiences free to exercise their own judgement in the light of the conviction of the participants and their own personal inclinations. Frequently, both public debates and private discussion groups (where a true difference of opinion was often difficult to generate) provided merely rituals of intellectual conflict, in which more attention was paid to the scoring of passing debating points than to the building up of a coherent and intellectually convincing case.[111] Nevertheless, there can be little doubt that this environment could act as a powerful solvent to the most firmly held views, as the weak points of personal convictions were sought out and exposed. Even within the emphatically demarcated lines of sectarian debating, firm religious commitment could be undermined and conversions made.[112] Unfortunately, as the successes of the Owenites in the 1830s and 1840s demonstrated, this was a double-edged sword which could as easily loosen as tighten the bonds of attachment to middle-class positions.

Discussions and debates also provided the greatest scope for the other significant brake on the lecturer's influence: active audience re-interpretation. It would be wrong to assume that access to the platform and the constant reiteration of middle-class ideology would by simple weight of repetition produce effective inculcation. The working classes were not passive recipients of the message of the platform, but actively participated in its reception and re-interpretation. The lecture

---

[110] Rev. Robert Steel, *The Literature of Labour*, (1856), 11.

[111] P. Ball, 'A Sketch of Our Society', 'Odds and Ends' (manuscript magazine of the St Paul's Mutual Improvement Society) (1855), 6–7, M38/4/2/1; cf. the warnings of Rawson in 'Mutual Improvement Societies', *PPL*, II (1856), 255.

[112] E.g. the case of the Catholic debater whose faith was fatally undermined by doubts prompted by a debate on 'freedom of the will' at the Ancoats Lyceum, *MCMM*, August 1855, 165–6.

hall was less a channel of ideas and more a battlefield of ideologies. Audiences disputed the authority of the lecturer in several ways. In the livelier atmosphere of debates, they cheered their agreement, and booed, hissed and whistled in dissension. In the normally more placid confines of lectures, they were still prepared to shout opposition to statements with which they strongly disagreed. The extent to which audiences could thus usurp the authority of the lecturer was not overlooked: lecture chairmen struggled hard to restrain audience responses, even to the extent of attempting to prevent spontaneous applause during addresses; after all, this also implied a sanctioning of the opinion of the lecturer, allowing even silences to be eloquent.[113]

In many cases the intellectual associations and their spin-offs served better in underpinning existing convictions and arousing action from the committed than in converting the uninitiated. Controversial lectures and debates played a key role as repositories of arguments and information upon which members of the working classes relied to bolster attitudes and beliefs which initially rested as much on emotion or group-identity as on intellectual conviction. Protestant workmen were fed with material which allowed them to counter the most popular arguments of Catholics, and take the initiative in discussions with them. City missionaries who appeared to be gaining the upper hand in debates over religion with Owenites were countered by the ultimate defence that they should go along to the Owenite lectures, 'and hear what they can say on the subject, and how they will tear your religion to flitters'.[114] Those who sought to demolish their opponents in this environment, often found that they merely hardened their convictions: hence the comment of cabinet-maker and eventually newspaper editor, Charles Hadfield, that his secularism had been 'burnt in' by the experience of a debate with a Catholic bishop.[115]

The ultimate form of audience response to lectures and addresses was simple non-attendance. Sectarian lecturers like the Anglican Rev. W.A. Darby gave Catholics the opportunity to reply to his lectures at their conclusion because he realised that without the intellectual

---

[113] E.g. Abel Heywood attempting to prevent applause during Gough's temperance orations, J.B. Gough and Rev. H. James, *Temperance Addresses*, (1858), 8.

[114] *MCMAR*, (1838), 22; see also the comment that another missionary found in one of the anti-socialist tracts he was distributing: Bembridge, 'Diary', 9 December 1843, MCLA.

[115] Hadfield to G.J. Holyoake, 25 November 1855, #805 Holyoake Papers, Hanover House.

gladiatorialism that this introduced, few would be likely to attend. And in this sense lecturers realised that in many cases they were speaking to the converted. As J.B. Gough, the celebrated temperance lecturer, told his audience in the Free Trade Hall in 1853, 'if I occupy your time in endeavouring to prove that drunkenness is an evil, it is a waste of your time, and an insult to your common sense'.[116] In this context lectures, particularly by eminent figures, could do much to stiffen the commitment of the members of any movement; as the Manchester merchant William Clegg told Robert Owen in 1833, at the time of the builders' strike, a lecture from him would 'raise the spirit of the unionists and prove the means of encouraging them to maintain the stand they have taken'.[117] Or they could be used for inspiring enthusiasm in the movement's workers, in Gough's words to 'say something that shall stir up those that hear me – not particularly to assent to this or that proposition, but to do something'.[118]

Gough's remarks hint, unintentionally, at a wider truth. While the institutions of intellectual culture were disseminators of ideology, they also offered a set of pastimes to compete with the traditional leisure activities of 'rough' culture. When Cooke Taylor expressed the hope in 1842 that public lectures would 'abate the fever of political excitement, by giving better occupation to the mind', he was uttering a contemporary platitude.[119] But the attempt to use institutes, associations and clubs to draw the working classes from the culture of drink was doomed to failure, because as the careers of leading autodidacts like Bamford and Brierley should remind us, intellectual self-culture was not like temperance, it did not necessitate the severing of all links with the pub, and there was nothing to stop those who spent Friday evening learning to write spending Saturday evening drinking, and even less to stop those who heard Nicholls lecturing on strikes from adjourning to the pub to discuss it.[120] The succumbing in the 1870s of the working men's club movement to the demand for drink in

---

[116] J.B. Gough, *J.B. Gough's Oration at Manchester, September 22 1853. Reported phonographically by William Rodger*, ([1853]), 3.
[117] Clegg to Owen, 2 November 1833, #612, Owen Papers, Hanover House. For a brief consideration of this role of lectures see E. Royle, *Victorian Infidels*, (1974).
[118] Gough, *Oration*, 4.
[119] W. Cooke Taylor, *Notes of a Tour*, 270.
[120] Of course this dovetails with the argument of Peter Bailey's suggestive article, 'Will the Real Bill Banks Please Stand Up? Towards a Role Analysis of Mid-Victorian Working-Class Respectability', *Journal of Social History*, XII, (1978–79), 336–53.

the clubs was merely the public defeat of an ideal which had scarcely operated in practice.

Unable to formalise any separation of spheres between those who actively participated in intellectual organisations, and those whose contact with them was more ephemeral, the impact of middle-class moral imperialism was always likely to be fragile and unstable. Its difficulties are encapsulated in the case of a certain Mr Greenhalgh, who found himself before the city magistrates charged with drunkenness in February 1849. The unfortunate Greenhalgh had attended a temperance meeting on the evening of his arrest, and had been, as he explained to the magistrate, 'musing on the observations to which he had listened, when, unfortunately for any embryo good resolutions which were forming, he met in Oldfield road with a friend, whose persuasions to take a drop of beer he could not withstand'.[121] For all their efforts, the mid-nineteenth century middle class were unable to neutralise the influence of working-class culture, and it is to that culture that it is now necessary to turn.

[121] *MX*, 27 February 1849.

Chapter Six

The resilience of
unrespectable recreation

The meagre returns from middle-class efforts in religion and rational recreation eventually forced social reformers to conclude that middle-class initiatives were being undermined by the constant attrition of working-class culture and the contradictory values which it promulgated; that, as the *Manchester Spectator* expressed it in 1856, '[w]e are all the products of a society, rather than a schoolmaster'.[1] The result, as Peter Bailey has suggested, was 'a significant retreat from unrelieved didacticism'.[2] This involved not so much the admixture of a little harmless entertainment to dilute the unrelieved diet of intellectual improvement, but rather a steady reversal of the priorities of middle-class reforming initiatives. By 1854 it was possible for Nathaniel Card, the founder of the United Kingdom Alliance, to remark of abstainers that 'I do not think that religious grounds lead them at first to abandon their habits. They principally get out of their habits, and that is the means of their receiving religious instruction afterwards'.[3]

Cultural barriers

A cursory glance at the comments of middle-class commentators reveals that they were all too keenly aware of the diversity of the environments within which working-class resistance to moral imperialism was stiffened. It had long been recognised that the workplace or the shopfloor generated strong solidarities and codes of behaviour subversive of bourgeois moral codes: this was often singled out as the root of the failure of Sunday school scholars to maintain their religious

---

[1] *MSp*, 17 May 1856.

[2] P. Bailey, *Leisure and Class in Victorian England: Rational Recreation and the Contest for Control, 1830–85*, (1978), 99.

[3] *PP*, (1854) XIV (367), 106-7. This shift is implicit in the organisation, although not explicit in the prose, in J.M. Golby and A.W. Purdue, *Civilisation and the Crowd. Popular Culture in England, 1750–1900*, (1984).

affiliations through adolescence.[4] The formalisation of workplace pressure in the case of strike sheets and their lists of contributors and blacklegs further emphasised the strength of work group pressure to conform.

What emerged steadily was a recognition of the ubiquitous significance of peer group pressure and peer group example. The calls by middle-class platform and pulpit speakers for their hearers to assume the role of witness and exemplar underline their growing recognition of the dynamics of group activity, particularly among adolescents. James Prince Lee, Bishop of Manchester, took the opportunity when delivering one of a series of sermons to the working classes in 1858 to underline the important duty the working classes had 'by precept, by example, by entreaty, by intercession, to seek to raise an interest in all around you for God and eternity'.[5]

For most observers, the imperviousness of working-class culture was rooted in two conditions: the material surroundings of the working-class neighbourhood, and the pattern of working-class leisure. In many cases the one was seen to derive from the other. The street and its culture acquired an evil reputation as the location in which youth was divested of innocence, and the weak converted to crime. But even more, the actual homes of the working classes were frequently identified as the root of the problem. The degradation of slum housing, it was argued, was such as to make the cultivation of standards of middle-class respectability almost impossible: as John Layhe commented in 1846, the efforts of the middle classes hitherto had been 'partial, irregular and unsatisfactory. No provision [had] yet been made to countervail the difficulties arising from vicious associations away from school, and particularly, from pernicious influences at home. Without something of this kind, however, we are likely to be thwarted at every step'.[6] The solution was clear: before the working classes could be made receptive to religion and rationality, they needed to be extricated from the slums: as the Rev. Angus McLaren told the annual meeting of the Ormond

[4] The theme of conflict between custom and discipline has been much studied; see for a classic expression, D.A. Reid, 'The Decline of St Monday', *Past & Present*, 71 (1976), 76–101, and for a recent study, C. Behagg, *Politics and Production*, (1990).

[5] J.P. Lee, *"Wash and be Clean", preached...in St. Andrew's Church, Ancoats, on Wednesday evening, January 6th, 1858, being the first in a course of twelve sermons to the Working Classes of Manchester and Salford*, ([1858]), 12. Cf. the comments of Richson in the same series that the working classes should become 'missionaries for [religion]', *Drunkenness*, (1858), 105.

[6] *MTPAR*, (1846), 25–6.

Street Sunday Evening Ragged School in 1864, 'It was no use deluging the people with tracts, drugging them with sermons, carrying them Bibles, or offering them Sunday School instruction, so long as they were left down in those dreadful holes where half of them lived'.[7] For some this led to the desultory interest in slum clearance common throughout urban Victorian Britain. For many more, it pointed to the need to begin the cultivation of the kind of provident habits which would enable the working classes to raise themselves from the slum.

Unfortunately, the pursuit of the provident lifestyle flew in the face of working-class leisure, which was rooted in institutions, such as the pub, and practices, such as gambling, which were antithetical to middle-class ideas of thrift. Moreover, it was accepted that these leisure activities were themselves crucial to the maintenance of distinct working-class cultural norms and value systems, and that their counter-appeal explained much of the difficulty experienced in attracting the working classes to church or institute. In this sense, both to bolster working-class providence, and enhance the attractiveness of the institutions of moral imperialism, it was necessary to transform the leisure patterns of the working classes.

Three overlapping strategies resulted. Firstly, the attempt, involving a fundamental shift from doctrine to style, to establish attractive alternatives to working-class leisure, to move from explicitly rational to merely innocent recreation. Secondly, the incorporation of such recreation into an overtly 'respectable' lifestyle, dominated by the cultivation of the full canon of Smilesian values as a means of elevation from the slums. Thirdly, to bolster the inherent attractions of these approaches, to tighten middle-class control and proscription of those elements of working-class culture deemed particularly offensive. Apparent at the outset, the confrontation with working-class culture became increasingly central to middle-class moral imperialism as the period progressed.

Recreation

In the early institute model, with its stress on self-improvement and the acquisition of knowledge, there was little room for recreation. Nevertheless, the relative failure of the institutes and the success of the

[7] *MG*, 6 December 1864.

Hall of Science with its combination of learning and entertainment, soon convinced at least the more progressive among the middle classes of the need to use recreational activities to make education more attractive.[8] The Lyceums, with their smoke rooms and newsrooms were the first move in this direction, and their initial success appeared to demonstrate the potential of this formula. But their subsequent collapse made it clear that while the primary focus remained didactic, working-class allegiance to middle-class institutions was likely to be only fleeting.

As a result, there is some evidence in the 1840s of a much broader shift towards the encouragement of respectable recreation patterns as at least a complementary strategy to direct proselytism. Noting the increasing popularity of music salons, reformers placed the encouragement of music in the vanguard of these efforts.[9] James Heywood told J.R. Beard in 1842 that of the various forms of wholesome amusements for the working classes which could be suggested, he favoured the provision of high class music 'to soften and civilise them by charming their ears'.[10]

As early as 1839 the Salford Mechanics' Institute was including concerts directed towards the working classes in its activities, and although these were quickly pronounced a failure, the experiment was copied in the 1840s by the Lyceums, the Manchester Mechanics' Institute, and by musical societies such as the Lancashire and Cheshire Philharmonic Institute, which grew out of the movement for working-class singing classes in Manchester.[11] By 1848 concerts were coming close to challenging lectures as the most common institute activity, culminating in the series of successful 'Concerts for the People' organised from 1848 onwards (at first independently and then under the auspices of the MMI), which at their peak attracted audiences of three to four thousand, although predominantly from the 'middle orders of society'.[12] Concert series for the working classes were organised

[8] See Benjamin Heywood to Henry Brougham, 3 January 1838, #14362, Brougham Papers, UCL.

[9] See David Russell, *Popular Music in England, 1840–1914*, (1987). For a Manchester example see 'A Friend to Rational Enjoyment', *MG*, 20 November 1841.

[10] James Heywood to J.R. Beard, 1 June 1842, Unitarian Mss, A.2.1, MJRL.

[11] For the early Salford concerts see *MG*, 27 April, 12 June 1839; for the Manchester institute see *MG*, 24 January 1844; the Philharmonic Institute concerts are described in *MG*, 29 July 1846.

[12] See the account of the Miles Platting Mechanics' Institute, *MX*, 21 March 1848; *MX*, 7 April 1849, 6 July 1850, 4 February 1852, *Chambers' Educational Journal*, 16 March

intermittently during the 1850s and 1860s, although the label 'popular' came to have less and less descriptive significance, as prices rose and the working classes stayed away.[13] By this stage, for specifically working-class audiences, the concert format had largely been replaced by the miscellaneous entertainment of music, recitations and short talks.

One of the main attractions of this approach was that it enabled full use to be made of the amateur choral groups and singing classes which had become by far the most significant element of the middle-class use of music. Prompted by the propagandising of both John Hullah and Joseph Mainzer, the Lancashire and Cheshire Workmen's Singing Classes were established in 1842, growing into the Philharmonic Institute in 1845.[14] Despite the formation of a 'normal school' by Mainzer in 1848, there was something of an organisational hiatus around 1850. Order was only re-established in 1856 under a new Tonic Sol-Fa Association. At the end of this year there were 16 elementary and two advanced classes under the association, mostly associated with Sunday Schools.[15] Indeed by this period, classes had become part of the normal offerings of the full range of working-class institutions from temperance societies to ragged schools. Singing classes appealed most often to children, but for many working-class men there was the parallel activity of the band, commonly associated with temperance societies, schools or works.

The refining potential of music maintained its appeal for moral reformers throughout the period, but it did have its limits. It was after all difficult to demonstrate directly the beneficial effects of music. As one commentator enquired during the controversy over Sunday bands in 1856, 'what is there in a band of music to "spread virtuous habits" in a people sunk in drunkenness and vice?'.[16] By the 1860s, such was the extent of enthusiasm for music in Manchester, that even the liberally-minded William McKerrow was prompted to question whether, despite the potentially refining influence of music, it was not

1850.

[13] *MX*, 7 February 1855, 'A Friend to Democracy', *MX*, 28 October 1856, *MG*, 10 November 1863.

[14] For Hullah see *MC*, 27 January 1841, *MG*, 23 September 1843; for Mainzer see *MG*, 2 June 1864. The papers of the Workmen's Singing Classes are at M400, MCLA.

[15] *MG*, 2 December 1856.

[16] 'J. Roberts', *MX*, 16 June 1856.

possible 'that they might have, in connection with their churches and congregations, too many of those pleasures'.[17]

Similar doubts were expressed at the periodic attempts of reformers to enlist the refining influences of art in their struggle to moralise the masses. The establishment of the Royal Manchester Institution and its annual exhibitions located the promotion of art as a central part of the assertion of middle-class cultural and civic leadership in Manchester, and this affirmation reached its apogee with the organisation of the great Manchester Art Treasures Exhibition of 1857.[18] The primary purpose of the exhibition was undoubtedly an affirmation of middle-class culture, but the use of art as a means of elevating the tastes and culture of the working classes remained an important subsidiary aspiration, one which surfaced periodically in this period. In the mid-1840s an abortive attempt was made to establish an institution of instructive art recreation for the masses in association with the Manchester School of Design.[19] This was followed in 1850 by the establishment, as a deliberate parallel to the Concerts for the People, of the 'Cosmorama', a series of art-related entertainments staged in a specially refurbished Free Trade Hall.[20] These, however, failed to attract sufficient numbers for the experiment to be repeated, and despite a number of works trips and Sunday school excursions, the Art Treasures Exhibition proved no more successful in attracting the working classes.[21] Perhaps as a result of this, when in 1860 Thomas Fairbairn launched a scheme to raise £100,000 to establish a public art gallery for Manchester there was considerable reluctance, even on the part of many active social reformers, to endorse the use of such a large sum for the provision of art, and after a long and often acrimonious public debate, the scheme was quietly abandoned.[22] Salford did have a public art gallery of sorts, in the collection of art displayed in the picture gallery in Peel Park, established by E.R. Langworthy in 1850,

[17] *MG*, 13 December 1865.
[18] See J. Seed, '"Commerce and the liberal arts": the political economy of art in Manchester, 1775–1860', in Wolff and Seed, *The Culture of Capital*, 45–81.
[19] See recollections of George Jackson, *MX*, 6 June 1856.
[20] See *MX*, 6 July, 16 October 1850, *MG*, 25 September 1850.
[21] Hawthorne, *English Notebooks*, 363; *MG*, 4 August 1857. Supporters were left claiming that despite obvious working class apathy the Exhibition must have done some good, 'AM', *MX*, 27 January 1858.
[22] For the text of the scheme see *MX*, 1 February, 16 March 1860; opponents included, for example, Robert Barnes, *MG*, 26 September 1860; for the collapse of the scheme see *MX*, 25 September 1860.

but Manchester had to wait until 1881 for the opening of its own permanent public art gallery.[23] In the meantime, popular consumption of art took place not at the usually poorly-attended annual exhibitions of the Royal Manchester Institution, but at the stream of travelling panoramas and dioramas which visited the city.

The Peel Park gallery was itself very much a subordinate element of the movement of the mid-1840s which was in the vanguard of the middle classes' attempts to reform recreation, the public parks movement. In the national concern of the early 1840s at the impact of rapid urbanisation and the growth of slums, the establishment of public walks was widely floated as one necessary response.[24] In Manchester the upshot of this concern was a movement, commenced by some of the social reformers, but soon capturing the imagination of all classes, for the establishment of several public parks in the city.[25] The amalgam of sanitary and moral aspirations which underlay the movement is best summed up by the address of a delegate meeting of Manchester operatives in August 1844, which commented that:

> Good air and exercise are as necessary to health as good food. Disease makes its abode in close, dark, pestilent dwellings; the gin palace glitters most temptingly in contrast with an unhealthy habitation, the mind not enough cultivated to appreciate outward nature and healthy sports, finds excitement at the gaming table; and man generally is so constituted that where the means of recreation are absent, vice becomes less odious and crime becomes less criminal...[26]

The opening of the three Manchester parks in the summer of 1846 was the excuse for ritual self-congratulation for the Manchester middle class. The hope was expressed that they would 'provide the greatest variety of rational recreations for the greatest possible number'.[27] Unfortunately, as might have been expected, the parks never came close to fulfilling the grand rhetoric with which they had been launched. After the novelty had departed, use of the parks dwindled considerably. Their distances from the most densely populated working-class districts, restrictions on their opening hours and on conduct within

[23] *MX*, 10 August 1850, *MG*, 7 September 1850.
[24] See Hazel Conway, *People's Parks. The Design and Development of Victorian Parks in Britain*, (1991), 26–36.
[25] For a good account of this movement see T. Wyborn, 'Parks for the People: The Development of Public Parks in Victorian Manchester', *MRHR*, IX (1995), 3-14.
[26] *MSA*, 24 August 1844.
[27] Conway, *People's Parks*, 81.

them, and the reluctance of the municipal councils to provide and maintain specific attractions (especially gymnastic equipment), all lessened their attractiveness.[28]

Nor was it clear that use of the parks had any significant impact on working-class leisure patterns: working-class behaviour outside the parks was quickly replicated inside.[29] The tensions between the park authorities and working-class users are nicely illustrated by a memorandum sent by the keeper of Philips Park to the Manchester Parks Committee in 1865, noting that in fine weather the park was visited by 'a number of exceedingly ill behaved young men whose dress, language and conduct were both disgusting and filthy'. He commented that attempts to discipline such working-class groups were routinely met with reference to the fact that the parks had been provided by the working classes themselves, and that keepers were even at times presented with copies of the inaugural placard which stated that the park 'was Purchased by the People, was made for the People and is given to the People for their protection'.[30] Conversely, other commentators suggested that the limited usage of the parks derived from the imposition of 'severe gentility' on the activities of park-users.[31] It is perhaps significant that it took over ten years of pressure from some of the inhabitants of Hulme and Chorlton to generate sufficient enthusiasm for a public parks movement to be put in train in these townships and then over two years more for the city council to be persuaded to establish a park there. Thomas Wright, the prison reformer, commented in 1854 that it was not unusual to see people coming from the parks and into the pubs, and in 1853 John Layhe concluded that if it was necessary to provide the people with moral outdoor recreation, the parks had failed to do this.[32]

Indeed it is instructive to compare the popularity of the public parks with the appeal of the private parks which were established in the vicinity of the city. By the time the public parks were opened, Manchester boasted two extensive pleasure gardens – modelled in part on London's long-established Vauxhall Gardens – Belle Vue Gardens,

---

[28] Complaints of this sort litter the newspapers from the time of the first establishment of the parks onwards.

[29] 'Anti-Narcotic', *MG*, 28 August 1852, 'Lectore', *MX*, 19 February 1853.

[30] Cited in Conway, *People's Parks*, 206. It is worthwhile noting here the way in which the vocabulary of the 'people' is being mobilised in a justification for resistance to constituted authority.

[31] *MCN*, 20 May 1871.

[32] *PP*, (1854) XIV (367), 123, *MTPAR*, (1853), 15–16.

and Pomona Gardens.[33] These offered not only promenades and gardens, but also menageries, boating lakes and refreshment houses, and during the 1850s and 1860s they developed a wide range of ancillary attractions, including exhibitions by well-known entertainers, brass band concerts, dog shows, and in particular (and at the Belle Vue Gardens especially), enormous and elaborate tableaux, involving huge painted panoramas of famous places and events, set off with spectacular firework displays. During Whit week, when these entertainments were first unveiled, huge crowds were attracted not just from Manchester, but throughout the district. In total 95,000 were estimated to have visited Belle Vue Gardens during the Whit week of 1859.[34]

By this stage, middle-class self-congratulation at the establishment of the public parks had directed attention to the more general provision of recreational activities. The parks having given the people a taste for improving recreations, commented the *Manchester Guardian* in September 1846, 'what shall be done to continue the beneficial influences during the inclement weather and the long dark evenings of winter?'.[35] One common answer, taking its cue from the activities of Joseph Brotherton in Salford, was the establishment of a public library. There were desultory attempts to organise a campaign in favour of a public library from 1845 onwards; in 1849 this finally generated the momentum necessary to sustain public interest. A successful subscription campaign followed and the Free Public Library at Campfield was opened in 1851.[36]

Although the library could be presented as having an educative function, its nature went against the deep-rooted suspicion of undirected and unsystematic reading. Despite the attempt to diffuse some criticism by the provision of a few lectures of advice on worthwhile reading, and the close attention which was paid to the material admitted, the library was always best seen in terms of encouraging a particular pattern of leisure, rather than inculcating certain doctrines. As one of the speakers at the opening of the Hulme branch of the Manchester Free Library commented, 'Reading makes a man thoughtful. It is the want of thought which is the great evil among the masses of the people. Let a man read and think for himself, and he is generally found a good member of

---

[33] For a brief account of the early years of the Belle Vue Gardens see *MG*, 8 August 1849.

[34] *MG*, 21 June 1859.

[35] *MG*, 28 September 1846; cf. *MC*, 16 August 1845, *MX*, 14 August 1852.

[36] W.R. Credland, *The Manchester Public Free Libraries*, (1899).

society'.[37] Or, as a working man commented in 1857, the boon of the library to the working classes was that 'it keeps them at home with their families'.[38]

As with the parks, however, the actual impact of the libraries on working-class leisure patterns was unspectacular. Although statistics of usage were impressive, the adoption of a system of recommendations, by which borrowers had to be endorsed, and the library indemnified against loss, by employers, clergymen or other respectable citizens, certainly operated to exclude many of the casually employed and the lower working class.[39] Limited opening hours (not at all on Sundays, and until nine o'clock only on weekdays), lengthy queues for borrowing books, the inability to obtain books wanted and too short a time allowed for books which were obtained, deficiencies in the catalogue, and the distance of many parts of the town from Campfield (before the opening of branch libraries from the late 1850s), all worked against general use of the library.

It also continued to face competition from other sources. Local neighbourhood libraries, often associated with newsagents or bookshops, often attacked for the low standard of literature which they supplied, continued to thrive in the 1850s.[40] The Free Library still had to compete, even as they declined in the 1860s, with the booksellers, both of the type described by the *Leisure Hour* in 1857, 'a little shop in a little house, doing a little business in a literary way in the midst of the homes of the factory workers', selling 'Seven Dials rubbish...dream books, fortune-telling books, and silly song books, [with] the broadsheet gory and supernatural romance, with pictures of cutting, stabbing and fighting', and the numerous second hand book stalls which congregated in Shudehill and Withy Grove, where, according to Waugh, 'the literary trash of Manchester...congregated'.[41]

Those that turned to the library often did so in search of similar reading material, so that rather than drawing the working classes out of their own culture, the free libraries merely supplemented it. Hence for

---

[37] *Report of the proceedings of a public meeting held..on the occasion of the inauguration of the new building for the Hulme branch*, (1866), 17–18.

[38] 'A Working Man', *MG*, 12 February 1857.

[39] *MX*, 9 October 1852; E. Edwards, 'Report', 11 December 1857, Letterbook of Free Library Committee, Township Records, MCLA.

[40] *MTPAR*, (1851), 45, (1852), 36; cf. W.E.A. Axon, *Handbook of the Public Libraries of Manchester and Salford*, (1877), 142.

[41] *Leisure Hour*, 7 May 1857, Waugh, 'Diary', 23 September 1848; by the 1870s these stalls had migrated to Smithfield, see *City Lantern*, V (1878–79), 319.

every booster of the libraries' successes there was another who was prepared to argue that they produced nothing more than what one critic termed 'mental thinklessness'.[42]

The encouragement of music, and the establishment of the Public Parks and the Free Library did not represent any substantial weakening of the promotion of rational recreation; rather they were conceived as supplementary activities, designed to fill in the gaps left by institutes and lyceums, and to strengthen their appeal by giving them a lighter, more relaxing face. The close relationship is demonstrated repeatedly in contemporary comment. The parks, for example, were presented as an outdoor lecture room in which lessons on geology, botany and other physical sciences could be pleasurably imbibed.[43] Nevertheless, they marked one stage on the journey towards the re-ordering of the priorities of rationality and recreation which becomes visible by the start of the 1860s.

The significance of developments in the 1850s was that they involved firstly internal alterations in the operation of the institutes, and then their abandonment in favour of the quite different ethos of the working men's clubs. An early indication of the former was the greater use of readings. Recitations and occasional readings by well-known itinerants such as Samuel Butler and Charles Kemble had been popular in the 1840s, but they had mostly been seen as money raising ventures and priced beyond working-class means. Reading lengthy extracts was also sometimes a feature of literary lectures. In the 1850s, however, a deliberate attempt was made, led by David Chadwick, Salford borough treasurer and a prominent social reformer, to encourage readings as an alternative to letting the working classes be 'repelled by dry moral platitudes, propounded in a still drier manner'.[44] A series of readings was presented by Salford Mechanics' Institute, and their popularity encouraged attempts to spread the model to other associations.[45]

---

[42] *Freelance*, XI (1876), 149, cf. *ibid*, 164,176–7; compare with the comment in 1879 of J. Taylor Kay, one of the assistant librarians, that the reading of novels obtained from the libraries and elsewhere had become 'a disease, a dissipation', H.R. Tedder and C.E. Thomas, eds, *Transactions and Proceedings of the Second Annual Meeting of the Library Association, 1879*, (1880), 45.

[43] Comments of John Watts, *MSA*, 28 September 1844.

[44] 'Nerva', *MG*, 22 September 1856; cf. 'Humanitas', *MG*, 15 September 1856; *MG*, 30 October 1856. For the wider popularity of penny readings in this period see V. Neuberg, *Popular Literature. A History and Guide*, (1977), 242–6, Meller, *Leisure and the Changing City*, 125–36.

[45] For example, the Angel Meadow WMA, *MG*, 12 November 1856.

Although attempts to provide overall co-ordination for this movement predictably came to nothing, penny readings became increasingly common in the 1860s. The initial intention of those who had promoted readings was that they should present working men with selections from works of 'taste and value'; in fact, working-class audiences were as little attracted to well-meaning reformers reading approved extracts to them as they had been to the same individuals attempting to lecture them, and it was only with the addition of music and singing, the removal of the 'great and the good', and the creation of a free and easy atmosphere, that penny readings proved successful.[46] What emerged was a specific recitation literature of working-class humour mingled with popular songs, and an atmosphere, captured in Brierley's 'The Goose Grove Penny Readings', which owed more to the music hall than the lecture hall.[47]

A similar process can be observed in respect to physical recreation, once again an occasional feature of the middle-class associations of the 1830s and 1840s, and acknowledged by the provision of outdoor gymnasia and games areas in the public parks, and which quickly became one of the necessary activities of any successful appeal to working men. In the mid-50s the cricket sections of congregational young men's associations were already threatening to swallow up their parent societies. In 1858 it was the introduction of games, particularly cricket, into the expiring St George's Church Mutual Improvement Society, which enabled it to grow into the successful 'Hulme Athenaeum'.[48] By 1859 the potential of physical recreations to revitalise the dwindling appeal of the city's literary institutions was being mooted publicly, and in the 1860s cricket, fencing, and increasingly football clubs and gymnasia, were becoming a necessary part of the offerings not only of clubs and institutes, but even of ragged schools.[49]

[46] See *Sphinx*, I (1868), 81–2.

[47] Ben Brierley, *Tales and Sketches of Lancashire Life*, (1863); 'R. Low Spence', *Sphinx*, I (1868), 96, *ibid*, III (1870), 140, 399. For examples of this literature see Joseph Cooper, *The Temperance Reciter*, (1856).

[48] *MX*, 21 January 1861. Similarly, the St Peter's Mutual Improvement Society found in 1857 that when it attempted to separate itself from an associated cricket club, the result was very nearly the demise of the association, and the club was rapidly brought back again, 'Minutes', 18 December 1857 to 26 April 1858, German Street School Papers, M12/8/1, MCLA.

[49] 'Patricus', *MX*, 21 February 1859; see the case of the Pendleton Mechanics' Institute, *SWN*, 12 March 1864, and for example the Heyrod Street Ragged School, *MG*, 29 November 1864.

Although by the 1860s readings had become interchangeable with lectures in most working-class associations, it is significant that the initial inspiration came from outside an associational structure which was still dominated largely by the institute model, and significant too that they were taken up first by the working men's associations. By the mid-1850s it was becoming increasingly apparent to those with intimate contact with the working classes that the weaknesses of the institute model could only be overcome by a fundamental change of emphasis. In Manchester the lead was taken by Rev. E.B. Chalmers, incumbent of St Matthias', Salford. In 1858 Chalmers took two adjoining cottages in his parish and established a working men's club. Explaining his philosophy in 1859, Chalmers argued that the old approach, '"cram them with education, stuff them with science" will not answer. The recipe reminds me of the celebrated directions of the cookery book "first *catch* your hare, then kill him". You cannot drive the labouring man to learning and to classes; *in very few instances* can you allure him'. Instead, Chalmers argued it was necessary to substitute the pub as the model which, with certain alterations, it was vital to follow: '...we must afford [working men] all the advantages of "the public" without its dangers – a place of resort where he shall be *as unconstrained*, where he can find his cheerful company, read his newspaper, and talk his politics'.[50]

The institutes were of little use for this. T.W. Marriott, another Anglican cleric who shared Chalmers' ideas, summed up the typical institute a year later as possessing no open fire, prohibiting smoking, providing no refreshments, and boasting an uncarpeted floor and uninviting seats 'of hard bare wood – an economical wood of peculiar hardness which no amount of use can wear out'.[51] Hence the attentions of middle-class reformers were switched to encouraging the formation of clubs and institutes, with sufficient success for Manchester to become a major centre of the national working men's clubs movement of which Henry Solly took the lead.[52] Working men's clubs

[50] Chalmers, *The Parson*, 9, 10 (emphasis in original).

[51] Marriott, *Some Real Wants*, 12–13.

[52] Solly's activities are fully covered in the pages of the *Occasional Papers of the Working Men's Club and Institute Union*, (1863–72). There are various studies of the movement, including L. Marlow, 'The working men's club movement 1862–1912: a study of the evolution of a working class institution', (PhD thesis, Warwick University, 1982), R. Price, 'The working mens' club movement and Victorian Social Reform Ideology', *Victorian Studies*, XV,2 (1971). For the movement in Manchester, see M. Harrison, 'Social Reform in Late Victorian and Edwardian Manchester with special

spread gradually throughout the Manchester district during the 1860s, as the middle classes rallied to the campaigns of Chalmers and Solly, and the working classes adapted their institutions in search of financial support and assistance. By 1865 there were at least eleven such clubs, the largest of which, St Matthias, was obtaining up to a thousand subscribers in the course of a year.

A survey of these institutions taken by Solly reveals the distance which had been travelled, even from the lyceums of the 1840s. The unifying feature of the clubs was their newsrooms, to which virtually all added a smoking room. Eight of the eleven sold refreshments. However, while five had some kind of a gymnasium, only six had libraries, and only three provided any kind of educational classes. By 1867 the range of games played included quoits, dominoes (much to the chagrin of some who thought it bound to lead to gambling),[53] and bagatelle, and according to more than half the secretaries, it was the newspapers and games which proved the main attraction.[54]

Where in the past the members of such institutions had been talked at from the lecturer's platform, lectures were now overshadowed by frequent and popular discussions, which provided instead a platform for working-class members to voice their own opinions. In the aftermath of the 1867 Reform Act, the club movement took on a distinctly political tone, with the establishment of numerous political ward clubs by both Conservatives and Liberals.[55] However, the return of political hectoring and the emphasis on party conflict only brought renewed signs of working-class resentment.[56] In consequence, instead of providing institutions 'to which', as Solly had hoped, 'the middle and upper classes might come...to bring their culture and refinement to bear upon the workmen and their wives', it was once again being recognised by the later 1870s that the clubs had largely to be accepted on the terms of their members, and welcomed simply as being better than constant resort to the pub.[57]

reference to T.C. Horsfall', (PhD thesis, University of Manchester, 1987), 212–40.
[53] *MCN*, 20 April 1867.
[54] *MX*, 31 October 1865; for at least one expression of concern at the wholesale replacement of the institute model with the working men's club model, see Lamb, *Free Thoughts*, I, 371.
[55] See J. Garrard, 'Parties, members and voters after 1867: a local study', *Historical Journal*, 20,1 (1977), 145–63.
[56] *MCN*, 20 January 1872, *The Critic* (Manchester), II (1872), 85.
[57] *MX*, 6 January 1865.

Thrift and self-help

The pub remained unchallenged in the demonology of the middle-class reformers because it epitomised working-class improvidence and rejection of respectability. The promotion of frugal, moral and sober habits was integral to moral imperialism from the beginning of the 1830s. Indeed, the first major city-wide response to the social cleavage and working-class unrest in the period after 1832, the District Provident Society, was explicitly designed to promote thrift and sobriety. Founded in 1832 by an interdenominational alliance ranging from high churchmen to unitarians, the DPS aimed to use domestic visitation by volunteers to bridge the social divide between rich and poor, save the working classes from the 'the guidance of unprincipled demagogues', and inculcate appropriate domestic virtues.[58] Unfortunately, the society never attracted sufficient visitors to move beyond the more prosperous districts such as Pendleton into larger working-class enclaves where middle-class inhabitants were few, and although the society's visiting continued into the 1850s, it was very soon peripheral to the main business of the society, which came to be the regulation of charity.[59]

Nevertheless, the ideal of the promotion of provident habits by domestic visitation was not abandoned. From the early 1830s temperance societies in Manchester not only organised regular visitation to society members, but also attempted to develop aggressive missionary activities, from the distribution of temperance placards and pamphlets outside pubs to the domestic visitation of drunkards.[60] By the early 1850s the Manchester and Salford Temperance Society employed two full-time temperance missionaries whose duties included addressing temperance meetings and visiting drunkards in their homes.[61] By 1860 there was even a separate Salford Temperance Missions Society, sponsoring visitation and tract distribution.[62] The missionaries of the Manchester City Mission and other parochial visitors also devoted a considerable amount of their time to the

[58] *MC*, 23 March 1833. For a brief history of the DPS see H.C. Irvine, *The Old D.P.S.*, (1933).
[59] District Provident Society, *Annual Report*, (1834–67), *passim*.
[60] *WMC*, 21 December 1833, *Preston Temperance Journal*, March 1834, July 1835.
[61] Manchester and Salford Temperance Society, *Annual Report*, (1853–54), 4, 9–14.
[62] *SWN*, 20 October 1860.

discouragement of profligacy and drunkenness.[63] Briefly in the early 1850s the Manchester and Salford Sanitary Association, and then more permanently from 1862, the Ladies Sanitary Association, visited the poor in an attempt to improve standards of domestic sanitation and those areas, particularly domestic management and expenditure patterns, which played a critical part in them.[64] By the 1860s scattered working-class adoption of such missionary activities is visible. The best example is the Pendleton Working People's Association, governed principally by working men from various local congregations, which in the mid-1860s developed both working men's club type activities and a band of 120 distributors, circulating tracts on religion, temperance and household economy to over three thousand houses in Pendleton.[65]

Considerable effort was also directed towards the provision of practical advice from the lecture platform. The success of the Sanitary Association lectures in the mid-1850s on various aspects of 'sanitary science' (the thrust of which was epitomised by one 1858 lecture, 'How to preserve Health and secure Wealth') encouraged the proffering of a welter of practical advice to working men and women.[66] This propaganda was accompanied by increasing attention to the support of the practical institutions of self-help, including clothing clubs, sewing classes, cooking depots, penny banks, temperance associations, bands of hope, and sick and burial societies.

The enthusiasm generated for preliminary savings or penny banks towards the end of the period provides an indication of the re-orientation of moral imperialism towards the low-level reform of manners. The encouragement of savings was in the 1840s very much the preserve of the DPS: its visitors were by this stage little more than deposit collectors, and as they dwindled the society introduced savings depots, usually associated with churches or Sunday schools.[67] The 1850s also saw scattered attempts to encourage savings through the establishment of independent institutions, such as the Hulme Preliminary Savings Bank (1853), or the annexation of savings banks to existing institutions.[68] There were, however, only five DPS depots

---

[63] *The Social and Physical Influence of the Mission*, [1856], in 266M21, MCL.
[64] For the Sanitary Association see its *Annual Reports*, (1853–70), *passim*; for the establishment of the Ladies Sanitary Association see *MX*, 1 November 1862.
[65] *SWN*, 23 May 1863, 23 April 1864, 27 January, 17 March 1866.
[66] Manchester and Salford Sanitary Association Papers, M126/5/1/106, MCLA; see above page 146.
[67] District Provident Society, *Annual Report*, (1846–48), 7–8, *Annual Report*, (1856), 6.
[68] *MG*, 27 February 1862, *MSp*, 13 April 1850, *MX*, 8 June 1850. For a general history

in 1856, and little sign of widespread activity elsewhere. The ensuing few years changed all this. Both the workmen's clubs and the ragged schools movements enthusiastically embraced the encouragement of provident institutions, particularly penny banks. Chalmers saw his club as a focus 'clustering around' which would be 'several organisations for the self-help of the working men and their families', and many of the subsequent clubs followed his lead.[69] Richard Johnson, the driving force behind the local Ragged School union, was even more enthusiastic, and by 1867 a penny bank was an integral element of ragged school work.[70] They were also being attached increasingly to Sunday Schools, and the number of DPS branch depots had jumped to seventeen by 1866.[71] Despite this effort, it is clear that the spread of such institutions in Manchester was slow. By 1870 there were only about 20 penny banks in Manchester officially connected to the Manchester and Salford Savings Bank, and the city was very much lagging behind other industrial cities in this regard.[72]

In many respects, if the penny banks provide an index of increasing effort, it was the middle-class-inspired sick and burial societies and temperance associations that remained at the heart of attempts to reform styles of life, because they both confronted directly the pub and the beerhouse, the focal institutions of unrespectable working-class culture. They are also more revealing because unlike the general self-help advice and associations considered hitherto (in which the working classes could obtain advice without being unduly challenged), in these cases the conflict was overt and middle-class success depended more fundamentally on the overthrowing of established cultural practices. In both cases, once the rhetoric is penetrated, what emerges is an area of culture in which the contradictory tendencies of middle-class and working-class visions produced a practice in which middle-class aspirations were crucially distorted.

In the case of friendly societies[73] the difficulties of the middle class derived from the firmly established presence, by the 1830s, of a group

of such efforts see P. Johnson, 'Credit and Thrift', in J. Winter, ed., *The Working Class in Modern British History*, (1983), 147–70.

[69] *Occasional Papers of the Working Men's Club and Institute Union*, (March 1863), 4.
[70] 'Richard Johnson', *MG*, 13 August 1862, *MG*, 21 April 1864.
[71] District Provident Society, *Annual Report*, (1866). 4.
[72] See later comments of Richard Haworth, *MCN*, 26 April 1879.
[73] Taken in the widest sense to include sick and funeral societies, as well as life assurance associations.

of institutions which had emerged from the uncertainties of working-class life which made some form of health and/or unemployment insurance highly desirable, and were impregnated with working-class notions of dignity and decency. The numerical strength of the various kinds of societies in the mid-century is difficult to gauge, but it was clearly substantial. In the Manchester district in 1848–49 there were an estimated 74 lodges and 6800 paid up members of the Manchester Unity of Oddfellows and 6000 members of the National Independent Order of Oddfellows, merely two orders among many, including Druids, Foresters, Shepherds, Gardeners.[74] In the 1860s, in addition to the large orders there were 38 simple friendly societies in Manchester with nearly 17,000 members.[75] In 1835 the *Manchester Courier* gave a figure of 60,000 members of burial societies in Manchester, and by the mid-50s this figure exceeded 100,000.[76]

For middle-class reformers the problem was that these were mostly not merely financial but also social institutions. The pervasive influence of the friendly societies proper, with their complicated hierarchies of officers and strange and mysterious rituals, has been demonstrated by P.H.J. Gosden.[77] The ceremonial culture of the burial societies was much less elaborate, but nevertheless, until the 1860s, when collecting societies became increasingly popular, most burial societies had quarterly or annual general meetings at which the books were 'audited'. In both cases meetings commonly took place in pubs, and drink was often purchased from the societies' funds.

The middle-class response to this activity was deeply ambivalent.[78] As institutions of working-class thrift, supporting working-class self-reliance, and reducing the burden on the machinery of the poor law or charitable institutions, they might be welcomed and supported. Unfortunately, the social life which developed around them, which seemed, in middle-class eyes, to be a wasteful profligacy perverting the original beneficial object, meant that they could not be so easily accepted. They were attacked as being actuarially unsound, even after the considerable efforts which the larger friendly societies made to improve their situation in the 1850s and 1860s. The friendly societies also prompted considerable distaste at their paraphernalia, ritual and

[74] *MX*, 30 September 1848, 21 November 1849.
[75] *MX*, 5 November 1864.
[76] *MC*, 10 January 1835, *MX*, 29 April 1854.
[77] P.H.J. Gosden, *The Friendly Societies in England, 1815–75*, (1961).
[78] Johnson, 'Credit and Thrift', 125.

bands, all considered to be a waste of money, if not a dubious means of lining the pockets of the leading officers.[79] Burial societies, meanwhile, were attacked because of middle-class distaste for the rituals of working-class funerals, with their elaborate wakes, involving a good deal of eating and drinking.[80]

In both cases, middle-class commentators were uneasy at the essentially working-class origins of the promoters and managers of such societies: although this was usually couched in terms of doubts as to the honesty of such promoters, the core of the attack, well illustrated in an editorial assault in 1860, was that the typical promoter was 'a man of no social standing'.[81] But above all, friendly and burial societies alike were attacked because they met almost entirely in public houses and were, because of this, enmeshed in the culture of drink which was the focus of so much middle-class reforming zeal.

Several avenues of reform were explored. The most prevalent was the establishment of rival, middle class patronised, sick and burial societies – on what were described as 'correct principles' – which usually included management vested in a nominated committee, meetings held, where at all, in school and chapel rooms rather than pubs, and clientele often drawn specifically from existing groups, such as Sunday school scholars.[82] The earliest Sunday school burial and sick society in Manchester probably dated from 1818, and although they were far from universal in the 1840s, the influence of bodies such as the Christian Mutual Provident Society, which co-ordinated their spread from the mid-1840s, meant that by 1854 it was possible to claim that they were attached to virtually every Sunday school in Manchester.[83] The problem was that these societies often remained very small, and found it difficult to compete with the more popular pub-based sick and burial societies, as the comparative sizes of the societies giving evidence to the 1872 Royal Commission makes clear.[84]

[79] *MX*, 30 March 1853.
[80] For example, Rev. Joseph Bardsley comments on the 'gigantic evil' of Sunday funerals, and the associated wakes, *MCMM*, December 1861, 5–9.
[81] *MX*, 17 March 1860.
[82] Comments of Dr Bardsley, *MC*, 8 February 1834; cf. W.J. Kidd, *MC*, 14 May 1836.
[83] For the Christian Mutual Provident Association see *MG*, 18 December 1847, *MX*, 23 September 1848, *PP*, (1854) VII (412), 85.
[84] See the comparative sizes of the public house and non-public house societies detailed in the evidence to the Royal Commission on Friendly Societies, *PP*, (1872) XXVI [514–I], 423–503.

A second strategy was the encouragement of national assurance societies, again usually under respectable patronage and paying particular care to the actuarial principles on which they operated. From the late 1840s considerable platform propaganda was devoted to attacking traditional working-class provident institutions and promoting societies such as J.R. Beard's Equitable Provident Association. Persistent attacks of this nature elicited indignant rebuttals, particularly from the leaders of the friendly societies proper, and the difficulties of some of the assurance societies which were established, such as the European Provident Association, more than balanced the extensive coverage given in the local press to defalcations of officers from working-class friendly societies.[85]

The third strategy was to encourage existing friendly societies to remove their meetings from the pubs. Here again, the evidence suggests an almost total lack of success: when David Chadwick surveyed the friendly societies of Manchester and Salford in 1860, he found that out of 105 courts of the Oddfellows and Foresters, only four did not meet in pubs, three using temperance hotels (where there was the potential for non-alcoholic refreshment) and only one a schoolroom.[86] Attempts to move established societies from pubs to schoolrooms were often fiercely resisted by the members.[87]

The prevalence of provident institutions does not indicate any great middle-class influence. Instead, they represented part of a distinct working-class culture of mutual aid, ranging from the kind of informal neighbourhood mutualism recognised by the more perceptive middle-class observers to the benefit functions of the craft unions. Not only did this sustain a more collectivist ethos than bourgeois notions of self-help, but it was also associated with practices (including pawnshops, shop credit and the regulatory functions of the trade unions) which were completely alien to them. Although by the 1860s it has been suggested that some of this culture was being eroded by the emergence of the national collecting societies, there is little sign in Manchester before 1867 that any significant modification of the patterns of working-class providence had been achieved.[88]

[85] Comments of Charles Hardwick in *Country Words*, (1866–67), 7–9. For the European see *European Assurance Society, Manchester Meeting, October 4th 1869*, [1869].
[86] *PP*, (1860) XII (455), 329.
[87] *PP*, (1872) XXVI [514–I], 447.
[88] Gosden, *The Friendly Societies in England*, 77–142.

Despite a contrasting history, the implications of the campaign for temperance are similar. Temperance, like the friendly societies, was originally a working-class movement. In the 1830s, the early temperance organisations in Manchester, as elsewhere, were generally greeted with suspicion by the middle class, concerned at their implication for religious activity and about the strength of grass-roots working-class control.[89] Partly as a result, although by 1839 the Manchester Total Abstinence Society had gained middle-class (including Anglican) endorsement, elite control over temperance organisations remained fragile. In the 1830s and 1840s there was a strong radical undercurrent to working-class temperance activity, and it would seem that by the mid-1840s initial middle-class attempts to establish a strong central authority over the various local temperance societies had foundered.[90] The temperance movement was thus left in the hands of largely working-class advocates, and the operations of the temperance halls were regarded with some suspicion.[91]

The upshot was determined effort between 1847 and 1851, led by Liberals such as Archibald Prentice, to counter the influence of the temperance advocates, reassert some measure of discipline with reference to Sunday operations and political content, and improve the standing of the temperance movement.[92] The success of these activities is demonstrated both by the unprecedented willingness of the religious authorities to provide schoolrooms and chapels as venues for temperance meetings, and by the outmigration of some of the more radical elements, alienated by what was seen as the 'cant and bigotry' of 'Esquires and Reverends'.[93] Nevertheless there was no firm central control over the individual societies or the temperance advocates, and the formation of the United Kingdom Alliance in 1853 further divided attention between the legislative campaign and the furtherance of active temperance. In consequence, only finally in the 1860s, largely through

---

[89] *Preston Temperance Journal*, January 1834, August 1835, 'Laicus', *MC*, 5 September 1840; see B. Harrison, *Drink and the Victorians,* (1971), esp. 137–44, and L.L. Shiman, *The Crusade Against Drink in Victorian England*, (1988), 23–7.

[90] For the tension within Manchester temperance, see the *Manchester and Salford Temperance Journal*, (1836); while official temperance remained aloof from chartism, the radicals established their own associations, such as the Universal Suffrage Total Abstinence Association, see 'Laicus', *MC*, 5 September 1840.

[91] 'Spec', *MSp*, 17 November 1849, 'Qui Vive', *MC*, 14 February 1849; plus comments of Lee, *A plea for the English operatives*, 43–5.

[92] *MC*, 25 March 1848, *MX*, 10 May 1851, 8 May 1852, and the *MSTR*, (1849–50).

[93] *MX*, 7 August 1850; 'Address' of the Age of Reason Total Abstinence Society, overtly committed to free speech and political discussion, *NS*, 10 May 1851.

the steady strengthening of its ties with religious institutions, did the temperance movement come under middle-class control.[94]

Until the mid-1850s the temperance movement was only uncomfortably hitched to middle-class moral imperialism. In the 1830s and 1840s temperance associations were often parts of the wider working-class search for social and political amelioration.[95] They encouraged a version of working-class self-reliance which was often positively hostile to middle-class control: during the chartist period, one of the commonly reiterated objections to the movement was its fanaticism and unwillingness to listen to middle-class calls for moderation, and the fact that, as one critic put it, 'what is gained in society in outward morality, is too often lost or exchanged for pride'.[96] In this respect it is significant that it appears that as ministerial control over the temperance movement was tightened in the early 1860s, so there was a shift in clientele, away from working-class adult men, and towards children and Sunday school scholars.[97]

It is perhaps merely coincidental that, judging by the evidence of drunkenness statistics, it is just at this time that drunkenness began to expand rapidly in Manchester.[98] Nevertheless, there can be little doubt that temperance propaganda had only a marginal impact on working-class leisure patterns in mid-nineteenth century Manchester. The example of those individuals who had used temperance as a means of social mobility was certainly a powerful (and much used) one, and, along with the kind of missionary activity engaged in both by other organisations, and the temperance societies themselves, it brought large numbers of the working classes into the temperance movement. But the movement was not well suited to the effective maintenance and support of converts. Despite the attempts to build up alternative temperance recreations centred on the temperance halls, including lecture meetings, recitations etc., the movement never really succeeded in establishing a recreational centre to rival the pub.[99] Layhe regretfully conceded that the influence of anti-drink campaigns, faced with the ever-present

[94] See, for example, the account of Rusholme Total Abstinence Society, *MG*, 14 November 1861; cf. *LL*, 10 June 1865.
[95] Shaw, *Replies*, 20.
[96] 'Ithuriel', *MC*, 31 October 1840.
[97] 'Screw Tator', *LL*, 28 May 1864.
[98] For figures and various interpretations of them, see evidence of Palin, Higson and Whitworth, *PP*, (1877), 6–11, 160–87,
[99] *LL*, 11 February 1865.

temptation which existed, was almost always temporary, and temperance advocacy always contained an intolerant streak which was reluctant to look sympathetically on such evidence of weakness.[100] '[A]fter many years of successful advocacy of total abstinence', regretted Henry Pitman in 1866, 'it was found that thousands of drunkards who had taken the pledge, and with every desire to keep it, were tempted to break their pledge again and again'.[101]

The assault on working-class culture

It is significant that by the late 1850s, middle-class enthusiasms for the temperance cause were being absorbed into the campaigns, most prominently of the United Kingdom Alliance, for some kind of legal prohibition of alcohol. In parallel fashion, attempts to draw the working classes to approved friendly societies were supplemented both by a steadily enlarging, though still minimal, legal regulation and by more direct attempts, such as the Hackney Coachmen's Lord's Day Observance Society, established in 1860 with the ulterior motive of suppressing what one of its promoters described as the 'gigantic evil' of Sunday funerals and the associated wakes, to suppress some of the practices with which rival working-class societies were associated.[102] In the cases both of recreation and of providence, middle-class moral imperialism had relied primarily on attraction and conversion to reform working-class practices. There always remained, however, a concurrent strand of activity which aimed at obtaining the direct repudiation of large elements of working-class culture, by the weight of social censure where possible, and by legal proscription where not.

The assault on working-class culture was of course integral to much of the activity of the religious bodies and the didactic institutions, although in many cases this was implicit rather than explicit, their focus being on the superiority of their activities rather than on the illegitimacy of existing working-class culture. The pulpit and the platform were clearly mobilised extensively to propagate middle-class perceptions of correct lifestyles. Unfortunately, as has been suggested, this kind of propaganda was of little use while that same culture acted as an

[100] *MTPAR*, (1844), 15; cf. 'James Cowburn', *SWN*, 14 July 1860.
[101] 'Henry Pitman', *SWN*, 7 July 1866.
[102] *MCMM*, December 1861, 5–9.

effective barrier between the minister or lecturer and the desired audience. Hence the perceived need for strategies of more direct confrontation.

Once again, missionary organisations presented particular advantages in this respect, requiring no prior co-operation on the part of the working classes. Particularly in the case of the Manchester City Mission the religious brief of the missionaries was interpreted sufficiently broadly to encompass a sustained attack on working-class culture. From the outset MCM missionaries targeted the annual fairs, such as Knott Mill fair, held in Manchester and Salford, the wakes, and the races while they were still being held on Kersal Moor, accosting the crowds which flocked to them, and distributing papers which urged them to shun such entertainments, often (as in the case of the fairs) not because they were intrinsically evil, but because they amounted to a waste of time which could be more profitably spent in mental and religious self-improvement.[103]

Indeed, what is striking about the domestic missionaries in general is the immoderate antipathy which they displayed towards working-class culture. Styles of life and patterns of belief were not so much gently questioned as peremptorily dismissed. The working classes were told that hobbies such as pigeon-fancying were merely a waste of time and a temptation to desecrate the sabbath, and should be abandoned.[104] The reading of non-religious books or newspapers on Sundays was loudly condemned, as was performing even the simplest of household duties, a constant source of resentment given the obvious way the wealthy relied on the labour of servants or cab-drivers on the same day.[105] So deep did the hostility run that the independent missionary James Bembridge could solemnly inform one man he visited who happened to earn a little money making dominoes, that this was a sin.[106] The extent of the missionaries' rejection of working-class culture in its entirety is perhaps epitomised by the writings of Alfred Alsop, a missionary in the Deansgate area from the late 1860s.[107]

---

[103] Whit week was the traditional time for working-class wakes etc., and thus the centre of such activities by the missionaries, see *MCMM*, July (1858), 4–5.

[104] *MCMM*, October 1857, 26.

[105] For example, *MCMM*, May 1849, 19, *MCMAR*, (1848), 26, which condemns washing and mending clothes on Sunday.

[106] Bembridge, 'Journal', 22 September 1845, MCLA.

[107] In particular, A. Alsop, *Ten Years in the Slums*, (1879), *passim*.

The activities of the missionaries both reflected and contributed to the numerous organised assaults on popular culture. The symbiosis is exemplified by the campaigns against Owenism in the 1830s and 1840s. From its foundation one of the prominent roles of the MCM was to preach against socialism, particularly outside the Hall of Science, after it was erected in 1840.[108] Their lack of success prompted the formation by several prominent Anglican clergy of the 'Anti-Socialist Committee' which attempted to use Napoleonic period anti-lecturing statutes and blasphemy laws to suppress socialism, a strategy which backfired spectacularly when the socialists riposted with a series of prosecutions of their own.[109] The response of the Stowellites was to revert to less controversial channels, establishing, with the co-operation of missionaries such as Bembridge, the Association for Counteracting Infidelity, which convened anti-socialist lectures and co-ordinated other anti-socialist campaigns, including participation in more general campaigns to mobilise the force of the state against socialist activity.[110]

The anti-Owenite campaigns were intense but transient. More persistent, and thus ultimately more revealing, was the undercurrent of sabbatarianism which surfaced periodically. Once again it would be possible to identify various institutional foci of sabbatarianism, including the Manchester Auxiliary of the London Society for the Better Observance of the Sabbath established in 1834, and operating intermittently throughout the period,[111] but the significance of the sabbatarian influence ran more deeply, and influenced the full range of middle-class patronage, leadership and management of cultural life. Campaigns in the 1830s ensured that all middle-class inspired working-class associations, with the significant and controversial exception of the Lyceums, were kept closed on Sundays; in the late 1840s, a similar constraint was placed on the Free Public Library, and considerable effort was focused on restraining the growth of Sunday cheap trips, and on closing the loophole which had allowed the parks to remain open. Although it could not close them, middle-class pressure, mobilised in

---

[108] *NMW*, IX (1841), 295.

[109] For the Anti-Socialist Committee see Maude to Normanby, 7 April 1840, HO44/35/nf, plus enclosures; also *NMW*, VIII (1840), 17–18, 29, 121, 156.

[110] Bembridge, 'Journal', 5 November, 10 December 1842, 4 February 1843, MCLA; *MSA*, 21 January 1843.

[111] *MC*, 22 February 1834, 30 September 1848.

this case through the Sunday schools, successfully suppressed Sunday band music in the parks in 1856.[112]

By the 1850s, sabbatarian pressure tended to be subsumed in the broader campaigns against the Sunday opening of the pub, and hence into the coercive branch of the temperance movement. Given the importance of the pub to working-class culture, it is not surprising that it attracted the attention of sabbatarians early. By the start of the 1840s pressure was already building for the regulation of the Sunday operation of pub music salons.[113] With the formation in 1850 of the Association for the Better Regulation of Public Houses, and then the increasing attention given by the Manchester and Salford Temperance Society to the legal control of Sunday drinking, this juncture was gradually strengthened.[114] Nevertheless, while the strategy of initiating the attack on the pub by obtaining complete Sunday closing remained popular, the success of the prohibitionist United Kingdom Alliance demonstrates the rapid shift of the movement to a much broader coercive approach. Controversial and hence ultimately unsuccessful as this more extreme policy was, the shift in focus of the temperance movement, both locally and nationally, did result in the tightening of magisterial control on public houses, and in the whittling down of beerhouse freedoms, both in the matter of opening hours, and in their connections with various working-class recreations.[115]

At the same time, by the 1860s the glance of the sabbatarians had also come to rest on the extent to which the weekly rhythm of working-class life involved the use of Sunday as a shopping day, the result being a determined campaign to enforce local by-laws which enabled the civic authorities to demand the closure of shops on Sunday, a campaign which was ultimately largely successful.[116] This case reminds us that after the establishment of the corporations, local by-laws established by local improvement acts provided a potentially highly effective mechanism of control of working-class culture. During the 1840s and 1850s the corporation acquired various powers of this sort, including the ability to regulate lodging houses, to enforce various sanitary

---

[112] Redford, *Local Government in Manchester*, II, 220-1.

[113] See comments of Stowell, *MC*, 18 February 1843.

[114] Manchester and Salford Association for the Better Regulation of Public Houses, *Annual Reports*, (1851-52); *MX*, 22 October 1851; Manchester and Salford Executive Council of Total Abstinence Societies, *Annual Report*, (1852-53), 11-12.

[115] Harrison, *Drink and the Victorians*, 247-61.

[116] WCM, 20 June 1861, *MG*, 17 July 1861.

standards, and to control the streets and the activities which went on within them, including playing and selling. Taken en masse, these powers represented a considerable authority over the working classes, but although the potential for control was great, it was never exploited to the full in mid-nineteenth century Manchester. Questions of coercion and prohibition could still touch the raw nerve of middle-class laissez-fairism. Alignments shifted, and there was no clear divide between the supporters of coercion and the supporters of conversion, but on each issue there was clearly divided opinion as to the policy and efficacy of coercion. In consequence the emergence of effective legal restraints was often either retarded or prevented completely.

In the final analysis, moreover, as the often strained relations between the civic authorities and the temperance movements suggest, the efficacy of such measures was determined by the enforcement mechanisms available to the civic elite, and in particular, of the police, who in some respects replicated the role of the missionaries, and were perceived, as Robert Storch has demonstrated, as part of the structure of moral control.[117] In the 1830s the magistrates and middle-class leaders realised that the police force available to them was insufficient for the job of restraining the more violent excesses of working-class life, and the desirability of improving the police was one of the justifications used by those in favour of incorporation in 1837. The threat the working classes perceived in a more efficient police was demonstrated by the frequency of attacks on constables in the early years of the new borough force which was established in 1839.[118] The willingness of some members of the working classes to take advantage of the reduced effectiveness of the police during the Manchester police strike of 1853 to pelt with stones or attack the police who remained on the beat suggests that this hostility persisted well beyond the mid-century.[119]

Moreover, except in the periods of particular chartist unrest, it is clear that the police were used to tighten the civil authorities' control of the streets and open spaces of the city, attempting to eradicate gambling, the playing of various traditional games, and even merely the

[117] Storch, 'Policeman as Domestic Missionary', 481–509, C. Steedman, *Policing the Victorian Community: The Formation of English Provincial Police Forces, 1856–80*, (1984), 53–64.
[118] S.J. Davies, 'Classes and the Police in Manchester, 1829–1880', in Kidd and Roberts, eds, *City, Class and Culture*, 26–47.
[119] *MG*, 6 July 1853.

assembly of miscellaneous crowds.[120] The weight of police presence is suggested by the periodic court cases involving over-zealous police activity, particularly in moving people on during the evenings.[121] During the 1840s the police also came to be used increasingly as the enforcement arm of various municipal regulations concerning issues such as the regulation of pubs and lodging houses, and the control of street obstructions, which also brought them into conflict with elements of working-class culture.[122] For instance, having done much to drive rough sports such as rat-baiting or cock-fighting out of the public arena and into pubs and beerhouses, the police were particularly active in attempting to suppress these organised elements of 'rough' leisure.[123]

The ultimate efficacy of the police as moulders of working-class culture is difficult to gauge. Those elements of street culture which proved most amenable to control were the host of marginal street hawkers and entertainers. Municipal prohibition, licensing and regulation, with the twin aims of clearing the thoroughfares and protecting the ratepaying shopkeepers, quite quickly pushed many of these figures from the streets. In the face of council hostility, Manchester never maintained a strong sub-society of hawkers and street sellers in the same way that Mayhew's London did.[124] Likewise, the evidence that rough sports tended to migrate indoors or beyond the city boundaries in the 1840s and 1850s suggests that within the borough policing was relatively effective.

Nevertheless, there were difficulties, as the endemic complaints of the more respectable citizenry demonstrated.[125] Centrally, the police were never sufficiently numerous to operate effectively as moulders of working-class culture. From the beginnings the Manchester borough police force was required to operate with fewer numbers per head of population than those in most other large centres of population, and as the population continued to expand, the size of the force struggled to keep pace.[126] One consequence was that beats were extended: in 1845

[120] *MSA*, 3 October 1840, WCM, 20 July 1848. In 1853 W.P. Roberts accused the police of being in the habit of breaking up innocent fun in the streets, beating the people etc., *MX*, 11 May 1853.
[121] 'Henry Johnson', *MX*, 18 May 1853, 'William Spreckley', *MX*, 29 September, 2 October 1863.
[122] For example, WCM, 25 July 1844.
[123] Davies, 'Classes and the Police', 38-40.
[124] See comments in *Leisure Hour*, 19 March 1857.
[125] See 'J.P.W.', *SWN*, 11 May 1867, 'E.B. Chalmers', *SWN*, 1 June 1867, to give but two examples from the end of the period.
[126] In 1842-44 the average strength of the Manchester police was 398 for a population

it was reported that some beats took three hours to complete on the double.[127] Another was that the disposition of the force often paid more attention to the protection of property than the imposition or preservation of civic order, concentrating on major thoroughfares to the neglect of many of the back streets and courts.[128] Indeed, some parts of the city were virtual 'no-go' areas for the police throughout this period.[129] The police, it was often complained, were frequently diverted to give particular attention to single issues which concerned the council at one time, such as the state of lodging houses, Sunday trading, or beerhouses. Moreover, the extra demands on their non-working hours caused by arrests and subsequent charges, discouraged the police from going beyond the policy of moving on. Detection rates in Manchester were very low.[130] As such, even where police action was successful, it merely placed constraints on popular culture; it did not in any sense reform it. As one reminiscing Manchester policemen put it, 'I don't mean to say that the policeman cannot restrain, but I do say he cannot cure'.[131]

Continuities of working-class culture

An examination of the continuities of working-class lifestyles during the 1850s and 1860s even begins to throw doubt on the efficacy of restraint. Without doubt, the presence of the police from the 1840s, and their moving on policy, did severely curtail the street-based 'rough' culture of gambling and brawling which had flourished into the 1830s. Nevertheless, even in the 1850s and 1860s, the street remained a focus

---

of 235,139, compared with a force of 543 for the City of London's population of 140,967, Redford, *Local Government in Manchester*, II, 67. By 1861, while the borough population had reached 390,127, the police force still numbered only 535, *MCCP*, (1861), 109. For the frequent demands of the chief constables for extra manpower see Willis, WCM, 2 July 1846, Palin, WCM, 8 March 1860, 'Report of the Watch Committee', *MCCP*, (1867), 195–6.

[127] Willis, WCM, 19 June 1845.

[128] In 1853 Willis commented that although there were four policemen on duty in the vicinity of Shudehill, these kept to the principal thoroughfares, and did not penetrate the back streets unless they saw something which specifically required their services, WCM, 19 October 1854.

[129] See comments of *MC*, 18 March 1846 on Little Ireland, comments on parts of Ancoats, *MCN*, 6 October, 1 December 1866.

[130] A. Aspland, *Crime in Manchester*, (1869), 6.

[131] 'Passages in the Life of a Retired Policeman', *MSp*, 3 April 1858.

Table 6.1 Pubs and Beerhouses in Manchester, 1840–67[132]

	1840	1850	1860	1867
Public Houses	502	481	485	484
Beerhouses	812	1298	1645	2016
Total	1314	1779	2130	2500

of working-class leisure, not only the playground of the young, with their kite-flying, hooping, and cricket, as well as stone throwing and snowballing in season, but also of the adults, who chatted from doorways or promenaded along popular thoroughfares, such as Oldham Road.[133] In the late 1860s and early 1870s, indeed, it is possible to discern the emergence of a forerunner of one element of inter-war youth culture identified by David Fowler, the 'monkey run', in which adolescents congregated on Sunday evenings in Oldham Street and Oxford Road for a form of semi-ritualised public courting.[134]

Closer police surveillance had only a very gradual impact on the position of the street at the fulcrum of the interlocking spheres of entertainment and retailing. It was here during the first half of the century that a large variety of casual sellers and performers entertained the people. Ballad sellers sang out the latest ballad, hawkers chanted their wares, patterers dilated on the merits of their goods – commercial activities which drew on popular attitudes and fed them.[135] Bands of Italian and German entertainers were common, later joined by the numerous temperance bands who rehearsed while marching through the streets; organ grinders ground out their tunes, and itinerant showmen traversed the city offering to show representations of horrible murders for a penny, or proclaimed the attractions of the giants, dwarves or flaxen-haired maidens they were exhibiting.[136] Reminiscing at the start of the twentieth century, one old Mancunian remarked on the

[132] *Chief Constable's Report of Police Administration*, (1842–67).
[133] *MG*, 6 December 1834, *MC*, 29 July 1846, *MG*, 25 August, 7 July 1858, *MX*, 21 July 1865, *MCN*, 21 April 1866, *MG*, 26 October 1859.
[134] *Freelance*, V (1870), 253, 279, IX (1874), 22–3. For the twentieth century 'monkey run' see D. Fowler, in Andrew Davies and Stephen Fielding, eds, *Workers' Worlds: cultures and communities in Manchester and Salford, 1880–1939*, (1992).
[135] 'W.M.H.', *MX*, 6 March 1858, *MSp*, 27 March 1858; cf. M. Vicinus, *The Industrial Muse: A Study of Nineteenth Century British Working Class Literature*, (1974), 13-38.
[136] *MC*, 13 December 1834, *MG*, 11 June 1858, *MSp*, 29 September 1849, *MX*, 7 February 1857, 2 February 1850.

numerous attractions which the streets had boasted during the 1840s when his memories began, not just the vendors but conjurors, acrobats, hurdy-gurdy players and the like.[137] The flavour of street life at its most intense is given by the descriptions of the *Morning Chronicle* in 1849:

> The gin shops are in full feather – their swinging doors never hang a moment still. Itinerant bands blow and bang their loudest; organ boys grind monotonously; ballad singers or flying stationers make roaring proclamations of their wares. The street is one swarming buzzing mass of people. Boys and girls shout and laugh and disappear into taverns together... Here a woman is anxiously attempting – half to drive and half to lure home her drunken husband: there a couple of tipsey fellows are in high dispute, their tobacco pipes in their hands, and a noisy circle of backers urging them on. From byways and alleys and back streets, fresh crowds every moment emerge.[138]

Although this aspect of working-class culture is even more shrouded in obscurity than most, it is apparent that such activity largely survived into the 1870s: a description of Saturday night in Hulme in 1872 provides a not dissimilar picture.[139]

Certainly the annual fairs, which increasingly spilled out from their traditional fairgrounds onto the streets as the period progressed, sustained the customs of irrational recreation. The largest of the local fairs were the Knott Mill Fair, held each Easter in Manchester, and the Salford Dirt Fair, which took place annually in December. The fairs provided the usual mixture of stalls, shows, menageries and circuses. Despite the hostility of city missionaries and shopkeepers, and the occasional outburst of the press, the fairs were tolerated uneasily, rather than subjected to a sustained campaign of middle-class opposition, and notwithstanding their ups and downs, were still thriving in the 1860s.[140] Indeed by the 1860s the traditional fairs were being

[137] Hayes, *Reminiscences of Manchester*, 12–19.
[138] C. Aspin, ed., *Angus Bethune Reach, Manchester and the Textile Districts in 1849*, (1972), 58.
[139] *MCN*, 7 September 1872.
[140] For various accounts of Knott Mill Fair see *MG*, 14 April 1838, 14 April 1852, 10 March 1853, 18 April 1865, *MCN*, 22 April 1865, *Freelance*, I (1867), 145–7, *Sphinx*, III (1870), 127–8, 133–4. For one outburst see the comment of the *Freelance* which described the Knott Mill Fair as 'that vile, festering abomination of vice, drunkenness, prostitution and theft...', *Freelance*, IX (1874), 113. See also J. Page, 'The story of Manchester's Fairs', *Papers of the Manchester Literary Club*, III (1877), 9-12; for a comparison see H. Cunningham, 'The Metropolitan Fairs: a case study in the social control of leisure', in Donajgrodski, ed., *Social Control in Nineteenth Century Britain*,

supplemented by commercially-motivated inventions such as the 'Hulme Wakes', celebrated by a fair in 1861.[141] The continued popularity of the fairs posed a constant reminder of the limited impact of reforming endeavours on working-class culture: as the *Manchester Examiner and Times* put it in 1856, '[i]t is somewhat staggering to the believer in the moral and intellectual omnipotence of the free libraries to raise and elevate the lower orders to find the success of this boisterous rival to our noble institution in Byrom-st, so much greater than what attends upon the library during these holidays'.[142]

The fairs were vulnerable to middle-class censure and in 1876 the Knott Mill fair was suppressed. However, police action and tightening municipal control was much less able to shake the hold of the pub and the beerhouse on patterns of working-class recreation.[143] Their importance is demonstrated by sheer numbers alone. The massive expansion of beerhouses in Manchester is detailed in Table 6.1; it was not surprising that the overriding image of working-class districts remained the pub on every street corner.[144] As the French observer Léon Faucher expressed it, '[t]he public house is for the operative, what the public square was for the ancients...it is there where they meet one another and where they discuss the topics in which they are interested. Their meetings, whether permanent or accidental, their masonic lodges, their mutual aid societies, their clubs and secret societies, are all held in public houses'.[145] While most middle-class reformers concentrated their attention on the dreaded evils of alcohol, for the working classes the relief that drink could bring to lives of hardship and uncertainty was only one of the attractions of the pub: most came not simply to drink, but to talk, and many who took temperance pledges were led to break them from having returned to the pub for its converse and comradeship rather than its drink.

Hence the pub was not simply a place of relaxation: it was also an arena for the development and circulation of ideas. Many pubs provided newspapers, some even having separate newsrooms attached, and

163-206.
[141] *MC*, 28 September 1861.
[142] *MX*, 25 March 1856.
[143] The classic picture is B. Harrison, 'Pubs', in H.J. Dyos and M. Woolff, eds., *The Victorian City: images and reality*, (1973).
[144] J. Roberton, *The Duty of England to Provide a Gratuitous Compulsory Education for the children of her poorer classes*, (1865), 3, (in MCLA M98, #170), which commented that in Deansgate '...at nearly every corner, a gin palace'.
[145] Faucher, *Manchester in 1844*, (1844), 52.

especially in the 1830s and 1840s, while the stamp duties kept the prices of newspapers high, and penny newsrooms and other similar institutions were still relatively scarce, those of the working classes who wished to keep abreast of the news resorted to the pub to do so.[146] The pub was the primary arena of political discussion and argument: as Cooke Taylor commented, 'it was part of the excitement which the operative seeks'.[147]

The content of this culture largely escapes the inquiring eye of the historian. Nevertheless, some feel for the atmosphere is given in later local writings, such as Ben Brierley's story 'Old Radicals and Young Reformers' written in the 1860s. Brierley's Manchester weavers are pictured complaining of the vague and insipid support for some measure of reform which was all that any newspaper reader was likely to give them at that time. In his day, comments one weaver, men where much more definitely either radical or tory: 'A aleheawse nook then wur like a cockpit. If a tory battut his wings, a radikil crowed, and fithers ud ha begun flyin in a minnit'.[148] Not that pub discussions always ended in pandemonium. As James Staton commented, '...awve yerd monny a fust-rate discusshun in a public house, unth'topics oth day, hondled wi a clivverness un a smetness that would ha done credit to th'Heawse of Commons'.[149] It was here, rather than in the staid atmosphere of the lecture hall, that political and economic attitudes were shaped and tempered.

As the infilling of the city and the increasing power of the police circumscribed elements of the old pre-industrial and increasingly 'rough' culture, the pub provided a natural alternative venue. Publicans began to take advantage of the desire for indoor venues in the 1830s: take, for example, the prize fight held in the General Chase beerhouse, New Market in 1836, which attracted large crowds.[150] During the 1840s the number of pubs catering for rat-hunting, cock-fighting and dog-fighting appears to have increased steadily, some providing purpose-built auditoriums or cockpits. Although such activities were by

---

[146] See comments of Thomas Hogg, secretary of the LCUMI, *PP*, (1851) XVII (558), 169, Cooke Taylor, *Notes of a Tour*, 130–1. Examples of pubs with newsrooms include the Bird in the Hand, Hulme, *MC*, 31 March 1849.

[147] Cooke Taylor, *Notes of a Tour*, 131.

[148] Brierley, *Tales and Sketches*, 224.

[149] *LL*, 20 February 1864; cf. comments on the topics of conversation in the early morning coffee rooms of Ancoats, *MSp*, 8 November 1856.

[150] *MG*, 11 June 1836.

the 1850s becoming to be associated more with the outtownships than Manchester itself, the steady stream of court cases evinces their persistence in the city.[151] And not only among the lower working class: dog-fights were also taking place in the room of the packers' union in the 1850s.[152] In 1866 the Unitarian domestic missionary James Harrop commented that until relatively recently dog- and cock-fighting had been quite common among the working classes, and that only lately had they become confined to the 'the lowest and most degraded portions of society'.[153]

In a similar fashion, pubs continued to service a thriving gamblers' community throughout this period; according to Robert Lamb, commenting in 1866, 'Manchester [was] notorious for its gambling character', betting mania being 'very general' in the city.[154] Although far from novel, gambling came to the fore in the mid-1840s when there was something of a gambling craze. During these years there was considerable participation in wheels of fortune, sweepstakes and raffles, and after these had largely been suppressed by police action, there was a renewed lottery craze in the mid-50s.[155] But the focus of working-class gambling remained sport, particularly horse-racing, and in Manchester this activity was centred around the pubs in the old Shudehill district, particularly Turner Street, Thomas Street and Charter Street. Despite periodic attempts to control this activity, especially in the early 1850s and 1860s, this district was still crowded with betting men in 1867.[156] Once again, although betting was clearly at odds with the philosophies of self-improvement and respectability, it was deeply entrenched across working-class culture. Not only was it a central element in many of the co-operative land and building society schemes

---

[151] See for example the account of an informal prize fight, with umpires etc., in a pub in Stretford, 'Nota', *MC*, 26 January 1864, or the case concerning the Pedestrian Tavern, Salford in 1867, where three bedrooms were found full of fighting cocks, and a cockpit with forms discovered in the garret, *SWN*, 22 June 1867.

[152] *MX*, 25 February 1852.

[153] *MTPAR*, (1866), 53.

[154] Lamb, *Free Thoughts*, I, 222.

[155] *MCCP*, (1847), 31–2, *MTPAR*, (1848), 33; *MX*, 23 December 1854, 'A Ratepayer', *MX*, 20 January 1857.

[156] *MC*, 29 November 1845, 'XYZ', *MG*, 20 August 1851, 'A.Z.', *MG*, 6 August 1857, *WCM*, 15 September 1853; for complaints about their continued prevalence in 1860 and the subsequent raids see *MG*, 3 March 1860, *MX*, 25,28 April, 27 November 1860, *WCM*, 15 March 1860. For the continued prominence of gambling see *MCCP*, (1867), 195, *Freelance*, II (1867), 179–80.

of the 1840s and 1850s, but in the 1850s it was also apparently an important part of coffee room and temperance hall life in the city.[157]

It was within the pub that the major forms of mid-nineteenth century working-class commercial leisure, the music halls and singing salons, developed. Folk and ballad music had always been an important element in popular culture, and continued to be so in rural communities where domestic outwork survived, continuing to serve the rhythms of production. In the cities the picture is less clear, although certainly informal singing within pubs did survive, particularly among the Irish, for whom it preserved a vital part of their cultural identity.[158] At the same time, musical culture developed along more commercial lines, as the pubs opened themselves up to the entertainers being gradually driven off the street, gradually regularising and professionalising their offerings; the first music salons appeared in the 1830s, and as early as 1841 it would seem that some pubs had gone as far as installing a stage and using scenery and made-up performers.[159] Music salons were already very popular in Manchester by this date: in 1842 there were already 54 salons in the city open on Sunday evenings (and it is likely that there were a further number closed on that night but open at other times during the week), and such rooms remained a constant thorn in the side of moral reformers throughout the period.[160]

The salons were quickly followed by the emergence of music halls proper. By 1846 both the Polytechnic Music Hall in Salford and the Casino in Manchester were in operation. These were joined in the 1850s by the Colosseum, and the Victoria, Shakespeare and Canterbury Music Halls, as well as by other venues which had some music hall content, like the Palladium and the Philharmonic Hall.[161] By the 1850s Manchester had thus developed a broadly based popular pastime, attracting large numbers: in 1854 one of the central Manchester City Mission districts contained eighteen assorted music halls and singing

[157] See P.H.J. Gosden, *Self-Help: Voluntary Associations in the Nineteenth Century*, (1973); *MTPAR*, (1852), 19.
[158] The survival is well evoked in M. Lynch, *The Streets of Ancoats*, (1985); for the persistence of the 'free and easies' see *Freelance*, I (1867), 81–3, IX (1874), 94–5.
[159] *Manchester and Salford Temperance Journal*, October (1836); R.W. Procter, *Memorials of Manchester Streets*, (1874), 50–1; *MC*, 11 December 1841.
[160] *NEM*, (1842), 348; comments of Hugh Stowell in *MC*, 18 February 1843. Cf. calls for action against Sunday evening singing and dancing salons to the council in 1869, *MCCP*, (1868–69), 299–300.
[161] *MG*, 11 July 1846, *MC*, 30 December 1846, *MX*, 11 January 1851, *MG*, 15 August 1857, 17 December 1859, 3 March 1860.

and dancing rooms attracting about five thousand people each Saturday night.[162] In the late 1860s it was estimated that fifteen thousand people attended the music hall every Saturday night, a figure not including the smaller concert rooms.[163] By this stage the halls appear to have had all the elements of the later more extensively documented London music halls, including a rapidly growing proportion of professional acts, booked through London agents.[164] While comic artists predominated, there were also singers and musicians, dancers, dissolving views, tumbling, juggling, feats of strength and other novelty items.[165] The clientele of the halls and salons varied. In many the young predominated, but in general it would seem that all age groups were attracted. Likewise, although some sections of the upper working class might have distanced themselves from the music hall, by the 1860s it would seem that, aided by the provision of galleries and separate sections in the halls, it had established cross-class appeal: when the Wolverhampton Music Hall opened in 1866 the prices of entry ranged up to 6/- for a box; at the same time the crowded concert rooms of Deansgate, where a couple of hundred crowded to watch similar entertainments, attracted those unwilling to pay the higher prices of the established halls.[166]

Indeed, middle-class reformers had difficulty with the music hall – it was attended in large numbers by artisans and the prosperous working class, often little in the way of drink was consumed, and thus it escaped some of the odium of the pub, yet it was clearly far removed from their ideals of rational recreation. In fact, patchy evidence suggests that even at this early date, the music hall maintained a consistently anti-bourgeois atmosphere, delighting audiences with song and dialogue which defied middle-class versions of taste and propriety, using satire and humour to ridicule those in authority while holding up an idealised picture of the working man and his qualities. Often this involved a direct and self-conscious reinterpretation of middle-class moral imperialism. When John Layhe visited a large casino in Mosley Street in 1850, he found performers singing a parody of the popular song 'There's a good time coming, boys!', which had been changed to 'There's a cold time coming boys, mix your dram the stronger!'.[167]

[162] *MCMM*, May (1854), 100.
[163] *Freelance*, III (1868), 237.
[164] *Freelance*, V (1870), 134.
[165] See description in 'J.W. Hudson', *MG*, 19 May 1852.
[166] *Freelance*, I (1866–67), 5-6, III (1868), 237, IV (1869), 41–2.
[167] *MTPAR*, (1850), 50, 41–2; cf. the later complaint that the music hall had sunk as low

Conclusion

Middle-class concern over the loosening of social bonds in the expanding mid-nineteenth century city inspired a multiplicity of campaigns and associations which, moving beyond religion or rational education, attempted to soften working-class recalcitrance by reforming or restricting the nature of working-class culture. However, the number and scope of these activities notwithstanding, it becomes apparent on closer scrutiny that the impact of this pressure was blunted by the very practices at which it aimed, by differences of emphasis within the middle class, and by the deficiencies of the mechanisms which they attempted to use. In consequence, working-class culture, although constrained, was never controlled, and its resilience shines through in the persistence of pub based activities, from rat-fighting to burial clubs to music hall. This culture both helped insulate the working classes from the brunt of middle-class didacticism, providing rival sources of learning and consciousness-formation. And ultimately, it was the shape of working-class consciousness which was to prove the acid test of middle-class moral imperialism.

as it could possibly go, *City Lantern*, IV (1877–78), 410. In this context Vicinus' comments about the switch to "mass culture", *Industrial Muse*, 238–80, in that they concentrate on a much later period, are not really applicable; nor would this fit in with the interpretation of L. Senelick, 'Politics as Entertainment: Victorian Music Hall Songs', *Victorian Studies*, XIX (1975), 149–180. For music hall history generally see also R. Mander and J. Mitchenson, *British Music Hall*, (1965).

Chapter Seven

The continuities of
working-class consciousness

The relative impotence of the agencies of middle-class moral imperialism, and their failure to effect any significant inroads into working-class culture, questions their influence over the development of working-class consciousness. In the 1960s and 1970s historians, observing the collapse of working-class politics after chartism, argued (although they relied on behavioural rather than attitudinal evidence) that there was a disintegration of working-class attitudes in this period.[1] In the later 1980s and early 1990s, prompted by Gareth Stedman Jones' 'Rethinking Chartism', focus began to shift towards the continuities of working-class radicalism, the motifs of radical patriotism, of free trade and anti-statism, and the franchise not as a mechanism of social and economic transformation but as a badge of citizenship.[2] In some cases, this re-evaluation has been taken to the extent of questioning the existence, even in the chartist period, of anything which can usefully be described as working-class consciousness, suggesting instead that populism provides a more fruitful framework for what thus become 'popular' rather than working-class attitudes.[3]

These revisions are welcome, because whereas in the past historians have been dissuaded from such an approach by the difficulties of obtaining adequate evidence, this current work has committed itself wholeheartedly to uncovering working-class or popular voices. Recognising that the public media filtered popular self-expression, particularly in those periods when the working classes were unable to maintain their own press or publishers, and that whereas at times government sources help overcome this problem, other periods produce silences whose interpretation is fraught with difficulty and voices whose

[1] See, for example, Burgess, *Challenge of Labour*, 19–20, Foster, *Class Struggle and the Industrial Revolution*, Kirk, *Working Class Reformism*.

[2] See above, page 1, note 4.

[3] See above, page 1, note 5, and also John Belchem, 'Beyond Chartist Studies: Class, Community and Party in Early Victorian Populist Politics', in D. Fraser, ed., *Cities, Class and Communication. Essays in Honour of Asa Briggs*, (1990).

typicality is far from assured, there has nevertheless been a new commitment to searching out and utilising the widest possible range of source materials, from banners to broadsides, from dialect poetry to scrapbooks and diaries.[4] It is becoming ever more apparent that extensive digging can turn up a wide variety of useful sources. Newspapers not only record the opinions of union and political activists, but also provide an occasional forum for the letters of the anonymous rank and file. Used with care, considerable insight can be gained from the opinions of middle-class figures such as John Layhe, who are in close contact with the working classes. Even the testimonies of the working-class autodidacts (such as, in this case, Samuel Bamford, J.B. Rogerson, John Teer, R.S. Chadwick, and Elijah Ridings), though unrepresentative, provide useful material from a liminal group.[5] Taken with the evidence of Home Office papers, parliamentary investigations, and occasional manuscript remains, these sources do provide the basis for an attempt to unravel the nature of working-class attitudes in this period.

It is important to emphasise at the outset, however, that we are not looking for (and would not find) something which could be described as a 'monolithic working class', and especially not a monolithic working-class consciousness. Indeed, this has been a weakness of much of the recent work on populism: that it has sought to deny the existence of working-class consciousness by establishing an over-schematic definition of what working-class consciousness must be. Applying the model developed in the first chapter,[6] working-class consciousness can exist on a number of different levels. At its most basic it can involve a shared sense of class identity. More significantly, this identity may be underpinned by a self-consciously distinct value system. This in turn *may* form the basis for a shared and distinct vision of an ideal society, of the means of bringing this ideal social order about, and an overall philosophy or *Weltanschauung*, but that it does not inevitably do so, does not of itself undermine the notion of class consciousness.

---

[4] The use of some of these is not without its difficulties: for the debate on the authenticity of the dialect voice see Brian Maidment, 'Essayists and Artisans – the making of Victorian self-taught poets', *Literature and History*, 9,1 (1983), 87, *idem, The Poorhouse Fugitives. Self-taught poets and poetry in Victorian Britain*, (1987), 366; M. Beetham, '"Healthy Reading": the Periodical Press in Late Victorian Manchester', in Kidd and Roberts, *City, Class and Culture*, 174, B. Hollingworth, *Songs of the People*, (1977), 5–7, Joyce, *Visions of the People*, 256–78.

[5] The point of Joyce's illuminating essay on Waugh in his *Democratic Subjects*.

[6] See above, pages 16–20.

Hence, evidence of disputes over strategies for change are themselves no basis on which to assert a collapse of working-class *identity*, or even of the subversion of working-class value systems. Nor, working in reverse, should the bitter class animosities in the 1830s be seen as evidence of a comprehensive critique of the capitalist system, complete with a developed sense of an alternative society, the absence of which has been deemed so significant for the post-chartist period. Instead, in recognising that chartism had always been predominantly a reformist movement, and that the post-chartist working class retained a strong sense of their working-class identity and value system, it is possible to construct a portrait of working-class consciousness which affirms the continuities rather than the discontinuities of the mid-century decades, without having to argue that the continuities reside in identities, values and ideologies which were naturally subsumed into some supra-class Gladstonian populism.

The working-class value system in the chartist period

At the heart of the working-class consciousness which existed in this period was a distinctive value system. Its core was an enduring egalitarianism. In part this was the assertion of a common humanity, a belief that, in the words of an address of the Manchester fustian cutters to their masters, 'we are men, and by nature equal to yourselves, springing from the same source and retiring to the same end, and that distinctions of rank are only circumstances necessary to order and government...'.[7] Such ideas drew strength from the rhetoric of the 'birthright of Englishmen' which was such an integral part of radicalism in the pre-chartist period, and which was made an integral part of Manchester chartism by R.J. Richardson's strenuous advocacy.[8] Christian beliefs reinforced these essentially secular ideas, providing a powerful picture of a common creation and common sinfulness, a sense that, as Rogerson prayed, 'we are all alike before Thee, weak and faulty things of dust'.[9] Within this tradition, the acceptance of a common humanity and common rights facilitated the assertion of the

---

[7] *MG*, 5 November 1836.
[8] Richardson published 'The Rights of Englishmen', *NS*, 21 December 1839; for Richardson see Sykes, 'Early Chartism', 187 n.17.
[9] J.B. Rogerson, *Musings in Many Moods*, (1859), 145.

primacy of the rights of man over the rights of property, not just in the allocation of power within the political system, but also in provision of economic and social conditions which enabled full human development.[10]

The acceptance of a common humanity and common rights also underpinned a strong sense of dignity and self worth, enhanced by a sense of exclusion and by the vision of the iniquities of the working classes which had developed. The working class confronted the perpetual small change of social life, different styles of dress, different modes of address, different pews in church or chapel, different seats in the Free Trade Hall, different carriages in the railway, with a nicely attuned sensibility to 'snobbery' and a prickly self-dignity.[11] 'With this correct idea of your own worth in your mind', thundered an address of the Manchester Political Union in 1838, 'with what indignation must you hear yourselves called...peasantry, rabble, mob, the "swinish multitude"...', and the resentment indeed came through again and again in working-class speaking and writing.[12]

This did not preclude the existence of a strongly developed sense of status differentials: the hierarchy of trades and occupations, and the emergence of cultural distinctions around trade unions, friendly societies and the temperance movement are in evidence in the 1830s.[13] It did not prevent the coexistence of other languages of identity which aligned the virtuous and industrious against the unvirtuous and the idle, or distinguished Anglican from Dissenter, Irish from English, in ways which could cut across class boundaries. Nor did it preclude the use of populist rhetorics in which sectional interests were disguised in appeals to the general good. However, such status distinctions and non-class identities coexisted, in most cases quite comfortably, within a social vision and a value system which emphasised working-class identities and distinctly working-class virtues of collective self-help and individual

[10] Cf. the claim of *Manchester and Salford Temperance Journal* that 'The rights of the poor do not seem to us to receive due consideration: they are men, and have minds, minds which ought to be cultivated, and poverty ought to be no bar to this', 17 September 1836.

[11] See M. Hewitt, 'Radicalism and the Victorian Working Class: the case of Samuel Bamford', *Historical Journal*, 34,4 (1991), 873–92.

[12] *NS*, 15 September 1838; cf., for example, 'A Working Man', *TUM*, 15 March 1851, 'A Hater of Partiality', *MX*, 27 September 1851.

[13] For example, the division between spinners and weavers, *MG*, 31 March 1832, within occupations, 'Address of the Fustian Cutters', [1833], Fustian Cutters Collection, #5, BR f331. 881722. Sc1, MCLA.

moral worth, and which did not challenge the underlying assumptions of equality.

In focusing on the worth of the individual, the working classes saw themselves as subscribing to a quite different set of values to those of the middle classes: they were concerned with the inherent worth of man, and with the virtues of the individual as individual, while middle-class values concentrated on externalities. The starkest expression of this wholesale repudiation of middle-class values comes, interestingly enough, in the writings of one of the figures most often used to exemplify the decay of working-class radicalism, Samuel Bamford. For all his failings, Bamford's commitment to a self-consciously working-class standard of ethics stands as a warning against too simple an interpretation of mid-century working-class consciousness.[14] The extent of this rejection is revealed in a remarkable chapter of his *Walks in South Lancashire*, entitled 'The Two Judgements'. This apocalyptic allegory on the state of Victorian England depicted a society divided into a small (middle-class) group marked by a hypocritical pretence of wisdom, meekness and saintliness (covering ignorance, pride and hypocrisy), and a large mass of the poor 'unaccepted'. (Social) acceptance was granted to the man who had accumulated vast sums of money, but not to him who 'has shared his bread with the hungry, and his garments with the naked' and who has 'protected the innocent'.[15] No worldly solution to this state of affairs was offered, but it is illuminating for the wholesale rejection which it demonstrates of the dominant values of mid-Victorian England, the individualism, the overriding preoccupation with wealth and external trappings as a measure of virtue, and the hypocritical double standards. Bamford was quite aware of the gap between the external image of a just society propagated by the middle class and the underlying reality, and his rejection of middle-class morality was total.

Frequent echoes of Bamford can be found in working-class repudiations of what they saw as the tendency of the middle classes to elevate wealth above humanity and virtue as the standard of worth. While the working classes sought competence and an escape from poverty, they generally looked on wealth with suspicion if not distaste. 'What is wealth' asked John Teer, 'but a gaudy show,/ A toy to please the proud and vain,/ A vessel filled with hidden woe,/ A constant

---

[14] Hewitt, 'The case of Samuel Bamford', 873–92, especially 888–90.
[15] S. Bamford, *Walks in South Lancashire*, (1844), 105–8.

spring of hidden pain'.[16] To working-class eyes, the wealth of the middle classes was the result of avarice, and obtained only at the expense of a repudiation of the wider nobility of humanity. For Rogerson, looking at the wealthy middle classes, 'the thirst for wealth [had] withered up their veins,/ They toil and grasp, and die - amid their gains'.[17] Indeed death, and the afterlife promised by religion, provided a useful motif for working-class rejection of judgements of worth based on wealth.

The priority given to the accumulation of wealth was disavowed not only because it was part of the influential language of romanticism, but because it led to inequality and injustice: while a few grew wealthy, many others were left starving. Hence more worthy was the aspiration to a simple competence: R.S. Chadwick, the chartist poet, rejected the use of money as a synonym for 'wealth': for him wealth was 'the peasant's cot', in its rural glade, with its frugal meal and homely comforts.[18] And certainly, the need for all to have access to the basic necessities of life claimed higher priority than the needs of the few to hold on to their riches. It was not that the working classes rejected the political economists' analysis of the role of supply and demand in fixing wages; in fact they realised only too well the impact of these forces under existing conditions. What they rejected was that the livelihood of people should be treated in the same way as other factors of production.[19]

In another sense middle-class emphasis on wealth could be contrasted with more universal virtues. Many of the working-class poets, as autodidacts, looked to education as a more appropriate standard of worth, in that, as Ridings put it, 'he is to be accounted the most worthy who subjects the passions and powers of the soul to the dictates of truth'.[20]

In particular, however, the working classes rejected wealth because they laid much greater emphasis on its use than its accumulation: the wealthy were perceived as indulging in an essentially self-interested search for money while in contrast, the greater virtue was to be found

---

[16] Teer, *Silent Musings*, (1869), 40. Teer was an Irish Catholic, radical, and secretary of the dressers and dyers union in the 1840s and 1850s.

[17] Rogerson, *Musings*, 117.

[18] R.S. Chadwick, *The Pleasures of Poetry. The purgatory of poets and other poems*, (1846), 6–7.

[19] 'Address of the Fustian Cutters', *NS*, 27 October 1838.

[20] Elijah Ridings, *Pictures of Life*, (1850), xii.

in ideals of mutuality and the ties of community. In working-class thinking, this was often absorbed into the idealised view of pre-industrial society which radical historians have until recently treated with such impatience. Visions of a past in which 'gentlemen were gentlemen indeed, and ladies were what they pretended to be, – loaf givers, dispensers of good' cannot simply be dismissed as backward-looking and regressive, for their significance lay in the way in which the working classes wished to invoke this myth to bolster their rejection of liberal individualism and their attempt to uphold notions of collective reciprocity.[21] The limits of such idealisation were well recognised. If there was an essentially selfish streak in most people, and if the middle classes could not always themselves be expected to recognise their duties, this only reinforced the need to use the political system, not for sectional gain, but for the benefit of the nation as a whole.[22] A good deal of working-class outrage during the 1830s was derived from the repudiation of the laissez-faire philosophy which underlay much of the Whig legislation, because it appeared to be 'legislating for individual benefit, and not for the benefit of the whole community', as R.J. Richardson, one of the leaders of Manchester chartism, expressed it.[23] Community, the direct corollary of universal citizenship, was the ideal which held such ideas together; as one factory reformer exclaimed in 1833, he did not believe that an effective Ten Hours Act would hinder trade, but if it did, '[p]erish trade and preserve community!'.[24] This is important, because much of the rhetoric of class which characterised chartism had little to do with any notions of the primacy of the working class. 'Class' in this context was synonymous with 'sectional', and class legislation was thus to be contrasted with national or community legislation.[25]

The implications of such attitudes were manifold: complete working-class rejection of middle-class connections of political power with property. It was the straightforwardness and self-evidence of the argument of the equality of men which cemented working-class commitment to the charter. In consequence the acquisition of the vote

[21] See 'Address of the Manchester Society for the Restoration of the Rights of Englishmen', *NS*, 14 March 1840, S. Bamford, *Early Days*, (1849), 20.
[22] See comments of James Leach, *NS*, 23 October 1841.
[23] *MC*, 13 March 1841.
[24] 'Address of the Ten Hours Sub-Committee for Chorlton upon Medlock', *MSA*, 26 January 1833.
[25] See the 'Address of the South Lancashire Delegates', *NS*, 21 January 1841. For a convincing analysis of this point, see Joyce, *Visions of the People*, *passim*.

remained central to the aspirations of most working-class groups. Support for the principles of the charter bridged virtually all working-class groups during the 1830s and 1840s.[26] In 1848 the glass-blowers were virtually the only group who made a clear statement of dissension from the stance of the charter on universal manhood suffrage, and even those working men who were sworn in as special constables to defend their places of work, were not averse to qualifying this by a statement that the distress of the working classes 'arises from class legislation', and that the working classes needed to be 'fully and fairly' represented in the House of Commons.[27] In 1848 John Watts, whose attitude to the charter had always been ambivalent at best, was prepared to admit that, rightly or wrongly, 'the working class as a mass had been taught to believe…that the enactment of the principles of the charter was the great measure that was to produce their salvation'.[28]

The motif of independence was also invoked widely in social relationships.[29] As has already been discussed, working-class reluctance to accept the heavy-handed intervention of middle-class patrons materially impeded attempts to establish control over working-class associational life. Their sense of their own self-worth left them very sensitive to what they perceived as slights on their status: as one Sunday school teacher put it in the 1850s, they 'too often experience[d], from such as are above them in worldly position, behaviour which remind[ed] them painfully of their situation'.[30] It also meant that positions of subordination, particularly at work, were a constant source of annoyance and were endured rather than accepted. Teer remembered his time in a cotton factory as one of 'great slavery, misery and privation'.[31] It was not simply the position of subordination which was irksome to working-class pride, but the sense in which it enabled employers to indulge in 'petty tyrannies', and the degree to which personal advancement appeared to be achievable only on the basis of sycophancy and toadying. Much trade union activity was

[26] Among the trades who identified themselves with the charter at one stage in this period were the dyers, fustian cutters, spinners, shoemakers, brickmakers, tailors, painters, engineers, hammermen, millwrights, boiler-makers.

[27] Resolutions of the railwaymen employed by the Lancashire and Yorkshire Railway Company, NS, 25 March 1848.

[28] MX, 11 April 1848.

[29] See Crossick, Artisan Elite, 134–8, Tholfsen, Working-Class Radicalism, 108–9, 243.

[30] 'A Late Teacher', MWA, 3 September 1859.

[31] MSA, 13 September 1845; cf. M. Vicinus, Edwin Waugh: The Ambiguities of Self-Help, (1984), 5.

sustained by working-class ascription to their right to control their own worth, and the sense of degradation which came with loss of control.

From this perspective, the workplace and wider social relationships appeared to trap the working classes into relationships which denied them their freedom. They thus treated with considerable suspicion, if not downright hostility, the attempts of middle-class groups to control working-class life outside those areas, such as work, where they were forced to submit to control. Given working-class belief in the value of their own opinions (the kind of attitudes which were discussed in the previous chapter), overt attempts to regulate their lives, whether by sabbatarian injunctions against Sunday sports, or sanitary reformers warning against cellar dwellings, were met almost universally with suspicion and hostility.

The maintenance of the working-class value system

In essence there is little evidence of any marked decay of this working-class value system in the mid-Victorian period. It had, perhaps, less opportunity of self-expression, but it apparently lost little of its vigour. Bamford's diary of 1858-61 is strewn with indications of its resistance to middle-class pressure: for example, on being challenged in 1859 for his pride by Jacob Bright, Bamford retorted that 'honest manly pride arising from conscious integrity was one of the best feelings we could cultivate'.[32] Indeed, the 'virtuous pride and self-respect' of the working classes, and the extent to which they clung to badges of self-esteem like their ability to survive without recourse to the Poor Law became a commonplace.[33] Such pride corroded practices of deference and respect to those in positions of authority. In consequence, 'the absence of that respect and deference which is due to superiority of rank and station' was a frequent lament of the conservative-minded through the 1850s and beyond.[34] If anything, the slightly greater tact which middle-class speakers adopted in dealing with the working classes after the 1840s, merely heightened working-class susceptibilities. When, during a Salford town's meeting in 1860, one speaker described all £6 householders as a 'parcel of fellows', working-

---

[32] Samuel Bamford, 'Diary', 19 May 1859, MS923.2 B99, MCLA.
[33] E.g. *BH*, 2 May 1863.
[34] 'Odds and Ends', 117, Bennett Street Sunday School, M38/4/2/1, MCLA.

class sentiment was outraged.[35] Similarly during the cotton famine a great deal of the unrest occasioned by the relief efforts was derived from the injured pride of the working-class applicants, who felt that they were being treated 'as if they were so many wild beasts, unworthy of sympathy and scarcely worth answering'.[36]

The working classes' resentment at their treatment under the Poor Law reflected not just persistence of robust pride at being working-class, but also their continued repudiation of the bourgeois individualism which it represented. While attempting to present their case in the best light as regards the principles of political economy, working-class groups at the same time continued to appeal to what the Manchester spinners called 'the far higher considerations of justice and humanity'.[37]

After mid-century the working classes refused to abandon their belief that, like the gentry before them, industrial masters had duties by dint of their position. Although these duties were conceived to include aid in the provision of education, leisure etc., it was not simply money which was wanted, and there was no time for charity which was merely a sop to avarice.[38] Nor is there any shortage of evidence that the provision of public parks, the Free Library, or other facilities for the working classes did not so much undermine class hostility and cement social collaboration in the way many supporters of the 'liberalisation' thesis have suggested, but rather served only to highlight the paucity and instrumentality of middle-class philanthropy, and provide a basis for further working-class demands. Hence both the parks and the library were used to justify demands for shorter hours, just as the mechanics' institutes had been before them. As the working-class secularist, James Robertson, commented in 1856, 'in Manchester we are too often in collision with the stern unbending doctrines of political economy not to know how little influenced our employers are by philanthropic motives...'.[39] What was required was a clear

---

[35] *SWN*, 28 April 1860.

[36] R. Timms, *MX*, 18 January 1861.

[37] Thomas Mawdsely, *MG*, 14 May 1861; cf. also the regrets of the minders and piecers, *Leader*, 8 December 1855.

[38] Charles Hadfield, 'How can mechanics' institutes be rendered more useful to the working classes', *Monthly Literary and Scientific Lecturer*, I (1850), 362–8, and poems like Rogerson's 'An Appeal for the Artisan' in *Silent Musings*; cf. Thomas Nicholson's criticisms of the avaricious man: 'His sins were as bare as the expiring year,/ His charity to cover them as cold', *The Sabbath Peal*, (n.d. [bound with his *A Peal for the People*, (1849) in MCL]), 6.

[39] 'James Robertson', *MX*, 24 June 1856; cf. the comment of 'A Working Man', that

acknowledgement of reciprocal duties within the nexus of employment, as well as within society at large. The plea of the working classes into the 1860s was for 'the rich [to] understand that the stability of society depends on the employers and their workmen understanding properly their relative duties'.[40]

The language of 'relative duties' was not without its dangers to a working-class identity; it implied a shared and even equal role in industry, a mutual reliance, a coincidence of ultimate interest (in the prosperity of the firm, etc.). However, that many employees recognised a degree of mutuality, and that this realisation helped bolster the rhetorics and rituals of workplace paternalism, cannot be taken as evidence of an abandonment of class identities. The rituals and the platitudes were acceptable as long as employers continued to operate within acceptable bounds – made no attempt to exercise rigid control over the work process, and did not get embroiled in a battle over wages or conditions. While the readers of the middle-class press were always ready to indulge the kind of comfortable self-delusion offered by accounts of works outings or presentations, these always existed in uneasy tension with the languages and rituals of the trades dispute and the strike, even if these are not so readily available in the press. It is symptomatic that there is no extant copy of a dramatic poem called *The Tramp*, published by a working man in Hulme in 1852. However, aided by a detailed review, it is possible to reconstruct the drama of the poem, which takes as its backdrop a dispute between the ironmasters and their men, and has as its main *dramatis personae* a tyrannical employer, his meddling wife, a couple of lick-spittle workmen 'who seek to betray the interests of their class', and some honest workmen of the right sort, who ultimately prevail.[41]

Nor is it clear that economic prosperity, stretching the income differentials within the working class, provided the foundation for the creation of sectional identities which subverted, rather than coexisted with, broader class identity. Hence, for example, the obvious reluctance of the overlooker, who wrote to the *Manchester Examiner and Times* in September 1862, appealing for support, to claim the distinction from

Robert Barnes, as demonstrated by his opposition to Gibson and Bright, was an enemy of the working classes, and providing water fountains, even if these were welcome, would not change this, *MX*, 19 May 1859.

[40] R. Timms, *MX*, 18 January 1861.

[41] Thomas Baker, *The Tramp: a dramatic poem*, (1852), not located, but reviewed in *RWN*, 11 April 1852; see also below, page 210–15.

the bulk of the working class that his function and higher wages might lead a devotee of ideas of the labour aristocracy to grant almost automatically.[42]

The persistence of class solidarities is best illustrated by the very limited signs of working-class abandonment of the basic radical belief in universal manhood suffrage. The solid commitment to this belief at the end of the 1840s even among those who had abandoned chartism has already been noted, and despite the accusations of conservatives that the lack of working-class enthusiasm for political agitation in the 1850s and 1860s demonstrated working-class indifference, the ability of the radicals to mobilise large numbers in franchise demonstrations in 1866 and 1867 demonstrates that there were other forces at work.[43]

Moreover, although the notion of meriting the franchise did gain currency in Manchester in the 1850s, this was far more a response to the needs to convince the middle classes of the policy of franchise extension, rather than from a deep-rooted switch to elitism. Radical leaders were sometimes prepared to lend their names to schemes for an educational franchise, but only when the standard was one to which all the working classes could lay claim, such as Hooson's 'honesty and commonsense'.[44] Indeed, as Charles Hadfield commented in a letter to Holyoake, one of the difficulties faced by working-class politicians in the 1850s and 1860s, in attempting to build a united middle-class/working-class campaign for reform, was the tenacity with which most working men clung to the principle of universal manhood suffrage.[45]

Nevertheless, there can be no doubt that the internal divisions within the working class which are clearly evident during the chartist period, were becoming more apparent particularly within the co-operative and trade union movements, as the distinction between the improving or the 'respectable' working class and the rest widened. Edward Hooson, the leader of Manchester chartism in the 1850s, who was increasingly drawn into the co-operative movement, found it necessary to distinguish between the B's and C's of the working class: the beer, 'bacco and

---

[42] 'An Overlooker', *MX*, 20 September 1862.

[43] See below, page 260.

[44] 'E. Hooson', *PPr*, 31 July 1858. There is little sign in Manchester of any increasing illiberality of working class ideas identified by Gray, *Labour Aristocracy*, 156–7.

[45] C. Hadfield to G.J. Holyoake, 3 November 1858, #1045, Holyoake Papers, Hanover House.

betting set and the co-operation, coin, comfort, and content set.[46] Nevertheless, such attitudes were not incompatible with chartist radicalism or with continued solidarity: despite their aristocratic status, the Manchester masons remained convinced in 1854 that they had a duty to 'render some further pecuniary aid to those patriots for labour's cause' who had taken part in the Preston struggle.[47] Similarly, Vicinus has pointed out the degree to which the central theme of dialect literature in the 1850s and beyond was 'the solidarity of the poor with the poor'.[48] There is little evidence that, except for those individuals who had actually raised themselves out of the working class, the respectable working classes ceased to identify themselves with the working class, or assumed a more petit-bourgeois identification.

Patrick Joyce has argued that while this kind of class language was still audible after mid-century, although 'the positive attributes of class were accepted, insofar as they contributed to the realisation of broader and more inclusive social and political identities...the negative and divisive aspects of class were anathematized'.[49] Undoubtedly, working-class and middle-class figures did attempt to annexe to themselves the national interest and the identity of 'the people'. However, they did so largely as a means of more effectively castigating the self-interested class sectionalism of their opponents, while being able to claim to have transcended narrow class interest themselves. The language of populism was not an alternative to the language of class, it was instrumental to it. Hence, despite all the optimistic noises which middle-class observers were in the habit of making about the improvement in the temper of the working classes during the late 1840s and 1850s, few inroads were made into the distinctive working-class value system which had emerged by the 1850s. The sense of class distinction which E.P. Thompson has identified as emerging in the first three decades of the century was still strong in the post-chartist period, and observers like Layhe were still forced to admit that 'class antipathies frequently come in our way'.[50]

---

[46] *Co-operator*, March 1863, 169.
[47] *OSMFR*, 6 April 1854; cf. *OSMFR*, 20 September 1855.
[48] Vicinus, *Edwin Waugh*, 41.
[49] Joyce, *Visions of the People*, 56.
[50] *MTPAR*, (1857), 24.

Working-class theoretical frameworks in the chartist period

It may well be that respectability is more clearly seen in its impact on working-class analysis of industrial society. Throughout the nineteenth century, the working classes were faced with conditions at odds with both their basic material needs and their broader value system. Industrial and urban development created an environment in which poor housing, overcrowding and increasingly insanitary conditions coexisted with an economic system which exerted an intensifying control over their lives, and demanded ever more extended and arduous work, while at the same time it proved incapable of providing stable employment at wages which could remove the spectres of poverty and starvation. As old community ties were ruptured and old hierarchies replaced by new stratifications based on industrial wealth, new social elites assumed more overtly the role of regulators of working-class existence, and the sense of working-class subordination and powerlessness grew.

The working classes were presented with two parallel puzzles: the need to come to an understanding of the way in which industrial society operated, and the need to comprehend the causes of the society's inability to provide for the basic wants of all its inhabitants on a stable basis. In consequence, by the 1830s they had developed (and continued to develop) a wide-ranging analysis of the nature of contemporary society and its problems. Considerable attention has been given in recent years, most particularly in the works of Claeys and Thompson, to presenting a sophisticated and nuanced account of the development of radical economic thought, identifying the contributions of the 'Smithian' and 'Ricardian socialists', the varieties of Owenism, and even their influence on the more economically-informed working-class radicals like Bronterre O'Brien and G.J Harney.[51] However, although these writings provided the context within which working-class theoretical frameworks were developed and sustained, they can tell us relatively little about the more functional and less sophisticated frames which served the bulk of the working class, and which underpinned most radical activity in the chartist period. To uncover these we need

[51] Claeys, *Machinery, money and the millennium, idem, Citizens and saints*, N. Thompson, *The People's Science: the popular political economy of exploitation and crisis, 1816–34*, (1985), *idem, The Market and its Critics: socialist political economy in nineteenth century Britain*, (1988); these build on earlier classics such as Maxine Berg, *The Machinery Question and the Making of Political Economy, 1815–48*, (1980).

to eschew the radical intellectuals, and focus on the politicians – both leaders and followers (and in this case on the Manchester politicians).

In the early 1830s, the attention of the bulk of the Manchester working class was still focused on the political system, believing that, in William Butterworth's words, the 'sole cause of their having to work so hard and so long was because they were not represented in parliament'.[52] During the pre-chartist years, the stance of the Manchester Political Union was still the long-standing radical analysis of Old Corruption, as the cause of poverty and social dislocation. As late as September 1838 its address urged that, 'No man possessing an ordinary understanding can entertain a doubt that the cause of our present suffering is the enormous amount of taxes which the government compels us to pay for the support of its army, its placemen, its pensioners etc., and for the payment of the interest on its debt'.[53] It was the burden of taxation which indicted the fundholders who soaked up the debt repayments, the crown, pensioners, placemen, clerics and the military who drained off government expenditure, and the aristocracy who were left tax free, while benefiting from the Corn Laws. The implication of Old Corruption analysis was that the state was an instrument for the elevation of class interest over that of the nation, and hence that the law it produced was class legislation.[54] When Sir Charles Shaw came to Manchester in 1839 he found 'the foundation of contempt and hatred for the law and magistracy' so deeply laid that he thought that all sense of allegiance to constituted authority had vanished.[55] Instead the government was portrayed as the fount of tyranny and oppression.

Attitudes of this sort bolstered rejection of the constitutional fictions that non-voters were represented, as part of the communities in which they lived, by the MPs chosen by the electors casting their vote as a trust for the whole community. The consequences of the 1832 Reform Act and the introduction of measures like the Poor Law Amendment Act had convinced even the reluctant, of the long-standing charge that the existing political parties and the MPs comprising them had equal

[52] Trade Union placard, HO40/38/199; *NS*, 30 November 1839.
[53] 'Address of the Manchester Political Union', *MSA*, 15 September 1838.
[54] For further examples see R.J. Richardson (as secretary of the Trades Union) to Earl Stanhope, *MSA*, 19 August 1837, 'Address of the [Manchester] United Trades Council', HO/40/38/199. This position has recently been argued with some force in M. Winstanley, 'Oldham radicalism and the origins of popular Liberalism, 1830-52', *Historical Journal*, 36,3 (1993), 622-4, 642-3.
[55] Shaw, *Replies*, 9.

disdain for the interests of the working classes.[56] Working-class radicals did not reject instrumental alliances with either Tories or Whig-Radicals, nor were they above supporting Radicals like Brotherton as being clearly better than their opponents, but in general it was accepted that little could be hoped for until the working classes themselves had the vote and could elect their own candidates. Only the Charter would produce a parliament which would bring relief by easing the tax burden, cheapening government and food, and enabling the establishment of a legal system which would treat all classes evenhandedly. It was thus the sense of exclusion from the political process which was at the heart of working-class radicalism in the 1830s.

Radical attitudes progressed during the chartist period, not so much by superseding this analysis as by expanding it to include more explicitly economic analyses of social ills. Traditionally, the Old Corruption analysis had little place for industrialists and employers, but the chartist period saw the incorporation of industrialists into the traditional canon of villainy of early nineteenth century radicalism, millocrats joining aristocrats as the bane of the working classes.[57] In some cases this was the preliminary to a move towards a full blown critique of the factory system. For example, the chartist P.M. M'Douall had by 1841 developed a comprehensive critique of the factory system *qua* system.[58] The strong Owenite movement in Manchester was based even more firmly on its analysis of the inherent evils both of the competitive industrial system, and the social and religious system which had developed with it. These analyses were not without support. M'Douall's factory critique struck a chord among those like the handloom weavers most affected by its rapid development, and while Manchester Owenism was dominated by the middle classes, drawn by its views on rational improvement, its theory of competition certainly attracted those like fustian cutter Richard Crowther, whose occupations suffered particularly from oversupply of labour and the constant driving down of wages through competition between the masters.[59] Crowther talked explicitly about the masters 'living partly or entirely on the profits derived from the labour of

---

[56] 'R.J. Richardson', *MSA*, 19 August 1837, *MSA*, 7 October 1837.
[57] A point well made by Sykes, 'Popular Politics and Trades Unionism', 345–52.
[58] See Kirk, 'In Defence of Class', 2–47.
[59] For Crowther's views see *NMW*, VII (1840), 1138–9. For the activities and attitudes of the fustian cutters see documents in the Fustian Cutters Collection, MCLA.

others' and throughout the 1840s continued to argue that under competition the good masters would always be at the mercy of the evil, and would ultimately be forced to follow the same path.[60]

In most cases, however, working-class analysis seems to have stopped short of wholesale rejection of capitalism as a system because of the inability of working-class leaders and thinkers to develop and effectively articulate any convincing theory of capitalist exploitation. The belief that labour was the source of all wealth, and that in consequence capitalists lived out of the profit of their workers had a well-established pedigree by the 1830s.[61] But the belief coexisted with the widespread acknowledgement of the role of the employer as worker, and even of the legitimate claims of the capitalist to 'reasonable' profits.[62] Without a precise theory of exploitation further progress was difficult. The writings of the *Northern Star* on the subject revealed only puzzlement. In its pages, the chartist leader Feargus O'Connor was left claiming that the manufacturers had contrived 'by some extraordinary process' to take advantage of the productive power of labour, or introducing his idea of the employers 'gambling on the labour of the poor'.[63]

The writings and speeches of Manchester chartists went no further. Working-class mutualism helped sustain the notion of interdependence, even if few accepted middle-class rhetoric about the identity of interests of employer and employed. The traditional division of the economic world into good and bad masters persisted, although those who were determined 'to grind them finer and finer in the mustard mill of starvation, hard labour and despair' might appear the majority.[64] Apart from the focus on the evils of competition, which itself encouraged solutions based on regulation, Owenite theorists concentrated on the systems of exchange, and in particular the currency, rather than the

---

[60] 'Richard Crowther', *NS*, 24 February 1844. Cf. comments of Richardson that 'competition is unnatural, and a competitive system is subversive of every legitimate principle of trade', *NS*, 26 December 1840 and *NS*, 23 January 1841.

[61] 'One of the Know-Nothings', *PMG*, 14 January 1832, 'One of the Oppressed', *PMG*, 14 April 1832.

[62] This weakness of chartist analysis has been frequently pointed out, e.g. Joyce, *Work, Society and Politics*, 230.

[63] *NS*, 28 September 1839; in this sense Manchester shared the general failure to mobilise the Ricardian socialist analysis noted by Thompson, *The People's Science*, 83–110.

[64] 'A Warehouseman', *NS*, 2 June 1839. Cf. comments of Kirk, *Working Class Reformism*, 21. Examples include 'A CUTTER to the Fustian Manufacturers and Merchants of Manchester and its Vicinity', (n.d.), Fustian Cutter's Collection, #10, MCLA; arguments of R.J. Richardson, *NS*, 5,12 December 1840.

productive process itself, and such ideas were often popularised and introduced into the arguments of Manchester chartists.[65] Between November 1839 and April 1840 R.J. Richardson published a long series of letters in the *Northern Star*, outlining in great detail his analysis of the ills of the currency system.[66] In many cases this itself was simplified into the traditional radical attack on the unproductive system of distribution. The nearest that the working classes came to an accepted theory of exploitation was their attack on the systems of sub-contracting and putting out: by 1848 the address of the trades delegates of Manchester was calling for the 'abolition of the middleman system, viz undertakers, squeezers, sweaters, etc..'.[67]

The failure of the working classes to develop an effective theory of exploitation did not necessarily weaken the extent of their dissatisfaction with the system, but it did mean that they lacked purchase for any effective rejection of existing economic structures, and were thus shepherded in the direction of regulation rather than repudiation, as the remedy for their ills. By 1840 there were already signs that most chartist rhetoric was switching from attacking industrialism *per se* to attacking its unbridled extension (and the advocates of this in the guise of the Anti-Corn Law League), and it was 'unprincipled' or 'unregulated' competition, and the pressure on wages which it produced, which bore the brunt of working-class hostility in the 1840s, rather than competition *per se*.[68] In the same way, although machinery and its introduction were subject to constant attacks during the chartist period, beneath the rhetoric it is clear that by the early 1840s, except in those trades like block printing where the impact of machinery was especially devastating, the working classes had come to accept the potential of machinery to cheapen goods and reduce their labour, and had switched their attack to what James Leach described as 'the crushing power of *misdirected* machinery', and to complaints that the benefits of advances in machinery were not being equitably shared between masters and men.[69] Again criticism was focused on the

[65] Stedman Jones, *Languages of Class*, 134–7, Claeys, *Machinery, morality and the millennium*, 136–42. For Manchester see James Clarke, *MG*, 6 March 1847.

[66] R.J. Richardson, *NS*, 1 June 1839, and series in *NS* from 7 March to 25 April 1840. For clearest expression of this view see 'The General Convention to the People of the United Kingdom', [12 July 1839], HO40/43/325.

[67] *MG*, 12 April 1848.

[68] Comments of the Manchester tailors, *NS*, 16 March 1844; resolutions of the fustian cutters, *NS*, 6 April 1844.

[69] *NS*, 10 May 1851 [emphasis added]: (Leach had been arguing this case for 10 years,

competitive system as a defective mechanism for governing economic decisions like the utility of investing in new machinery.

In both cases working-class analysis of the impact of competition returned to the dynamics of underconsumption. Just as taxation sapped the ability of the home market to sustain demand at the level needed to maintain wages, so the vicious cycle of competition, mechanisation, and wage reduction crucially undermined the demand of the working classes. According to the South Lancashire chartist delegates in 1841, it was the employers' 'greedy, grasping and grinding propensities... their overspeculation, competition, improvements in machinery, reduction of wages, taking money out of circulation, glutting the foreign market, and destroying the best market, namely home consumption, by preventing the people from purchasing...' which lay at the root of the problems of the working class.[70]

Yet because the dangers of the economic system were seen to be open to sanction or regulation by the state, these economic attitudes remained firmly wedded to an analysis which gave politics primacy. The solution was not the abandonment of the system, but the introduction of regulation to allow the underlying mutuality of interests of employers and employed to be institutionalised and protected. While trade unions looked in general to achieve this regulation through industrial strength whereas other groups focused much more consistently on politics, the underlying assumption was the same. When Edward Curran, the radical handloom weaver, asserted that the function of the government was to 'dignify mankind, to harmonise society' he was affirming his faith in its regulative functions. As did all the rest of the radical rhetoric of the responsibility of the government for the protection of labour. And as did the various schemes for national legislation, or for national and local wages boards, or for the provision of government allowances or training for those displaced by machinery, which were the currency of specific working-class solutions to the problems of the chartist period.[71] From this perspective as well, it was

---

see *NS*, 25 April 1840), 'A Worker', *MG*, 17 June 1846; Berg, *Machinery Question*, 269–90.

[70] 'Address of South Lancashire Delegates', *NS*, 24 December 1841, Richard Crowther, *MG*, 19 October 1842.

[71] See S.A. Weaver, *John Fielden and the Politics of Popular Radicalism, 1832–47*, (1987), 114–39; for the Manchester handloom weavers see *MSA*, 18 December 1839; see also below, pages 223–5.

the exclusion of the people from the political process which sustained the evils under which they suffered.

The maintenance of working-class theory

It has become a central plank in the explanation of the collapse of chartism that its essentially pre-industrial critique, focusing as it did on the state, was unable to survive the changing nature of political activity from the 1840s and the growing realisation that the difficulties of the working classes were at root economic rather than political.[72] Yet this interpretation fails to take proper account of the extent to which the radical critique of the political system did in fact prove remarkably durable. While it is clear that the reforms of the 1840s did deny purchase to some of the more extreme anti-state ideas, at the same time the move to a gradually more interventionist local and national state probably created greater focus for hostility, not less. Indeed, the collapse of radicalism in the post-chartist period owed perhaps much more to continued commitment to the established analysis coupled with growing disillusionment with the strategies available to the working classes, than to its renunciation.

Hence, although there is no doubt that as the burden of indirect taxation declined in the 1840s and 1850s taxation became less central to working-class political attitudes, it continued to exercise working-class as well as middle-class radicalism through the mid-century period, and it was still important enough in 1857 to be described by Charles Hadfield, one of the most politically active of Manchester's trade unionists in this period, as one of the 'great questions' of politics.[73] It did not seem anachronistic for John Frost to announce in the People's Institute in 1856 that '[t]he principal object of government is to take from those who work, and give the proceeds to those from whom the people receive no value in return'.[74] The church did not escape: as Rev. W. O'Connor, the rector of St Simon and St Jude, regretted in 1860, visiting clergy were frequently faced

---

[72] Stedman Jones, 'Rethinking Chartism', *passim*.
[73] Charles Hadfield, *MSp*, 11 April 1857; cf. 'A Manchester Plebian', *MSp*, 15 August 1857, 'Livingston Gordon', *MG*, 23 September 1858.
[74] *MX*, 27 August 1856; *vide* the persistence of the picture of the state as a huge machine for fleecing the poor to keep the rich wealthy in C.J. Haslam's *How to Make the People Virtuous*, (1857), *passim*.

with arguments about 'the overgrown wealth of the Establishment, the inequalities of our livings, the usurpation and taxation which our system engenders...'.[75] Nor did the aristocracy: Joseph Barker's anti-aristocratic rhetoric made his periodical *The People* the most popular of the radical journals in the early 1850s, and the stranglehold which the aristocracy continued to exercise on political power during the period between the reform acts was a theme which exercised radicals of all hues.[76]

It is clear that at moments of crisis such as that occasioned by the House of Lords' attempted opposition to the repeal of the paper duties in 1860, such attitudes could encourage the sublimation of a distinct working-class identity into a demotic identity which incorporated the middle classes.[77] The chronic conflicts of the mid-century, however, served rather to highlight distinctions between working and middle classes. Suggestions of the emergence of the 'neutral state' must be tempered with a recognition that the legislative concessions of the 1840s were not universally satisfactory, and the sense of exclusion, although diminished, was far from removed. After 20 years of struggling, the factory operatives, despite the various factory acts, had been denied the ten hours they had sought, and were left resentful at what Robert Holmes, secretary of the Fielden Association, called 'the combined treachery of those in whom they trusted' and the stupidity of the Whigs.[78] The rhetoric of 'class legislation' might merely express a sense that there was one law for the rich and another for the poor, but this was not a formulation emptied of class distinctions; just as easily the law could be identified as an instrument of middle-class domination. As Malcolm McLeod put it in 1867, '[u]nder a system of class legislation, many laws were made by capitalists to oppress working men'.[79]

---

[75] 'W. O'Connor', *MX*, 29 May 1860.
[76] 'John Beatie', *The People*, I, 292. The Lords' rejection of the repeal of the paper duties created perhaps the biggest anti-aristocratic outburst in the post-chartist period, but even in periods bereft of controversy, the evils of aristocratic influence were still adjudged worthy of comment, *MSp*, 24 January 1857, cf. comments of E. Hooson, *SWN*, 19 January 1867.
[77] As suggested by Joyce, *Visions*, 70–3; the one chronic resentment which drew working and middle classes together in any kind of sustained fashion, was that over the game laws, see Biagini, *Liberty, Retrenchment and Reform*, 56–9.
[78] *Factory Operatives Guide and Labour's Advocate*, 18 June 1853, in HO45/5128/160–7; cf. 'A Card Room Factory Operative', *MWA*, 14 February 1857.
[79] McLeod, *MCN*, 25 May 1867, 'W.W.', *MG*, 14 March 1859, 'A Baker's Man', *MX*, 8 October 1867; 'F.B.' (probably Frederick Booker), *MCN*, 26 October 1867; *LL*, 23

At the same time, the contrast was often drawn between employers' willingness to accept shorter hours and the steady pressure to increase the work-pace, and there is no doubt that the movement towards an increasingly economic analysis of poverty and deprivation apparent during chartism, was continued in the years afterwards.[80] The focus remained the need for collective organisation to blunt the impact of the competitive economic system, and for all the pragmatic appeal of the co-operative movement and the despair of some of its activists at the lack of enthusiasm of the membership as a whole for its sense of mission, it is significant that it was co-operation, both manufacturing and retail, which claimed so much enthusiasm in the 1850s and 1860s. Both co-operative and trade union movements, however buried this was by the immediate problems of their operations, built on the foundation of a wide-ranging critique of the operation of the unregulated economy.[81] The comment of Middleton weavers encountered by a correspondent of the *Bolton Loominary* in 1856, that 'it isn't the machinery dooin th'werk ut we should faw cawt abeawt, its th'competishun wi separate un opposin individual interests uts sappin un undermoinin, wi its selfishness, th'morals oth foak', was typical of working-class sentiment.[82]

Apart from the moral critique of the competitive system, and the feeling that it brought about the demoralisation of the working classes, the weight of dissatisfaction was aimed at its inability to produce what seemed an equitable adjustment between wages and profits. The complaint was that 'wages [were] screwed down to the lowest point,...even in seasons of the greatest prosperity, but few masters, unless urged by some plea of necessity or afraid of a strike of the hands, will voluntarily grant the smallest advance'.[83] In times of

January 1864. As Rohan McWilliam has argued, the Tichborne claimant case demonstrated 'a popular culture contemptuous of the law as a corrupt force in society...', 'Radicalism and popular culture: the Tichborne case and the politics of "fair play"', in Biagini and Reid, *Currents of Radicalism*, 56.

[80] As one man told the Manchester correspondent of *RWN*, 'some of the masters, you know, who were for the Ten Hours Bill, got great praise for their humanity, were the very first to adopt this system of forcing work, and thus profited by their philanthropy [sic]', 9 November 1851.

[81] In the case of co-operation, the negative interpretation of Pollard has been challenged by recent work such as S. Yeo, 'Introductory: Rival Clusters of Potential: Ways of Seeing Co-operation', in his *New Views of Co-operation*, (1988), 1–9.

[82] *Bolton Loominary*, 12 December 1856. For a wider discussion of the criticisms of the market and its role in competition see Thompson, *The Market and its Critics*.

[83] 'Eureka', *RWN*, 12 October 1851.

prosperity, the working classes quickly became what master spinner George Clarke described as 'refractory', and there was little evidence that those employers who invested most heavily in the paraphernalia of factory paternalism thereby overcame the undercurrents of working-class hostility.[84] Instead the wealth which facilitated paternalism was further resented. As W.H. Wood, the secretary of the Manchester and Salford Trades Council put it in 1867, the resulting '[g]igantic fortunes, princely residences, and vast landed estates obtained in an ordinary lifetime, must of necessity be the result of exorbitant profits'.[85] The size of the fortunes which the middle classes accumulated continued to cause what one Sunday school teacher described as 'a widespread feeling of discontent...powerful for mischief', and despite the weight of middle-class propaganda that profits produced only a fair rate of return, as one manufacturer lamented, 'no argument will convince them to the contrary'.[86] Although institutionally focused on co-operative stores, much of the campaigning force of Lancashire co-operation in the 1860s concerned working-class claims to a share in 'profits', claims only partially reflected in E.O. Greening's Partnerships of Industry movement.

There were changes of tone. The working classes were less likely to challenge *in toto* the contours of the existing system, and as unions established a more stable foothold within an emerging system of industrial relations, the heat of the antagonism between unions and employers was considerably cooled. Nevertheless, although unions were readier after 1850 to acknowledge some degree of shared interest, this acknowledgement was often purely conventional, and there is little evidence that the basic stance of unionism had changed.[87] When Alexander Forrester told an Amalgamated Society of Engineers festival at Belle Vue in 1866 that the interests of men and employers were identical, he added, 'at all events...to [the] extent that each was trying

---

[84] *MWA*, 16 April 1859; comment of 'A Manufacturer' that 'There is no spinner or manufacturer who is not now smarting and suffering under the ill-usage and tyranny of the last 12 months, and none more so than have done most for their workpeople in personal kindness, providing places of worship, schools, libraries, baths and wash-houses', *MG*, 26 January 1861.

[85] W.H. Woods, *Trades Unions Defended*, [1867?], 8.

[86] 'Odds and Ends' I (1855), 117, M38/4/2/1, cf. comments in John Roberton to Richard Cobden, 23 May 1855, Add Mss, 43665, ff310–11; *RWN*, 25 September 1853; 'A Spinner and Manufacturer', *MG*, 18 March 1859.

[87] See C.G. Hanson, 'Craft Unions, Welfare Benefits, and Trade Union Law Reform, 1867-75', *Economic History Review*, XXVIII (1975), 243–59.

to secure as much as they could of the loaf'.[88] Even when the language was fully embraced, it was often in a way which implied that shared interests meant that the interests of the employers were the same as those of the men, rather than vice versa.[89]

While accepting the survival of industrial pluralism, it has been suggested that the real transformation in working-class attitudes post-chartism was the rejection of structural explanations of poverty and inequality, and a slide into what John Belchem has called 'the alluring improvement ethic', which ascribed most social problems to personal moral failings.[90] Undoubtedly, there were individuals whose personal success led them to alter their economic and political beliefs and propound an increasingly individualistic creed. As one working man commented in 1850, although he used to think that the upper and middle classes were guilty of causing the privations of the working classes, he could by then see clearly that this was not the case: '[t]o me, self-inflicted misery – self-imposed taxation, are everywhere visible, improvidence rides rough-shod, prudence and economy are at a discount among working men, [and]…the more I read and think, the more firmly I am convinced that 'self-reform' must be the watchword of working men'.[91] The official temperance movement in Manchester increasingly took up this stance, disengaging itself from political radicalism and establishing a firm commitment to the motto emblazoned on the *Manchester and Salford Temperance Reporter* that 'the only government which can ensure prosperity to the people is self-government. The most effective of all reforms is INDIVIDUAL REFORM'.[92] Without individual reform, Elijah Ridings commented, parliament is 'not worth a fleeting breath'.[93]

---

[88] *MCN*, 8 September 1866.
[89] 'Memorial of the Factory Operatives of the Northern Counties', *MG*, 22 January 1859, complaints of the *MG*, 20 December 1860; cf. the call of the Manchester glassmaker to 'try to teach our masters that in studying our own interests we are taking care of theirs', *Flint Glass Makers Magazine*, (1850), 38–9.
[90] J. Belchem, *'Orator Hunt': Henry Hunt and English Working Class Radicalism*, (1985), 9. Perhaps the best expression of this is R. Cooter, *The Cultural Meaning of Popular Science*. Of course the popularity and significance of the Smilesian doctrine of self-help is well documented: see not only A. Briggs, 'Samuel Smiles and the Gospel of Work', in his *Victorian People*, (1954), but also R.J. Morris, 'Samuel Smiles and the Genesis of Self-Help: The Retreat to a Petit Bourgeois Utopia', *Historical Journal*, 24,1 (1981), 89–109.
[91] 'A working man', *MSp*, 30 November 1850.
[92] *MSTR*, 26 January 1850.
[93] Ridings, *Pictures*, 169.

In turn this could prompt a re-assessment of the need for political reform and a retreat from democratic beliefs. As 'A True Reformer' explained in 1858, from having 'attended chartist meetings and shouted lustily for the five [sic] points', and finding that it didn't work, he had decided he would 'remodel [him]self', and obtained a £15 house and a 'snug little freehold'; 'I now see...that property has its rights and must be respected and protected, and if I should ever be induced to advocate an extension of the franchise, I could not conscientiously go one jot beyond "household suffrage"'.[94]

But it is interesting that in almost all cases such sentiments came from the small, if growing minority who had raised themselves out of the working classes; those that remained in the working class, as Archibald Prentice found in 1851, were reluctant to accept middle-class versions of temperance as the panacea for social problems.[95] The sense of difference and of superiority which developed among the respectable working class did not eradicate the long-standing belief that however it might be possible in many cases to raise oneself away from the foot of the social pyramid, this did not mean that the social system itself was not both ultimately at fault for the extent of poverty and deprivation, and incapable of providing equality of opportunity and treatment to different social groups.

In most cases, what emerged was not rampant individualism, but a recognition that political reform alone could not be the panacea that some had thought it, and that, as the Manchester masons put it in 1850, 'no reform, however democratic, can improve the condition of those who are not willing to make an effort in their own amelioration'.[96] But while pragmatism might incline the working classes to ameliorative strategies, this was a priority accepted only reluctantly, and the innate working-class sense of justice continued to convince many that, as one 'rough workman' put it in 1851, '[s]elf-reform is all very well where it is needed...but give me my political rights, and let me feel and know that I am a man among my fellow men, and then I may take a pride in rising upwards'.[97]

Likewise, at the root of union activity was the assumption that collective organisation at the workplace represented, in practice, the

[94] 'A True Reformer', *MG*, 27 December 1858.
[95] Cf opposition to Prentice's views, *MX*, 1 November 1851.
[96] 'Proposition of the Manchester Masons', OSM Papers, Modern Records Centre, Warwick; cf R.J. Richardson in *MSp*, 3 March 1849.
[97] 'Eureka', *RWN*, 16 November 1851.

best weapon available in the fight for better social conditions; and if political activism was likely to weaken collective solidarity, it should be eschewed. However, unionism, in its various guises, like Owenism and the land schemes, remained collectivist responses to working-class deprivation, and as such they were quite distinct from the kind of individualist ameliorism which is often blamed for the collapse of political radicalism. Moreover, the union movement never entirely lost its commitment to the assumption that '[t]o fight the battle of trades reform with any hope of success, we...must have political power – the right to assist in legalising the means of our defence'.[98] The revival of union involvement in political activity in the mid-1860s marked not the rediscovery of the political dimension of unionism, but a re-evaluation of the need to acknowledge institutionally this dimension in the face of what seemed to be a renewed government onslaught.

Similarly, it would be a mistake to invoke working-class citation of classical economists, their use of arguments of supply and demand, or their advocacy of expedients such as emigration, as illustrative of an acceptance of classical political economy. Largely, such formulations represented the realisation that with the defeat of chartism there was no rapid path to the legislative regulation of the industrial system, and in consequence some kind of strategy had to be developed for action within this unjust system. Unionists accepted that without political protection for labour, supply and demand conditions did have an impact on the availability and remuneration of employment. As the Salford working man W. Taggart remarked in 1865, it was ridiculous to 'allow a fellow mortal to rob you of your fair day's wage, whilst you look "stoically" on, observing to yourself as he pockets your cash, "Just wait a bit till I get my co-operative engines at work, and you don't do that any more"... I am a co-operative [sic] myself, but...I am certainly afraid that that Utopian age...exists only in...imaginations'.[99] As a result, working men were prepared to accept the law of supply and demand, particularly when they could be applied to their own benefit during times of prosperity. William MacDonald, the house-painters' leader, called for 'fearless economists to tell the employer who is resisting what is fair and just', and argued that people 'who teach us

---

[98] 'W.W.' *NS*, 3 January 1852.
[99] *BH*, 29 April 1865. As MacDonald argued later, although he was not against co-operation, '...at no time can the profits of capital become a substitute for the earnings of industry. It is to this source that the vast majority of people must look for their support and comfort', *MCN*, 15 December 1866.

political economy and the laws of supply and demand, should know that these laws are no respecters of persons – are not partial to masters and abusive to men'.[100]

These formulations were also a sign of the increasing sophistication with which middle-class analysis was turned back on itself. Realising the extent to which it had an unassailable status as orthodoxy among large sections of the non-working-class public, working-class spokesmen avoided, where possible, outright opposition. Instead, elements of the thought of the leading economists were used to re-interpret their conclusions and especially the conclusions of the economists' more vulgar popularisers. 'We revere *true* political economy', announced *Weekly Wages* in 1861, 'and only protest against the narrow fanaticism that declares that man was made for political economy and not political economy for man'.[101] As one correspondent told the *Salford Weekly News* in 1866, '...we *do* know something of political economy and we are fully aware of the great divergence of opinion on its tenets revealed in the writings of Smith, Malthus and Ricardo. But we do not believe that the canons of this economic creed are exhausted when the parrot cry of "supply and demand" has been uttered'.[102] 'Working men had found out', another added, 'that there was another view of political economy, relating not only to the acquirement of wealth, but to its distribution also...'.[103]

Smith and Ricardo were also cited to demonstrate that even orthodox economists accepted that in fixing the rate of wages (and conversely the rate of profit), master and man were fundamentally at odds, so that while stable employment was ultimately in the interests of both, this by no means implied identity of interest.[104] This allowed union spokesmen, even prior to the full scale demolition of the wage-fund theory which took place in the late 1860s and early 1870s, to assert that unions had been inserted into political economy as a necessary counterweight to the masters' natural desire to maximise their profits at the expense of wages.[105] According to an 1867 circular of the

[100] *MX*, 5 October 1866, *MCN*, 15 September 1866.
[101] *Weekly Wages*, October 1861, [emphasis in original].
[102] 'A Trades Unionist', *SWN*, 27 October 1866, [emphasis in original].
[103] *MCN*, 23 February 1867.
[104] See, for example, Woods, *Trades Unions Defended*, 14–16, McLeod in his lecture, 'Trades Unions a Necessity', *MCN*, 1,8 December 1866.
[105] For the debates within political economy on these issues, and their reflections in union attitudes see E.F. Biagini, 'British Trades Unions and Popular Political Economy, 1860–1880', *Historical Journal*, 30,4 (1987), 811–40.

Association of Operative Cotton Spinners of Lancashire, '[e]conomic writers tell us there is a point above which wages cannot rise without driving capital from the trade, and also a point below which wages cannot fall without driving labour from the country, or starving it out of existence. These positions being granted, it is not difficult to see that if trades unions did not exist, the wages of the labourer would always be this starvation rate'.[106]

The occasionally fierce debate conducted in the press and on the lecture platforms of Manchester during the 1860s provides further evidence of the pragmatic and utilitarian nature of working-class adoption of political economy, and the degree to which it was persistently denied the status of unchallengeable orthodoxy. In the face of middle-class propaganda, led by the writings and platform appearances of John Watts, three lines of resistance were adopted.

First, the version of economics being propagated was attacked as a class-based mockery of reality. According to William MacDonald, the leading protagonist of Manchester's unionists, much of political economy was 'class dogmas and one sided morals', part of a 'vicious system and false opinions, propagated to maintain class interest'.[107]

Second, the propagandists' status as teachers and guides of working-class opinion was undermined by portraying them as the servants of class interests. Watts was dismissed as one of 'the school that urges that labour would be better off if it were defenceless', he was part of the 'Newall's Building clique', and his methodology confirmed his bias: '...as he declines to consider the justice of the strike and overlooks the lock-out, he negatively adopts the side of the masters, whether he intends it or not', MacDonald pointed out.[108] When the leading place on the platform was taken by an ex-smallware weaver who was eventually discovered to be receiving funds from Watts and his Liberal backers, this lesson was even more starkly drawn.[109]

Third, working-class thought invoked experience as the universal standard by which mere theory could be evaluated and, if necessary,

---

[106] *MCN*, 28 December 1867.
[107] 'William MacDonald', *MCN*, 27 October 1866, 3,10 November 1866. See also 'A Trade Unionist', *SWN*, 27 October 1866.
[108] *Weekly Wages*, October 1861; *MX*, 5 October 1866. Compare with the ironic commentary in *LL*, 11 February 1865; see also *LL*, 4 June, 23 July 1864.
[109] *BH*, 22 December 1866, 'Thomas Evans', *MCN*, 21 January 1867; comments of McLeod, *MCN*, 2 November 1867.

rejected. William Wood put the case clearly in his pamphlet *Trades Unions Defended*:

> The union is denounced and the workman is endeavoured to be cajoled into the belief that it is no friend to him. But it is preferable to accept the honest expression of the working man's convictions of the fruits of his faith in Union, than all the learned disquisitions of the ablest professors of political economy that the country can produce. The latter is but theoretical, based upon an ordinary accountant's calculation that any school boy can accomplish; the former is founded on the daily teachings of common life, practically tested and proudly achieved; for whenever a Trade Union has passed through the fiery ordeal of either a strike or a lockout, it has confirmed the faith of its adherents in the rectitude of their policy.[110]

In this way, via a selective re-interpretation of classical political economy, coupled with a more fundamental rejection of its authority, (denying its scientific objectivity, and presenting it as a class-inspired perversion which failed to provide solutions to the actual problems of society), the working classes were able to erect barriers which intellectuals such as Watts were unable to breach; and the more urgently they tried, the more determinedly the working classes clung to the dictates of their own reason.[111] As James Staton, editor of the *Lankeshur Loominary* commented laconically, 'Its a subject thats often cum before th'public, un a greight deol has bin said on booath soides; but mitch as has been said ogern combinashuns un stroikes, thoose ut have believed in um un do believe in um seem as far off beein converted as ever'.[112]

The limits of the chartist vision

The stunted vision of late nineteenth century labour movements has long been seen as a central aspect of the inhibition of socialism.[113]

---

[110] Wood, *Trades Unions Defended*, 6. Cf. the comments of Robert Last in the 1866 'Annual Report of the General Union of Carpenters and Joiners', *BH*, 1 December 1866, W. Macdonald in the *Monthly Reports of the Amalgamated Society of Carpenters and Joiners*, (November 1866), 17–18; and W.H. Fraser, *Trade Unions and Society*, (1974), 167–84.

[111] As Wood commented at a meeting of the Manchester and Salford Trades Council in 1867, 'The more frequently they were assailed, the more powerful their antagonists, the more firmly did they believe in the principles of union', *MCN*, 19 January 1867.

[112] *LL*, 23 July 1864.

[113] See Savage, *Dynamics of Working Class Politics*, R. McKibben, 'Why was there no

Implicitly and explicitly this lack of vision has been contrasted with the chartist years, during which, as Neville Kirk has put it, working-class radicalism was 'held together by a vision of a new social order'.[114] However, the revolutionary implications and rhetoric of chartism should not be allowed to obscure the fact that even the relatively attenuated social vision of the working-class movements of the early 1830s, such as the National Union of the Working Class and the Grand National Consolidated Trades Union, persisted only in diluted form within O'Connorite chartism.[115] Even contemporaries recognised the confusion of radical and chartist thought. Joseph Smith, a Salford Owenite, commented that 'they see not, they know not their position as men in society and their worth and power when their energies shall be properly directed, so they seem quite at a loss, and wonder at their own ignorance'.[116]

In the pre-chartist period, the language of the working classes was studded with the confined phrases of pragmatism. The General Builders Union of 1833 was supported because it would 'secure by industry a comfortable livelihood for future generations'; the United Trades of 1834 wanted 'Fair Play - a clear stage and no favour'; the ten hours cause was summed up as '[t]hat all may have an honest living,/ That none may e'er be wanting food'.[117] Chartism brought a greater sense of confrontation but not a more ambitious conception of the ultimate goal. Its appeal remained prosaic and essentially reformist. It is of course in some senses a truism to argue that chartism was, in J.R. Stephens' words, 'a knife and fork question'. Nevertheless, what is striking about the utterances of chartists in Manchester, is how much they returned to this motif. R.J. Richardson described chartism as 'a bread, beef and ale question', and promised that it would satisfy the wants of the people for 'a fair share of the good things in life'.[118] The Manchester Female Reformers claimed that the 'charter...will protect labour, and secure plenty, comfort, and happiness to all'.[119] Even

Marxism in Great Britain?', *English Historical Review*, XCIX (April 1984), 297–331.
[114] Kirk, *Working Class Reformism*, 65–6; or what James Epstein has described as 'increased awareness of the possibility for fundamental social and political change', *The Lion of Freedom*, 115.
[115] For one of the very few studies to recognise fully the implications of this see R.A. Sykes, 'Trade Unionism and Class Consciousness', in J. Rule, ed., *British Trade Unionism 1780-1850: the formative years*, (1988).
[116] Joseph Smith to Robert Owen, 18 July 1836, #805, Owen Papers, Holyoake House.
[117] *MSA*, 25 May 1833; HO/40/32(4)/291; *MSA*, 27 April 1833.
[118] 'R.J. Richardson', *NS*, 19 January 1839.
[119] 'Address of the Female Chartists of Manchester', *NS*, 24 July 1841; compare with the

chartists like O'Brien, with a more developed social critique, are to be found extolling the virtues of the charter in terms of vague promises that it will bring 'more and greater ease'.[120]

What is particularly noticeable is the virtual absence of any fully-fledged rejection of property *per se*, an almost inevitable consequence of the dominance of labour theories of value. Another of Richardson's visions looked to the time when 'England [will] flourish, the poor become happy, and the rich [be] safe in the enjoyment of their prosperity'.[121] Hence, even when ostensibly 'socialist' ideas began to penetrate chartism, under the slogan 'the charter and something more', the extra was often a banal summing up of the good life: according to Manchester chartist Thomas Jones, taking up the traditional radical motif of 'freedom', 'freedom meant something more substantial than a vote in an election; it meant clothes, fire, food, education, and amusement for the people'.[122] In large part chartist utopianism did not move beyond this vague belief in the possibility of a better life with the charter.

Although chartism was able, particularly at times of crisis, to attract support from organised labour, this support was often based on a narrowly confined view of what the charter was hoped to gain. For many unionists chartism was a mechanism of change, an alternative to trade unions, rather than an alternative social vision. Hence the address of the chartist mechanics of Manchester spoke of their desire to use the charter to establish 'a proper remuneration of labour, security of capital, [and] create confidence and goodwill betwixt employers and workmen'.[123] Neither in trade union chartism, nor in the subsequent moves to establish non-chartist political trade union alliances was there ever any aspiration to overthrow the existing economic system: as John Gash told an aggregate meeting of the Manchester unions in 1846, what they wanted was not to prevent the employer from acquiring capital,

Manchester-issued placard 'The Executive Committee of the National Chartist Association to the People', HO45/247C/215.

[120] HO40/43/239-46.

[121] R.J. Richardson, *NS*, 6 January 1838.

[122] *MG*, 28 September 1850; George White, who by 1850 had come under the influence of Harneyite ideas of social reform, was in 1848 still telling audiences around Manchester that chartism meant 'a full cupboard and plenty of clothing', *MC*, 21 June 1848; for White see S. Roberts, *Radical Politicians and Poets in Early Victorian Britain. The voices of six Chartist leaders*, (1993), 11-38.

[123] *NS*, 9 July 1842; for a more extended discussion of this see R. Gray, 'Languages of factory reform..', in P. Joyce, ed., *The historical meanings of work*, (1986), especially 150-156.

but the power to ensure that it would not be 'turned out and round' on the workers who had aided its acquisition.[124] The horizons of at least some chartists were even narrower than this: of Manchester chartists in the aftermath of the Plug Plots, one letter intercepted by the Home Office declared, 'we want the wages paid 1841 if they wont give it us Revolution is the consequence [sic]'.[125]

The exiguousness of such visions of transformation was unsurprising. The radical analysis of social ills made social and economic revolution unnecessary. If prevailing evils were due to imbalance and maladjustment, what was needed was merely a mechanism to ensure readjustment. The appeal of the political power which the charter offered was that it promised the ability to establish government as this regulator, and the concrete aspirations of the working classes in the chartist period focus on the regulatory power of government.

Working-class attitudes to the state in the chartist period were deeply ambivalent. Certainly the state as it was constituted was increasingly seen as an alien and hostile force; the New Poor Law, the new police, amongst others, all helped to bolster hostility to the state. At the same time, the tradition of looking to government for the establishment of minimum wages or in some cases for the regulation of hours, was well-established, and continued to prevail.[126] According to David Roberts, one of the Manchester chartist rank and file, 'until there was a law enacted by the legislature of this country, that the people must work for so long in the day, and that they must receive so much for it, they would never be happy or contented'.[127] As the pace of technical change accelerated in the 1830s and 1840s, the threat of technological unemployment added control over the introduction of new machinery and the provision of training and employment for those thrown out of work by it, to the responsibilities of the government. As nightsoil man John Smith told a Manchester court in 1848, '[b]y the law of England every man...should be furnished with the means of an honest

---

[124] *MC*, 27 May 1846, 'A Worker', *MG*, 17 June 1846.

[125] Intercepted letter, HO45/264/100. The weavers as a body had resolved to strike for the 1840 rates and, if they were not ceded, then for the charter, *NS*, 13 August 1842.

[126] For an introduction to some of these tensions, see P. Richards, 'The State and Early Industrial Capitalism: the case of the Handloom Weavers', in Rule, *British Trade Unionism, 1780–1850*.

[127] *MSA*, 7 March 1840; cf. Layhe's comments in 1843 that the general feeling of the working classes he met was 'that democracy would cure the evils of society by regulating both machinery and wages', *MTPAR*, (1843), 23, 'A Working Man', *MG*, 28 February 1846.

livelihood..'.[128] It is thus in complete consistency with the tenor of working-class aspiration throughout the chartist period that the 1848 movement to establish what was grandly christened the 'Northern Trades Association for Obtaining Political and Social Reform', should have attempted to add to the charter various policies such as national and local boards of trade, limitation of hours of labour, effective sanitary laws, unsectarian education, the abolition of entail and primogeniture laws, and the application of crown and waste lands to the absorption of surplus labour.[129]

The prominence still given to the land was significant, because it was certainly in their attitudes to the land that the working classes came closest to envisaging social transformation.[130] The co-operative thinkers came closest of all: undoubtedly for the Owenites, the land represented an opportunity to reshape the whole basis of society. Yet the ideal of Owenite communities never gained more than the fleeting adherence of anything but a small minority of the working classes, even before the collapses of the 1840s finally disillusioned even its most ardent supporters. Moreover, even with Owenism, the vision was often limited. For all its utopian language, the programme of the Regeneration Society in the early 1830s was merely to effect a reduction in the hours of labour to eight. The attack on competition was often by inference on unfair or unrestricted competition, and there was only patchy evidence of any wholesale rejection of the competitive system, or of any suggested alternative.[131] With the collapse of the land communities, the visionary elements of Owenism receded: the associative labour ideas of the Christian Socialists after 1848 could envisage only slow gradual reform.[132] Despite his sympathy, from his close contacts with Manchester Owenites, Engels was forced to admit that they had no sense of 'a definite policy culminating in the dissolution of the existing social order'.[133]

This was true even of later chartist and trade union schemes of land colonisation. The appeal of the land was associated indelibly with the

---

[128] *MSA*, 26 August 1848; state provision could avoid the stigma of 'charity', 'A Working Man', *MG*, 21 April 1847.

[129] *MSA*, 8 April 1848, *MX*, 22 April 1848.

[130] See M. Chase, *The People's Farm: English Radical Agrarianism, 1775–1840*, (1988).

[131] See Stedman Jones, *Languages of Class*, 123–4.

[132] As Noel Thompson has argued, they no longer aimed to remove the market, merely to moralise it, *Market and its Critics*, 121–5.

[133] Engels, *Condition of the Working Class*.

appeal of pre-industrial England, and appeared to offer the chance to escape the 'slavery of the factory' for an environment of natural plenty. Yet once industry and mechanisation had been accepted, as they were by the 1840s, it might provide individuals with an autarchic defence from the market, but it could provide no alternative to capitalism.[134] It was significant that while Owenite schemes had envisaged communal land ownership, the chartist land plan operated on the basis of the establishment of peasant proprietors, via regular contributions. In this context, the land had become merely a strategy to cope with capitalism either by reducing the supply of labour, and thus improving the bargaining position of the working class, or by providing industrial workers access to land which would free them from the position of having to choose starvation or the wages offered by the employer.[135]

The practical aspects of co-operation always proved popular with the Manchester working classes. They provided a promise of immediate, if gradual improvement, in contrast with the less certain gains of political action. By appealing to individual action in co-operation for the common good, they helped bridge individual aspirations for improvement and working-class mutuality. Hence the considerable popularity which land schemes did have in Manchester during the 1830s and 1840s.[136] But any wider conception of the creation of an alternative economic system was violently rejected. For the Manchester masons, suggestions that their union should use funds to begin contracting for business in their own right were 'wild and visionary' and 'about a century too soon'.[137]

---

[134] For a good discussion of the limitations of working class attitudes towards the land see Thompson, *Market and its Critics*, 86–93.

[135] E.g. Thomasson, *Regenerator and Chartist Circular*, 26 December 1840, *NS*, 8 July 1843, 5 September 1846, J. MacAskill, 'The Chartist Land Plan', in Briggs, *Chartist Studies*, 305–7.

[136] Several working class groups attempted to establish land schemes, e.g. the smallware weavers and the wireworkers, *MSA*, 18 January 1845; though note the comment of Riley of the plasterers at the March 1845 NAUT conference that the trades of Manchester 'were not ready for the land question', *NS*, 29 March 1845. The land was also a central motif of the 'Kirkdale pamphlets', issued by the Manchester chartist leaders from Kirkdale Gaol, see Roberts, *Radical Politicians*, 27–8.

[137] *OSMFR*, 27 August 1840.

Sense of an alternative society in the post-chartist period

In the post-chartist period, the simmering frustration, and the sense of their own power, which led the chartists to talk revolution, certainly waned. But this was not because of any great change in working-class visions of an ideal society. Ironically, as O'Connorite chartism began to disintegrate as a movement at the end of the 1840s, strenuous efforts were made by chartists like Harney and Jones to develop a much more comprehensive social chartism.[138] However it is clear that this had little impact amidst the working class generally, and by 1853 Jones was forced to revert to a more gradualist and less 'utopian' version of social change, accepting the need to make the best of the existing system for the time being, while hoping eventually to replace it with a better one. The limited, gradualist nature of working-class aspirations have been the subject of much study, and it is not necessary here to duplicate this.[139] It is worth emphasising, however, the extent to which this 'reformism' was consistent with the attitudes of the chartist period. There was the same desire for 'sweet competence', or 'a fair day's work and a fair day's wage, and no Bastille to keep our wives and children from starvation', as one banner of 1863 put it.[140] Working-class groups continued to look to government regulation of hours and wages, and for the protection of and provision for those made unemployed by the advance of machinery, while this search was still tempered by suspicion of what the Manchester Chartist Association called in 1851 'the officiousness of centralised power'.[141] The desire for change remained strong, and in the 1850s Layhe noted the degree to which revolutionary theories and ideas continued to ferment below the surface of the working classes.[142] The difficulty was, as the *Manchester Guardian* put it in 1857, although the masses wanted change, they were not sure what form it ought to take.[143]

Nevertheless, change can be detected in the nature of working-class vision in the post-chartist period. Just as the memory of the Peterloo

---

[138] See Claeys, *Citizens and saints*, especially chapter 8.

[139] See in particular Kirk, *Middle Class Reformism, passim*.

[140] *MG*, 8 August 1859, *MX*, 24 November 1863.

[141] *NS*, 3 May 1851; Thomas Hackney of the packers, *NS*, 10 May 1845, Manifesto of Operative Dyers, *MX*, 18 November 1854; see 'An Operative Painter', *MG*, 27 October 1856; address of the delegate hand mule spinners, minders, etc., *PPr*, 2 February 1856.

[142] *MTPAR*, (1857), 24.

[143] *MG*, 4 June 1857.

era had dulled the sense of the power and the immediacy of change for the radicals of the post-1815 era, so the defeat of chartism prompted a certain reluctance to speculate on an ideal future of which there was clearly little hope of implementation in the foreseeable future. For some the lesson of chartism was the need to distrust the visionary, with his castles in the air, and looking back Rogerson mused on the time when 'o'er Utopian schemes my fancy ran,/ By which my aid might liberty advance', until 'manhood's day dispelled my waking trance'.[144] Even within the co-operative movement, better circumstanced than most for sustaining wider visions, there are signs of impatience with visionary aspirations. For W. Taggart, quoted above, the repudiation of visions was the necessary precondition for action; but for others it may well be that there was a constriction of their sense of the possibility of an alternative or even a markedly improved social system, which encouraged the development of the kind of fatalistic conservatism, rooted in the struggle for daily existence, which has been much observed among the casually-employed and low paid working class in the late nineteenth century.[145]

As the possibility of political and social change receded, so of course did the function of the articulation of visions of an ideal society. Nevertheless working-class utopias can still, as Patrick Joyce has argued, be uncovered in the formulations of popular art and literature.[146] Joyce's study of ballads, popular melodrama, and dialect literature rightly stresses the constrained and in many respects quite conservative utopias of this literature in the second half of the nineteenth century. Nevertheless, this conservatism was born of frustration not contentment, and ultimately the labourist (or 'demotic') vision was not so much a retreat from chartism, as the reassertion of chartist ideas shorn of the apocalyptic means for obtaining them to which the chartists had looked.

---

[144] 'A scheming visionary./ His castles in the air were all he could bequeath./ Hope ever charmed him with her gilded snares', Nicholson, *The Sabbath Peal*, 8; Rogerson, *Musings*, 106.

[145] James Harrop spoke of the working classes 'looking upon events, the cause and prevention of which are in their own power, as matters of course, simply to be submitted to without either question or consideration', *MTPAR*, (1868), 25; see, for a classic formulation, Stedman Jones, 'Working-class culture and working-class politics in London, 1870-1900: Notes on the remaking of a working class', in his *Languages of Class*, 179–238.

[146] Joyce, *Visions of the People*, chapters 9 and 10.

Conclusion

In order to uncover the changes in working-class consciousness in these years, this chapter applies the distinctions between the normative, theoretical, visionary, and strategic elements of consciousness which were developed in chapter one. It argues that working-class radicalism in the chartist period was based on a distinctly non-bourgeois value system, and that this value system survived largely intact into the mid-Victorian period. Persistence is also very much in evidence in the theoretical frameworks with which the working classes sought to make sense of socio-economic and political deprivation. Where attitudes changed here was in the recognition of changing conditions, not in the theoretical assumptions on which analysis rested. Furthermore, it is suggested that interpretations of the collapse of radicalism have exaggerated the extent to which the working classes in the chartist period adhered to a vision of a coherent and well-developed alternative society.

From this perspective, there is little to be gained from an interpretation of the post-chartist period which speaks of the 'collapse' of radical thought or implies a retreat from class consciousness. The heart of working-class consciousness, its value system and visionary thought, remained virtually untouched by the collapse of chartism and the ostensible improvement in social and economic conditions at mid-century. What underwent change were in part working-class theoretical knowledge, and, in particular, beliefs as to the feasibility of the various strategies of change open to them. But these changes were not the result of a failure to comprehend the circumstances in which the working classes found themselves, but rather the consequence of a realistic assessment of changing social, economic and political conditions. If we were to divide working-class thought between universal and contingent elements, it was the contingent elements which changed, and changed in response to changes in the conditions upon which they were contingent.

Chapter Eight

The strategic contradictions of mid-nineteenth century radicalism

Neither the change in the material circumstances of the working classes nor the attempts at moral imperialism of the middle classes appear to provide sufficient cause for the sort of political demobilisation which took place in the 1840s and 1850s. Part of the explanation may lie in the fact that working-class consciousness in the chartist period was never as 'revolutionary' as has often been suggested, and that as a result the contrasts between the chartist and the post-chartist periods have been overdrawn, and the continuities of working-class norms and values underestimated. By invoking the notion of strategic consciousness, this argument can be taken one stage further: while the continuities in much working-class thought were strong, what the period did see was a progressive collapse of the fragile and partial strategic consensus which was the primary achievement of O'Connorite Chartism.

The move to chartist radicalism

In the years after the 1832 Reform Act, the general consensus that the effects of the Act would have to be given time to work themselves out effectively undercut attempts to sustain the mass platform campaign for universal suffrage. Attention turned to factory reform, the New Poor Law and the municipal corporations. Attempts by the Huntite radicals to maintain the focus of radicalism on further franchise reform were ineffectual, despite the early efforts of O'Connor.[1] Instead, most working class activity concentrated on attempts to build bridges with tory-radicals like Oastler, or whig-radicals like Fielden, and centred on the local politics of the vestry and the police commission. While these movements retained some semblance of coherence, the frustrations of radicalism proper prompted the formation of a series of rival

[1] Epstein, *Lion of Freedom*; Sykes, 'Chartism and the Trades', 395–415.

associations.[2] At the same time there were signs that disillusionment with the outcome of the reform campaign of 1830–32 encouraged some who had been drawn into radicalism to turn once again to unionism, and in the mid-1830s Manchester saw a number of fierce union struggles.[3]

Increasing frustration with action on both wings gradually encouraged a return to agitation for the franchise. The 1833 Factory Act was a bitter disappointment to the factory reformers, and the lack of encouragement which the campaign received gradually forced its supporters back to the lessons of 1832 and the franchise campaign.[4] Likewise, as the government pressed on with the implementation of the Poor Law after the arrival of the commissioner in Manchester in October 1836, bodies like the South Lancashire Anti-Poor Law Association gravitated steadily towards political solutions. The defeat of Fielden's anti-Poor Law motion in February 1838 confirmed this change in strategy, which was affirmed at the great Kersal Moor meeting of September 1838 which marked the commencement of the chartist mass platform agitation in Lancashire.[5]

For the trade unions, the New Poor Law, with its thinly disguised attack on wage rates, was merely one of a series of incidents which seemed to demonstrate that political power was being used to undermine union effectiveness. By 1838 incidents such as the Glasgow spinners' case had convinced many unionists that the government '[had] sworn enmity against our order'.[6] By the end of 1837 a general organisation of the trades had been established which provided a platform for the development of a trade union inspired chartism. As organisations, the unions stayed aloof from the first wave of chartism, but by 1840–42 an increasing sense of failure meant that the unions themselves were committing themselves to political action.[7] In March 1842 the address of the trades and political associations conceded that

[2] See Weaver, *John Fielden*; for local politics in Manchester see Fraser, *Urban Politics*, 38–41, 61–5.
[3] See R.G. Kirby and A.E. Musson, *The Voice of the People: John Doherty 1798–1854, Trade Unionist, Radical and Factory Reformer*, (1975), 272–98. While it is true, as Winstanley has recently commented, that 'radicalism should not be conflated with unionism' ('Oldham Radicalism', 621–2), neither should the overlaps be ignored.
[4] J.T. Ward, *The Factory Movement, 1830–55*, (1962).
[5] Weaver, *John Fielden*, 179–96.
[6] Trade union placard c.20 June 1838, HO40/38/59.
[7] This process is dealt with in R.A. Sykes, 'Early Chartism and Trade Unionism in South-East Lancashire', in J. Epstein and D. Thompson, eds, *The Chartist Experience. Studies in Working-Class Radicalism and Culture, 1830–1860*, (1982), 169–74.

it seemed that only politics could 'secure labour from the aggression of capital', and, announcing their affiliation to the National Charter Association in July 1842, the Manchester mechanics conceded that trade unions 'h[ad] been tried and found wanting'.[8]

Nevertheless, this activity did not mark either the development of essentially new aspirations for the working classes, or the abandonment of non-political or non-chartist strategies. In his lectures to the trades which did much to bring the unions into the chartist fold in 1842, James Leach, one of the Manchester chartist leadership, had been careful to emphasise that in calling for political activism he was not advocating the abandonment of trade unionism, merely recommending necessary safeguards for their operation. Certainly, the unions who joined were careful to retain their independent identity, in most cases establishing separate political societies, and while pressure for piecemeal legislative reform was swamped by the enthusiasm for the charter, there was little evidence that the old demands had been abandoned. Chartism was embraced because it appeared to offer new hope of providing the power to obtain these demands. Its support depended on the extent to which it could maintain a convincing character as the most effective option for working-class action.

The dilemmas of radicalism

The problem was that the success of chartism in achieving the general support of the Manchester working classes between 1839 and 1842 did not itself mean that radical leaders had successfully generated a consensus on the correct strategy for change. The fate of chartism only makes real sense if it is recognised as an umbrella movement which covered a wide range of strategic options. These divisions have long been recognised, and a variety of conceptualisations have been advanced. Two linked alternatives dominate much of the literature: conflict or collaboration, and revolution or reform (not always expressed in this vocabulary).[9] Although centrally concerned with strategy, judgements about policy are inherent: Marxist convictions that collaboration leads inevitably to the dilution of class goals has meant

---

[8] *NS*, 26 March, 9 July 1842.
[9] In place of the second couplet, for example, John Belchem has talked about 'fundamentalist' and 'opportunist' strands of radicalism, see *'Orator Hunt'*, 9–10.

the virtual exclusion of the possibility of collaborative strategies in pursuit of transformative goals.

The problem is that the historical reality was more complex, even perhaps than the contemporary rhetoric of moral force versus physical force would allow. Historians like T.H. Kemnitz have pointed out that this dichotomy is too simplistic, but the extent of the divergence has never been fully discussed.[10] Within traditional 'physical force' it is possible to distinguish between those who sought political change by armed insurrection, those who sought to bring down the existing system by tactics of unarmed resistance, including general strike or non-payment of taxes, and those who saw physical force as a threat which would intimidate the ruling classes into conceding change. In essence 'moral force' chartism rejected these insurrectionary and intimidatory overtones and looked to the power of reasoned argument and the force of example to win over the ruling classes.

However, what has been insufficiently acknowledged is that this alternative moral force tradition must also be divided. Some radicals saw moral force as a strategy of conversion aimed primarily at the rest of the working class, to remove the differences of opinion which prevailed and create a united working-class voice. The implication, left deliberately vague, was that a united working class would quickly draw concessions ('moral force' proper). For others, however, moral force chartism was seen as using rational platform argument, and the example of an increasingly respectable working class, to create a public opinion, particularly among the enfranchised middle classes, in favour of the charter (what we can term 'moral suasion'). As the Manchester Chartist Council put it in 1851, chartism rather than 'a roar of defiance', would be 'a philosophical appeal to the good sense of the nation'.[11]

The strategy of moral suasion was thus one of alliance, in that it recognised the need for the support of the middle classes if the charter was to be passed. The difficulty was that the attempt to gain middle-class support was inevitably met by offers of compromise, and it was more against compromise than alliance *per se* that chartist anti-middle-class rhetoric was directed. Hence, here too, increasingly clear lines of division can be drawn, between those who stressed the vital integrity

[10] T. H. Kemnitz, 'Approaches to the Chartist movement: Feargus O'Connor and Chartist strategy', *Albion*, V (1973), 67–73.

[11] *NS*, 8 March 1851; for an interesting picture of a suasionist, which brings out much of the character of the type, see the chapter on Charles Clarke in Roberts, *Radical Politicians*, 77–88.

of the charter and the need for universal manhood suffrage to be introduced at one step (the 'fundamentalists'), and those who, recognising the implications of alliance with the progressive middle classes, accepted the need to take the largest possible reform as an instalment, and then renew the agitation for more (whom O'Connor attacked in 1841 as the 'instalment men', and whom we might term the 'incrementalists').[12]

Paralleling the strategies of radicalism proper were a range of essentially non-political strategies, which prompted various gradualist and ameliorative movements, including temperance, self-education, co-operation and trade unionism. Not that the distinction was clear in practice. Neither physical force nor moral force chartism were ever completely divorced from ameliorative movements. Activities of personal betterment such as temperance could be seen as an adjunct to political movements in several ways. Apart from being urged as part of a general abstinence from excisable goods, temperance was often adopted by radicals who recognised that the money which they could save in this way was vital to the support of radicalism, just as trade unionists realised that expenditure on drink might rob them of 'the sinews of war'.[13] Temperance and the concern for rational recreation and self-improvement which went with it, were also seen as a vital part of the campaign to spread working-class knowledge of politics and economics and hence to increase support for radicalism.[14] Self-improvement was endorsed as part of the tactics of moral suasion, as a means of convincing the middle classes that there was nothing to fear in granting the charter, or of meeting middle-class demands that the workers should merit franchise.[15]

At the same time, strategies of amelioration could derive from a growing disillusionment with platform politics, a frustration that after years of agitation little had been achieved, and a belief that it was necessary for action to be reorientated towards more practical ends. This was likely to be particularly true when it appeared that a consensus on the need for reform existed, and all that remained to be

[12] NS, 15 May 1841, cited in Winstanley, 'Oldham Radicalism', 924–5.
[13] For temperance chartism see account of Griffen's lecture, NS, 24 October 1840, 6 February 1841.
[14] P.M. M'Douall address, NS, 15 August 1840.
[15] Comments of O'Brien in Manchester, MSA, 11 December 1841; G. Chambers, NS, 24 May 1851.

decided were the details: in this case the platform might be marginalised almost completely.

It would be foolish to imply that there is no natural link between such strategic choices and political goals. The more transformative or revolutionary the ultimate aim, the less suasionist tactics are likely to promise success, and the greater the appeal of physical force solutions. However, if we accept that, except at the margins, working-class demands in the chartist period were essentially limited, then two conclusions must follow. First, that there was no inherent advantage in adopting fundamentalist and class-conflict models of political action, and second, that changes in strategic choices are just as (if not even more) likely to reflect changes in perceptions of the available opportunities for successful political action as some more fundamental transformations in class consciousness. Unless we are determined to bow down to the Marxist teleology that class action must be class conflict, then there is nothing sinister in the drift to collaborative politics, and there is nothing in this drift which undermines the utility of the concepts of class or class consciousness.

The divisions of Manchester chartism: physical force

Few would deny that working-class radicalism in the chartist as well as the post-chartist period was deeply divided. Historians have, however, tended to approach this division from extreme positions: those of the left identifying those individuals or factions who diverged from orthodoxy as renegades or class traitors; those on the right seizing on the divisions as evidence that there was no working class or at least no general working-class consciousness.[16] The truth lies somewhere in between: working-class unity in the chartist period derived from its shared sense of values, understandings and prescriptions for reform. The task of working-class radicalism, as of all political movements, was to mobilise and institutionalise this unity around a specific programme of reforms, and specific strategy and tactics for their achievement. Despite the magnitude of O'Connor's achievement, this was something which even he could not sustain.

---

[16] For an example of the former see Belchem, *Orator Hunt*; for the latter see E.H. Hunt, *British Labour History, 1815–1914*, (1981), and A.E. Musson, *British Trade Unionism, 1800–1875*, (1982).

Working-class radicalism in the 1830s was dominated by the realisation that the 1832 Reform Act had been extorted from the ruling class only by the threat of revolutionary violence, thus providing tangible confirmation of the assertions of the Huntites that 'the ministers would not give the people such a measure as they wanted unless through fear'.[17] Oastler's comment to the Manchester Regeneration Society in 1836 that it was useless to appeal to the humanity of the middle classes, that 'the only appeal was to their fears', set the tone of the chartist agitation.[18] From this perspective the function of the platform was to generate a convincing image of a revolutionary threat by mobilising what appeared to be revolutionary fervour, by showing a 'bold front'.[19]

The majority of chartists little expected the language of revolutionary violence to be translated into action. The strategy was based on the assumption that in the end the demonstration of popular will would be enough, that, as the Manchester Political Union put it in an 1838 address, 'it is when the people can overthrow everything that they never need to move'.[20] Hence the ambiguity of the notion of 'physical force', (deliberately maintained by the mystifying abstractions used by the leadership), and its ability to draw together both those who accepted and those who rejected the actual use of violence. The rhetoric of physical force acknowledged that the priority of chartism was to explore all possible avenues of constitutional redress of grievances. It was able to present itself as the preserver of social peace by arguing that it was only the mindless resistance to change of the authorities which allowed pressure to build to exploding point. It appealed, for example in its stress on the right to bear arms, to those radicals for whom the Englishman's birthright struck a particular chord. In doing so, it brought together violent revolutionaries and moderate reformers.[21]

O'Connor's version of physical force radicalism clearly had considerable appeal in Manchester. Almost as soon as the chartist alliance had been cemented by the great Kersal Moor meeting of

[17] Gilchrist, *MSA*, 4 February 1832.
[18] Thomas Clegg to John Fielden, 10 July 1836, Fielden Papers, MJRL.
[19] Police deposition, 31 July 1838, HO40/43/475-6.
[20] 'Address of the Manchester Political Union', *NS*, 2 December 1838.
[21] For a rhetorical analysis of the chartist physical force platform, see A. Clark, 'The Rhetoric of Chartist Domesticity: Gender, Language and Class in the 1830s and 1840s', *Journal of British Studies*, 31 (1992), 62–88.

September 1838, there was a deliberate move away from the moderate stress on 'union, knowledge and perseverance' which had previously characterised the campaigns of that year.[22] By November torchlight meetings were being regaled with calls to be well armed and ready to petition no more. Richardson, the leading figure in Manchester chartism at this time, was quite open about his tactics, acting to restrain the movement when it appeared there might be any real move towards violence, and even boasting to the magistrates that his intention was to intimidate, rather than foment immediate insurrection.[23] During the sittings of the Convention and the run up to the presentation of the petition, the language of violence became increasingly specific, and the practice of public drilling, in overt defiance of the authorities, became common.[24] The symbolic nature of this activity is clear: for example, chartist companies would parade openly through the streets of the city, even having a band at their head.[25]

Nevertheless, even at this stage it is clear that Manchester radicalism was not completely united behind the O'Connorite stance. Many of the old radicals of the Peterloo vintage, including Elijah Dixon, continued to ally themselves with the Manchester Political Union, which stressed its desire to 'collect and organise the peaceful expression of public opinion', in opposition to the Manchester Chartist Political Union.[26] The divisions were confirmed by the repudiation of the initial Manchester delegates to the 1839 Chartist Convention, including R.J. Richardson, in favour of the much more aggressive William Butterworth and William Tillman.[27] Although the physical force party prevailed in the matter of delegates, it would seem from the falling off of support for chartist mass demonstrations and among organised labour after this split, that a considerable proportion of the rank and file had inclined against physical force also.[28]

Such indications should warn against the temptation to play up the decidedly revolutionary element of chartism, and urge caution in what

---

[22] *NS*, 18 August 1838.

[23] Egerton to Russell, 16 December 1838, HO40/37/40–43.

[24] See, for example, police deposition, 23 April 1839, HO40/43/177–9.

[25] *MC*, 27 July 1839, Wemyss to Philips, HO40/43/423–5.

[26] *MSA*, 11 August 1838, Manchester Political Union, *Rules*, (1838), 'Address', *NS*, 22 December 1838.

[27] *NS*, 11 May 1839.

[28] *MG*, 29 May 1839, *MC*, 1 June 1839. Cf. also the publication by Bamford of his *La Lyonnaise* (1839) with a long introduction warning against the futility of the appeal to arms, reprinted in his *Homely rhymes, poems and reminiscences*, (1864), 242–5.

appears at times to be a tendency to dwell on revolutionary fragments as a key demonstration of chartist virility.[29] Certainly, judging the strength of the real revolutionary wing of chartism is fraught with difficulty. As the language of the chartists was deliberately ambiguous, the extent of any revolutionary threat can only be gauged by the amount of underground organisation. In Manchester there is little evidence of any widespread revolutionary underground. After the replacement of Richardson, the public demonstrations continued as before, although there was some move towards smaller private meetings.[30] Arming did take place, and many of those arrested in 1839 were found to possess arms, but no move was made towards establishing a specific plan of action.[31] It is thus significant that in Manchester, as in the manufacturing districts generally, the breakup of the Convention in Birmingham and the rejection of the petition in July was met not with an escalation of military preparation, but instead with attempts to organise the Sacred Holiday.[32]

The general strike was the foremost weapon in the armoury of the second strand of physical force chartism, akin to non-violent civil resistance. The assumption behind this strategy remained the need to force concession out of the ruling classes; however, in place of the threat of direct armed rebellion, it sought alternative ways of threatening to undermine the political and economic system: as the Manchester Political Union put it, 'if the working men of England were to stand aloof from work for one week, the social compact would be broken, [and] anarchy, robbery, and confusion then reign'.[33] Several traditional radical tactics were supported in this cause: the non-payment of taxes or abstention from all excisable goods; engineering a run on the banks by demanding gold; exclusive dealing; alternative elections to a convention or anti-parliament; as well as the general strike. Together they might have provided a progression of tactics with which pressure could have been gradually increased on the authorities. Unfortunately, many required nationally co-ordinated action which was

[29] This might be said of Thompson, *The Chartists*, 67–87, or of Goodway, *London Chartism*, and certainly of M. Jenkins, *The General Strike of 1842*, (1980).
[30] Police deposition, HO40/43/177–9, Evidence of witnesses, c.23 July 1839, HO/40/43/479–81, Wemyss to Phillips, 6 August 1839, HO40/43/493–6.
[31] Foster to Russell, 4 May 1839, HO40/43/197–9, Wemyss to Phillips, HO40/43/493–6, *MC*, 17 August 1839, Police deposition, HO40/43/475–6.
[32] Wemyss to Phillips, 1 August 1839, HO40/43/436–8; *NS*, 3 August 1839.
[33] 'Address of the Manchester Political Union to the Working Classes in Birmingham', *NS*, 22 December 1838.

beyond the control of the Manchester chartists, and those offering the opportunity of local success, such as exclusive dealing, were ill-suited to the scale and impersonality of Manchester.[34]

In consequence, the strike tactic, just like the recourse to arms, presented the chartists with the insurmountable problem of how to generate the solidarity and unanimity necessary for success; and once again, despite the rhetoric, there was little concrete preparation among the Manchester chartists. Nor, apart from a little sporadic effort to turn out mills, was there much sign of revolutionary activity during the attempted 'sacred month' in August 1839, and despite the arrest of some chartists discovered with arms, the authorities expected no trouble.[35] The confusion which existed in the popular mind between the strategy of overthrow and the strategy of threat, coupled with chartist propaganda about the inability of the authorities to resist the will of a united people, had merely encouraged a lack of preparedness and Manchester chartism was left to collapse amid recriminations over the failure of the national and local leaders to develop an effective plan of campaign.[36]

The disappointments of 1839 brought the swift collapse of physical force chartism in Manchester. In November Butterworth commented that 'the silence of the people of Manchester had been more dreaded for the last few weeks than their noise was some time ago'.[37] From then until the spring of 1842 the authorities in Manchester remained confident that physical force supporters were few.[38] The failure of the first petition campaign and the 'sacred month' had generated a clearly defined group, centred on T.P. Carlile and his *Regenerator and Chartist Circular*, who rejected the threat/overthrow strategy, and called for more ameliorative strategies.[39] A police spy present at a chartist committee meeting noted a feeling of 'mutual distrust' and 'much and quarrelsome discussion' between the two groups.[40]

---

[34] Few attempts were made to implement exclusive dealing in the town, and those that were tended in fact to be small scale co-operative retail schemes rather than communal boycotts, *NS*, 29 June, 27 July 1839, 19 November 1842.

[35] *NS*, 17 August 1839, Thomas Potter to Russell, 9 August 1839, HO40/43/519–20, Maude to Russell, 13 August 1839, HO40/43/544–6.

[36] 'Address of the Salford Radical Association', *NS*, 23 May 1840.

[37] *NS*, 2 November 1839.

[38] Shaw to Phillips, 2 December 1839, HO40/43/740–2, Shaw to Phillips, 1 March 1841, HO45/46/9–10, Arbuthnot to Fitzroy Somerset, 17 September 1832, HO45/268/177–80.

[39] *Regenerator and Chartist Circular*, 7 December 1839 [at HO40/43/776–83].

[40] Neale to Shaw, 17 December 1839, HO40/43/835–8.

Symptomatic of this split, the circulation of the *Northern Star* in Manchester fell off considerably, and various other chartist papers, particularly the *Northern Liberator,* became increasingly popular.[41] Nevertheless, widespread agreement was gradually accorded to James Leach's opinion that physical force was 'worse than madness', and that while standing firm on the principles of the charter, it was necessary to concentrate on the proselytisation of the working classes.[42] The establishment, at a national delegate meeting held in Manchester in July 1840, of the National Charter Association (NCA), on an impeccably moral force stance, marked the acceptance of Leach's analysis, and prevented any institutionalised split in Manchester chartism.[43] Certainly as a result of this redirection of chartist action in the early months of 1840 it remained possible for moderate chartist figures who had kept aloof from the agitation during 1839, including Abel Heywood and James Scholefield, to maintain a loose affiliation with organised chartism, acting as treasurers to committees, appearing on the platform at large meetings, and giving occasional lectures, while retaining a strictly moral force stance. Heywood's essentially Lovettite position is made clear in the lecture he gave in aid of the chartist prisoners in September 1840, and he did all that he could to distance himself from physical force doctrines, apparently even undertaking to inform Charles Shaw, the police commissioner, of any threatened revolutionary outbreaks.[44] Likewise Scholefield used his position as chairman of the Hunt Monument Committee to act as a moderating force.[45]

During 1840 and 1841 Manchester chartism channelled its energies into the conversion of the working classes.[46] The NCA programme included 'the diffusion of political knowledge', and considerable effort was invested in extending the range of chartist meeting places and the amount of chartist propaganda. In the fifteen months up to the end of October 1841 seven chartist meeting rooms were opened.[47] These

[41] Shaw to Phillips, 9 December 1839, HO40/43/795–802.
[42] *NS*, 16 May 1840.
[43] *NS*, 1 August 1840.
[44] *NS*, 19 September 1840, Shaw to Phillips, 20 May 1840, HO44/35/H/nf, Shaw to E. Chadwick, 8 February 1842, Chadwick Papers 1794/30-2, University College, London.
[45] Cf. evidence in the *Trial of Feargus O'Connor and Fifty-eight others,* [1843], 199–214.
[46] It seems that as early as March 1839, R.J. Richardson had been seeking support for the establishment of a 'Constitutional Society for Promoting Political Instruction', see Richardson to John Fielden, 20 March 1839, Fielden Papers, C353 827a, WYRO, cited in Weaver, *John Fielden,* 223.
[47] *NS*, 6 November 1841. It was later claimed that before the concentration on Carpenters

rooms housed chartist libraries and provided discussion groups and lectures.[48] The rhetoric of chartist addresses concentrated on calls to 'dig our foundations deep by spreading extensively political information'.[49] The South Lancashire delegate meeting appointed James Leach as a full-time lecturer for the district, and established a comprehensive lecturers' plan to ensure that the various chartist localities were regularly served with voluntary lecturers.[50] By the start of 1841 Leach and M'Douall were concentrating their efforts on organised labour, attempting to persuade Manchester unionists of the limitations of unionism without political power.[51] Associated with all this activity was a prominent place for temperance and co-operative ideas, and every effort was made to stress the moderation and legality of the chartist position.

During 1841 and particularly during the early summer of 1842 this stance succeeded in effecting the affiliation of several of the trades, and in establishing a healthy local membership of the NCA.[52] When Charles Shaw attended a chartist meeting in March 1842 he was 'much struck with the great change in the appearance' of the chartists; whereas the previous winter they had been 'of the most dirty, ragged and disorderly class', now 'they were well dressed and as well conducted as in a Church'.[53]

The apparent revival of 1848 cannot disguise that from this time physical force ideas were effectively abandoned in Manchester. Although during the early months of 1848 the authorities became concerned at the spread of revolutionary feeling among the Manchester working classes, this activity was quite distinct from earlier chartist physical force in the extent to which it relied on the Irish repeal movement.[54] Even in 1843 it is clear that the remnants of the physical force faction in Manchester had recognised that the Irish repealers

---

Hall, the chartists had ten different rooms open in Manchester, *NS*, 15 August 1846.

[48] These discussions focused not on indignance subjects, but on issues such as the impact of burial societies on the political institutions of the country, *NS*, 31 October 1841.

[49] 'Address of the South Lancashire Delegate Meeting', *NS*, 17 October 1841.

[50] *NS*, 5 November 1840.

[51] *NS*, 1 February 1841.

[52] Cordwainers and tailors, *NS*, 6 February 1841, carpenters and joiners, *British Statesman*, 8 May 1842, mechanics, *NS*, 4 June 1842.

[53] Shaw to Phillips, 10 March 1842, HO45/249C/25-6.

[54] See W.J. Lowe, 'The Chartists and the Irish Confederates: Lancashire 1848', *Irish Historical Studies*, 24 (1984), 172-96, *idem, The Irish in Mid-Victorian Lancashire*, 184-8.

formed the group most likely to endorse violent action, and the events of 1848 bore this out.[55] In the early months of the year chartist and repeal movements formed a close alliance which fed not only on news of the revolutions in Europe, but also on developments in Ireland where events were moving rapidly towards the rebellion of the United Irishmen.[56] However, despite the delegate of the London chartist insurrectionists finding Manchester ready for insurrection in August 1848, the chartist-repeal alliance had already foundered on Irish disgust at the pusillanimity of the majority of the chartists, and the only sign of revolutionary activity in Manchester by this time was within the repeal clubs.[57]

The actions of the railwaymen, in agreeing to be sworn in as special constables to protect property, but at the same time stressing their commitment to the charter, indicates that the revival of physical force touched only the peripheries of Manchester chartism. Certainly, in contrast to 1839 and 1842, there was little doubt among the Manchester middle classes that the bulk of the workers would have no truck with violent solutions in 1848.[58]

Intimidation or suasion?

However, the repudiation of direct action as premature and then as impracticable, did not of itself imply any lessening of chartist hostility to the middle classes. The chartist leaders, in particular, were still determined to force the charter in its entirety on the middle classes, and from the outset the NCA maintained the commitment of O'Connorite chartism to a confrontational approach. This involved chartism in the pursuit, in tandem, of a series of tactics.[59]

[55] NS, 3 June 1843, Police report on chartist meeting of 8 June 1843, HO45/350/95.
[56] NS, 19 February, 11,25 March 1848, MSA, 18 March 1848.
[57] Foster to Grey, 6 April 1848, HO45/2410A/99–103, (although in contrast see Elkanah Armitage's comments that there appeared to be no definite plans, HO45/2410A/113–4), Goodway, London Chartism, 89–93; for the later repeal activity see MG, 29 July 1848, Arbuthnot to Waddington, 17 July 1848, HO45/2410D/AD/546–7, and idem, 26 July 1848, HO45/2140D/AD/591–2. See also details in the brief for the trial of George Archdeacon, in TS11/137/374 Part 1.
[58] M. Goffin, ed., The Diaries of Absalom Watkin. A Manchester Man 1787–1861, (1993), 271–8.
[59] 'Address of Salford Radical Association', NS, 26 October 1839.

On one level, the chartists still hoped to use education as a strategy of intimidation. The weakness of chartism had been the authorities' confidence that the working classes were not united: the NCA was intended to broaden and deepen working-class commitment to chartism, to create the kind of united working-class support which would, as William Tillman, one of the first NCA executive put it, 'strike terror into the hearts of the poor man's oppressors'.[60]

At the same time, perhaps more effective than intimidation would be the practice of paralysing the effectiveness of traditional middle-class pressure group politics, especially the Anti-Corn Law League (ACLL), by seizing control of the local platform.[61] The intention was to ensure that at all public meetings on political questions, amendments in favour of the charter were passed, both to generate evidence of the solidarity of the working class for the priority of the charter and in the hope that this thwarting of rival radical movements would force the concession of franchise reform and the charter. This kind of platform censorship was initiated almost as soon as the 1839 Sacred Holiday collapsed. Public meetings for other movements, like the Peace Society or the anti-slavery movement, were similarly taken over by the chartists.[62] Throughout 1840 and early 1841 constant chartist spoiling tactics brought local ACLL activity to a virtual standstill, the chartists boasting that it was impossible to hold any public meeting in Manchester without a chartist amendment being passed.[63]

Nationally, to complement this platform struggle, again on the model of the League, the chartists attempted to mobilise the electoral power of the working classes to gain the election of chartists, both on local bodies and to parliament. In Manchester, the size of the constituency and the strength of middle-class Liberalism made this a formidable task, and at this time there was little electoral activity. Similarly, while the Salford chartists did make a concerted effort to elect chartist police commissioners, Manchester remained reluctant to act.[64] O'Connor made it clear that his electoral strategy was based on refusing any close

[60] NS, 19 December 1841, William Thomasson, NS, 9 January 1841.

[61] 'A Member of the Manchester Chartist Association', Regenerator and Chartist Circular, 7 December 1839; NS, 14 December 1839. This was a common chartist tactic, see W. Hinde, Richard Cobden. A Victorian Outsider, (1987), 127, for Norwich, R.J. Morris, Class, Sect and Party, 189–91.

[62] MC, 7 November 1840, NS, 12 December 1840.

[63] NS, 4 April, 8 August 1840, 15 May 1841; for the ACLL perspective see N. McCord, The Anti-Corn Law League, 1838–46, (1958), 51–3, 96, 99–102.

[64] NS, 29 October 1842, 24 August 1844.

alliance with existing political groups, and on using the power of the chartists to harm local electoral prospects and obstruct parliamentary business in order to bid for support from the middle classes.

Not all radicals were happy with continued confrontation. Many of those, like William Butterworth, who had supported the strategy of overthrow in 1839 were now convinced that 'they must have a greater number of wealthier classes on their side than they had at present' and turned to the line of Richardson, Cleave and Hetherington at a national level, of a more conciliatory policy towards the middle classes.[65] Furthermore, during 1840 and 1841, the sheer negativity of the chartist opposition to the ACLL seems to have disillusioned many, who wished to see the policy of confrontation with the middle classes abandoned in favour of a more conciliatory strategy which attempted to win over the middle classes by force of argument rather than by intimidation, coupled with an attempt to establish firmer political foundations by renewing links with other strands of working-class activity including the unions and the ten hours movement.[66] There are signs that sections of working-class radicalism were willing to look favourably on the olive branches such as the Household Suffrage Association of 1841 and the Complete Suffrage Union (CSU) proffered by middle-class Radicals, despite the hostility of O'Connor and official chartism.[67] It would seem that these groups had been convinced along with Richardson that 'without union, their great and noble ends could never be attained'.[68]

At this stage, however, the activities of the League only served to bring out chartist anti-industrialism. Relations reached a low point after May 1841, when the Leaguers turned for support to the Manchester Irish, whom O'Connell was able to mobilise in favour of repeal, and a series of confrontations between the chartists and the Irish occurred, at which the chartists were generally bested, and the Leaguers were able to pass anti-Corn Law resolutions.[69] However, organised chartism remained determined to oppose middle-class political initiatives. Attempts to gain endorsement for the CSU platform at public meetings in Manchester were successfully thwarted, and after the bitter defeat of

[65] NS, 14 March 1840.

[66] 'A Radical of Twenty-five years' standing', MSA, 20 March 1841, 'A Huntite Radical', MSA, 27 March 1841.

[67] MSA, 5 March 1842, 'Address of the Trades Delegates of Manchester' (dated 15 March 1842), Commonwealthsman or Chartist Advocate, 2 April 1842.

[68] British Statesman, 16 April 1842.

[69] MG, 19 May 1841, Shaw to Phillips, 5 June 1841, HO45/46/22-3, MG, 27 October 1841.

the Plug Plots in the autumn of 1842, the chartists returned to their attempts to nullify the League's platform agitation.[70]

Nevertheless, the renewal of trade union involvement in chartism in 1840 and 1841 meant that the possibility of direct action in support of the charter was never completely discountenanced. Indeed as economic conditions worsened markedly in late 1841 and early 1842, it was placed on the agenda again.[71] Hence the rapidity with which the August 1842 strike in the out-townships became a general strike for the charter. Undoubtedly the chartist leadership played no part in the initial strike, but the alacrity with which they attempted to seize the opportunity to mobilise a general stoppage demonstrates an essential continuity of strategy from 1839 to 1842. Unfortunately, the readiness of the trade delegates to advocate a general strike for the charter represented the application of conventional union methods to broader goals rather than full acceptance of physical force chartism. There is little evidence that the unionists had thought through the implications of their decision and once the spectre of anarchic revolution had been raised and firm action taken by the authorities, the organised trades quickly abandoned their stance, leaving the weavers and fustian cutters to struggle on.[72]

The failure of the 1842 strikes did encourage some recourse to private meetings at which violent action was discussed, but once again, apart from the prevalence of casual talk about the desirability of the armed seizure of government there is no sign of any attempt to put these ideas into practice.[73] Moreover, the persistence of violent mutterings among the chartists should not disguise the fact that the fright taken by organised labour had once again rocked the movement back on its heels. Indeed, it could be argued that 1842–43 marked the effective end of intimidatory chartism in Manchester, accelerating a movement away from this form of politics which had been visible since the early 1830s. In 1845 John Layhe observed that although the

---

[70] 'John Campbell', *NS*, 5 November 1842, *MG*, 7 December 1842. We must thus be careful not to over-exaggerate the impact of the Stevenson Square defeat of June 1841 (see Hinde, *Richard Cobden*, 88).

[71] Shaw to Phillips, 16 February 1842, HO45/249C/9–10, which talks about a meeting passing resolutions in favour of the passive resistance system.

[72] For the Plug Plots see A. Rose, 'Truckling Magistrates of Lancashire in 1842', *Transactions of the Lancashire and Cheshire Historical Society*, 83 (1985), 40–70.

[73] Arbuthnot to Phillips, 10 August 1843, HO45/434/76–8; cf. comments of Brierley that the men who met in his father's house were in the habit of talking about the need for 10,000 trained pikemen to establish a republic, *Home Memories*, (1887), 23.

working classes still laboured under what he called 'long-cherished misconceptions and prejudices', nevertheless, 'bitter experience' had taught many that '...they had gained nothing by listening to violent counsels'.[74] Certainly, Manchester chartist audiences in 1848 demonstrated little patience with the violent rhetoric of figures such as G.J. Mantle.[75]

Fundamentalism or incrementalism?

The fate of the Plug Plots brought into question again the nature of radical strategy, and further widened the divisions appearing within Manchester radicalism. The uneasy truce which had prevailed within the chartist ranks since the spring of 1841 was fractured as the early converts to moral suasion went one stage further and abandoned fundamentalism in favour of support for the kinds of gradualist strategies advocated by the CSU.

The division between fundamentalists and incrementalists stretched back to 1832 and it had been O'Connor's most important achievement to revive working-class confidence in the Huntite platform strategy as a viable mechanism for achieving all the chartists desired at one swoop. Nevertheless, from the failure of the 1839 Convention onwards, it is clear that the Manchester working classes, although increasingly committed to the charter itself, became more and more disillusioned with the strategy which O'Connor followed. While dissentients in the 1839–40 period tended to concentrate their fire on the intimidatory nature of chartists tactics, there is a clear undercurrent of gradualism beneath the ideas of the Carlile group.

The chartist challenge to the ACLL brought these divisions increasingly into the open. Despite the success with which the chartists were able to organise opposition to the ACLL at its public meetings, the success of the Operative Anti-Corn Law Association demonstrated a considerable vein of working-class support for the ACLL stance, and

[74] *MTPAR*, (1845), 10, *ibid*, (1843), 23–4; the previous year he had commented that 'The repeated failure of political nostrums to effect the regeneration and happiness of the British people has, I believe, taught some that their personal welfare and social rank depend much more on their own foresight, economy and good conduct, than on the measures of any government, however enlightened', *ibid*, (1842), 22.

[75] J. Belchem, 'Radicalism as a "Platform Agitation" in the periods 1815–21 and 1848–51. With special reference to the leadership of Henry Hunt and Feargus O'Connor', (PhD thesis, University of Sussex, 1974), 215–6.

a minority of working-class radicals, identified with the *Manchester and Salford Advertiser*, remained perturbed by this strategy which struck radicals like Bamford as being like 'the fruit grower who says he will not pick any of his berries until all of them are ripe, and can be brought down with one shake of the tree'.[76]

The failure of the Household Suffrage Association in Manchester, the reluctant conversion of the League Radicals to the universal suffrage stance of the CSU, and the ability of the chartists to persuade even an aristocratic trade like the mechanics to stick with the chartist line, demonstrates the continued strength of fundamentalist attitudes. Indeed the gradual extension of middle-class reform schemes was taken as the clearest proof of the success of holding out for the charter without compromise.[77] The anti-alliance rhetoric of this period was thus in part a reflection of the deep distrust which the working classes had of middle-class intentions and consistency, but in essence a rejection not of alliance, but of alliance on any platform which marked a retreat from the six points.

The failure of the Plug Plots undoubtedly caused a re-think of this attitude.[78] In December, the chartists had to physically throw CSU supporters out of the meeting held to elect delegates to the CSU conference to be sure of electing 'whole hog' men, and by the start of 1843 a clear division within the working class was developing on this issue.[79] R.J. Richardson asserted that his conversion was one mirrored by 'a vast body of the intelligent people', who differed from the chartists, 'not upon principle, but upon their policy'.[80] 'The radicals with whom I am "immediately connected"', announced Richardson, 'are in favour of every measure of reform, no matter how small the amount'. In May 1843 this group established a rival Democratic Chartist Association, and although there is little concrete evidence of the operation of this body, the 'sturgite rump' appear to have continued to be active through the year.[81]

Tensions also remained within the Manchester NCA, but the rapidity with which the Leaguers abandoned the CSU, and the reversion of the NCA to gentle moderation during 1843 meant that the issues of alliance

---

[76] *MSA*, 27 March 1841, see also the letter of 'A Huntite Radical' in the same issue.

[77] 'Address of South Lancashire Delegates', *NS*, 26 February 1842.

[78] Cf. the letter of 'An Old Chartist', *NS*, 3 September 1842.

[79] *MG*, 17 December 1842.

[80] *MSA*, 22 April 1843.

[81] *NS*, 27 May, 9 December 1843.

and incrementalism were by-passed.[82] Indeed in the ensuing years, the bulk of working-class effort was channelled once more into various ameliorist or practical movements, ranging from the Oastler Freedom Fund and the Ten Hours agitation at one extreme to the campaign against the Master and Servants bill at the other.[83] Over the next few years, the activities of the working-class gradualists centred on the interventions of figures like Heywood, John Watts, and John Teer, who built up a kind of working-class Cobdenite group, which as well as providing working-class support for various League meetings, was itself active in calling for more rapid action on the Corn Laws, and for an extended removal of taxes on articles such as tea, butter and cheese.[84] Although the chartists never evinced great enthusiasm for free trade ideas, by 1847 individual chartists like James Leach were acting with this group, and there were signs that they were moving towards closer co-operation over reform matters.[85]

At the same time, the leaders of Manchester chartism remained convinced that the strategy of opposing middle-class political movements needed to remain central to chartist activity. According to John Nuttall, one of these leaders from 1843, 'it [was] by meeting the Leaguers on their own dunghills, that [the chartists] achieved in Manchester their proud position'.[86] Similarly, although they were willing to court the support of middle-class groups, the Manchester chartists remained convinced that 'this movement must never be permitted to merge into a middle class movement'.[87] Such attitudes reveal the contradictions which bubbled beneath the surface of working-class politics in the mid-1840s.

---

[82] Cf. the suppressed attack of Thomas Heames on some of the chartist leaders, *NS*, 27 May 1843. Heames remained a member of the NCA Manchester council throughout 1843, but was apparently not active thereafter, and appears to have drifted towards protectionism.

[83] See Weaver, *John Fielden*, 250–74.

[84] *MC*, 6 December 1845, 14 October 1846, 24 February 1847.

[85] E.g. the joint meeting to call for the repeal of the ratepaying clauses of the 1832 Reform Act, *MC*, 17 February 1847.

[86] *NS*, 27 December 1845.

[87] *NS*, 17 April 1847.

The acceptance of alliance

The events of 1848 revealed the divisions which remained; but the subsequent rapid collapse of popular support for the surviving chartist groups made clear that the bulk of the working class had finally abandoned the policy of opposition to middle-class reformers to which the dwindling chartist rump clung. Once again, largely for tactical reasons, at the height of the chartist 'revival' of 1848, the divisions between fundamentalists and incrementalists often remained blurred, but it is clear that while chartists like Donovan and Leach were carried along on the Irish tide, the moderates reverted to explicit attempts to build up a middle-class alliance, and in particular to rally the shopkeepers into calling for the charter.[88] While a few individuals toyed with a reversion to revolutionary tactics in alliance with the Irish repealers, many ex-chartists, including prominent figures such as G.H. Smith, William Tillman and Thomas Whittaker, were increasingly being drawn out of the O'Connorite camp and into groups such as the old Universal Suffrage Association (USA).[89]

Although the moderates in the Association attempted to use the atmosphere of crisis to press for middle-class support for the whole charter, and initially differentiated themselves from the O'Connorites on the basis of their moral force strategies, the commitment of its leading lights to incrementalist strategies was soon apparent, and faced with the emergence of a Cobdenite Parliamentary and Financial Reform Association, it quickly amalgamated with the more progressive Leaguers within Vincent's People's League, on a manhood suffrage and lower taxation programme.[90] This moderate movement was stifled by the strong discouragement of public meetings which the authorities thought it necessary to introduce at the end of May. Nevertheless, for the first time incrementalists had not just indicated a willingness to settle for an instalment of reform, but had begun to explore local avenues to the institutionalisation of class collaboration. The new realism of 1848 even encouraged a formerly model O'Connorite such

[88] *MX*, 11 April 1848, *MSA*, 15 April 1848: a shopkeepers' committee was briefly established, *NS*, 22 April 1848.
[89] *MX*, 9 May 1848, *MG*, 13 May 1848, *MSA*, 20 May 1848. The USA was also able to attract many who accepted the charter but were deeply suspicious of chartist organisation, cf. 'A Shopkeeper', *MX*, 10 June 1848.
[90] *MSA*, 10 June 1848. For Richardson's reiteration of his incrementalist stance see *MX*, 22 April 1848.

as Thomas Clark, originally from Stockport, but increasingly a central figure in Manchester chartism, not only to publicly embrace collaborationist and incrementalist strategies, but even to join the Parliamentary and Financial Reform Association (PFRA).[91]

The PFRA, with its feeble commitment to franchise reform, was not a comfortable home for ex-chartists, and not for the first time, rather than attempt to maintain a rival working-class organisation committed to collaboration, many of the USA leaders took the decision to move back into the chartist mainstream after the collapse of the chartist-repeal alliance. With many of the 1848 leaders in prison, the incrementalists were able to obtain a tenuous control over the semi-autonomous Manchester Chartist Council, which had been set up in late 1848 as a sign of dissatisfaction at the failure of the NCA to hold a properly organised election for its new executive. The incrementalists had little affection for the Manchester chartist prisoners, and the result was a series of increasingly bitter exchanges. During late 1848 and early 1849, the Manchester Chartist Council, while clearly rejecting moral force outright, was racked by disputes between the split supporters of rival suasionist strategies. When Leach was released from prison in September 1849 he was able to rally a deeply divided council around his stance of support for middle-class alliance, but rejection of 'juncture' with any association which did not embrace all the points of the charter.[92]

The immediate result was the decision, in April 1850, of Thomas Clark, Philip McGrath and William Dixon, all of whom had close links with Manchester, to set up the National Charter League (NCL) on explicitly incrementalist and moral suasionist lines.[93] Although the NCL fared little better in Manchester than it did elsewhere, it undoubtedly had the (at least) tacit sympathy of many of the Manchester Chartist Council, and the tensions which this created prompted the formation of a rival pro-NCA faction which although it admitted the necessity of alliance, opposed the incrementalist leanings of the Council. In the early months of 1851 the establishment of a new Manchester locality of the NCA, and the reformation of the Chartist

[91] Roberts, *Radical Politicians*, 97–100.

[92] *NS*, 4 August 1849, cf. comments of Doyle as Manchester representative to the Chartist conference, *NS*, 15 December 1849.

[93] The initial address of the NCL noted that 'it appears that the only hope of the democratic movement is in a sincere co-operation with that section of the middle classes, who are anxiously promoting the cause of freedom', *NS*, 6 April 1850.

Council into the Manchester Chartist Association confirmed this split.[94]

Despite the resolution of the dispute over the status of the rival 1851 London and Manchester conferences, relations between the two groups remained strained until the autumn of that year, when reunification was effected. Ostensibly, this was the result of a relaxation of the NCA position so that, without making any commitment to support incrementalist movements, chartists could attend meetings called to express public opinion, and test that opinion by proposing amendments in favour of the charter, but not attempt to disrupt them or actively oppose other reform movements.[95] If this moderation was encouraged by hopes for the newly established National Reform Association, the pusillanimity of the reform proposal eventually agreed upon quickly brought disillusionment.

Within Manchester itself, the lines of division at this stage became further confused by the emergence of the issue of 'social rights', and the overlaying of strategic issues with splits based on loyalty to O'Connor, who at this stage began his brief flirtation with the middle-class political reformers. Certainly, by the time Manchester chartists began to draw battle lines over the call of the Manchester Chartist Council for a conference in Manchester to revive the movement, it became clear that Leach and many of the 1848 leaders were aligning themselves with O'Connor and the NCL leaders in favour of what Leach called 'a new organisation upon a more intelligent, tolerant and conciliatory basis'.[96] However, when the extent of O'Connor's debility became apparent, and Ernest Jones and his supporters tightened their grip on chartist organisation both nationally and in Manchester, the incrementalists once more drifted away. At this juncture there can be little doubt that the reluctance of the chartist movement to accept the implications of the final collapse of physical force strategies, as demonstrated by the internal struggles of 1850–51, completed the alienation of working-class radical opinion which had been spread during the 1840s. By 1852 organised chartism in Manchester was confined to a handful of loyalists, sustained only by Jones' *People's Paper*, and preoccupied with internal organisational disputes; sporadic

---

[94] *NS*, 1 February 1851, 'Address of the Manchester N.C.A.', *NS*, 15 February, *NS*, 8 March, 5 April 1851.
[95] *NS*, 13 September, 1 November 1851.
[96] *NS*, 1 February 1851.

attempts to rekindle a wider activism were singular failures.[97] By the autumn of 1853 little more than a committee remained, and despite chartist attempts to make capital out of the Preston Strike of 1853, with Jones' Labour Parliament movement, there is little evidence that this had any beneficial knock-on effect on chartism itself.[98] During the following years, Manchester chartism remained in this parlous condition. Its significance was not so much in its activity, but in its persistent refusal to move towards an acceptance of the needs of alliance. Despite its numerical importance, Jones and the NCA localities remained the spiritual guardians of the chartist cause, and by maintaining their exclusive stance they succeeded only in extending middle-class suspicion of reform, confirming working-class alienation, and preventing any possibility of the creation of a united reform opinion, as a result undermining any attempts at a general working-class/middle-class reform movement.[99]

From 1852 this and the impact of the Crimean War effectively silenced working-class radicalism in Manchester. Nevertheless, the extent of underlying sympathy can perhaps be gauged by the ability of chartists with a national reputation to attract considerable numbers to meetings at the People's Institute, and the readiness with which old patrons like Abel Heywood and W.P. Roberts returned to the chartist platform once the outright opposition to compromise had been abandoned by the chartist conference of November 1857.[100]

The setbacks to radicalism (in all its forms) in the 1857 general election, and Jones' increasing difficulties with the *People's Paper*, coupled with the particularly galling victory for conservative Liberalism in Manchester, finally broke the tenuous hold of fundamentalist chartism in Manchester. Announcing his conversion to incrementalist strategies in February 1858, Edward Hooson, a leading figure in Manchester chartism from 1850, and by 1858 its acknowledged leader,

[97] *MG*, 28 July 1852, *PPr*, 25 December 1852, 16 April 1853.

[98] *PPr*, 24 September 1853; despite the presence of chartists on the trades committee, and relatively successful fund raising, only 13 votes were recorded from Manchester in the election of the executive in the spring of 1854. Manchester was in any case only lukewarm in its support for the Preston strikers, see letter of Lyon Playfair in HO45/5244/nf.

[99] The difficulties of the mid-1850s were encapsulated by Joseph Cowen, in his *Northern Tribune* (1854): Cowen argued that the working classes recognised the need for alliance with the middle classes, but had grown apathetic because of the failures of the chartist campaigns, while 'those of the working-classes who are not apathetic are foolishly exclusive', 37–9.

[100] 'Edward Hooson', *PPr*, 18 April, 9 May, 7 November, 5 December 1857.

commented that '[i]f anyone could show how the Charter could be gained at one stride better than it was now proposed to gain it by two, he would yield and adopt that course; but he believed that the course now recommended would amount to this – one step with the middle classes and then the Charter'.[101] Despite the continued reluctance of Jones, leading Manchester chartists Hooson and William Longmaid were at the forefront of the new move. With Longmaid commenting that as most of the working classes were clearly determined to stand aloof from chartism there was little use in retreating into extremism, the Manchester chartists voted for alliance with the middle classes on the basis of universal suffrage, abandoning for the time being their insistence on the other five points. At this stage the alignment of chartism nationally remained unclear: despite the fact that the February 1858 chartist conference accepted the alliance stance, relations with Morley's Parliamentary Reform Association remained tepid because of Roebuck's ratepayer suffrage stance, and Hooson's attempt to obtain an explicit repudiation of platform disruption failed.[102] In Manchester, however, it is clear that, with Hooson in the lead, class-conflict chartism was dead.

Radicalism reunited? 1857-67

Despite the opportunities created by the chartist change of heart, the achievements of the years between 1857 and 1865 were profoundly disappointing for radicalism. The proliferation of reform associations in Manchester between 1857 and 1862 was a sign of weakness not of strength; it was also a further indication of the difficulties of the radicals' position. Having demonstrated their willingness to compromise with the progressive Liberals, the radicals were left with the problem of how to ensure that the most extensive measure of reform possible was to be extracted within the new alliance. Unable to mobilise the degree of support necessary to impose themselves on the alliance, working-class radicals struggled to reach agreement as to the best means of exerting pressure within the broader movement. The inclination of Hooson, and more firmly of Jones (of increasing local significance after his move to Manchester in 1861), was to oppose all

---

[101] *MG*, 14 February 1858; for a brief notice of Hooson, see *MCN*, 18 December 1869.
[102] *PPr*, 13 February, *RWN*, 14 February 1858.

programmes which did not include universal manhood suffrage.[103] Unfortunately, since there was clearly no middle-class enthusiasm for such a platform, this was tantamount to a repudiation of collaboration. Yet the logic of simply accepting whatever middle-class reformers were able to sell to moderate Liberals (the stance of figures like Robert Cooper, the ex-Owenite) led only as far as the abdication of influence which typified his role.[104]

The difficulty of the position was made clear by the end of 1858. At the start of the year, studiously avoiding chartist overtures, the Manchester Liberals established the Manchester Reform Association on the lines of the moderate Parliamentary Reform Association.[105] Hooson's attempts to conciliate the middle classes by focusing his agitation on the surrounding villages brought no response and the resulting frustration of Manchester radicals eventually brought Hooson to establish a local working-class reform committee on the more democratic Parliamentary Reform League stance, which renewed the pressure on the middle-class reformers and managed to obtain agreement to a reform conference at the Union Chambers in November.[106] This conference, despite the strident calls of Edmund Potter (the leading figure among the middle-class reformers) for a rating suffrage, agreed to a programme of registered manhood suffrage, triennial parliaments, and new electoral districts, and put in train the establishment of the Manhood Suffrage Association (MSA), with Abel Heywood as president. Undaunted, however, Potter simply formed the rival Lancashire Reformers Union, which incorporated most of the radical wing of the old ACLL, dismissed the MSA as 'limited in its object, contracted in its sphere' and (more importantly) as too democratic, and plumped instead for ratepayer franchise, triennial parliaments, the ballot and electoral redistribution.[107]

[103] See the 'Address of the Manhood Suffrage Association', *Cabinet Newspaper*, 15 March 1859.
[104] For Cooper see A.D. Taylor, 'Modes of Political Expression and Working Class Radicalism, 1848-74: the London and Manchester examples', (PhD thesis, University of Manchester, 1992), 403-405, *NR*, 19,26 July 1868, and R.Cooper to Joseph Cowen, 28 July 1862, C1738, Cowen Papers, Tyne and Wear Archives.
[105] 'A Working Man', *MSp*, 23 January 1858, *MX*, 2 February 1858.
[106] Editorial, *MSp*, 13 February 1858, 'One of the Disappointed', *MSp*, 6 March 1858, *PPr*, 10 July 1858, *MX*, 27 October 1858.
[107] *MX*, 28 October 1858, *RWN*, 21 November 1858, *MG*, 11,16, December 1858, *MX*, 17 December 1858.

As a result, 1859 was marked by skirmishing between the two groups, first in a series of rival ward meetings, then in town meetings in both Manchester and Salford, and ultimately during the 1859 election. The MSA bitterly attacked early supporters who subsequently expressed a willingness to accept the more moderate instalment of Bright's 1859 bill, while the LRU faction ostentatiously avoided supporting the candidature of Heywood at the 1859 Manchester election, even though he, like most other ultra-Liberals, had ultimately announced themselves willing to support the LRU stance, and Bright's bill, as an instalment.[108] The subsequent victory of the conservative Liberals in Manchester, and the staunchly anti-reform Palmerston in the country as a whole, in that it highlighted the weakness of the radical position, not only discouraged further attempts to press for a larger measure of reform, but even forced the revival of the Manchester Reform Association on a platform even more moderate than that of the LRU in an attempt to attract the support of the moderate Liberals.[109] When Russell's Reform Bill of 1860 was published, some reformers, such as John Watts, were willing to accept it reluctantly: for Watts it was 'a very little effort', but at least its passage would distinguish the genuine from the 'microscopic' reformers.[110] Others took a different view: '[s]ome "Liberal" politicians think that this miserably meagre measure should be accepted as an "instalment"', noted one, 'but, in my opinion, it ought to be rejected as an insult'.[111]

Furthermore, at the Leeds reform conference of November 1861, Hooson, representing the Manchester radicals, was once again left isolated by the moderate consensus. The result was yet another reform association, Cooper's Manchester Working Men's Parliamentary Reform Association (MWPRA), with the moderate ultimate aim of at least a poor-rate franchise, ballot, redistribution, and shortened parliaments, but a commitment to support any instalments.[112] As each new association appeared, so were the ex-chartist radicals thrown back

---

[108] *MX*, 16 February, *MG*, 19 February, 16,17 March 1859, *Cabinet Newspaper*, 25 December 1858, 22 January, 5, 12, 26 February 1859.

[109] *MX*, 30 November, 7 December 1859, 10 March 1860, 'Spectator', *MG*, 12 March 1860. The MRA was later presided over by T.B. Potter, *BH*, 2 April 1864. Meanwhile the pages of the *Cabinet Newspaper* suggest that the brief renewal of working-class agitation had once again collapsed by the summer of 1859, to revive only briefly in the autumn of the year, 3, 10 December 1859.

[110] *MG*, 10 March 1860.

[111] 'F.G.', *MX*, 20 March 1860.

[112] *MG*, 20 November 1861, *MX*, 23 January, 25, 27 February 1862.

on the belief that the only way to prevent the paring of reform measures down to the point at which they collapsed through popular apathy was to rest any programme on what Hooson called 'the sure ground of principle'.[113] Unfortunately, their stance only created a picture of ill-tempered division and dissension within reformers' ranks.[114] Hence, the paradoxical result of acceptance of incrementalism by the chartists in 1857 had become not reunion of working-class radicalism, but its further fragmentation.

After the disruption of the reform movement by the Cotton Famine, and the slavery and emancipation issue, the revival of the reform agitation in Manchester in April 1864, with the long-planned reform conference called by the MWPRA, presented a virtual carbon copy of previous campaigns. Once again universal suffrage motions (this time from Jones) were rejected in favour of the 1862 London programme, and on this basis the National Reform Union was established. In turn the moderation of the NRU platform and the sluggishness of its local operations drove the radicals to the formation of the National Reform League, for which a Manchester branch had been formed by the end of March 1865, under whose aegis most of the local universal suffrage associations were brought during 1866.[115] Once again, the overriding need to present some kind of a united front prevailed over disappointment at the extent of reform offered. Leading NRL figures like E.O. Greening finally acceded to the need for temporary union for moderate reform. Jones, defiant to the last however, remained one of the few determined to stand out for universal manhood suffrage.[116]

The abandonment of platform politics, 1832-67

The course of radical campaigns in the 1850s and 1860s demonstrated that the working classes could no longer be mobilised behind a traditional platform agitation. A closer study of the chartist period suggests that general working-class commitment had in any case been

---

[113] 'Edward Hooson', *MX*, 14 June 1862.

[114] 'E. Longfield', *MX*, 24 May 1862, 'F. Clayton', *MX*, 31 May 1862, 'R. Cooper', *MX*, 3 June 1862, *MX*, 5,11 November 1862.

[115] *MX*, 20 April, 26 October, 29 November 1864, *BH*, 1 April 1865, *MX*, 10 May 1865, *MCN*, 11 November 1865.

[116] 'J.D. Morton', *BH*, 2 December 1865, Greening, *SWN*, 7 April 1866, 'E. Jones', *MX*, 5 May 1866.

more fleeting than the public successes of chartism suggested, and that the successive failures of chartist campaigns to obtain any redress from governments soon convinced those who had turned to the movement as the only option left to them, that it had little to offer.

The disillusionment with the platform is not easy to trace: it was less likely to draw forth discussion than merely to lead to a dwindling away of support. But there remains sufficient evidence of its gradual spread to see it steadily eroding support for political agitation from as early as 1839. In November 1839 Bamford was selling the weekly issues of his *Passages in the Life of a Radical*, not simply to warn against the follies of physical force, but also as a broadside against what he described as the 'vanities of vanity' of the chartist platform.[117] For old radicals like Bamford, with long experience of the platform, the platform appeal to the emotions and the passions created only transient enthusiasm, and prevented the building up of a firmly grounded rational support for franchise reform. Likewise the fustian cutters' leader Richard Crowther took as the lesson of 1839 that it was 'the greatest folly imaginable for working men to expect to derive any extensive relief from their burdens from measures which cannot be carried into effect by their own exertions'.[118]

The failures of 1839 demonstrated to many that the platform encouraged the reliance on rhetoric as a substitute for the hard graft needed to build up working-class political strength. As one disillusioned radical put it in 1841, '[c]ertain it is that without organisation they may "talk a dog's leg off", but they will never progress a single inch in the right way'.[119] Sentiments like this did much to encourage the proliferation of chartist self-help groups and non-platform movements, such as the Universal Suffrage Total Abstinence Society, which so worried O'Connorite chartists in the early 1840s.[120] The recovery of O'Connorite chartism in 1841 and 1842 owed less to mass demonstrations then to the appeal of the new style of local self-improvement to the educated sections of the working class and the trade unions.[121]

---

[117] Bamford, *Passages*, 277.
[118] 'Richard Crowther', (1 December 1839), *NMW*, VI (1839), 951–3.
[119] 'An Old Republican', *MSA*, 9 January 1841.
[120] *MG*, 30 September 1840; see for example the warnings about those who 'pretended' to be chartists given by the Salford Radical Association, *NS*, 23 May 1840.
[121] Redfern Street report, *NS*, 5 February 1842; see Sykes, 'Early Chartism' 169–76.

However, the unions had always been uncomfortable about their links with chartism, and the renewed reverses of 1842 caused organised labour to take fright, so that by 1843 organised chartism had been reduced to a small faction, with little sign of general working-class commitment.[122] By this stage, to concern over the impermanence of radical agitation and its inability to sustain organisation had been added a growing disillusionment with the inability of platform chartism to provide some material reward and to offer encouragement for further endeavour. It was a hard road to follow, and as the years passed by and no advance was obtained, it was not surprising that a certain weariness set in. After the failures of 1839–42, the chartist lecturer David Ross, on a tour of south-east Lancashire, found 'people anxiously looking forward to some...practical development of our principles as would yield them some true advantage, some positive good. Men are tired of unceasing agitation, of again treading the same devious path of uncertainties only to be again attended with future disappointments'.[123]

It was in this context that O'Connor began formulating his land plan. There is no doubt that, along with the profile gained by chartists attaching themselves to other working-class movements, such as unionism and the ten hours campaign, it was the land plan which sustained chartist appeal in Manchester in the mid-1840s. It took advantage of a broad tradition in working-class thought of recourse to the land as the basis of strategies for coping with industrialisation (and was only the most grandiose of the various home colonisation schemes, both local and national, which attracted the Manchester working class in this period).[124] The land plan quickly engineered a revival of chartist fortunes in Manchester, and in total there were over 3000 Manchester members.[125] Yet, as James Leach pointed out in 1845, many of the land plan members were never chartists in the traditional sense, having little interest in the agitational wing of chartism, despite O'Connor's stress that the two were inseparable.[126] By early 1847 the Manchester Land Company shareholders had established a entirely distinct organisation, and their complete lack of interest in the political

---

[122] Arbuthnot to Fitzroy Somerset, 7 July 1843, HO45/434/60–1.
[123] NS, 15 July 1843.
[124] See for example, the wireworkers' and smallware weavers' schemes, MSA, 10 January 1845, spinners MG, 29 January 1845; see also Chase, The People's Farm.
[125] NS, 21 June 1845; Thompson, The Chartists, 299–306, MC, 13 September 1848.
[126] NS, 13 December 1845.

side of the movement drove chartist activists to distraction.[127] As a result, 1848, bringing as it did not only a return to violent agitation from the O'Connorite chartists, but also the first signs of the difficulties into which the Land Company was getting, and O'Connor's talk of establishing a second company brought a double disillusionment. Although the local land subscribers continued until 1850 in an attempt to rescue their investment, by the end of that year nearly all had clearly given up their investment as lost.[128]

At the same time, the events of 1848–49 confirmed the working-class rejection of the platform. 'Idle talking, the war of words which may tend to protract our day of deliverance from political thraldom and social bondage, ought now to cease for ever', wrote one factory operative in the wake of the re-emergence of physical force rhetoric in March 1848.[129] Despite the widespread support for the charter, except among the youths who had not suffered the disappointments of 1839–42, there was little wider working-class support for the renewed platform agitation, and those older chartists who did join, did so in large part because of their frustration with agitation, and their hope that this time there would be a swift move to insurrection.[130]

Unsurprisingly, the failures of 1848 dispelled any lingering support for the platform from all but a few die-hards. As one working man explained in 1849, while his support for the principles of the charter remained, he had lost all faith in the methods of the movement: he '[d]efied the most enthusiastic chartist...to prove to me that during those fifteen years of agitation for, and subscribing money to obtain, the six points, one single step was gained towards the attainment of [the] object'.[131] In 1850 the Manchester Chartist Council itself admitted that it could see nothing in the platform but the folly of 'its senseless vapouring, its platform braggadocio and its private cowardice'.[132] During the 1850s and 1860s, whenever the lack of working-class support for reform movements was alluded to by opponents of reform, there was usually some spokesman ready to

---

[127] *NS*, 13 February 1847; see complaints of the Manchester correspondent, *NS*, 24 July 1847.
[128] See resolutions of Land Company meeting, *NS*, 21 December 1850.
[129] 'A Factory Operative', *MX*, 1 April 1848.
[130] Maude to Grey, 19 April 1848, HO45/2410A/132–4, police deposition, HO45/2410A/139–41.
[131] 'A Working Man', *MSp*, 24 November 1849.
[132] 'Address of the Manchester Chartist Council', *NS*, 14 December 1850.

justify working-class quietism: 'to be continually talking about reform is to my mind preposterous unless something is done towards obtaining that for which we talk and labour', as one sceptic expressed it.[133]

Inevitably attention turned to activities with a material return. In 1848 even the stalwart chartist lecturer and activist James Leach admitted that after agitating for fifteen years in his own case, and with many having struggled even longer, 'he now wished them to stay agitation and do something for their own practical good'.[134] After dallying with the co-operative movement, Leach, like several other leading Manchester chartists, became involved in the British Industry Life Assurance Society.[135] Others (such as Thomas Ormesher) moved into the co-operative movement, or (such as R.S. Chadwick) the temperance movement.[136] Many others of couse, returned to trade unionism. Yet, as Hooson was to demonstrate in the 1860s, the recourse to practical reforms did not necessitate an abandonment of chartist aspirations, and disillusionment with the platform did not produce complete working-class apathy. When reform looked a distinct possibility, and the lack of popular support was clearly damaging its prospects, the working classes were prepared to appear in their thousands, as they did at the huge open air demonstration in Manchester in September 1866 at which up to 200,000 people were present.[137]

Conclusion

'It is not enough that an uniformity of opinion should obtain among the people', the *Northern Star* told its readers in 1842, 'there must also be an uniformity of energy and determination universally manifested'.[138] Unfortunately, for all its success in rallying the working classes to its banner, the chartist movement never achieved this successful mobilisation of working-class consciousness into 'movement consciousness'. Instead, the failures of chartism brought both a

---

[133] 'A Working Man', *SWN*, 7 June 1862.

[134] *MC*, 13 September 1848.

[135] For the scandals surrounding this society see *RWN*, 23, 30 October, 13 November 1853.

[136] For Ormesher see *RWN*, 29 February 1852; for Chadwick see *MSp*, 31 August 1851.

[137] *MX*, 11,25,27 September 1866.

[138] *NS*, 23 July 1842.

fragmentation of working-class radicalism between various strategies for political change, and ultimately the gradual repudiation of the platform itself and the subsequent embroiling of working-class politics in the kind of consensus pressure politics in which there appeared little place for mass mobilisation. It is a tribute to the symbolic power of the charter, and the leadership abilities of first O'Connor and then Jones, that it survived as long as this. In retrospect it can be seen that from 1843 onwards, this version of chartism held little real prospect of success, for during the period 1843–57 chartist organisation had been able to move beyond its hard core support only by attaching itself to other social and industrial movements of the working classes. This kind of reasoning provides the most convincing explanation of the decay of radical activism in the post-chartist period. Not that there was any loss of working-class awareness of the failings of the economic system, nor any retreat from their vision of a democratic society: but rather that the platform as a means of progress had finally been repudiated.

The resulting demobilisation of working-class radicalism in the post-chartist period thus derived not from a transformation of working-class aspirations, but from changes in working-class strategic consciousness. The argument of the penultimate chapter is that the causes of this shift in strategy can be found in large part in changes in the intellectual morphology of the city, and the ways in which these served to restrict the potential for political action on the early nineteenth century model, and to channel working-class politics into arenas in which the middle classes were able to re-establish a greater measure of control.

Chapter Nine

The restraint of working-class politics

Any comprehensive explanation of the dynamics of the repudiation of platform radicalism during the chartist period would probably draw in many of the conventional theories of chartist decline. The willingness of working-class radicals to come to terms with the middle classes and seek to work in alliance with them was certainly encouraged by the various manifestations of a more conciliatory stance which have been given the label 'liberalisation'. The search for common ground upon which strategies of alliance were predicated was also eased by the consensus, whether purely linguistic or more fundamental, which existed between middle and working-class versions of radicalism. In particular, notions of respectability enabled those working-class leaders drawn from the more prosperous echelons of the working class to ape some of the manners of the middle classes and thus find acceptance in middle-class circles largely on middle-class terms. And beneath all this, the greater stability and emerging prosperity of the economy did constrict the supply of the large groups of unemployed or underemployed which had been the bedrock of the chartist movement at times of crisis, and blunt the urgency of chartist demands.

Nevertheless, these explanations cannot tell the whole story, for at least in part, the dynamics of the changing strategic directions of working-class radicalism in Manchester need to be sought in the changing nature of the city's intellectual morphology, and corresponding transformations of political culture. In his *Politics and the People*, James Vernon has gone a long way towards delineating the breadth of popular political culture in this period, and the crucial significance of its shape in moulding the politics of the people. However, it is important to develop the insights of Vernon's work, and in particular to examine the complex interaction between the forms of political culture, the range of tactical possibilities these encourage or preclude, and wider considerations of strategy. The changes in political culture which Vernon traces were, to a much greater degree than he would allow, a product of this interaction.

The difficulties facing working-class radicalism were straightforward, although not easily solved. Unrepresented (or at least without direct representation) after the 1832 Reform Act, the working classes were forced to attempt to influence the political system from without. Fundamentally, two strategies were available. One involved the direct use of the threat of revolution or massive social and economic dislocation to extort change out of those with political power, the other involved juncture with the progressive elements of the middle classes via appeals to their self-interest, the need to preserve legitimacy, and the desirability of an extension of the suffrage.

Pressure from without involved not simply a shared perception of the roots of social, economic and political ills, but also the development of political programmes designed to eradicate them, and the mobilisation of opinion behind such programmes. In the former case, consensus was required for the presentation of a united, numerous and widespread group, committed, if their demands were not met, to the forcible overthrow of the existing political system. In the latter case the programme needed to present progressive elements of the middle classes with an attractive means of achieving common objectives, and overcoming the persisting biases in the political system. The various strands of physical force thus relied on the conversion and mobilisation of the working classes in a movement of protest with convincing revolutionary overtones, and the willingness and ability to demonstrate in large numbers, to arm, and to project this image to those in power. The various strands of moral suasion relied on the conversion of middle-class opinion, and then the ability to articulate this consensus as the opinion of the community in the national arena.

Whichever strategy was adopted, the contexts within which working-class political movements operated deteriorated crucially during this period. In the 1830s the mechanisms of urban discipline were still sufficiently feeble, and the shape of urban society sufficiently open, to enable the conventional methods of early nineteenth century radicalism to flourish. However, during the course of the period, the spaces (both literal and metaphorical) in which these methods had flourished were filled in or brought under middle-class control, with the result that by the 1860s, the environment of radicalism, and hence its practices, was quite distinct. These processes thus had their part to play in the history of radicalism in the chartist and post-chartist period.

Physical restraints

In the early 1830s the revolutionary threat of working-class radicalism
was sustained by the inadequacy of the mechanisms for the enforcement
of law and order. In 1832 there were only 25–30 day police in the city
and, as F.C. Mather has demonstrated, the maintenance of law and
order rested heavily on the military.[1] In ordinary times Manchester had
the protection of a detachment of troops stationed at Hulme barracks,
and reinforcements were available when trouble threatened. The troops
were used regularly during the 1830s and 1840s. Generally, they were
deployed to curtail specific acts of violence, or to defuse threatened
outbreaks. They were also used, however, as a means of controlling
political action, including breaking up meetings.

Furthermore, at times of heightened tension, the magistrates also had
the ability to call upon the services of pensioners and special
constables. The pensioners were of limited value, but the special
constables, through sheer numbers alone, could, on occasion, make a
substantial contribution to the assertion of the rule of law. About 2500
constables were enrolled during August 1842, mostly collected by
merchants and warehouse owners, and in April 1848 as many as 6000
special constables were sworn in and organised on a street by street
basis, with further numbers sworn in at their places of work.[2]
However, given only the most rudimentary of instruction, and often
unwilling to serve beyond the immediate environs of workplace or
home, special constables had a strictly limited utility. The Watch
Committee confessed in 1846 that it had 'generally found special
constables an obstacle rather than an assistance'.[3]

The military thus remained a crude and insensitive weapon with
which to combat and control working-class radicalism, useful at times
of particular tension, and effective in demonstrating the ability of the
authorities to repulse any direct assault on law and order, but of little
use in exerting the kind of constant and flexible control which could
have prevented the eruptions of political and economic sentiment which
they were eventually called upon to suppress. This kind of control
required the regular and close surveillance which could only be

[1] Mather, *Public Order in the Age of the Chartists*, 62–75.
[2] *MG*, 13,17 August 1842, 8 April 1848; see Goffin, *Diaries of Absalom Watkin*, 277–8,
for their use not only to keep out mobs from the out-townships, but also to occupy
central squares to prevent meetings taking place there.
[3] WCM, 30 July 1846.

effectively provided by an adequate police force. Convinced by the events of the Reform Bill crisis of the deficiency of the police, the local authorities mooted various schemes of improvement, and the size of the force gradually increased.[4] Nevertheless, in 1837 there were still only 30 regular day police (along with 150 nightwatchmen) in the town.[5] Even after incorporation, when the new Watch Committee force numbered well over 300, the confusion created by the persistence of the old police commissioners in maintaining their own police, and the constant attacks on the new police by the working classes meant that law enforcement remained in a state of near-chaos.[6] Hence Manchester chartism developed very much within the context of a traditional lack of effective policing.

However, after Charles Shaw was appointed commissioner of police in October 1839, much of the confusion was removed and the efficiency of the police improved rapidly, despite the sniping of the anti-incorporationists.[7] By 1841 the police were being deployed to prevent the holding of political meetings, and by the next year they were operating successfully to keep the streets clear and prevent any undesirable political demonstrations taking place.[8] The police still needed to be reinforced by special constables and the military during times of crisis (and were even then not always able to maintain order), but considerable effort was devoted to drilling them into a disciplined force, which, armed with staves, could be used in part as a substitute for the military in crowd control.

Shaw himself remained keenly aware of the acute problems posed by Manchester's position, surrounded by a number of populous out-townships, and the riots of August 1842 confirmed his fears of the limitations of the police; but after the miscalculations of the first day, he was able relatively quickly to reassert order in the city, and the lesson, once learnt, was not forgotten.[9] In similar circumstances in

[4] *MSA*, 11 February 1832, *MC*, 11 January 1834.

[5] Wemyss to Jackson, 18 April 1837, HO40/35/7–8.

[6] *MC*, 27 April 1839, *MG*, 1 June 1839, *MC*, 26 June 1839, *MG*, 12 October 1839; see Shaw, *Replies*.

[7] *MCCP*, (1840), 36–41; for the rule of Shaw in Manchester see Mather, *Public Order*, 119–27.

[8] *MG*, 24 September 1842, *MSA*, 14 September 1842, Neild to Graham, 19 October 1842, HO45/247C/369.

[9] C. Shaw to Edwin Chadwick, 28 September 1841, 1794/51, Chadwick Papers, University College, London; for full details see E.G. Rose, 'The Plug Riots of 1842 in Lancashire and Cheshire', *Transactions of the Lancashire and Cheshire Antiquarian Society*, LXVII (1958), *idem*, 'Truckling Magistrates of Lancashire in 1842',

1848, joint police and military action successfully prevented the incursion of chartist mobs at the end of May, and in general had asserted tight control over the public space of the city.[10]

Perhaps even more significantly, Shaw was able to develop the force into a comprehensive information-gathering network. It was not just that uniformed police became an increasingly visible presence at chartist public meetings and rallies; more that by 1841 plain-clothes police observers were present at most chartist meetings.[11] This considerably strengthened the magistrates' use of the law to curb chartist activity. The equivocation of chartist attitudes to physical force, combining the need both for a credible revolutionary threat, and a high platform profile for revolutionary rhetoric, left chartist leaders vulnerable to the law in any case; but the new police provided the authorities with accurate information as to the state of the movement on which to base their decision of when it was politic and safe to act, the organisation required to mount the simultaneous arrests of all the leaders, and the evidence with which to ensure committal. Hence, even in those cases where a conviction was not eventually obtained, the magistrates could use high levels of bail either to keep leading chartists in prison, or at least put severe constraints on their actions while they awaited trial. As Gatrell has argued, the use of mass arrest was one of 'the buttress[es] upon which, in critical months, the survival of Manchester society depended'.[12] It decapitated the chartist movement at crucial times, leaving it without necessary direction: in 1842 and in 1848 the Manchester magistrates used arrests, once they had imposed their control on the streets, to remove local leaders such as James Leach. Mass arrests forced the dissipation of chartist energies on prisoner support schemes: as John Sutton commented in 1848, the arrests of that year had 'depressed their spirits and exhausted their funds'.[13]

Transactions of the Lancashire and Cheshire Historical Society, 83 (1985), 40-70.

[10] Arbuthnot to Phillips, 10 March 1848, HO45/2410AD/84-8, Armitage to Grey, 31 May 1848, HO45/2410A/187-9; see later successful mass deployment in 1858, Steedman, *Policing the Victorian Community*, 36.

[11] Wemyss to Phillips, 4 November 1841, HO45/43/62-3. The extent of police surveillance is clear in the detailed accounts in TS11/137/374 Part 1.

[12] V.A.C. Gatrell, 'A Manchester Parable' in J.A. Benyon, et al., eds, *Studies in Local History*, (1976), 30.

[13] *NS*, 11 November 1848. After the arrests in 1848 the national Victim Defence Fund was attempting to collect £10 per week for the support of prisoners, *NS*, 24 March 1849.

In some respects, the military threat of the chartists had always been insubstantial. The importance of the Irish to physical force activity in Manchester highlighted the lack of any tradition of revolutionary violence, or even of personal violence, in England.[14] When chartist orators talked of violence, they had to look back to the career of Cromwell, or even the Britons and Anglo-Saxons; as a result, it took evidence of the possibility of successful revolution from overseas to generate any momentum for physical force doctrines, and the impetus produced was temporary.[15] The failure to act on the rejection of the first chartist petition in 1839 was also significant because after the reverses of 1839 much of the naive early enthusiasm of chartism was lost, never to return.[16] However, there can be little doubt that it was the greater strength and organisation of the police and the military by the early 1840s which did much to undermine the power of the physical force rhetoric of chartism.

What prominent suasionists like G.H. Smith realised was that as the police force was brought to efficiency to supplement the troops, the forces at the deployment of the authorities would always be too powerful for a divided working class: without 'a plan to go on, or a system to work upon' he asked his fellow chartists, 'what chance will we stand against the soldiers and against the police'?[17] The history of the 1848 revolution in France appeared to demonstrate that even if the rhetoric of violence could intimidate the ruling classes and topple existing governments, it would only produce a period of anarchy during which employment and prosperity would be badly hit and an even more despotic regime might establish itself.[18] The failures of May and June 1848 marked the final abandonment of physical force ideas: there was, according to Layhe, 'a growing conviction, which the issue of all our disturbances has tended to confirm, that it is hopeless for mobs to contend against the organised authorities of the state...'.[19]

---

[14] Noted by Palmer, *Police and Protest in England and Ireland, 1780–1850*, (1988), 482.
[15] *NS*, 7 September 1839.
[16] Cf. comments of Robert Lowery, in B. Harrison and P. Hollis, 'Chartism, Liberalism and the Life of Robert Lowery', *English Historical Review*, 82 (1967), 503–35.
[17] Police deposition, HO40/43/475–6.
[18] For example, see the ideas of Bamford in *Cassell's Weekly Newspaper*, 28 January 1854; Sam Collins' warning that 'A nation should pause long ere it arise/ To strike the ruthless, rash and random blow./ A maddened people know not well to choose:/ Sometimes a double despotism ensues', Collins, *Miscellaneous Poems and Songs*, ([1859]), 37; see also John Teer, *MSA*, 15 April 1848.
[19] *MTPAR*, (1849), 11. For the development of the Manchester police see Davies, 'Classes and the Police', 26–47.

In large part, the failure of non-revolutionary physical force strategies was bound up in the failure of revolutionary ideas themselves, for the same obstacles, in particular the growing strength of the forces of law and order, and the increasing surveillance which the authorities were able to exercise over the chartists, told equally in this case. The failures of 1839 and particularly of 1842, despite the lapses which allowed out-township strikers to bring out the Manchester mills in August 1842, demolished the credibility of working-class intimidation, for English chartists at least.

In this sense, the stiffening of the coercive power of the state, particularly in the local context of Manchester, is vital in explaining the renunciation by the working classes of the intimidatory elements of early nineteenth century radicalism. However, the power of the state was limited, and would have been no match for a fully united working class determined to challenge established authority. As such, although rightly stressed in recent work on chartism,[20] coercion was itself contingent on the failure of radicalism to achieve a strongly held strategic consensus, and to explain this failure, it is necessary to examine the barriers to effective mass proselytisation which the intellectual morphology of Manchester placed in the way of working-class radicals.

Control of intellectual life

Not surprisingly, given the continuities of working-class consciousness, not all elements of working-class intellectual culture fell under middle-class control. The radical culture of the streets, for example, was resistant to such uncomplicated discipline, and it would be wrong to suggest that the politics of public space was in any way more successfully 'sterilised' than the elements of working-class culture discussed earlier. During the 1830s and 1840s Great Ancoats Street in the heart of the factory district remained the traditional meeting place for the city's Irish: here Irish papers would be read, dissected and debated by large crowds of Irishmen. Throughout the period Stevenson's Square was a focus of working-class activity. Its corners were a frequent stomping ground for orators and propagandists of all shapes, often participating in long-running debate over issues such as

---

[20] Goodway, *London Chartism*, 99–149, Saville, *1848*, 219–21.

the role of temperance or drink within the community, often to large audiences.[21]

To Stevenson's Square and New Cross (a smaller square at the heart of Ancoats) the working classes would gravitate at times of excitement to pick up the latest news, and to assess its significance. During the 1840s it was here that chartism and Irish nationalism brooded and smouldered, fanned by a constant round of debates and declamation. It was here in the 1850s that religious issues were subjected to similar scrutiny: Protestant and Catholic working men mixed indiscriminately, contending publicly over religious doctrines of all types.[22] During the Fenian crisis of 1867, 5000 Irishmen were able to convene at New Cross and process, headed by a drum and fife band, to the houses of executed Fenians, without police intervention.[23]

These spots provided the 'Speakers' Corners' of Manchester, their status sufficiently accepted for open air addresses there to be advertised in the press by the 1860s. James Staton commented in 1863 that the working classes 'could yer lectures on aw subjects awmooast any neet at th'New Cross un sitch loike places'.[24] And what happened slightly more in the public eye in these squares was replicated to a lesser extent on more obscure street corners throughout the city.[25]

Nevertheless, police concession of the right to hold organised political meetings in such areas was more the exception than the rule, confined usually to specific cases, or periods such as the Cotton Famine, when the ability of the working classes to let off steam was deemed less likely to sustain opposition, than its suppression. As much as a result of these pressures, as from the kind of search for radical respectability noted by Vernon, radicalism was pushed indoors. Although this did sometimes present serious problems to working-class groups in search of a venue, Manchester never had the kind of closed intellectual culture typical of places such as Cheltenham.[26] In the 1830s radicalism had fought successfully to break the hold which the

---

[21] *MG*, 27 September 1834, T. Swindells, *Manchester Streets and Manchester Men*, Second Series, (1889), 159.

[22] 'A Catholic', *MC*, 12 July 1845, *MG*, 15 March 1848, *Freelance*, XI (1876), 270.

[23] *MCN*, 27 November 1867.

[24] *LL*, 10 October 1863.

[25] *MTPAR*, (1850), 40, *MC*, 4 July 1863.

[26] Though see the tribulations of the Irish repealers, *MG*, 5 March 1834; for Cheltenham, infamous in the 1840s in radical circles for prosecutions of Owenites, see O. Ashton, 'Clerical Control and Radical Responses in Cheltenham Spa, 1838–48', *Midland History*, VIII (1983), 121–47.

civic elites had possessed on public rooms and halls.[27] The availability of the Dyers Union room in Spier Street, then Bywater's Rooms after 1836, followed in turn by the Salford Social Institution, the Carpenters' Hall and later the Hall of Science, provided radicals with a range of venues; Joseph Smith the Salford Owenite, commented that the opening of the Social Institution, 'quite mortifyes [sic] our opponents the clergy'.[28] In general, beerhouses, less under the influence of the magistrates, also provided potential bases, where political meetings could be integrated into the wider culture of radical newspapers and discussion.[29]

In the 1790s a considerable framework of press regulation, with the stamp laws as the corner stone, had been developed, but by 1832 it was clear that the vibrancy of the unstamped press was beginning to threaten this apparatus of control. At a national level, the conflicts over the unstamped press and their influence on radical politics have been studied in depth by several authors.[30] However, the unstamped press was also a key element in local radical activism: it provided an organisational focus, recruitment material, and funds for local radical leaders. Hence, first its centralisation and then its demise proved a serious blow to local radicalism, only partly cushioned by the successes of the *Northern Star*.

In the early 1830s Manchester radicalism was undoubtedly sustained by the unstamped press. According to one 1834 estimate, nearly 3000 copies circulated.[31] In consequence, attempts, particularly by a wave of prosecutions in 1836, were made to uphold the stamp laws in Manchester; occasional use was made of the libel laws; and several sellers of unstamped periodicals were imprisoned.[32]

The impact of this activity was unclear. Certainly it did not destroy the radical press. During the late 1830s as many as twelve unstamped radical periodicals circulated in Manchester, including two, the

[27] For indications of the pressures which were exerted see Robert Bellringer, *WMC*, 28 April 1832, William Newall, *MG*, 19 October 1833, Joseph Robinson, *MG*, 17 August 1834.

[28] Smith to Owen, 17 April 1836, #790, Owen Papers, Hanover House.

[29] 'J. Barrowclough', *MSA*, 1 August 1840; for the role of the pub see Vernon, *Politics and the People*, 214–20.

[30] P. Hollis, *The Pauper Press, a study in working-class radicalism of the 1830s*, (1970).

[31] HO40/32(1)/49–52.

[32] *MC*, 5 October 1833, 4 January 1834, 23 August 1834, *MG*, 30 January 1836, *MSA*, 20 February 1836; see the case of Doherty in May 1832, Kirby and Musson, *Voice of the People*, 435–8.

Regenerator and the *Political Register*, which were published in the city, and including up to 9,000 copies of the *Northern Star*.[33] Similarly, it would seem that little could be done to prevent the circulation of other forms of radical literature, whether the blasphemous and seditious pamphlet *His Satanic Majesty's Proclamation and Form of Thanksgiving for the Downfall of the Tories*, which circulated in great numbers during the 1835 election, or more substantial works from the radical pantheon, including Paine and Cobbett.[34] Such radical literature circulated in a variety of ways, and examples were even turned up by school inspectors in the 1840s being used as copy books.[35]

Nevertheless, the pressures on radical literature were not entirely ineffectual. The securities required by the libel laws presented a formidable barrier to the establishment of new periodicals. Advertising and stamp duties increased price and restricted circulation, forcing a greater reliance on newsrooms and communal reading. The relaxation of the duties on the press was introduced in such a way that the pointed radicalism of the chartist-period papers was superseded by the diffuse, mass-consumption radicalism of the new national papers, *Lloyds, Reynolds, Weekly Times*, and *News of the World*.[36] The reduction in prices consequent on the removal of the stamp duties, and the increasing costs of newspaper technology meant that during the late 1840s and 1850s the costs of commencing a newspaper escalated rapidly, and the circulation required to enable cheap periodicals to break even became substantial.[37] In 1849, Archibald Prentice, an ex-newspaper owner himself, estimated that a circulation of 4,000 would be needed to keep a projected temperance journal solvent, and the *Sunday School Penny Magazine*, edited in Manchester, did not make any profit until its circulation exceeded 5,000.[38] When a group

---

[33] Shaw to Phillips, 9 December 1839, HO40/43/795–802.

[34] *MC*, 2 May 1835; the investigators of the Manchester Statistical Society estimated that Cobbett's *Legacy to Parsons* had sold about 1800 copies in Manchester over the course of 6 weeks in 1835, despite costing 1/6 each, and that about 800 copies of Paine's *Rights of Man* and 400 of his *Age of Reason* had been sold in the previous three years, 'Report of the Committee inquiring into the number of immoral and irreligious works sold in Manchester', Appendix to the Minutes of the Manchester Statistical Society, #45, Ms F310.6M5, MCLA.

[35] *PP*, (1845) XXXV [622], 123, *PP*, (1850) [1215] XLIII, 180–1.

[36] *MTPAR*, (1852), 33.

[37] Alan J. Lee, *The Origins of the Popular Press in England, 1855–1914*, (1975), 50–89.

[38] *MX*, 31 August 1850, *XR*, June (1850), 370; various temperance journals established in Manchester around 1850, including the *Manchester Temperance Reporter* and The

of Manchester trade unionists attempted to establish a working-class paper, *Weekly Wages*, in 1861, despite some support from local unions, it survived for only three monthly issues, and the *Co-operator*, also published in Manchester for the growing co-operative movement, was never really solvent throughout the ten years of its existence, despite serving an identifiable, numerous and expanding group.[39]

Radicals also faced difficulties in selling what was a particularly perishable commodity. Often booksellers and newsvendors were unwilling to stock radical titles.[40] In the early 1830s Doherty found it difficult to sell his unstamped *Poor Man's Advocate*, and had to employ his own street vendors to sell them.[41] During the 1840s chartist periodicals were largely circulated through chartist leaders turned newsagents, like John Campbell of Salford, and in 1853 the Manchester Chartist Committee was forced to take Ernest Jones' *People's Paper* themselves as a speculation, giving them out to the newsvendors, and agreeing to buy them back if unsold.[42] As a result, even relatively successful radical papers were simply unknown, even by politically aware members of the working class: despite its having been in existence for over a year, with an established circulation in Manchester, it was still possible for a Manchester joiner to confess in January 1865 to being previously unaware of the existence of the *Beehive*.[43]

In some cases, as well, it could be difficult to find a printer for material likely to offend middle-class sensibilities. In 1849 Charles Southwell's *Lancashire Beacon* ran into this problem, before being rescued by a local radical publisher.[44] The role of radical printer-publishers cannot be underestimated; circulation was important, but it was predicated on the ability to publish. In this sense the consolidation of the press in the 1840s and 1850s was a blow to local radicalism. Moreover, difficulties of circulation meant less revenue,

Teetotaller, quickly folded, see *MCN*, 27 July 1878.

[39] For the background of the *Weekly Wages* episode see A.J. Lee's entry on Charles Hadfield in the *Dictionary of Labour Biography*, and *MCN*, 18 May 1878. For the plight of the *Co-operator* see *Co-operator*, 20 May 1868, H. Pitman to Brougham, 23 October, 7,20 November 1865, #11446–48, Brougham Papers, UCL, and W. Morrison to Holyoake, 20 May 1868, #1781, Holyoake Papers, Hanover House.

[40] This might have been a business rather than a political decision, cf. the comments of Henry Turner that he was not able to get a Homeopathy journal in Manchester, Epps, *Diary of the late John Epps* ([1870]), 428.

[41] Kirby and Musson, *Voice of the People*, 367–8.

[42] *PPr*, 15 October 1853.

[43] 'Sam Ramsbottam', *BH*, 7 January 1865.

[44] *Reasoner*, VIII (1850), 21–2.

and as the case of the *Manchester and Salford Advertiser* demonstrates, the newspaper office had served as a general radical publisher and bookseller, particularly of ephemeral literature like pamphlets and handbills. In the 1830s and 1840s radical literature was readily published and circulated in Manchester; Abel Heywood built up his publishing business on the basis of Owenite tracts, and T.P. Carlile, the brother of Richard Carlile, had little difficulty in publishing a Manchester version of Macerone's *A New System of Defensive Instructions for the People*.[45] Printers such as James Wheeler enabled the radicals and chartists, as well as the Anti-Corn Law League, to provide a steady stream of handbills for circulation around the city.[46] As newspaper publishers and the lesser printers and stationers succumbed to the dual pressures of the collapse in the demand for their goods consequent on the disintegration of chartism in the 1840s, and the increasing sophistication of the remaining publishing and newspaper offices, an important source of diversity was removed.[47]

It was not simply a question of the lack of a market: although he was able to sell over 12,000 copies of *Dr Cahill's Fifth Letter to Lord John Russell* at the height of the Ecclesiastical Titles controversy, it was generally accepted in the Catholic community that Manchester Catholicism owed much to the efforts of publisher and bookseller Thomas Smith, to sustain a cheap Catholic literature for Manchester.[48] Publishers often had to be willing to gamble on the creation of a market for their products, and without the level of commitment evinced in the early decades of the century it was easy to decline the risk, particularly when it was becoming increasingly important to maintain an unsullied reputation in order to retain the confidence and the purchases of the middle classes. It is indicative that by the mid-1850s, despite his early career, and although he continued to situate himself on the radical fringes of Liberalism, Abel Heywood eschewed all participation in radical publishing.

---

[45] Francis Macerone, *A New System of Defensive Instructions for the People*, (Manchester, T.P. Carlile, 3rd edition, 1839), see copy in HO40/37/1000–48.

[46] J. Reilly, *History of Manchester* (1865), 410. In Manchester the best known of these was probably James Wheeler, who flourished in the 1830s and 1840s, publishing radical and chartist handbills and placards; for a reprint by Wheeler of a pamphlet originally printed in Newcastle see HO40/43/421, HO40/37/752.

[47] Cf. the complaints of Maude in 1840 of the publication of (Owenite) pamphlets by 'stationers of a very low class', Maude to Normanby, 7 April 1840, HO44/35/nf.

[48] *Tablet*, 17 January, 14 February 1852.

This left working-class groups or individuals forced to rely either on the subsidisation of works by organisations, by collections at public meetings, or via advance subscription. The third route had exactly the same drawback as straightforward commercial appeal to the (middle-class) book-buying public – it involved an at least tacit, and often quite explicit, submission to the codes of middle-class morality.[49] Moreover, it was far from foolproof in itself, as Edwin Waugh and his publishers found when attempting to collect money from the subscribers to Waugh's *Lancashire Sketches* in 1855.[50] The second, although possible over the occasional emotive incident (like the outrage which the Sunday lecturer, the Rev. Arthur Mursell, caused by an outspoken attack on Feargus O'Connor in 1859), was no substitute for the sustained existence of the first. But this was a catch-22 situation, as organisations sufficiently established to sustain their own publicity usually needed such publicity to establish themselves in the first place.

The decline of the radical printer-publisher was mirrored by that of the radical bookseller (in many cases the same person). As Brian Harrison has suggested, the bookseller was a basic resource of nineteenth century radical activity, facilitating the circulation of radical ideas, as well as providing a living for leaders debarred from other employment, and often serving, in consequence, as an organising focus.[51] In the 1830s the city was well-provided with radical booksellers, including John Doherty, James Wroe, Abel Heywood and William Willis; later James Leach, John Campbell and other chartists can also be found attempting to establish businesses of this sort. These booksellers were a vital channel for the circulation of radical literature, particularly given the unseen control which could operate over middle-class booksellers.[52] This position was enhanced by the frequent attachment of newsrooms or circulating libraries to these shops: in the 1830s Doherty's newsroom catered to an extensive readership of the

---

[49] Hence, in the introduction to *Fawse Jimmy an'th'Cattle Plague*, (1868), Tom Kershaw expressed the hope 'that the truthfulness to real life, and the careful avoidance of everything bordering on coarseness and vulgarity, which will invariably be adhered to, may secure that patronage which he desires', 2.

[50] Dunhill and Palmer to Waugh, 21 February 1855, Waugh Papers, MS427.72W89, MCLA.

[51] B. Harrison, *Peaceable Kingdom. Stability and Change in Modern Britain*, (1982).

[52] See, for example, the 1835 controversy surrounding Clarke's bookshop, 'J.R. Beard', *MG*, 21 February 1835; for a portrait of one of these, William Willis, see *MCN*, 8 November 1879.

unstamped press.[53] From the 1840s the situation deteriorated: although individuals such as Heywood and J.R. Cooper survived, they became much more circumspect in their dealings with working-class radicals. Meanwhile, death or bankruptcy removed many of the others. Of course, this deterioration was due in large part to the falling popularity of radicalism by the end of the 1840s: working-class (largely second hand) booksellers did survive and regret was frequently expressed at the amount of 'inflammatory trash, made up of mystery and murder, debauchery and madness' which continued to circulate in the 1850s and 1860s.[54] Nevertheless, in the wider context of the post-chartist period, the loss of the radical bookseller was a further restriction on the capacities of revival of the working-class movement.

The radical newsroom-bookshop was encouraged during the 1830s by the extreme reluctance of the middle classes to countenance newspapers (as part of the general proscription of politics) within the associations they sponsored for the working classes. During the 1840s the admission of newspapers into the institutes and even church-based societies broadened their appeal, and enabled them to begin to replace the private newsrooms. Similarly, the opening of the Free Public Library in 1851, and the steady extension of temperance, religious and institute-based libraries in the 1850s and 1860s provided a threat to local subscription libraries. In both cases, the opportunity was provided for a certain degree of control over the content of these institutions. In 1841 the managers of the Christian Institute ensured that only the 'most unobjectionable' of the newspapers appeared in their library.[55] The managers of the Free Public Library exercised a similar, if more private, surveillance. Sir John Potter had laid down in 1851 the principle that the library would contain only 'books of real bona fide value, not trash, not rubbish...but really useful books', and the attempt was made to put these principles into practice.[56] Holyoake's secularist publication, *The Reasoner*, was excluded from the library, and books which did not meet the librarian's standards of decency and good taste were rejected.[57]

[53] HO40/32(1)/4952.

[54] *MTPAR*, (1851), 44; *PP*, (1856) XLVII [2079], 115.

[55] Love and Barton, *Manchester Handbook* (1842), 179.

[56] *Report of a Public Meeting to effect the establishment of a Free Public Library*, ([1851]), 8.

[57] For the *Reasoner* case see Edward Edwards, 'Diary', 14,24 February, 2 June, 21 September 1854, 5,12,26 January 1855, BL (Printed Books Section); an illuminating example from R.W. Smiles, Edwards' successor, can be found in Smiles to Charles

Similarly, the managers of cultural institutions were concerned to exercise close control over the ideas which circulated within them. Their libraries were vetted to ensure the exclusion of undesirable volumes. Lecturers were carefully chosen and often directly given details of proscribed areas.[58] Often, under considerable pressure from middle-class opinion,[59] clear limits were placed on the operations of discussion or mutual improvement societies, although this was not always easy, as the running conflict which the directors of the Athenaeum had with its essay and discussion society demonstrated.[60]

This did not necessarily create what R.J. Morris has recently described as a 'neutral space' for the propagation of middle-class values; the bitterness of the conflicts over the lectures of George Dawson and Ralph Waldo Emerson in the 1840s bear witness to the extreme difficulties of creating a consensus over the bounds of acceptable utterance, and then policing it effectively.[61] Unable to control their own public discourse, in no sense can it be argued that middle-class control over the circulation of radical ideas was ever effected, and as a result, for all the weight of middle-class propaganda, there continued to be available to the working classes a corpus of oppositional ideas and analyses. Nevertheless, the combined action of the changing intellectual morphology of the city, and the continuing efforts of the middle classes to impose some kind of ideological control did succeed in restricting the amount and the accessibility to the working classes of radical propaganda. Moreover, much greater success was achieved in sterilising the middle-class intellectual world. In combination, this goes some way to explain the frustrations of radical attempts to build a general radical consensus, either among the working classes alone or between working and middle classes, in the 1840s and 1850s.

Dyall, 25 March 1859, Out Letter Book, I, MFPL Archive, MCLA.

[58] Hence when George Thompson was invited to lecture to the Athenaeum, his invitation contained a specific instruction to avoid politics, Athenaeum 'Minutes', 25 February 1841, M2/1/2, MCLA.

[59] See for example, the furore caused by the appearance of a discussion on socialism in the Athenaeum in 1840, H.H. Birley to the Directors, 3 April 1840 (copy), Athenaeum 'Minutes', 30 April 1840, M2/1/1, MCLA.

[60] See Athenaeum 'Minutes', 7 November 1839, 29 February 1840, 26 April 1848, 18,31 January 1856, 29 April 1857, M2/1/1-5, MCLA. For the context of these struggles see Wach, 'Culture and the Middle Classes', 382-7.

[61] See my as yet unpublished paper 'Ralph Waldo Emerson, George Dawson, and the control of the lecture platform in mid-nineteenth century Manchester'.

The trials of platform politics

Besides the problems of creating a unified sentiment, the radical movement also found the mobilisation of such sentiment as did exist more and more difficult as the period progressed. In part, the difficulty was the cost of personal participation in the radical movement for both rank and file and leadership. The strengthening of the police had much to do with the re-evaluations which took place: the greater likelihood of successful prosecution restrained the activities of prominent chartist orators, and dissuaded others from following a similar course.[62] The experience of prison itself often demoralised those who had initially been determined enough to become prominent chartists: some, like Christopher Dean, being persuaded that the necessary sacrifices were too much to be born.[63]

In this respect, the power of the agents of the law was reinforced by the discipline of work. It is not necessary to go as far as does Patrick Joyce to establish the significance of employer-employee relations in explaining the tightening of civic discipline during the chartist period. At one level it was simply a question of the nature of work: as the workshop and the factory replaced the outworker, so working-class freedom to participate in political action was curtailed. Various incidents in the 1830s when employers made clear their opposition to their hands absenting themselves from work to take part in demonstrations, backed up by court cases in which the magistrates took great pains to underline their willingness to enforce agreements as to periods of notice, even for only temporary absences, emphasised the greater discipline expected.[64] In the chartist period this discipline was still uneven: some employers remained willing to allow their hands to please themselves whether they attended important meetings, and the existence of widespread unemployment provided further freedoms.[65]

Nevertheless, the trend was clear. Mirroring the tradition of the trade unions, by the early 1840s many chartist activists were reluctant to be identified by name in the local press. It was a middle-class

---

[62] Cf. comments of R.J. Richardson, *MSA*, 2 January 1841.
[63] Letter of C. Dean, dated 15 March [1841] in HO45/46/15–6.
[64] *MG*, 11 January 1834, *MSA*, 16 September 1837.
[65] Thomas Clegg to [John Fielden], 22 August 1838, Fielden Papers, MJRL; the comments of Charles Shaw in his reports to the Home Office stressed repeatedly the fact that in Manchester, 'the operatives are under such a complete subjection to, and dependence on the factory proprietors, that no political disturbance...is to be apprehended from the labouring classes' unless there was widespread unemployment, 1 May 1841.

commonplace in the 1830s and 1840s to call on employers to assume greater control over the extra-work life of their employees, and to dismiss those who would not conform, and scattered evidence suggests that this practice increased steadily.[66] Many prominent chartists fell foul of informal employer blacklisting.[67]

Outside the employment relationship, pressure could often be exerted via various social and commercial sanctions. John Watts, a leading Owenite of the 1840s, despite the fact there is no evidence that his views had changed in any fundamental way, clearly distanced himself from Owenism in the 1850s and 1860s as he became integrated into the ultra-liberal group. This progression was common enough for Thomas Ellis, one the leaders of secularism in Manchester in the 1860s, to bemoan the fact that many who had become eminent then dropped away; having obtained success, he commented, 'society expects of them to isolate themselves from all Freethought societies'.[68] Such pressures were sustained through the period: when in 1864, John Russell, who had played a leading part in a farriers' dispute, attempted to circumvent the proscription on his employment which the Manchester employers enforced, by setting himself up in a shop, the vendetta against him was pursued to the extent of attempts to oust him from his premises by out-bidding him.[69]

No doubt in some cases employer paternalism did build deferential responses from workforces, but it is necessary to treat sceptically the ritual platitudes of the works meeting and the workmen's testimonial. Strong, and sometimes overt, pressure would have existed to participate in such practices.[70] The picture presented in T.G. Lee's *Trade Union Magazine* was that:

> so tremblingly aware are some of the millowners that they are surrounded by heaps of inflammable materials, that they are afraid of the least spark of intelligence falling upon the easily ignitable mass of human combustibles by which their machinery is attended... We know that the system of intimidation is so fearfully acted upon, that there is scarcely one man in five hundred who thinks himself

---

[66] See T. and R. Barnes' attempts to prevent their hands sending children to chartist Sunday School, *NS*, 6 April 1844.

[67] Cf. comments of Teer, *NS*, 27 December 1845; for desire for anonymity see *MX*, 5 September 1849.

[68] *NR*, 5 December 1863.

[69] 'John Russell', *BH*, 3 September, 8 October 1864, 'Thomas Greaves', *BH*, 1 October 1864.

[70] E.g. 'A Goods Porter', *MSp*, 25 October 1856.

safe in speaking, even to a friend, of the abuses by which the operatives are victimised.[71]

Nor was the problem confined to union activity: as agent of the Lancashire Public Schools Association in 1850, Edwin Waugh found working men reluctant, because of fear of employer reaction, to get involved even in the educational movement.[72]

In the face of pressure of this intensity, there needed to exist compelling reasons for participation in radical politics. The mass platform strategy of the mainstream chartist movement provided such reason: the demonstration of the commitment of the working classes to the chartist programme and their willingness to mobilise in favour of it, was a central element of the underlying sense of crisis and intimidation which the leadership hoped to provide. But this justification largely collapsed once the decision was made to switch to suasionist approaches in which rational argument and the attempt to create a communal opinion in favour of reform were predominant.

It is thus possible to interpret the demobilisation of radicalism after chartism as due, in part, to the new constraints (of external force and internal logic) on widespread popular participation. In 1832 the political culture of Manchester shared the vibrant forms of popular participation, particularly at election times, described so vividly in James Vernon's study of 'electoral poetics'.[73] The public sphere was still very much defined by the public spaces of the town, and the candidates' meetings for the 1832 election took place almost wholly out of doors.[74] However, as Vernon has suggested, after 1832 this public outdoor popular political culture was increasingly constrained by new definitions of the public. In the following years three significant developments occurred. First, middle-class political culture, apparently anxious to distance itself from popular politics, moved rapidly indoors, so that by the mid-1840s the election hustings in St Ann's Square was the only outdoor platform sanctioned (and increasingly reluctantly) as respectable by middle-class opinion.[75]

At the same time, the radical movement found the changing morphology of public space within which it had to operate increasingly

---

[71] *TUM*, 18 January 1851; viz *TAHP*, 14 September 1850.

[72] Waugh, 'Diary', 1 April 1850, MCLA.

[73] Vernon, *Politics and the People*, especially 80–102.

[74] Although already by 1832 there were signs that open air meetings were no longer considered entirely respectable, *MSA*, 17 March 1832.

[75] *MCN*, 7 September 1872.

uncongenial. As the municipal authorities became ever more efficient, they began to impose their own authority on the streets, squares and fields within which radicalism had previously thrived unmolested. Although the informal political culture of the streets survived, from the 1840s it is clear that first the nuisance inspectors, and then from 1846 the police, became increasingly anxious, if not to stamp out the more formal elements of open air politics, then certainly to ensure that only those permitted and regulated by the police went ahead.[76] In 1848–49 chartists and trade unionists were being forced to apply for police permission (which was not always given) to hold outdoor meetings or processions, and radicals were increasingly informed that they would be held responsible by the police for any disturbances at such meetings.[77] Largely as a result, the only reliable venues for open air meetings came to be outside the borough boundaries.[78]

Over time, urban spread completed the work of the police: as Manchester grew, the vacant plots and open areas common in 1832 were gradually built upon. St Peter's Field, for example, the site of Peterloo, was steadily encroached upon during the 1830s and 1840s by buildings such as the Hall of Science (later, symbolically, the Free Public Library); maps of Manchester in the 1870s show that it, and many other spaces like it, had disappeared. Even Kersal Moor, described by Engels as the 'Mons Sacer' of Manchester radicalism, was enclosed in the early 1850s.[79]

There remained the network of pubs, beerhouses, and trade union rooms which were integral to the working-class radical culture of the 1830s. The problem was that these rooms were less suited to sustaining general political mobilisation. They were often small, and even the larger were by their very nature sectional or local in identity: it was difficult to use them as the focal point for collective radical politics. As one sympathetic observer put it, a few lectures in the Free Trade Hall would 'produce more effect than a hundred of your little, detached, grumbling meetings', and save the waste of placards for meetings

[76] Cf. comments in Bembridge's 'Journal', 6 June 1847, MCLA.
[77] *MX*, 13 June 1848, *MG*, 12 May 1849; cf. pressure by the mayor to prevent Stevenson's Square meeting, *MX*, 21 April 1852, *PPr*, 31 July 1852.
[78] Cf. moving of Ernest Jones meeting from Pin Mill to Stretford New Road, *PPr*, 28 June 1856.
[79] Engels, *The Condition of the Working Class in England*, 256; *MG*, 15 February 1851.

which 'scarcely a thousandth part of Manchester even hear of, or care for'.[80]

A step could have been taken in the right direction had the radicals been able to construct a comprehensive framework of ward and district meetings as a means of providing the building blocks of a comprehensive expression of public opinion. Unfortunately, throughout the period, the working classes found it very difficult to gain access to the multiplicity of chapel rooms and schoolrooms which were the staple of district politics for the middle classes. Likewise, they failed in their attempts in the 1840s to lay some kind of claim to municipal buildings, and found that even where appropriate middle-class venues were not closed off, the cost of hiring them on the regular basis needed to generate an effective educative campaign, was prohibitive.[81]

The socialists got round these problems by building the Hall of Science, and the chartists followed suit with the Carpenters' Hall and then the People's Institute. Unfortunately in all cases a compound of initial indebtedness and high running costs meant that working-class control was not maintained and by 1849 all three were entertainment halls of various degrees of ill-repute.[82] This meant that after 1848 the radicals found it difficult to sustain an independent platform, and were inexorably sucked into dependence upon middle-class reform movements.

The difficulties of the platform were compounded by the problems of the press. It seemed equally impossible to obtain favourable comment, let alone support, from local newspapers. Sympathetic middle-class observers admitted that 'few newspapers dare advocate your cause. Proprietors of newspapers are obliged to be politically expedient in order to be commercially honest'.[83] Where coverage was given, it was often deliberately misleading, and working-class attempts to correct the picture were refused or accepted only on payment for them as advertisements.[84] Hostile reporting had the effect of dissuading readers from attendance at the very meetings where the

---

[80] 'J. Mee', NS, 23 January 1847.

[81] NS, 31 July 1841, TUM, 15 March 1851, MG, 17 July 1841; cf. Burton's complaint that hiring even the Hall of Science cost £4, MSA, 17 June 1848.

[82] 'C.F.', MSp, 22 September 1849. The Hall of Science, for example, cost £6000; by 1840 (when it was opened) half of this figure had been raised; at the end of 1842 the Owenites were still £2000 in debt to friends on account of the Hall, New Moral World, VII (1840), 1244–5, XI (1842–43), 218.

[83] TUM, 4 January 1851.

[84] See comments of 'John Easby', MG, 18 April 1846.

radicals hoped to put over their point of view.[85] Even more crippling was middle-class indifference. Papers not only ignored radical activity except at times of crisis, and judged information on trade union activity as private and of no wider public interest, but also deliberately glossed over radical participation or intervention in meetings and events which it did wish to report.[86] Working-class frustration about what *Weekly Wages* called the 'systematic distortion and forgery of facts by the moneyman's press', and despondency over the chances of mobilising it on the side of radicalism, persisted into the 1860s.[87]

Of course, as Joyce and Vernon have recently pointed out, newspapers by no means exhaust the range of printed technologies available to the working classes. Handbills and placards were extensively used. At the height of the chartist period large announcements of the latest radical meeting informed the working classes of the progress of the movement, and the practice was even extended to the painting of large chartist slogans on the walls of the city.[88] But such placards, even had they not been treated with mild disdain by the middle classes, could do little to overcome the inherent weakness of the radicals' position once the mass platform was abandoned.[89] Pamphlets and tracts had more potential, and at times (particularly in 1849 when an ambitious scheme of chartist tract publication and distribution was embarked upon), working-class radicals did try to use this method to create the informed opinion they sought; but the cost of publication and the difficulties of distribution made these more envious glances at parallel middle-class pressure groups than sustained policies.[90]

Moreover, from the CSU initiative in 1842 onwards, the emergence in Manchester of a strong progressive element in middle-class liberalism, which tended to accept, at least in principle, the justice of universal suffrage, and at least some of the other points of the charter,

---

[85] *MC*, 6 June 1846.

[86] As the *MG* said on one occasion, 'we published the legitimate proceedings of the day, but we do not profess to publish all the nonsense which absurd or mischievous intruders may think proper to vent on such occasions', *MG*, 15 August 1837.

[87] *Weekly Wages*, August 1861; cf. the 'Manchester Carpenters and Joiners', *MG*, 28 June 1851; as one correspondent told *SWN*, 'Working men have an impression that the press is only open to these wealthy employers', 'One not present', 27 April 1861.

[88] *MG*, 4 May 1839.

[89] See the comments of 'S', *MG*, 30 September 1840; for a later successful use of placards see the account of the Union and Emancipation Society placard, *MG*, 27 August 1863.

[90] *MSp*, 3 March 1849.

blurred the lines of political opposition on which radicalism had thrived. As the staunch chartist E.C. Cropper bemoaned in 1856, 'they had been dying in the last couple of years for want of agitation, having no foe to grapple with'.[91] Once the issue, at least locally, had become merely the practicability of certain reforms, or what it was realistic to expect the middle classes to accept, the battle for reform had become a matter of argument and negotiation within the middle classes, a process in which it was difficult to find a place for mass radical agitation.

The imperatives of the alliance with middle-class reformers, particularly the need to accept compromise measures of reform to ensure unity, but also the necessity of working with laissez-faire liberals, also undercut the ground of any agitation. The working classes proved repeatedly unwilling to agitate for watered down versions of reform: as W.E. Adams of Hulme pointed out in 1862, there was so little active support for the reform movement in Manchester at the time because, '[a]ll attempts to evoke an agitation on behalf of mere expedients have been a lamentable failure'.[92] Among those sections committed to protective labour legislation, there was also an understandable lack of enthusiasm for an alliance with ACLL liberals who remained firmly opposed to trade unions, factory reform and state regulation.[93]

The stifling of suasionist politics

This was the nub of the radical problem. For the chartists, the core of the political task was to mobilise the working classes around a shared programme and agreed strategy, and the platform necessary for this could only be a class platform, committed to an indivisible programme. Once the central assumptions of moral and physical force strategies came under question, however, and the working classes shifted towards tactics of suasion and collaboration, the platform and the press could form the basis of political action only if they integrated reformers from across the classes, and operated as a mechanism both for the creation of a new inter-class political consensus, and then for its organisation

---

[91] *MX*, 27 August 1856.
[92] 'Caractacus' [W.E. Adams], *NR*, 31 May 1862.
[93] For example, 'A Manchester Operative', *MC*, 16 June 1860.

and presentation as the genuine and widely-held sentiment of the community. This did not remove the need for effective working-class organisation; rather it presented in a particularly acute form the problem of creating organisations in which working-class radicals could effectively influence policies while carrying midddle-class reformers along with them. The intense pressures were only too well recognised. '[I]f our organisation is not effected now we have little hopes of being able to make ourselves heard at all', confessed James Robertson to the Newcastle Radical Joseph Cowen in November 1858.[94] And thus it proved: at the Union Chambers conference in November 1858 the working-class radicals prevailed, only to see the middle-classes ignore the Manhood Suffrage Association in favour of the quickly-established and much more moderate Lancashire Reformer's Union. Although the MSA strove valiantly during 1859 to make good its claim to speak for a new reforming consensus, it was progressively marginalised.[95] As the *Weekly Wages* recognised with regret in 1861, '[t]he people are finding out the power of organisation and of concerted action, but they have hardly yet discovered the secret of influencing public opinion'.[96]

The secret, if such it were, lay in the operations of the press and the platform. The closure of the press was a telling blow against radical strategies of suasion. Newspapers were the working classes' most accessible channel to the middle-class mind: as Richard Crowther confessed in 1842, '[a]s I am only a working man, [I] have no means of giving publicity to my ideas, except in the cheap form of a "correspondent"'.[97] Moreover, as the *Church of the People* commented in 1858, 'the greater number of Englishmen look at the world not with their own eyes, but through the medium of the daily journal'.[98] More importantly, the mid-nineteenth century newspaper was overtly an organ of public opinion. Editorials were seen as reflecting in some senses the attitudes of the readership. The prominent accounts of public meetings were given as representations of local sentiment. The most prestigious would be taken up by other regional papers and the national press, enhancing their status and significance. By giving undue prominence to favoured issues, and ignoring radical

[94] James Robertson to Joseph Cowen, 4 November 1858, *idem*, 10 November 1858, C258, Cowen Collection, Acc. 634, Tyne and Wear Archives.
[95] See above, pages 250-53.
[96] *Weekly Wages*, August 1861.
[97] 'Richard Crowther', *MG*, 19 December 1842.
[98] *Church of the People*, n.s. III, (1857–58), 186.

activity, the press could be seen as responsible for what *Weekly Wages* called 'the adulteration of public opinion by subsidised, or conscienceless, or reckless, or ignorant public writers...'.[99] Certainly, without its own press, any shade of political opinion risked marginalisation and impotence. As the *Manchester and Salford Temperance Reporter* put it, without newspaper support, 'meetings have passed off unreported, and as far as the general public were concerned, unheeded and unknown'.[100]

Unfortunately, as the survival of the *Northern Star*, the *People's Paper*, and then the success of the *Beehive*, demonstrated, merely having its own press profited radicalism little in the era of collaboration. Radical papers like the *Northern Star* circulated among the working classes, but they were shunned by middle-class readers. O'Connor commented in 1845 that because of the attitude of the press, 'we must force, we must thrust...we must drive our policy down the very throat of faction', and this call was taken up in Manchester.[101] Manchester radicals and trade unionists realised the necessity of a local paper which would advocate their interests while achieving an inter-class readership, but had not the resources to establish one, and instead were left trying to encourage the reluctant editors of the established press to espouse their cause and raise public awareness of it.[102]

However, although the press was perhaps central in the creation of public opinion, in its articulation it played second fiddle to the platform, and in the long run the platform proved almost equally impervious to radical activity. There were two basic difficulties: getting the articulation of the necessary opinion, and ensuring that this took place at meetings of sufficient prominence and status to be able to lay claim to being 'public opinion'. In the 1830s, before incorporation in Manchester and Salford, the bitter political rivalries within the middle classes attenuated any attempts to control the platform, and the multiplication of local authorities maximised the opportunities for popular participation.[103] Once the towns had been incorporated, the political map was simplified, and the platform focused on the *ad hoc* public meeting which was so characteristic an element of Victorian public culture.[104] And while it may well be true, as Joyce has

---

[99] *Weekly Wages*, August 1861.
[100] *MSTR*, 4 August 1849.
[101] *NS*, 27 December 1845, cf. the comment of J.G. Clarke, *NS*, 25 March 1848.
[102] Thomas Salter, *MX*, 1 October 1853, 'Tenax', *MX*, 27 June 1856.
[103] See complaints of middle-class figures cited in Garrard, *Leadership and Power*, 212.
[104] For some interesting comments on the public meeting see Morris, *Class, Sect and*

suggested, that in this period the most formal of the types of public meeting, the 'town's meeting', was developed by the civic elites as being 'emblematic of shared urban community', in practice the public meeting remained a central site of political conflict.[105] This conflict brought working-class radicals face to face with an impressive array of control mechanisms. Although public meetings had the forms of deliberative assemblies, and the conscience of liberalism made overt legal control increasingly untenable after 1832, in fact this was largely symbolic; more and more the meeting was carefully staged and manipulated to ratify and demonstrate public backing not for the opinions of the community in general, but of its promoters.[106]

The Manchester practice of calling public meetings by circular, allowed the organisers to shape their composition, and by holding a pre-meeting of the influential supporters of the movement, drawing up the resolutions to be presented to the meeting, and allocating the speakers who were to speak to them, it was possible to present the meeting with a rigidly defined agenda, which it was difficult if not impossible to alter.[107] This straitjacket was reinforced, through the chairman, by the application of a series of unwritten 'laws' of public meetings. The one most often used was that matter which was foreign to the purpose of the meeting could not be introduced; this was often extended to the more contentious assertion that '[t]hey could not call a meeting for a specific purpose, and carry resolutions opposed to the purpose for which it was called'.[108] The importance of the chairman was acknowledged by the frequent struggles which marked public meetings in the chartist period over who should occupy the chair.[109]

Moreover, whenever there might be any doubt as to the vote of the assembly, the organisers could apply a series of stratagems. The time

---

Party, 184–95.

[105] Joyce, *Visions of the People*, 43–4.

[106] For the difficulties of the liberal conscience with the control of the platform see W.L. Arnstein, 'The Murphy Riots: A Victorian Dilemma', *Victorian Studies*, XIX (1975), 59–68.

[107] *MC*, 23 May 1840; *MG* commented that 'our public meetings are fast becoming a means of announcing to all the decisions of a few...the work for which such meetings are avowedly called is really done elsewhere, by a few individuals conferring in secrecy, and forming a self-appointed committee, which delegates to itself the duties of the assembly which is afterwards called to ratify its acts', 15 September 1858.

[108] *MC*, 18 May 1847; for their mature expression see 'The Rights of Public Meetings', *Freelance*, VII (1872), 213.

[109] For the most vivid illustration of this see A. Prentice, *History of the Anti-Corn Law League*, (1853) I, 192–3; see also *NS*, 27 March 1841, *Freelance*, I (1867), 115.

of the day at which meetings were called could be used to good effect. Town meetings were traditionally called during the day, and the continuation of this practice of course restricted the ability to attend of those who needed to be at work. In the chartist period, widespread unemployment and less effective work disciplines had obscured this problem, but during the campaigns of the 1850s and 1860s, the inability of the working-class voice to be heard at daytime public meetings was a frequent source of radical frustration.[110]

Where the endorsement of the meeting was thought to be in doubt, it was always possible to ensure that only the right kind of participants were admitted. Ticket-only meetings were the most effective method here, and this practice was widely adopted, although meetings so overtly limited could scarcely claim to be 'public', and the issue of tickets was not always easy to control.[111] Instead considerable effort was often devoted to mobilising supporters, ensuring that they gained favoured access to the hall, and were able to dominate the platform and assume the positions of prominence from which the minority might appear as the majority.[112] If this was not enough, then vigorous policing could ensure that obvious opponents were ejected for 'disturbing' the meeting, and although Charles Shaw had been unwilling for his force to become involved in the internal policing of meetings, it is obvious that after his departure the police and magistracy were prepared to seek a much tighter control.[113] In any case, once committed to consensus, it was difficult to see what radicals could achieve by forcing themselves on the attention of the middle classes by the old chartist tactic of disrupting public meetings.

Such constraints helped stifle radical opinion, particularly within collaborationist movements. Although radicals might hold local meetings to present their case, and even get motions in favour of their programme accepted, the dynamics of collaboration meant that effectively, the important decisions were made at the large general meetings which ostensibly established the consensus of informed

---

[110] MG, 20 March 1841, 'A Working Man', MG, 15 March 1859, Manchester Weekly Times, 6 June 1863.
[111] Despite the impression of Vernon, Politics and the People, 225–9, ticketing was almost exclusively used as a method of exclusion against, rather than by, radicals. See, of many examples, MG, 19 August 1840, 26 February 1857, 25 September 1839. For an example where lack of care in controlling tickets brought difficulties see 'James Lowe', NMW, V (1838–39), 539.
[112] 'Hater of Partiality', MX, 27 September 1851, 'Fair Play', MG, 16 March 1859.
[113] See the comments of Maude, MG, 20 February 1844; MX, 28 January 1857.

opinion. Hence the radicals were still forced to shape their activities to suit the wishes of middle-class liberals, whose participation at such meetings, as the promoters and seconders of resolutions, was critical to the achievement of the necessary tone.

While many of the working classes remained disenfranchised, and the expectation remained that the political behaviour of at least some of the rest was considerably influenced by the activities and opinions of a few prominent citizens, the number and size of public meetings was of less importance than their character, the extent to which they enjoyed the participation of the influential, and could to some degree be said to represent their opinion. During the chartist period, the official stamp of character and representativeness was reserved for the 'town meeting'. Unfortunately for the working classes, such a meeting could only be called on the agreement of the boroughreeve and then the mayor, and these men exercised this prerogative to refuse applications, or to alter the motions to be put to the meeting.[114] Similarly ward meetings were deemed to have official sanction only when called and chaired by the council representatives. In the 1830s and 1840s this allowed radical meetings, however numerously attended, to be dismissed as merely 'the mob' and hence politically insignificant, if not illegal.[115]

From the 1830s, however, the role of the official 'town meeting' declined as it became accepted that in a town the size of Manchester, the conventional fiction of the assembly of citizens was wearing rather too thin, and the fear grew that they were degenerating into 'sheer tumultuous clamour'.[116] Instead, the weight of a public meeting came to depend less on its official status, and more on the influence and significance of its leading participants. By the conventions which surrounded public meetings, the correct tone required prominent 'requisitioners' who would put their name to the placard calling such meetings, a suitably respected man to act as chairman, and preferably some sign of the sanction of the appropriate local authorities.[117]

[114] *MC*, 22 November 1834, Shaw to Phillips, 29 December 1841, HO45/46/66–7.
[115] *MG*, 2 March 1833; see Russell's comments on unlawful meetings, *PP*, (1839) XXXVIII (448).
[116] *MG*, 31 March 1841, 4 May 1860; for a more positive evaluation see *MC*, 9 February 1864.
[117] 'XYZ', *WMC*, 20 April 1833, *MC*, 14 October 1846, deliberations of Athenaeum committee, 'Minutes', 30 December 1835, M2/1/1 MCLA; hence in 1864 it was even possible for the *Manchester Courier*, (albeit from transparent party motives) to dismiss a meeting which had all the forms of a town meeting because 'not a single man of any

It was also vital that the meeting was held at the right place, for by mid-century the local platform was strictly defined by a steep hierarchy of venue. The Town Hall was the traditional venue for a town's meeting, but increasingly the Free Trade Hall, partly because of its greater size, assumed the position of premier venue; the Corn Exchange also had a certain cachet, and was often favoured by Conservative groups; but meetings held in the Carpenters' Hall, the People's Institute, or the Co-operative Society's Downing Street Hall, had little chance of engrossing community attention.[118] In particular, the politics of the street and the moor was rendered impotent, because these were not sites on which class alliances could be built and sustained: redefinition of the street as unrespectable meant that it could play little part in radical movements committed to strategies of moral suasion and alliance with the middle class.

The cumulative effect of these conventions was to tie the hands of radical leaders and hand over control of the reform movements of the 1850s and 1860s to the middle-class Radicals. Ironically this control redounded to the detriment of the Liberals, although this provided no comfort for radical leaders, because it called into question the ability of the platform to effectively articulate community opinion, and severely damaged the credibility of all forms of pressure politics. In Manchester, the crisis of the platform was highlighted by the bitter conflict between the rival schemes of educational reform fought tooth and nail in ward and town meetings between 1848 and 1852, prompting a spate of claims and counter-claims as to the validity of the demonstrations mounted by the rival camps, or the verdicts of the occasional direct clashes. Meetings were held which had been advertised only to the carefully selected supporters of one side, to ensure unanimity, and then passed off as general local opinion.[119] Elaborate efforts were made, via the printing of special tickets of admission, with carefully controlled distribution and backed up by heavy police presence, to ensure that the meetings moved comfortably and without disturbance along prearranged channels. Inordinate efforts were made to organise supporters to attend debates between the two sides to ensure victory.[120]

mark took part in the proceedings', *MC*, 12 February 1864.

[118] Cf. comment of Jones, *PPr*, 21 November 1857.

[119] Cf. E. Waugh, *Local Heddicashun Meetings*, (1849), 'John Watts', *MX*, 19 November 1851.

[120] The positions taken during this conflict were reprised during the disputes over various

The result was little more than a farce, and one which did significant damage to the role of the public meeting. The sense of disillusionment which resulted is best summed up by R.J. Richardson, who finally bowed out of active participation in politics in this period, for reasons which would undoubtedly have been echoed by many other chartists and radicals. Richardson commented that he was asked to take part in the agitation over education but refused because:

> the parties who were getting up the meeting were purely of the religious class, and ministers of the Gospel of the different churches and chapels, who have at their call the visitors and teachers of the Sunday Schools, and they can pack a meeting at any time. There is no chance of a fair and free discussion at any meeting where religion comes into question.

'I believe', Richardson continued, that 'all those who have been in the habit of taking part in the public meetings in Manchester have abstained from attending for that very reason'.[121]

This may have been something of an exaggeration, but there can be little doubt that there was a growing sense of frustration among influential middle-class opinion at the stultification of the public meeting which the almost universal 'management' of the late 1840s and 1850s had produced. According the *Manchester Guardian* in 1859, '[p]ublic meetings are always a nuisance and generally a farce', and as a result, '[a] valuable organ of public opinion is thus mutilated, silenced, or falsified'.[122] A year later it confirmed that 'public meetings...often represent nothing more than the determination and activity of a small minority advocating unpopular opinions'.[123] The declining reputation of the public meeting, and its dwindling importance was noted with regret by leading ultra-liberals, many of whom settled for less public modes of political action in the 1850s, and were still, in 1861, looking anxiously for a 'time when public meetings will be more common [and] more important than of late'.[124]

Liberal and Constitutional Association meetings in Manchester in 1867, see *MX*, 28 February, 1 March 1867.

[121] *PP*, (1854) XIV (367), 201; compare with the very similar ideas of 'A Working Man', *SWN*, 7 June 1862.

[122] *MG*, 19 May 1859.

[123] *MG*, 4 May 1860.

[124] For the shift to personal politics see Cobden to Henry Ashworth, 7 December 1850, Ashworth to Cobden, 22 October 1851, Cobden Papers, Add Mss 43653 ff.169, 184-5, BL; Bright to Wilson, 21 January 1861, Wilson Papers, MCLA, reiterated in Bright to Wilson, 10 July 1866, cited in Vincent, *The Formation of the Liberal Party*, 193;

The practice of public meetings was too much ingrained in the fabric of Victorian political mores for it to be abandoned overnight, and both they and controversies over their status continued into the 1860s. Nevertheless, it is significant that from the mid-century onwards, there was a definite move towards other, more manageable and less impeachable forms of opinion demonstration, in particular the conference. The Anti-Corn Law League had made much use of conferences in the early 1840s, partly as a response to chartist obstruction at public meetings, partly as a way of projecting its national identity. The ACLL address of October 1842 placed conferences second behind publications in the hierarchy of the League's propaganda activities.[125] The educationalists in the early 1850s, the United Kingdom Alliance in the late 1850s, and in particular the National Reform Union in the 1860s, all turned to the conference. In the early 1870s it was possible for one local journal to announce 'the age for conferences', and for another to protest at the 'number of so-called "conferences"'.[126] By deriving its status from the standing of carefully invited participants, rather than from some doubtful claim to represent any specific local or regional opinion, the conference by-passed many of the drawbacks of the meeting, while at the same time fulfilling the function of providing the semblance of deliberation and endorsement which was necessary to give legitimacy to an adopted programme. Of course it did this in an environment in which the influential elite was able to outvote the delegates of the many. In May 1865 Ernest Jones complained bitterly to Karl Marx at the middle-class manipulation of the reform conferences of 1864 and 1865, and in particular the manufacturing of sufficient moderate delegates to outvote supporters of universal manhood suffrage.[127]

A similar process of decay can be discerned in the case of petitions, the long-standing complement to the platform in the articulation of public opinion. The efficacy of petitioning was dealt a severe blow in 1832, when the process of the House of Commons was altered to deny MPs presenting petitions the right, which they had previously

---

Freelance, XI (1876), 201, 386.

[125] Prentice, *History*, 395. The CSU also made prominent use of conferences, which in this period can be seen partly as a self-consciously less threatening version of the radical 'convention'.

[126] *Freelance*, V (1871), 400, *MCN*, 27 January 1872.

[127] See Jones to Marx, 22 May 1865, Marx-Engels-Lenin Institute, Moscow, cited by Taylor, 'Modes of Expression', 493-5.

possessed, to speak to the petition. O'Connor and the chartist leadership recognised the weakness of petitioning in these circumstances, and this contributed to their rhetoric of 'the last petition' in 1839.[128] Within the confines of suasionist politics, shorn of its intimidatory undertones, petitioning laboured under further disadvantages: problems associated with the status of petitions; the accuracy of the numbers signing; the standing of the signatories; and the extent to which they had done so from conviction and without compulsion. All of these were raised not only by the chartist petitions themselves, but also during other campaigns, including those associated with the conflict between the National Public Schools Association and the Manchester and Salford Education Bill Committee. Largely discredited by the end of the chartist period, petitions, like public meetings, needed reform and rehabilitation in the 1850s.[129] Hence the experiments with 'family petitions', and hence the switch to alternative procedures, particularly canvassing, pioneered by the Maine Law campaigners.

At the end of March 1861 a public meeting was held in the Manchester Town Hall to consider the latest reform bill, Lord Derby's proposal of that year. The bill was roundly condemned; but the speeches, particularly that of John Watts, vividly anatomised the tactical bankruptcy of mid-Victorian radicalism. Watts' opposition to the bill was determined, and he made the conventional plea that the radicals should seek all constitutional means to achieve a more satisfactory bill. But then his tone changed. 'He was', he confessed,

> almost tired of what were called constitutional remedies and had begun to ask himself how often it would be necessary to lift up one's voice and send petitions to parliament, and hold public meetings, which took working men and bankers and merchants away from their ordinary business at a cost of their time and wages? What did constitutional remedy amount to after all?... How was the remedy to be got? Petition? Petitions were laughed at. Hold public meetings? Public meetings were no value till they were riotous, and if they were riotous they must be put down. How were they to go to work...?[130]

In 1841 such a speech would likely have been the prelude to a rousing call to arms; in 1861 it was a confession, by one of the most

---

[128] Epstein, *The Lion of Freedom*, 104–5.
[129] Belchem, 'Radicalism as a Platform Agitation', 144; the rehabilitation did bring a renewed use of petitions – Parry has noted that in numerical terms, the period 1862–72 saw the peak of petitioning, Parry, *The Rise and Fall of Liberal Government*, 223.
[130] *MC*, 30 March 1861.

indomitable advocates of extensive parliamentary reform, of radicalism's deep-seated feelings of impotence in the face of the obstacles to effective platform politics in pursuit of strategies of suasion and collaboration.

From this perspective, what is crucial about working-class politics in the 1850s and 1860s is the class' loss of a sense of agency, of its confidence in being able to effect change, which sowed the seeds of the fatalism, the 'culture of consolation', and the strategy of warrening capitalism, which historians such as Stedman Jones, Meacham and Saville have identified in the years after 1870. This loss did not derive from the dramatic defeats of chartism in 1839, 1842 or 1848; it emerged gradually, although not inevitably, from the frustrations of collaborationist politics in the period from the late 1830s to the early 1860s, when the institutional forms of politics became increasingly uncongenial to working-class radicalism.

Conclusion

In this sense, we must supplement the traditional explanations of radical decay in the period after 1848 by examining the role of the changing intellectual morphology of the mid-Victorian city. The dissonance between working-class normative and theoretical consciousness on the one hand, and working-class strategic consciousness on the other, and the slide of radical strategy towards moral suasion can be explained in part by the rapid erosion of the working-class revolutionary threat by the strengthened coercive armoury of the state, in part by the difficulties faced by radicals in achieving either working-class consensus or effective influence over the middle classes, and in part by the weakened position of extra-parliamentary politics generally, (itself a result of the crisis of confidence in the traditional organs of the articulation of public opinion which emerged in the 1850s and 1860s). In this situation, and given the pressures against political activism which existed, working-class non-participation in the radical movement is explicable without the need to assume a drastic transformation of consciousness.

Chapter Ten

Conclusion

Summary

Though it is often disguised by a concentration on political activity, the traditional picture of mid-nineteenth century working-class history involves a belief in the transformation of working-class consciousness which was, therefore, at base an intellectual process. This implies that a fundamental dimension of the explanation of change around mid-century must involve the operation of the structures and contexts within which consciousness was formed (which I have termed the 'intellectual morphology').

Yet historians have remained uneasy with the notion of consciousness: some have ignored it, some have subsumed it under 'culture', and some have even considered it and then neglected it as of little explanatory use. Predominantly, this is a response to two problems, the difficulty of obtaining evidence of working-class attitudes, and the lack of a generally accepted and heuristically-useful framework of consciousness and its formation. This study has attempted to develop such a framework, and to use extensive newspaper and archival research to overcome, as far as possible, the difficulties of sources.

Consciousness becomes more readily analysed, and also more readily integrated into explanations of action, if the distinction between its different elements (particularly cognitive, normative, theoretical, visionary and strategic) is made. These provide a basis on which the nature of consciousness at any point in time can be examined. The dynamics of consciousness formation and change, and hence the factors influencing its change, can only be studied historically if it is accepted that attitudes were the results of processes of *learning, reflection* (the analysis of experience), and political action. Hence understanding the nature of change in working-class politics must include an examination of the nature of working-class experience, and the changing shape and operation of the intellectual morphology.

In the case studied here, the nature of the intellectual morphology was influenced by the socio-economic structure of Manchester, by changes in its local government and the forces of law and order, and most of all by the confrontation between the institutions and practices of working-class culture, and the incessant pressure of middle-class activities designed to reform and reshape that culture. In Manchester, from the 1830s to the 1860s there was an active, and sometimes a frantic search for appropriate mechanisms with which the middle classes could establish a degree of cultural, and hence economic and political control over the working classes. This middle-class 'moral imperialism' ranged from institutions of religious or politico-economic propagandism to associations and mechanisms of control designed to inculcate and enforce bourgeois standards of conduct.

The motivation for these activities is clear. What is less certain is their efficacy, and at least in the case of Manchester, their singularly disappointing results makes it impossible to use them as the foundation of any general explanation of the restabilisation of the social order. Despite the massive efforts particularly of the Church of England, religious provision could do little more than keep pace with the expanding population of the city, and few inroads were made into the gaps and insufficiencies which had been opened up in the first thirty years of the century. The fragility of the social stability was only too apparent to observers in the 1860s. In 1864 the Rev. J.C. Paterson told the annual meeting of the Manchester Ragged and Industrial Schools that he believed 'that by churches and schools and the individual efforts of Christian men, we are doing nothing more than simply banking up and preventing an overflow of the vice and wickedness which is all around us...we are every day in danger of the moral embankment we have thrown up being overturned and carried away by the flood of vice and wickedness which is all around us...'.[1]

Similarly, there is little evidence of progress being made towards the stubbornly held aspiration to dispel the working classes' 'ignorance' of politics and economics, convince them of the rectitude of classical political economy and elite views of a limited representative government. The schools, it seems, had neither the resources nor the inclination for this kind of education. The mechanics' institutes and their various successors were supported by the working classes only to the extent that they abandoned this kind of overt proselytism and the

---

[1] Manchester Ragged and Industrial Schools, *Annual Report*, (1864), 17.

middle-class patronage and control which had made it possible. The experience of these clubs and institutes was paralleled by the difficulties of the less institutionalised activities of the lecture platform, the periodical propagandist or the tract distributor. In 1864, Edward Brotherton, driving force behind the Education Aid Society, confessed that 'immense mischiefs are growing about us, and eating into the heart of society, because we are so lax in this matter of education'.[2]

So unsuccessful were middle-class initiatives in these directions that it is apparent that throughout the period the focus of moral imperialism turned increasingly onto the promotion of provident habits, and the 'respectable' lifestyle with which they were associated. The direction opened up by the District Provident Society in the 1830s was followed by the various missionary organisations and propagandising bodies such as the Sanitary Association in the 1840s and 1850s, supplemented in turn by the rapidly expanding provident institutions of churches, chapels and day, Sunday and ragged schools. Yet here again, the working classes did not so much repudiate middle-class initiatives, as imbue them with a distinct working-class ethos, often embodied in their own institutions of self-help. The limited success of the temperance movement, and the tensions within it over control and direction, epitomise the frustrations middle-class reformers faced. Despite their efforts, a distinctive, and often overtly anti-middle-class working-class culture not only survived but developed. Within it, the working classes retained the intellectual space to sustain and develop their own values and ideology.

The inefficacy of middle-class efforts was the combined result of the weaknesses of the mechanisms they developed, and the formidable range of obstacles with which they were faced. Despite considerable middle-class patronage, the number and diversity of the institutions of moral imperialism, and the absence in most cases of any effective structures of co-ordination, left them reliant on the financial support of the working classes. This in turn created vulnerability to working-class pressure. Moreover, middle-class reformers were often surprisingly open about their hostility to working-class culture and attitudes, and rather than attempting gradual change sought frontal demolition. Antagonism and rejection were the not unnatural results.

The inherent difficulties of the reform effort were in any case immense. The size of the city, its residential segregation, and the sense

---

[2] 'E.B', *MG*, 5 December 1864.

of neighbourhood solidarity which prevailed, overwhelmed even those organisations like the City Mission which were specifically constructed to achieve a comprehensive geographical coverage. The greater portion, including schools and their ancillary activities, which relied on locally- or congregationally-generated finance and facilities were even more hamstrung. By 1870 the ragged school and mission hall movements were only beginning to rectify the maldistribution of resources which had hitherto prevailed. In any case, the divisions were more than simply geographic. Working-class culture had by mid-century generated a largely separate structure of intellectual life, in which learning took place informally in home and street, in pub and music hall, as much as it did in school, church or institute. Progress towards the kind of *modus operandi* best suited to operating in this territory, for example in the provision of open air lecturing, was faltering and uneasy. Even the accent and language of working-class speech was distinct from that of the middle classes: comprehension could not always be assured.

The ultimate consequence of this unequal contest was the diversion and the dilution of middle-class aims, and the continued survival of the attitudes and practices which they had been attempting to reform. The evidence is clearest in the case of working-class culture: the prominence of the pub, the success of the music hall, the persistence of the old 'rough' sports such as dog-fighting and the growth of new interests, including pedestrianism, and above all the overwhelming presence of the unreconstructed life of street and local community, all bear witness to its continued vibrancy.

It is the journey from culture to consciousness which creates the problems. The collapse of independent working-class politics during the 1840s, and the diversion of working-class activism into trade unions, friendly societies and co-operative associations both provide *prima facie* evidence of a transformation in working-class attitudes. The paucity of working-class testimony complicates the task of penetrating beyond activity and towards a clearer understanding of the beliefs on which it was based. However, the picture which emerges from the Manchester evidence is of the predominance of continuity in working-class consciousness through the mid-century decades. The nature of this continuity becomes clearer if one makes distinct working-class norms, utopias, theoretical understandings, and strategic and tactical beliefs. Applying this categorisation, it is clear that there is relatively little change apparent in working-class norms and values in this period: the egalitarian, fiercely independent rejection of middle-class values which shines through in the chartist period, is equally apparent, if less vociferous, in the 1850s and 1860s. Given that the social vision of rank and file chartists was much less revolutionary than has often been suggested, working-class conceptions of their ideal society also remained remarkably constant, as did the perception of the sources of the social and political evils which they suffered and upon which these visions were largely based. The accepted picture of a transformation of working-class consciousness around mid-century is in this sense an illusion.

What altered in this period were conceptions of the appropriate strategies for change, precisely, of course, the element of working-class attitudes most likely to be reflected in the nature of working-class politics. In essence, the early nineteenth century model of radicalism, which sought to impose immediate democratisation by means of irresistible popular pressure on a reluctant polity, was abandoned in favour both of alliance with progressive elements in the polity in furtherance of incremental advances towards democracy, and of the pursuit of other ameliorative movements which could produce improvements irrespective of the need for political change.

In both cases it is important to emphasise that change occurred not because the working classes were hoodwinked by middle-class propaganda, but rather in response to a largely rational re-evaluation of their activism as the environment within which they operated changed. Hence, as the greater efficiency of the military and the massive potential of the new police for the maintenance of law and order became apparent, and the realisation grew that the threat of revolution which had sustained early nineteenth century radicalism became more difficult to sustain, so opinion swung in favour of strategies of alliance with middle-class reformers, rather than antagonism to them. This in turn encouraged the acceptance of piecemeal reform as a more realistic aspiration. Similarly, the politicisation of the working classes in the chartist period had derived from the recognition that in a period of massive structural change coupled with cyclical instability (although of course contemporaries did not think in these terms), systemic change through political action was the only realistic strategy available to them. As economic conditions became more stable and more favourable from the middle of the 1840s, so it became increasingly possible to recognise the efficacy of temperance, co-operation and trade unionism as mechanisms of economic and social advance. Therefore, where change is visible in working-class attitudes, it is change derived from the rational reactions to changing conditions.

This is not to suggest that over the longer term it is not possible to discern more fundamental changes in working-class consciousness. After mid-century there is an increasing willingness for the upper echelons of the working classes to ascribe poverty to individual failure rather than a flawed social structure. Such attitudes, and the cultural differences which were constructed on the growing economic divergence between craft and non-craft sections of the working class, did begin to erode the sense of class solidarity which had marked the chartist period (although it did not eradicate the sense of working-class identity which had been established by the 1830s). However, these attitudes had existed in the 1830s and 1840s, and their spread was slow and uneven, too much so for them to be seen as causes of the post-chartist transformation of working-class politics. They were more consequence than cause. They developed because the environment of crisis and antagonism of the 1840s had given way to the more conciliatory years of the 1850s and 1860s.

Yet if all this was so, why is there so little evidence of working-class enthusiasm for political reform in the 1850s and 1860s? There are several reasons. Most significantly, after the abandonment of the platform, the role of mass participation in the reform movement became unclear, and even, if the priority was seen as convincing middle-class waverers of the safety as well as the policy of further political reform, undesirable. The dominant role assumed by middle-class Liberals, such as Edmund Potter, also created frustration and disillusionment among the working classes when such leadership seemed to result merely in prevarication and delay. This was particularly the case when the measure of reform which was being mooted might not, in any case, benefit considerable numbers of the working classes: it was easier to accept the need to work with the middle classes than it was to summon up any enthusiasm for the restricted measures which were all they seemed prepared to accept. For the leaders of working-class radicalism this created a particular problem of strategy: were they to constantly press for a greater measure of reform in order to ensure that what they actually obtained was the most that was possible, or, mindful of the dangers of perpetually dividing what was never more than a fragile alliance, should they knuckle under and accept that they could only go at the speed of their most unwilling ally. The divisions between

Cooper, Hooson and Jones on this issue could only harm their ability to mobilise the people.

Nevertheless, just as injudicious attacks on heroes of the chartist period were likely to elicit resounding demonstrations of popular reverence of their memory, so, despite the carping of conservatives, critical junctures in the reform process brought periodic evidence of the persistence of support for reform among the working classes. The crowds which packed the streets of Manchester during the great reform demonstration of 1866 speak eloquently of the reservoir of commitment to the old chartist ideal of political reform.

Epilogue

The period of this study was chosen because for working-class politics it was dominated by the struggle to revise the political settlement embodied in the 1832 Reform Act. Unexpectedly, although not entirely by default, the second Reform Act provided the Manchester working class, at least in purely local terms, with a considerable instalment of their demands. The context of politics after 1867 was different, and needs to be studied on its own terms. Nevertheless, a brief glance must be given to the city's subsequent political history because on superficial acquaintance, it would seem to throw doubt on the argument which has been advanced here.

Between 1832 and 1867, with one short-lived aberration, Manchester had been a liberal city, had indeed become inextricably associated with progressive liberalism, the 'Manchester School'. In 1868 in the new two-vote, three-member constituency, the Liberals captured only two of the three seats, with the third going to a Tory, and Ernest Jones, the acknowledged leader of working-class radicalism in the North, could manage only a dismal fifth place.[3] Jacob Bright, brother of John and the new leader of progressive Liberalism was himself defeated in 1874, and in 1885 only one of the six Manchester divisions returned a Liberal. Without the sectarian heat of Liverpool, or the factory paternalist – and church-based – politics of the Lancashire mill towns, Manchester nevertheless repudiated progressive and radical Liberalism in the decade and a half after 1867.

---

[3] For a detailed study of the 1868 general election in Manchester see Taylor, 'Modes of Expression', 610-31.

Moreover, when the socialist revival emerged in the 1880s and early 1890s, it struggled hard to establish a foothold in Manchester, and made painfully slow inroads into popular support for the Conservative and Liberal parties. It is also significant that the socialism which did appear to resonate most among the city's working class was Blatchford's idiosyncratic and almost tory 'Clarion' socialism.[4] Indeed, Manchester did not elect its first Labour MP until after 1923 (although Labour won Salford North in 1918). Radicalism as a political force seems scarcely to have existed after 1867. Surely this throws doubt on its vigour before 1867?

Not necessarily: it is in fact a picture consistent with the analysis of working-class consciousness advanced here. During the chartist period there was little underlying consensus among the working classes as to the most effective programmes for social and economic reform: chartism succeeded precisely because it concentrated on the need for political power as the prelude for the implementation of any reform programme. Once this unifying standard had been removed by Disraeli in 1867, just as in the 1830s, working-class activism was fragmented by the pursuit of various specific reforms. And because the aspirations of the working classes beyond the charter had been strictly limited, it remained feasible to look to the established political groupings as the means of further change.

In the context of this utilitarian evaluation of the main political parties, the Conservatives could claim considerable advantages. By being responsible for the 1867 act they had not only removed the most important obstacle to working-class support, but had also called into question some traditional assumptions as to the undemocratic and anti-popular nature of the party. This allowed them to solidify the appeal which they had possessed since the 1830s and 1840s as supporters of social reform, and opponents of the laissez-faire excesses of the Manchester School.[5] Manchester Conservatives such as W.R. Callender, with his support of trade unionism and social reform, and the Birleys, with their extensive support for working-class interests, particularly education, provided a political face with considerable appeal. This is not to suggest that sectarian tensions and the influence of Anglican dominance of the school system did not play an important

[4] J. Hill, 'Manchester and Salford politics and the early development of the Independent Labour Party', *IRSH*, (1981), 171–200; P.F. Clarke, *Lancashire and the New Liberalism*, (1971), 40–2.
[5] Cf. the appeal of Horner in 1875, Clarke, *New Liberalism*, 32.

role in sustaining working-class toryism, or that nonconformity and traditions of independence did not support Liberalism. Nor is it to suggest that the post-1867 working classes were instrumental voters from election to election. It is merely to argue that Liberal and Conservative voting traditions could be consistent with pre-1867 radicalism and the nature of working-class consciousness in the chartist period.

Implications

How far does the experience of Manchester force a reassessment of current approaches to the post-chartist period? The immediate objection to any grandiose revisionism is that Manchester is far from typical of England at this time, and it is certainly true that being neither artisanal like London or Birmingham, nor factory-dominated like the textile towns of the North, Manchester possessed an unusually variegated occupational structure. Yet in some sense this is its advantage. Lacking occupational solidarity, and of a size and structure which effectively blunted processes of paternalism or social control, Manchester was already by mid-century beginning to develop the urban morphology which in the late nineteenth century has been identified as one of the bases of the re-emergence of independent labour politics.[6]

In any case, the search for a single explanation of mid-Victorian stability is undoubtedly misguided. Historians have long accepted chartism as an uneasy combination of various local movements; the logical corollary of this is that we need to seek for different patterns of decline, in which the relative importance of the processes at work varied from place to place. Even in Manchester, the influence of intellectual structures and the environment of political action do not provide in isolation a satisfactory explanation. However, the history of Manchester chartism demonstrates, with perhaps particular clarity, the need to incorporate into all accounts some assessment of the role of the structures of intellectual life and politics, too often in other studies neglected or submerged.

The fragmentation of chartism in Manchester which emerges from a close analysis of the strategic debates within working-class radicalism also points to the difficulties which have been created by the conflation

---

[6] See, for example, Savage, *The Dynamics of Working Class Politics*, chapter 5.

of a multiplicity of different local movements into one national movement. While rejecting the reductionist excesses of historians such as Gash and Hunt, it must be accepted that there was no unitary chartist movement in Britain, either from town to town, or even within individual localities. As such, the use of a framework for nineteenth century British history which includes a chartist movement from 1838 to 1848, and then defeat and quiescence from 1848 to the mid-1860s at least is highly misleading. In the past, it has sanctioned the two most serious weaknesses of nineteenth century labour historiography: the neglect, in the search for the roots of chartist failure, of the events of the period 1839-42, and the tendency to examine mid-century stability from the vantage point of the 1870s and 1880s, parading as causes of chartist decline conditions which were in fact a consequence of it.

This kind of backward projection provides unwarranted support to many of the most often invoked mechanisms of the decline of chartism. It is possible to divide these into two sorts, those which involve some kind of change in the environment in which the working classes lived and working-class politics operated, and those which involve some kind of externally induced alteration in working-class culture and consciousness itself. Theories in the latter group, social control, hegemony, embourgeoisiement, the labour aristocracy, are all on their weakest ground when attempting to account for changes in the crucial 1839-48 period. Their explanatory force is limited for precisely this reason. It is the dynamics of the former group, economic improvement, changing middle-class attitudes in national and local politics, the increasing potency of the forces of law and order, which provide the most effective explanations of events in this period. Examination of the processes of intellectual change provides the key to linking the two: the decline of chartism was a rational working-class response to changes in the environment and it was the altered strategies and institutions that resulted which enabled the gradual penetration of the forces of hegemony or social control and the development of a labour aristocracy ready to adopt some elements of middle-class ideology.

In this way, perhaps, it is possible to begin to reconcile the rival approaches to mid-nineteenth century labour history. Historians have tended to incline to either a positive view of chartism, coupled with a negative view of the succeeding decades, or have sought to re-evaluate the mid-Victorian labour movement by wholesale questioning of the significance of the chartist movement. While the former have invoked large scale theories of decline, the latter have denied the need to look beyond basic material changes. It has come to seem essential for contributors to the debate to nail their colours to one mast or the other. The irony is that it is the works most committed to maximising the ideological, political and cultural achievement of chartism which, in the face of the disintegration of the late 1840s and 1850s, have the most pessimistic implications for the resilience of working-class culture and politics. The more powerful, united and revolutionary in outlook was the working class of the 1830s and 1840s, the more cataclysmic was its subsequent defeat, and the more cataclysmic the defeat, the more powerful must be the historical processes at work. The steady stream of theories that seek to explain the mid-century hiatus which have jostled for academic position over the past 40 years and more can provide solutions only by developing a picture of a working class confronted, defeated and converted by the middle classes and the state.

Chartism has been zealously guarded, particularly by the left, as a symbol of the revolutionary potential of the industrial working class. The implications of this work are that only by questioning the icon of chartism can we come to a clearer understanding of the resilience of working-class consciousness, a more balanced evaluation of the achievements of the working classes during the middle decades of the nineteenth century, and a greater understanding of the emergence of stability in the industrial city.

Bibliography

Manuscript Sources

Manchester Central Library Archives

Samuel Bamford Papers
Bennett Street Sunday School Papers
James Bembridge Journals
Edward Brotherton Papers
Edward Edwards Papers
German Street Sunday School Papers
Manchester Athenaeum Papers
Manchester and Salford Sanitary Association Papers
Manchester School Board Minutes
Manchester Statistical Society Papers
Manchester Township Records
St Paul's Literary and Educational Society Papers
Edwin Waugh Diary
George Wilson Papers

University of Manchester, Institute of Science and Technology

Manchester Mechanics' Institute Minutes

John Rylands University Library, Manchester

John Fielden Papers
J.C. Street Diary
Unitarian Correspondence

Hanover House, Manchester

G.J. Holyoake Papers
Robert Owen Papers

Modern Records Centre, University of Warwick

Union of Construction, Allied Trades and Technicians: Friendly
Society of Operative Stone Masons, 'Fortnightly Returns'

British Library of Political and Economic Science

Henry Solly Papers

British Library

Richard Cobden Papers
Edward Edwards Diaries

National Library of Scotland

George Combe Papers

Public Records Office

Home Office Papers
Treasury Solicitor's Papers

Printed Primary Sources

Newspapers and Periodicals

Beehive (1862–67)
Champion of What is True and Right for the Good of All (1849–50)
Christian Reformer (1848–67)
Church of the People (1856–58)
Co-operator (1860–70)
Freelance (1866–78)
Home (1851–53)
Home Mission Field (1859–70)
M'Douall's Chartist Circular and Trades Advocate (1841)
Manchester City Mission Magazine (1853–61)
Manchester City News (1864–80)
Manchester Courier (1832–49, 1858–64)
Manchester Examiner and Times (1846–67)

Manchester Guardian (1832–67)

Manchester Illuminator and General Catholic Record (1850)

Manchester and Salford Advertiser (1832–48)

Manchester and Salford Temperance Reporter and Journal of Progress (1849–50)

Manchester Spectator and Commercial Gazette, (1848–51, 1856–58)

Manchester Weekly Advertiser (1855–61)

Manchester Weekly Times (occasional issues)

Monthly Literary and Scientific Lecturer (1850–53)

New Moral World (1834–43)

North of England Magazine (1840–43)

Northern Star (1838–52)

Northern Tribune (1854–55)

Occasional Papers of the Working Men's Club and Institute Union (1863–75)

Oddfellow's Magazine (1850–70)

People (1848–49)

People's Paper (1852–58)

Pitman's Popular Lecturer (1855–64)

Poor Man's Guardian (1832)

Reynold's Weekly Newspaper (1850–67)

Salford Weekly News (1859–67)

Tablet (occasional issues)

Trades Advocate and Herald of Progress (1850)

Transactions of the Manchester Statistical Society (1853–70)

Wheeler's Manchester Chronicle (1832-33)

Working Men's College Magazine (1859–61)

Official Publications

Factory Inspectors' Reports (1832–67)

Report of the Select Committee on Combinations (1837–38)

Report of the Royal Commission on Large Towns and Populous Districts (1844)

Reports of the Select Committee on Public Libraries (1850–52)

Report of the Select Committee on Newspaper Stamps (1851)

Reports of the Select Committee on Manchester and Salford Education (1852, 1852–53)

Report of the Select Committee on Public Houses (1852–53)

Report of the Select Committee on Friendly Societies (1854)

Report of the Select Committee on the Franchise (1860)

Report of the Royal Commission on the State of Popular Education (1861)

Returns of Parliamentary Boroughs (1866)

Report of the Royal Commission on the Organisation and Rules of Trade Unions (1867)

Report of the Select Committee on Schools for the Poorer Classes (1870)

Reports of the Royal Commission on Friendly Societies (1871-74)

Report of the Royal Commission on Drunkenness (1877)

Primary Published Works[1]

Abram, W.A., 'Social Conditions and Political Prospects of the Lancashire Workman', *Fortnightly Review*, New Ser. IV (1868), 426-41.

An Account of the Extraordinary, Arbitrary and Illegal Proceedings of the Wesleyan Sunday School Committee, Manchester South Circuit, in the expulsion of conductors and consequent resignation of the teachers in Chancery Lane Sunday School, (Manchester, 1835).

Adshead, Joseph, *Distress in Manchester: Evidence (tabular and otherwise) of the state of the Labouring Classes in 1840-2*, (Manchester, 1842).

___, *State of Education in the Borough of Manchester. Tables and Documents relative to evidence to be given by Mr. J. Adshead...before the Select Committee of the House of Commons*, (Manchester 1852).

___, *Reformatories and Ragged Schools. A Paper*, (Manchester, 1858).

Alsop, Alfred, *Ten Years in the Slums*, (Manchester, 1879).

Ancoats Lyceum, *Annual Report*, (Manchester, 1849-52).

Aspland, Alfred, *Crime in Manchester, and police administration*, (Manchester, 1868).

Atkinson, Charles, *Ninety Years of Sunday School Work in Saint John's Parish. A Centenary Address given at St. John's Church, Manchester*, (Manchester, 1880).

Axon, W.E.A., *Handbook of the Public Libraries of Manchester and Salford*, (Manchester, 1877).

___, *The Annals of Manchester*, (Manchester, 1886).

Baker, Henry, 'On the growth of the Commercial Centre of Manchester', *TMSS*, (1871-72), 87-106.

Bamford, Samuel, *Passages in the Life of a Radical*, (Oxford, n.d. [or.1841]).

___, *Walks in South Lancashire and on its borders: with letters*,

---

[1] Most of the primary published sources cited are available at the Manchester Central Library. Occasional items may only be available at the British Library, London or the Bodleian Library, Oxford.

descriptions, narratives and observations, current and incidental, (London, 1972 [or.1844]).

___, *Early Days*, (Manchester, 1849).

___, *Homely rhymes, poems and reminiscences,* (Manchester, 1864).

Bazley, Thomas, *National Education. What should it be?*, (Manchester, 1858).

Bremner, John A., 'Education of the manual labour class', *Transactions of the National Association for Promoting Social Science,* (1866), 307–17.

Brierley, Benjamin, *Tales and Sketches of Lancashire Life*, (Manchester 1863).

___, *Home Memories*, (Manchester, 1887).

[Brotherton, Edward], *Popular Education and Political Economy. Six Letters by 'E.B.' reprinted from the Manchester Guardian,* (Manchester, [1864]).

___, *The Present State of Popular Education in Manchester and Salford. The Substance of Seven Letters reprinted from the Manchester Guardian, January 5th to January 26th 1864,* (Manchester, 1864).

Bullock, Charles, *Hugh Stowell: a life and its lessons,* (London, [1882]).

Butterworth, Edwin, *A Chronological History of Manchester brought down to 1833, including descriptions of the boroughs of Manchester and Salford,* (Manchester, 1834).

Callender, William R., *The Commercial Crisis of 1857: its causes and results,* (London, 1858).

___, *Historic Conservatism. An Address,* (Manchester, 1867).

Chadwick, David, *Free Public Libraries and Museums: their usefulness in the promotion of the education of the working classes and the improvement of their social position, as compared with the library of Sunday schools, and of Mechanics' and other institutions,* (London, 1857).

___, *On the Rate of Wages in 200 trades and branches of labour in Manchester and Salford, and Lancashire during 1839–1859,* (London, 1860).

___, *The Progress of Manchester, 1840–60,* (Manchester, 1861).

___, *On the Social and Educational Statistics of Manchester and Salford,* (Manchester, 1862).

Chadwick, Richard Sheldon, *The Pleasures of Poetry. The purgatory of poets and other poems,* (Manchester, 1846).

Chalmers, Rev. E. Botelier, *The Parson, the Parish and the Working Men,* (London, 1859).

Chorlton-on-Medlock Mechanics' Institute, *Report of the Temperance Hall and Mechanics' Institute...Chorlton-upon-Medlock,* (Manchester, 1851, 1854).

A Christian Observer, *Papers on the present condition of Congregationalism in Manchester and Salford,* (Manchester, 1853).

Collins, Samuel, *Miscellaneous Poems and Songs,* (Manchester, [1859]).

Cooper, Joseph, *The Temperance Reciter,* (Manchester, 1856).

Corbin, John, *Ever Working, Never Resting, a memoir of John Legge Poore,* (London, 1874).

Credland, W.R., *The Manchester Public Free Libraries. A History and Description and Guide to their contents and use,* (Manchester, 1899).

Easby, J., *Manchester and the Manchester People,* (Manchester, 1843).

Edwards, Edward, *Three Reports on the Origin, Formation and First Year's Working of the Manchester Free Library with an Introduction on the results and the defects of the Public Libraries Act of 1850,* (Manchester, 1853).

Epps, John, *Diary of the late John Epps, M.D., embracing autobiographical records, notes on passing events, [etc],* (Edinburgh, [1870]).

Evans, Thomas, *An Address to Working Men on the Evils in Trades Unions and Strikes,* (Manchester, 1867).

Faucher, Léon, *Manchester in 1844: Its Present Condition and Future Prospects,* [trans. J.P. Culverwell], (Manchester, 1844).

Gaulter, Henry, *The Origin and Progress of the Malignant Cholera in Manchester,* (London, 1833).

Goffin, M., ed., *The Diaries of Absalom Watkin. A Manchester Man, 1787–1861,* (Stroud, 1993).

Gough, J.B., *J.B. Gough's Oration at Manchester, September 22 1853. Reported phonographically by William Rodger,* (Manchester, [1853]).

___, *Temperance Address, by the Rev. Horace James and J.B. Gough, Esq., in the Free Trade Hall, Manchester, on Sunday Afternoon, August 8th, 1858,* (Manchester, [1858]).

Griffen, Rev. James, *Memories of the Past: Recollections of a Ministerial Life,* (London, 1883).

Grundy, C.S., *Reminiscences of Strangeways Unitarian Free Church, June 1838 to June 1888,* (Manchester, 1888).

Halley, R., *Lancashire, its Puritanism and Non-conformity.*   2 vols, (Manchester, 1869).

Haslam, C.J., *How to Make the People Virtuous; showing that the Clergy do not take the proper means to make the people virtuous,* (Manchester, 1857).

___, *A Letter to the Working Classes, on the course of conduct they ought to pursue in order to acquire the ELECTIVE FRANCHISE,* (Manchester, 1857).

Hatton, John, *A Lecture on the Sanitary Condition of Chorlton-upon-Medlock,* (Manchester, 1854).

Hawthorne, Nathaniel, *Passages from the English Notebooks of Nathaniel Hawthorne,* (London, 1870).

Hayes, L.M., *Reminiscences of Manchester and some of its local surroundings from the year 1840,* (Manchester, 1905).

Herford, Brooke, ed., *Travers Madge. Memoirs,* (London, 1867).

Heywood, J., *Address to the Members of the Manchester Athenaeum,* (Manchester, 1836).

___, 'State of Poor Families in Miles Platting, Manchester', *Journal of the Statistical Society of London,* I (1838), 34–6.

Ireland, Alexander, *Recollections of George Dawson and his lectures in Manchester in 1846–7,* (Manchester, 1882).

Jevons, William S., *A Lecture on Trade Societies: their objects and policy. Delivered by request of the Trade Unionists' Political Association, in the Co-operative Hall, Upper Medlock-st, Hulme, Manchester, 31 March 1868,* (Manchester, [1868]).

[Johnson, Joseph], *Popular Preachers: three lectures by Argus the Younger,* (Manchester, [1859]).

___, *People I have Met,* (Douglas, 1906).

Jones, Ernest, *Labour and Capital: A lecture delivered in 1867,* (London, 1867).

Kay[-Shuttleworth], J.P., *The Physical and Moral Condition of the Working-Classes employed in the Cotton Manufacture in Manchester,* (London, 1832).

___, *Sketch of the Progress of Manchester in Thirty Years from 1832–62,* (London, 1862).

Kershaw, Tom, *Bits o'Skits i'th Lancashire Dialect,* (Manchester, [1867–68]).

Kirkham, T., *A History of German St. Church of England Sunday School, St. Martins,* (Manchester, 1876).

Lamb, Robert, *Free Thoughts on Many Subjects,* 2 vols in 1, (Manchester, 1866).

Leach, James, *Stubborn Facts from the Factories by a Manchester Operative,* (London, 1844).

___ et al., *Chartist Tracts for the Times,* (Manchester, 1849).

Lee, James Prince, (Bishop of Manchester), *'Wash and be Clean', preached...in St. Andrew's Church, Ancoats, on Wednesday evening, January 6th, 1858, being the first in a course of twelve sermons to the Working Classes of Manchester and Salford,* (Manchester, [1858]).

Lee, Thomas Gardiner, *A Plea for the English Operatives, in which the means of elevating the working classes are humbly suggested,* (Manchester, [1850]).

___, *The Dignity, the Objects, the Rewards, and the Triumphs of Labour, discussed in 4 lectures at the Pendleton Mechanics' Institution, in November 1860,* (Manchester, [1860]).

Leigh, John and Gardiner, Ner, *History of the Cholera in Manchester in 1849,* (Manchester, 1850).

Lester, C.E., *The Glory and Shame of England,* 2 vols, (New York, 1841).

Love, Benjamin, *Manchester as it is,* (Manchester, 1842).

___, *Chapters on Working People: How to Elevate their morals and to Improve their social condition,* (London, 1843).

MacDonald, W., *The True Story of Trades' Unions: Being a Reply to Dr. John Watts, Professor Jevons and Others,* (Manchester, 1867).

Manchester and Salford Education Aid Society, *Annual Report* (Manchester, 1865–72).

Manchester and Salford Executive Council of Total Abstinence Societies, *Annual Report,* (Manchester, 1853).

Manchester and Salford Sanitary Association, *Annual Report,* (Manchester, 1853–70).

Manchester and Salford Temperance League, *Annual Report,* (Manchester, 1857).

Manchester and Salford Temperance Union, *Annual Report,* (Manchester, 1868, 1871–72).

Manchester and Salford Temperance Society, *Annual Report,* (Manchester, 1852–54).

Manchester Athenaeum, *Annual Report,* (Manchester, 1848–67).

Manchester Bookbinders' Consolidated Union, *The Bookbinders' Consolidated Union Trade Circular and Reports from March 1855 to June 1856. Issued by the C.C.,* (Manchester, 1862).

Manchester Church Education Society Working Committee, *Annual Report,* (Manchester, 1844–48).

Manchester Corporation, *Proceedings of the Council,* (Manchester, 1840–70).

Manchester Corporation, Watch Committee, *Chief Constable's Report on police administration,* (Manchester, 1842–70).

Manchester City Mission, *Annual Report,* (Manchester, 1837–70).

Manchester District Association, *Report of the Manchester District Association of Literary and Scientific Institutions, with observations upon the plan and management of mechanics' institutions, and suggestions for their improvement...,* (Manchester, 1840).

Manchester District Provident Society, *Annual Report,* (Manchester, 1837–70).

Manchester Mechanics' Institution, *Annual Report,* (Manchester, 1832–67).

Manchester Ministry to the Poor, *Annual Report,* (1835–70).

Manchester People's Institute Association, *Laws of the Manchester People's Institute Association,* (Manchester, 1844).

Manchester Public Libraries, *Annual Report,* (Manchester, 1851–67).

Manchester Statistical Society, *Report of a Committee of the Manchester Statistical Society on the state of education in the borough of Manchester in 1834,* (1837).

___, *Report of a committee of the Manchester Statistical Society on the state of education in the borough of Salford in 1835,* (Manchester, 1836).

Marriott, Rev. William Thackeray, *Some Real Wants and Some Legitimate Claims of the Working Classes,* (Manchester, 1860).

Marsden, J.B., *Memoirs of the Rev. Hugh Stowell,* (London, 1868).

Mursell, Rev. Arthur, *Lectures to Working Men, delivered in the Free Trade Hall, Manchester*, (Manchester, [1858-64]).

[Nicholls, J.A.], *The Strike, by a Lancashire Man. A Letter to the Working Classes on their present position and Movement*, (Manchester, 1853).

___, *A Lecture on Strikes*, (Manchester, 1856).

Nicholson, Thomas, *A Peal for the People: with sundry changes. A poetical miscellany*, (Manchester, 1849).

Nightingale, B., *Lancashire Non-conformity*, 6 vols, (Manchester, 1890–93).

Parkinson, Rev. Richard, *'The Church of England a bulwark between superstition and schism': two sermons preached in the Collegiate Church of Christ, in Manchester, on Sunday 4th day of October, 1835, being the third centenary of the Reformation*, (Manchester, [1835]).

___, *On the Present Condition of the Labouring Poor in Manchester*, (Manchester, 1841).

Prentice, Archibald, *Historical Sketches and Personal Recollections of Manchester: The Progress of Public Opinion, 1792–1832*, (London, 1851).

___, *History of the Anti-Corn Law League*, 2 vols, (London, 1968 [or.1853]).

Prince, J.C., *Hours with the Muse*, (Manchester, 2nd ed., 1841).

___, *Miscellaneous Poems*, (Manchester, [1861]).

Procter, R.W., *Memorials of Manchester Streets*, (Manchester, 1874).

Ransome, A. and Leigh, J., *Report Upon the Health of Manchester and Salford*, (Manchester, 1867).

Reach, A.B., *Manchester and the Textile Districts in 1849*, C. Aspin, ed., (Helmshore, 1972).

Reilly, John, *History of Manchester*, (London, 1865).

Report of a public meeting to effect the establishment of a Free Public Library and Museum in Manchester; to which are prefixed leading articles on the subject from the Manchester newspapers, (Manchester, 1851).

Report of the proceedings at the public meeting held in the Library, Camp Field, Manchester, on Thursday September 2nd 1852, to celebrate the opening of the Free Library; Sir John Potter in the chair; also leading articles on the subject from the Manchester newspapers, list of subscriptions etc., (Manchester, [1852]).

Report of the proceedings of the meeting...presenting an address from the Catholic Sunday school teachers to Thomas Wyse, (Manchester, [1837]).

Report of the proceedings of a public meeting held...on the occasion of the inauguration of the new building for the Hulme branch, Manchester Free Public Library, (Manchester, 1866).

Richson, Canon Charles, *A Sketch of some of the causes which induced the abandonment of the voluntary system in the support of schools, and the introduction of the Manchester and Salford Education Bill*, (Manchester, 1851).

___, *Educational Facts and Statistics of Manchester and Salford, being a summary of some of the most important statistical tables presented in evidence before a committee of the House of Commons on Manchester and Salford education, May and June 1852,* (Manchester, [1853]).

___, *'Drunkenness and other moral and social evils'. Sermons to the working classes, preached in St. Philip's Church, Salford, on Wednesday evening, February 24th, 1858,* (Manchester, 1858).

Ridings, Elijah, *Pictures of Life,* (Manchester, 1850).

___, *The English Tribune. A Rhyme of Liberty and Progress,* (Manchester, 1860).

Roberton, John, *The Duty of England to Provide a Gratuitous Compulsory Education for the children of her poorer classes,* (Manchester, 1865).

Rogerson, J.B., *Musings in Many Moods,* (London, 1859).

Shaw, Sir Charles, *Replies of Sir Charles Shaw to Lord Ashley, M.P., regarding the Education and Moral Condition of the Labouring Classes,* (London, 1843).

Shaw, W., *Manchester Old and New,* (London, 1894).

Silver, A.W., ed., 'Henry Adams' Diary of a Visit to Manchester', *American Historical Review,* LI (1945–46), 75–89.

Slugg, J.T., *Reminiscences of Manchester Fifty Years Ago,* (Manchester, 1881).

Steel, Rev. Robert, *The Literature of Labour,* (Manchester, 1856).

Sumner, Rev. John Bird, *District Visiting Societies Recommended,* (Chester, 1832).

___, *Sermon on District Visiting Societies in The Fourth Annual Report of the General Society for Promoting District Visiting, [delivered at] Portman Chapel, Baker-st. [May 10 1830],* (London, 1832).

Swindells, T., *Manchester Streets and Manchester Men,* Second Series, (1889).

___, *Old Deansgate,* (London, 1905).

Taine, H., *Notes on England,* trans. W.F. Rae, (London, 1872).

Taylor, W. Cooke, *Notes of a Tour in the Manufacturing Districts of Lancashire,* (London, 1842).

Teer, John, *Silent Musings,* (Manchester, 1869).

Templar, Benjamin, *A Paper on the importance of teaching social economy in elementary schools,* (Manchester, 1858).

___, *The Religious Difficulty in National Education,* (Manchester, 1858).

___, *A Paper on the religion of secular schools and their claims on government aid,* (Manchester, 1859).

___, *A Paper on Ten Years Experience of the Manchester Free School, (formerly the Model Secular Schools),* (Manchester, 1866).

Thompson, Rev. Patrick, *Sermons... with a brief memoir,* J. Radford Thompson, ed., (Manchester, 1872).

The Trial of Feargus O'Connor and Fifty-eight others on a charge of sedition, conspiracy, tumult and riot, (New York, Agustus Kelley, 1970 [or. 1843]).

de Tocqueville, A., *Journeys to England and Ireland, 1835,* G. Lawrence and J.P. Mayer, eds, (London, 1958).

Twelve sermons to the Working Classes of Manchester and Salford, by Twelve Ministers of the Church of England, (Manchester, 1858).

Wade, Richard, *A Sketch of the origin and progress of the Lower Mosley Street Day and Sunday Schools,* (Manchester, 1867).

____, *The Rise of Non-conformity in Manchester, with a brief reference to the history of Cross St. Chapel,* (Manchester, 1880).

Waters, T.H., *Report on the Sanitary Condition of Certain Parts of Manchester, being a letter addressed to the committee of the Manchester and Salford Sanitary Association,* (Manchester, 1853).

Watts, John, *Report of a statistical enquiry of the Executive Committee of the N.P.S.A. in St. Michael's and St. John's wards; Manchester. Now and December 1852,* (Manchester, 1853).

[Watts, John], *The Associated Mechanics, etc. Institutes of Lancashire and Cheshire. A Controversial Correspondence, reprinted from the Manchester Examiner and Times*, (Manchester, 1862).

Waugh, Edwin, *Temperance and Education,* (Manchester, 1850).

Wheeler, J., *Manchester: its political, social and commercial history, ancient and modern,* (London, 1836).

Whitehead, James, *The Rate of Mortality in Manchester,* (London, 1863).

Wood, William Henry, *Trades Unions Defended,* (Manchester, 1870).

Secondary Published Works

Abercrombie, Nicholas, *Class, Structure and Power, Problems in the Sociology of Knowledge,* (Oxford, Blackwell, 1982).

____, et al., *The Dominant Ideology Thesis,* (London, George Allen and Unwin, 1980).

Altick, Richard D., *The English Common Reader: A Social History of the Mass Reading Public 1800–1900,* (Chicago, University of Chicago Press, 1963).

____, *Victorian People and Ideas,* (London, Dent, 1974).

Anderson, Gregory, *Victorian Clerks,* (Manchester, Manchester University Press, 1976).

Anderson, Perry, 'Origins of the Present Crisis', *New Left Review*, 23 (1964), 26–53.

____, 'Socialism and Pseudo-Empiricism', *New Left Review*, 35 (1966), 2–42.

Archer, M.S., *Culture and Agency. The place of culture in social theory,* (Cambridge, Cambridge University Press, 1988).

Bailey, Peter, *Leisure and Class in Victorian England: Rational Recreation and the Contest for Control, 1830–1885,* (Toronto, Routledge and Kegan Paul, 1978).

____, 'Will the Real Bill Banks Please Stand Up? Towards a Role Analysis of Mid-Victorian Working-Class Respectability', *Journal of Social History,* XII (1978–79), 336–65.

Belchem, J., '1848: Feargus O'Connor and the Collapse of the Mass Platform', in Epstein and Thompson, eds, *The Chartist Experience, 269-310.*

____, *'Orator Hunt': Henry Hunt and English Working Class Radicalism,* (Oxford, Oxford University Press, 1985).

____, 'Beyond Chartist Studies: Class, Community and Party in Early Victorian Populist Politics', in D. Fraser, ed., *Cities, Class and Communication. Essays in Honour of Asa Briggs,* (London, Harvester Wheatsheaf, 1990).

Berg, Maxine, *The Machinery Question and the Making of Political Economy 1815–1848,* (Cambridge, Cambridge University Press, 1980).

Biagini, Eugenio F., 'British Trades Unions and Popular Political Economy, 1860–1880', *Historical Journal,* 30,4 (1978), 811–40.

____, *Liberty, Retrenchment and Reform: Popular Liberalism in the Age of Gladstone, 1860–1880,* (Cambridge, Cambridge University Press, 1992).

____ and Reid, A., eds, *Currents of Radicalism: Popular Radicalism, Organized Labour and Party Politics in Britain, 1850–1914,* (Cambridge, Cambridge University Press, 1991).

Breuilly, J., *Labour and Liberalism in Nineteenth Century Europe. Essays in Comparative History,* (Manchester, Manchester University Press, 1992).

Briggs, Asa, 'The Background of the Parliamentary Reform Movement in Three English Cities, 1830–2', *Historical Journal,* 10 (1950–52), 293–317.

____, ed., *Chartist Studies,* (London, Macmillan, 1959).

Burgess, K., *The Challenge of Labour. Shaping British Society 1850–1930,* (London, Croom Helm, 1980).

Cardwell, D.S.L., ed., *Artisan to Graduate: Essays to Commemorate the funding in 1824 of the Manchester Mechanics' Institution,* (Manchester, Manchester University Press, 1974).

Catling, H., *The Spinning Mule,* (Newton Abbot, David and Charles, 1970).

Chapman, Stanley D., *The Cotton Industry in the Industrial Revolution,* (London, Macmillan, 1972).

Chase, Malcolm, *The People's Farm. English Radical Agrarianism, 1775–1840,* (Oxford, Oxford University Press, 1988).

Church, R.A., 'Labour Supply and Innovation, 1800–60: The Boot and Shoe Industry', *Business History,* XII (1970), 25-45.

____, ed., *The Dynamics of Victorian Business,* (London, Allen & Unwin, 1980).

Claeys, George, *Machinery, Money and the Millennium. From moral economy to socialism,* (Cambridge, Polity, 1987).

____, *Citizens and Saints. Politics and anti-politics in early British Socialism,* (Cambridge, Cambridge University Press, 1989).

Connolly, G.P., 'Little brother be at peace: the priest as Holy Man in the nineteenth century ghetto', in W.J. Sheils, ed., *The Church and Healing...Studies in Church History Volume 19,* (Oxford, [Ecclesiastical History Society], 1982).

____, 'The Transubstantiation of Myth: towards a New Popular History of Nineteenth Century Catholicism in England', *Journal of Ecclesiastical History,* 35,1 (1984), 78–104.

Conway, Hazel, *People's Parks. The Design and Development of Victorian Parks in Britain,* (Oxford, Oxford University Press, 1991).

Cooter, Roger, *The Cultural Meaning of Popular Science: Phrenology and the organisation of consent in nineteenth century Britain,* (Cambridge, Cambridge University Press, 1984).

Crossick, Geoffrey, 'The Labour Aristocracy and its values: a study of Mid-Victorian Kentish London', *Victorian Studies,* XIX,3 (1976), 301–28.

____, *An Artisan Elite in Victorian Society: Kentish London, 1840–80,* (London, Croom Helm, 1978).

Cruikshank, M.A., 'The Anglican Revival and Education: a study of school expansion in the cotton manufacturing areas of North-West England, 1840–50', *Northern History,* 15 (1979), 176–90.

Davies, S.J., 'Classes and Police in Manchester, 1829–1880', in Kidd and Roberts, eds., *City, Class and Culture,* 26–47.

Richard Dennis, *English Industrial Cities of the Nineteenth Century. A Social Geography,* (Cambridge, Cambridge University Press, 1984).

Donajdgrodski, A.P., ed., *Social Control in Nineteenth Century Britain,* (London, Croom Helm, 1977).

Edsall, N., *Richard Cobden. Independent Radical,* (London, Harvard University Press, 1986).

Eley, G., 'Reading Gramsci in English: Observations on the Reception of Antonio Gramsci in the English-speaking world, 1957–1982', *European History Quarterly,* 14 (1984), 441–78.

Epstein, James, *The Lion of Freedom. Feargus O'Connor and the Chartist movement,* (London, Croom Helm, 1982).

____, and Thompson, Dorothy, eds, *The Chartist Experience,* (London, Macmillan, 1982).

Farnie, D.A., *The English Cotton Industry and the World Market, 1815–1896,* (Oxford, Oxford University Press, 1979).

Finn, Margot, *After Chartism. Class and nation in English radical politics, 1848–74,* (Cambridge, Cambridge University Press, 1993).

Floud, R.C., *The British Machine Tool Industry, 1850–1914,* (Cambridge, Cambridge University Press, 1976).

Foster, John, *Class Struggle and the Industrial Revolution. Early Industrial Capitalism in three English Towns,* (London, Weidenfeld and Nicholson, 1974).

Fraser, D., *Urban Politics in Victorian England. The structure of politics in the Victorian cities,* (Leicester, Leicester University Press, 1976).

Fraser, W.H., *Trade Unions and Society, The Struggle for Acceptance, 1850–75,* (London, Allen and Unwin, 1974).

Gadian, D.S., 'Class Consciousness in Oldham and other North-West Industrial Towns, 1836–50', *Historical Journal,* XXI,1 (1978), 161-72.

Garnett, Jane, and Howe, A.C., 'Churchmen and Cotton Masters in Victorian England', in D.J. Jeremy, ed., *Business and Religion in Britain,* (Aldershot, Gower Press, 1988), 72–94.

Garrard, J., *Leadership and Power in Victorian Industrial Towns, 1830–80,* (Manchester, Manchester University Press, 1983).

Gatrell, V.A.C., 'A Manchester Parable', in J.A. Benyon, et al., eds, *Studies in Local History,* (Oxford, Oxford University Press, 1976), 28–36.

____, 'Labour, Power, and the Size of Firms in Lancashire Cotton in the Second Quarter of the Nineteenth Century', *Economic History Review,* 30,1 (1977), 95–125.

____, 'Incorporation and the Pursuit of Liberal Hegemony in Manchester 1790–1839', in D. Fraser, ed., *Municipal Reform and the Industrial City,* (Leicester, Leicester University Press, 1982), 15-60.

Gillespie, F.E., *Labor and Politics in England, 1850–67,* (Durham, N.C., Duke University Press, 1927).

Goodway, D., *London Chartism, 1838–48,* (Cambridge, Cambridge University Press, 1982).

Gosden, P.H.J., *The Friendly Societies in England, 1815–75,* (Manchester, Manchester University Press, 1961).

____, *Self-Help: Voluntary Associations in the Nineteenth Century,* (London, Batsford, 1973).

Gray, R.Q., 'Styles of Life: the "labour aristocracy" and class relations in later nineteenth century Edinburgh', *International Review of Social History,* XVIII (1973), 428–52.

____, *The Labour Aristocracy in Victorian Edinburgh,* (Oxford, Oxford University Press, 1976).

____, 'Bourgeois Hegemony in Victorian Britain', in J. Bloomfield, ed., *Class, Hegemony and Party,* (London, Lawrence and Wishart, 1977), 73-94.

Gunn, S., 'The "failure" of the Victorian middle class: a critique', in Wolff and Seed, eds, *The Culture of Capital,* 17-43.

Haber, L.E., *The Chemical Industry in the Nineteenth Century,* (Oxford, Oxford University Press, 1958).

Hanham, H.J., *Elections and Party Management. Politics in the time of Gladstone and Disraeli,* (London, Longmans, 1959).

Hanson, C.G., 'Craft Unions, Welfare Benefits, and Trade Union Law Reform, 1867–75', *Economic History Review*, XXVIII (1975), 243–59.

Harrison, Brian, *Drink and the Victorians. The Temperance Question in England, 1815–72,* (London, Faber and Faber, 1971).

____, *Peaceable Kingdom. Stability and Change in Modern Britain,* (Oxford, Oxford University Press, 1982).

____, and Hollis, Patricia, 'Chartism, Liberalism and the life of Robert Lowery', *English Historical Review,* 82 (1967), 503–35.

Harrison, J.F.C., *Learning and Living 1790–1900. A Study of the English Adult Education Movement,* (London, Routledge and Kegan Paul, 1961).

Harrison, Royden, *Before the Socialists. Studies in Labour and Politics 1861–81,* (London, Routledge and Kegan Paul, 1965).

____, and Zeitlin, J., eds, *Divisions of Labour. Skilled workers and technological change in nineteenth century England,* (Brighton, Harvester, 1985).

Hewitt, M., 'Science as Spectacle: Popular Science Culture in Saint John, New Brunswick, 1830–1850', *Acadiensis,* XVIII,2 (1988), 91–119.

____, 'Radicalism and the Victorian Working Classes: the case of Samuel Bamford', *Historical Journal,* 34,4 (1991), 873–92.

Hinde, Wendy, *Richard Cobden. A Victorian Outsider,* (London, Yale University Press, 1987).

Hobsbawm, Eric J., *Labouring Men: Studies in the History of Labour,* (London, Weidenfeld and Nicolson, 1964).

____, *Worlds of Labour. Further Studies in the History of Labour,* (London, Weidenfeld and Nicolson, 1984).

Hollis, Patricia, *The Pauper Press: A Study in Working-Class Radicalism of the 1830s,* (Oxford, Oxford University Press, 1970).

____, *Pressure from Without in early Victorian England,* (London, Edward Arnold, 1974).

Houghton, Walter E., *The Victorian Frame of Mind,* (London, Yale University Press, 1957).

Howe, A.C., *The Cotton Masters, 1830–1860,* (Oxford, Oxford University Press, 1984).

Huberman, Michael, 'Invisible Handshakes in Lancashire: Cotton Spinning in the First Half of the Nineteenth Century', *Journal of Economic History,* XLVI,4 (1986), 987–98.

____, 'The economic origins of paternalism: Lancashire cotton spinning in the first half of the nineteenth century', *Social History,* 12,2 (1987), 177–92.

James, Thomas Theophilus, *Cavendish St. Chapel [centenary commemoration], 1848–1948,* ([Manchester, n.p. 1948]).

Johnson, C.H., 'Economic Change and Artisan Discontent: The Tailors' History 1800–1848', in R. Price, ed., *Revolution and Reaction: 1848 and the Second French Republic,* (London, Croom Helm, 1975), 87–114.

Johnson, P., 'Credit and Thrift', in J. Winter, ed., *The Working Class in Modern British History. Essays in honour of Henry Pelling*, (Cambridge, Cambridge University Press, 1983), 147–70.

Jones, Stuart, 'The Cotton Industry and Joint-Stock Banking in Manchester 1825–50', *Business History*, XX,2 (1978), 165–85.

Joyce, Patrick, *Work, Society and Politics, the Culture of the Factory in Later Victorian England*, (London, Harvester, 1980).

_____, *The Historical Meanings of Work*, (Cambridge, Cambridge University Press, 1987).

_____, *Visions of the People. Industrial England and the question of class 1848–1914*, (Cambridge, Cambridge University Press, 1991).

_____, *Democratic Subjects. The self and the social in nineteenth century England*, (Cambridge, Cambridge University Press, 1994).

_____, 'The end of social history?', *Social History*, XX,1 (1995), 73-91.

Kargon, Robert, *Science in Victorian Manchester: Enterprise and Expertise*, (Baltimore, Johns Hopkins University Press, 1977).

Kellett, J.R., *The Impact of Railways on Victorian Cities*, (London, Routledge and Kegan Paul, 1969).

Kidd, Alan J., and Roberts, K.W., eds., *City, Class and Culture: studies of social policy and cultural production in Victorian Manchester*, (Manchester, Manchester University Press, 1985).

Kingsford, P.W., *Victorian Railwaymen: the Emergence and Growth of Railway Labour, 1850–70*, (London, Cass, 1970).

Kirby, R.G., and Musson, A.E., *The Voice of the People: John Doherty 1798–1854, Trade Unionist, Radical and Factory Reformer*, (Manchester, Manchester University Press, 1975).

Kirk, Neville, *The Growth of Working-Class Reformism in Mid-Victorian England*, (London, Croom Helm, 1985).

_____, 'In Defence of Class. A Critique of Recent Revisionist Writing Upon the Nineteenth Century English Working Class', *International Review of Social History*, 32 (1987), 2–47.

_____, 'History, language, ideas and post-modernism: a materialist view', *Social History*, XIX,2 (1994), 221-40.

Koditschek, Theodore, *Class Formation and Urban-Industrial Society. Bradford 1750–1850*, (Cambridge, Cambridge University Press, 1990).

Lancaster, Bill, *Radicalism, Co-operation and Socialism. Leicester Working Class Politics, 1860–1906*, (Leicester, Leicester University Press, 1987).

Laqueur, T.W., *Religion and Respectability. Sunday Schools and working class culture 1780–1850*, (London, Yale University Press, 1976).

Lawrence, Jonathan, and Taylor, Miles, 'The poverty of protest: Gareth Stedman Jones and the politics of language – a reply', *Social History*, XVIII (1993), 1–16.

Lee, Alan J., *Origins of the Popular Press in England, 1855–1914*, (London, Croom Helm, 1975).

Lee, C.H., *A Cotton Spinning Enterprise, 1785–1940: A History of*

McConnel and Kennedy, Fine Cotton Spinners, (Manchester, Manchester University Press, 1972).

Lloyd, Christopher, *Explanations in Social History,* (Oxford, Blackwell, 1986).

Lloyd-Jones, R., and le Roux, A.A., 'The Size of Firms in the cotton industry in Manchester, 1815–41', *Economic History Review,* 2nd Ser. XXXIII (1980), 72–82.

____, and Lewis, M.J., *Manchester and the Age of the Factory. The Business Structure of Cottonopolis in the Industrial Revolution,* (London, Croom Helm, 1988).

Lowe, W.J., *The Irish in Mid-Victorian Lancashire. The Shaping of a Working Class Community,* (New York, Lang, 1989).

McKibbin, Ross, 'Why was there no Marxism in Great Britain?', *English Historical Review,* XCIX (1984), 297–331.

Maidment, B.E., 'Essayists and Artisans – the making of Victorian self-taught poets', *Literature and History,* 9,1 (1983), 74–91.

____, *The Poorhouse Fugitives. Self-taught poets and poetry in Victorian Britain,* (Manchester, Carcanet, 1987).

Maltby, S.E., *Manchester and the Movement for National Elementary Education, 1800–1870,* (Manchester, Manchester University Press, 1918).

Mann, Michael, *Consciousness and Action among the Western Working Class,* (London, Macmillan, 1973).

Marshall, Gordon, 'Some Remarks on the study of Working-Class Consciousness', *Politics and Society,* 12,3 (1983), 263–301.

Marshall, L.S., 'The Emergence of the First Industrial City, Manchester 1785–1850', in C.F. Ware, ed., *The Cultural Approach to History,* (New York, American Historical Association, 1940), 140-61.

Mather, F.C., *Public Order in the Age of the Chartists,* (Manchester, Manchester University Press, 1959).

Mayfield, David, and Thorne, Susan, 'Social history and its discontents: Gareth Stedman Jones and the politics of language', *Social History,* XVII (1992), 167–88.

Meacham, Standish, *A Life Apart. The English Working Class, 1870–1914,* (London, Thames and Hudson, 1979).

Meller, Helen, *Leisure and the Changing City, 1870–1914,* (London, Routledge and Kegan Paul, 1976).

Morris, R.J., 'The Middle Class and British Towns and Cities of the Industrial Revolution, 1780–1850', in D. Fraser and A. Sutcliffe, eds, *The Pursuit of Urban History,* (London, Edward Arnold, 1983), 286-305.

____, 'Voluntary Societies and British Urban Elites, 1780–1850', *Historical Journal,* 26,1 (1983), 95–118.

____, *Class, Sect and Party. The making of the British middle class. Leeds, 1820–1850,* (Manchester, Manchester University Press, 1990).

Musson, A.E., 'Class Struggle and the Labour Aristocracy 1830–60', *Social History,* 3 (1976), 335–56.

Nairn, T., 'The English Working Class', *New Left Review*, 24 (1964), 43–57.

____, 'The Fateful Meridian', *New Left Review*, 60 (1970), 3–35.

Neale, R.S., *Class and Ideology in the Nineteenth Century*, (London, Routledge and Kegan Paul, 1972).

____, 'Cultural Materialism: a critique', *Social History*, 9,2 (1984), 199–215.

Palmer, Stanley H., *Police and Protest in England and Ireland, 1780–1850*, (Cambridge, Cambridge University Press, 1988).

Parry, J.P., *The Rise and Fall of Liberal Government in Victorian Britain*, (London, Yale University Press, 1993).

Parsons, G., ed., *Religion in Victorian Britain*, 3 vols, (Manchester, Manchester University Press, 1988).

Parssinen, T.M., 'Association, Convention and Anti-Parliament in British Radical Politics, 1771–1848', *English Historical Review*, 88 (1973), 504–33.

Pons, V., 'Contemporary interpretations of Manchester in the 1830s and 1840s', in J.D. Wirth and R.L. Jones, eds, *Manchester and Sao Paulo: problems of rapid urban growth*, (Stanford, Stanford University Press, 1978).

Pooley, M.E., and Pooley, C.G., 'Health, Society and Environment in Victorian Manchester', in R. Woods and J. Woodward, eds, *Urban Disease and Mortality in Nineteenth Century England*, (London, Batsford, 1984), 148–77.

Price, Richard, 'The working mens' club movement and Victorian Social Reform ideology', *Victorian Studies*, XV,2 (1971), 117–48.

____, 'The other face of respectability: violence in the Manchester brickmaking trade 1859–70', *Past & Present*, 66 (1975), 110–32.

____, *Labour in British Society*, (London, Croom Helm, 1986).

Ratcliffe, B.M., and Chaloner, W.H., *A French Sociologist Looks at Britain: Gustave D'Eichtal and British Society in 1828*, (Manchester, Manchester University Press, 1977).

Redford, A., *The History of Local Government in Manchester*, 3 vols, (London, Longmans, 1939–40).

Reid, Douglas, 'Religion, recreation and the working class: Birmingham, 1844–1885', *Bulletin of the Society for the Study of Labour History*, 51,1 (1986), 9-10.

Roberts, Jacqueline, *Working Class Housing in Nineteenth Century Manchester*, (Manchester, Neil Roberts, 1975).

Roberts, Stephen, *Radical Politicians and Poets in Early Victorian Britain. The voices of six Chartist leaders*, (Lampeter, Edward Mellon Press, 1993).

Robinson, W.G., *A History of the Lancashire Congregational Union, 1806–1956*, (Manchester, Lancashire Congregational Union, [1955]).

Rodgers, H.B., 'The Suburban Growth of Victorian Manchester', *Journal of the Manchester Geographical Society,* LVIII (1962), 1–12.

Rose, Arthur G., 'The Plug Riots of 1842 in Lancashire and Cheshire', *Transactions of the Lancashire and Cheshire Antiquarian Society*, LXVII (1957), 75-112.

____, 'Truckling Magistrates of Lancashire in 1842', *Transactions of the Lancashire and Cheshire Historical Society,* 83 (1985), 40–70.

Rothstein, T., *From Chartism to Labourism: historical sketches of the English working class movement,* (London, Martin Lawrence, 1929).

Royle, Edward, 'Mechanics' Institutes and the Working Classes, 1840–60', *Historical Journal,* 14 (1971), 305–21.

____, *Victorian Infidels,* (Manchester, Manchester University Press, 1974).

____, *Radicals, Secularists and Republicans. Popular freethought in Britain, 1866-1915,* (Manchester, Manchester University Press, 1980).

Rule, John, ed., *British Trades Unionism, 1750-1850: the formative years,* (Harlow, Longman, 1988).

Russell, David, *Popular Music in England, 1840-1914*, (Manchester, Manchester University Press, 1987).

Saul, S.B., 'The Market and the Development of the Mechanical Engineering Industries in Britain, 1860-1914', *Economic History Review,* 2nd Ser. XX (1967), 111–30.

Savage, Mike, *The Dynamics of Working Class Politics. The Labour Movement in Preston, 1880-1940,* (Cambridge, Cambridge University Press, 1987).

Saville, John, *Ernest Jones: Chartist,* (London, Lawrence and Wishart, 1952).

____, 'The Ideology of Labourism', in R. Benewick, et al., eds, *Knowledge and Belief in Politics: the Problem of Ideology,* (London, Allen and Unwin, 1973), 213–26.

____, *1848. The British State and the Chartist Movement,* (Cambridge, Cambridge University Press, 1987).

Searle, G.R., *Entrepreneurial Politics in Mid-Victorian England*, (Oxford, Oxford University Press, 1993).

Seed, John, 'Unitarianism, political economy and the antinomies of liberal culture in Manchester, 1830–50', *Social History,* 7,1 (1982), 1–26.

Senelick, L., 'Politics as Entertainment: Victorian Music Hall Songs', *Victorian Studies*, XIX,2 (1975), 149-80.

Shapin, Steven and Barnes, Brian, 'Science, Nature and Control: Interpreting Mechanics' Institutes', *Social Studies of Science,* 7 (1977), 31–74.

Shiman, L.L., *The Crusade Against Drink in Victorian England*, (Basingstoke, Macmillan, 1988).

Sicot, John Henry, ed., *St. Andrew's Church, Travis St., Ancoats, Manchester, consecrated 6th October 1831. A commemorative booklet for the centenary,* (Manchester, Holt Publishing Services, 1931).

Simon, B., *Studies in the History of Education,* (London, Lawrence and Wishart, 1960).

Simon, S.D., *A Century of City Government in Manchester, 1838–1938,* (London, George Allen and Unwin, 1938).

Smail, John, *The Origins of Middle Class Culture. Halifax, Yorkshire, 1660–1780,* (Ithaca, Cornell University Press, 1994).

Smith, Dennis, *Conflict and Compromise: Class Formation in English Society 1830–1914,* (London, Routledge and Kegan Paul, 1982).

Smith, Roland, 'Manchester as a centre for manufacturing and merchandising cotton goods 1820–30', *University of Birmingham Historical Journal,* IV (1953–54), 47–65.

Steedman, Carolyn, *Policing the Victorian Community: The Formation of English Provincial Police Forces, 1856–80,* (London, Routledge and Kegan Paul, 1984).

____, 'Linguistic Encounters of the Fourth Kind', *Journal of Victorian Culture,* 1,1 (1996), (forthcoming).

Stedman-Jones, Gareth, 'Working Class Culture and Working Class Politics in London, 1870–1900: Notes on the Remaking of a Working Class', *Journal of Social History,* 7 (1973–74), 460–508.

____, 'Class Expression versus Social Control? A Critique of Recent Trends in the Social History of "Leisure"', *History Workshop,* 4 (1977), 163–70.

____, *Language of Class. Studies in English Working Class History, 1832–1983,* (Cambridge, Cambridge University Press, 1983).

Storch, Robert D., 'The Plague of the Blue Locusts: Police Reform and Popular Resistance in Northern England 1840–1857', *International Review of Social History,* 20,1 (1975), 481–509.

____, 'The Policeman as Domestic Missionary: Urban Discipline and Popular Culture in Northern England, 1850–1880', *Journal of Social History,* 9,4 (1976), 481–509.

Sykes, R.A., 'Some aspects of Working-Class Consciousness in Oldham, 1830–42', *Historical Journal,* 23,1 (1980), 167–80.

____, 'Early Chartism and Trade Unionism in South-East Lancashire', in Epstein and Thompson, eds, *The Chartist Experience,* 169–74.

____, 'Physical Force Chartism: "The Cotton Districts and the Chartist Crisis of 1839"', *International Review of Social History,* XXX,2 (1985), 207–36.

____, 'Trade Unionism and Class Consciousness: the revolutionary period of General Unionism, 1829-34', in Rule, ed., *British Trade Unionism 1780–1850,* 178-99.

Taylor, Miles, *The Decline of British Radicalism, 1847–1860,* (Oxford, Oxford University Press, 1995).

Thackray, Arnold, 'Natural Knowledge in Cultural Context: The Manchester Model', *American Historical Review,* 79 (1974), 682–3.

Tholfsen, Trygve R., 'The intellectual origins of mid-Victorian stability',

Political Science Quarterly, LXXXVI (1971), 57–91.

___, *Working-Class Radicalism in Mid-Victorian England,* (London, Croom Helm, 1976).

Thompson, Dorothy, *The Chartists,* (London, Pantheon, 1984).

Thompson, Edward P., *The Making of the English Working Class,* (London, Penguin, 1964).

Thompson, Noel W., *The People's Science. The popular political economy of exploitation and crisis, 1816–34,* (Cambridge, Cambridge University Press, 1984).

___, *The Market and its Critics. Socialist political economy in nineteenth century Britain,* (London, Routledge, 1988).

Trainor, R., *Black Country Elites. The Exercise of Authority in an Industrial Area, 1830–1900,* (Oxford, Oxford University Press, 1993).

Turner, Michael J., 'Gas, Police and the Struggle for Mastery in Manchester in the 1820s', *Historical Research,* LXVII (1994), 301–17.

___, 'Manchester Reformers and the Penryn seats, 1827–1828', *Northern History,* XXX (1994), 139–60.

Tylecote, M. *The Mechanics' Institutes of Lancashire and Yorkshire before 1851,* (Manchester, Manchester University Press, 1957).

Vernon, James, *Politics and the People. A Study in English Political Culture, c.1815–1867,* (Cambridge, Cambridge University Press, 1993).

Vicinus, M., *The Industrial Muse: A Study of Nineteenth Century British Working-Class Literature,* (London, Croom Helm, 1974).

___, *Edwin Waugh: The Ambiguities of Self-Help,* (Littleborough, Kelsall, 1984).

Vigier, F.J., *Change and Apathy: Liverpool and Manchester during the Industrial Revolution,* (Cambridge Mass., M.I.T. Press, 1970).

Vincent, David, *Bread, Knowledge and Freedom. A Study of Nineteenth Century Working Class Autobiography,* (London, Europa, 1981).

Wach, H.W., 'Culture and the Middle Classes: Popular Knowledge in Industrial Manchester', *Journal of British Studies,* 27 (1988), 375-404.

Wahrman, Dror, *Imagining the Middle Class. The Political Representation of Class in Britain, c.1780-1840,* (1995).

Ward, W.R., 'The Cost of Establishment: Some Reflections on Church Building in Manchester', in C.J. Cumming, ed., *Studies in Church History,* III (London, Ecclesiastical History Society, 1966), 277–89.

___, *Religion and Society in England, 1780-1850,* (London, Batsford, 1972).

Weaver, S.A., *John Fielden and the Politics of Popular Radicalism, 1832-47,* (Oxford, Oxford University Press, 1987).

Werly, J.M., 'The Irish in Manchester, 1832–49', *Irish Historical Studies,* 18 (1973), 345–58.

Williams, Raymond, *Marxism and Literature,* (Oxford, Oxford University Press, 1977).

Winstanley, Michael, 'Oldham radicalism and the origins of popular Liberalism, 1830–52', *Historical Journal*, 36,3 (1993), 619–44.

Wolff, Janet, and Seed, John, eds, *The Culture of Capital; art, power and the nineteenth century middle class,* (Manchester, Manchester University Press, 1988).

Secondary Unpublished Works

Belchem, J., 'Radicalism as a "Platform Agitation" in the periods 1815–21 and 1848–51. With special reference to the leadership of Henry Hunt and Feargus O'Connor', (PhD thesis, University of Sussex, 1974).

Gatrell, V.A.C., 'The Commercial Middle Class in Manchester, 1820–1857', (DPhil thesis, Cambridge University, 1972).

Gunn, S., 'The Manchester Middle Class, 1850–1880', (PhD thesis, University of Manchester, 1992).

Harrison, M. 'Social Reform in Late Victorian and Edwardian Manchester with special reference to T.C. Horsfall', (PhD thesis, University of Manchester, 1987).

Hassall, J., 'The Bennett Street Sunday School, Manchester. A study in nineteenth century Educational and Social Improvement', (PhD thesis, University of Manchester, 1986).

Hewitt, M., 'Structures of Accommodation: the intellectual roots of social stability in mid-nineteenth century Manchester, 1832–67', (DPhil thesis, University of Oxford, 1991).

Marlow, L., 'The working men's club movement 1862–1912: a study of the evolution of a working class institution', (PhD thesis, Warwick University, 1982).

DeMotte, C., 'The Dark Side of Town: Crime in Manchester and Salford, 1815–1875', (DPhil thesis, University of Kansas, 1976).

Nenadic, S., 'The structure, values and influence of the Scottish urban middle class: Glasgow 1800–1870', (PhD thesis, University of Glasgow, 1986).

Rushton, P., 'Housing Conditions and the Family Economy in the Victorian Slum: a study of a Manchester District, 1790–1871', (PhD thesis, University of Manchester, 1977).

Sykes, R.A., 'Popular Politics and Trade Unionism in S.E. Lancashire, 1829–42', (PhD thesis, University of Manchester, 1982).

Pons, V., 'Housing Conditions in Manchester and Sao Paulo', (unpublished paper, Manchester Central Library).

Tiller, Kate, 'Working Class Attitudes and Organisation in Three Industrial Towns 1850–1875', (PhD thesis, University of Birmingham, 1975).

Taylor, A.D., 'Modes of Political Expression and Working-Class Radicalism, 1848-74: the London and Manchester examples', (PhD thesis, University of Manchester, 1992).

Wach, H.W., 'The Condition of the Middle Classes: Culture and Society in Manchester, 1815–50', (PhD thesis, Brandeis University, 1987).

Index